Sustainable Tourism Management

This book is dedicated to Susan and
'little' John, perfect travelling companions
on the journey of life.

Sustainable Tourism Management

John Swarbrooke
Principal Lecturer in Tourism
School of Leisure and Food Management
Sheffield Hallam University
Sheffield, UK

CABI *Publishing*

CABI Publishing is a division of CAB International

CABI Publishing
CAB International
Wallingford
Oxon OX10 8DE
UK

CABI Publishing
875 Massachusetts Avenue
7th Floor
Cambridge, MA 02139
USA

Tel: +44 (0)1491 832111
Fax: +44 (0)1491 833508
Email: cabi@cabi.org
Web site: www.cabi-publishing.org

Tel: +1 617 395 4056
Fax: +1 617 354 6875
Email: cabi-nao@cabi.org

A catalogue record for this book is available from the British Library, London, UK

Library of Congress Cataloging-in-Publication data
Swarbrooke, John.
 Sustainable tourism management / by John Swarbrooke.
  p. cm.
 Includes bibliographical references and index.
 ISBN 0-85199-314-1 (alk. paper)
 1. Ecotourism. 2. Sustainable development. I. Title
 G156.5.E26S88 1998
 338.4′791—dc21   98–42296
                                                             CIP

ISBN 0 85199 314 1

First published 1999
Reprinted 2000, 2002, 2004, 2005

Printed and bound in the UK by Biddles Ltd, King's Lynn

Contents

Preface

In recent years, the concept of sustainable tourism has taken centre stage in the tourism world. It has stimulated numerous conferences, textbooks and corporate policy statements. So much has been written and spoken about sustainable tourism that one could be forgiven for thinking there is nothing left to say on the subject.

However, for all the words, there are still relatively few examples of successful sustainable tourism initiatives to inspire both students and practitioners. In other words, we have failed, to date, to put theory into practice. Even where attempts have been made to turn words into action, the results have generally been very limited.

The aim of this book is to focus on the practical side, to explore the ways in which tourism could be managed in ways that would make it more sustainable.

It is underpinned by a range of underlying principles, including the following:

1. Sustainable tourism is not just about protecting the environment; it is also concerned with long-term economic viability and social justice.
2. Initiatives designed to achieve sustainable tourism bring benefits to some people and costs to others. It is thus a highly political, rather than just a technocratic, field.
3. Sustainable tourism cannot be separated from the wider debate about sustainable development in general.
4. There is a need for more critical evaluation of existing thinking and techniques in the area of sustainable tourism. There are too many 'sacred cows' that are not being challenged rigorously enough or often enough. For example, where is the evidence that small-scale tourism is inherently more sustainable than mass tourism, regardless of the nature of the environment in which it takes place?
5. Progress towards more sustainable forms of tourism will depend far more on the activities of the industry and the attitudes of tourists, than on the actions of public sector bodies.

The book is designed to be contentious and to stimulate critical debate in this important field.

To achieve its aims, the book is divided into a number of sections, as follows:

(i) **Part One** sets the scene for the rest of the book by:
   - offering a historical perspective on the broader concept of sustainable development

- defining the term, 'sustainable tourism' and looking at its scope
- providing a critique of current thinking in the field
- setting out a range of principles that the author believes should underpin any strategy aimed at developing more sustainable forms of tourism.

(ii) **Part Two** focuses on the three dimensions of sustainable tourism, namely:
- the physical environment
- economic viability
- social justice and equity.

(iii) **Part Three** concentrates on the key actions of shareholders in sustainable tourism, notably:
- the public sector, in other words, government departments and agencies
- the tourism industry
- voluntary sector organizations
- the host community
- the media
- the tourist.

(iv) **Part Four** looks at sustainable tourism in different geographical settings, including:
- coastal environment and the sea
- rural areas
- towns and cities
- mountainous areas
- islands
- developing countries.

(v) **Part Five** covers the relationship between sustainable tourism and the four main areas of functional management, in other words:
- marketing
- human resources management
- operations management
- financial management.

(vi) **Part Six** focuses on the different sectors of the tourism industry:
- destinations
- visitor attractions
- tour operators
- transport
- hospitality.

It also looks at four specific types of tourism that are growing currently, namely:

- cultural tourism
- ecotourism
- all-inclusive and self-contained resort complexes
- business tourism.

(vii) **Part Seven** offers a range of conclusions

(viii) **Part Eight** consists of a chapter which relates to the future of sustainable tourism, including:

- sustainable tourism and the wider debate on ethics in business
- the links between sustainable tourism and the concept of sustainable development
- the potential role of 'virtual reality' technologies and the anticipated rise of 'virtual tourism'
- the issue of implementation, notably monitoring systems and performance indicators
- whether or not, in the future, sustainable tourism will prove to be an impossible dream or an irrelevant issue.

The book offers a range of case studies of good practice drawn from all over the world. It also includes a number of discussion points and exercises, designed to reinforce the reader's understanding of the key issues.

While it is written by a British author, the book attempts to offer an international perspective on the subject of sustainable tourism management, for this is a global challenge for a global industry.

It is hoped that this book will be useful reading for a variety of audiences, including:

- students on undergraduate and postgraduate courses in tourism, hospitality, leisure, urban and regional planning, geography, and environmental management
- academics and researchers in the field of sustainable tourism
- managers in the tourism industry who want to understand why and how they should be attempting to make their organization's activities more sustainable
- public sector practitioners who are responsible for developing and implementing tourism strategies for cities, regions, and countries.

I hope this book on a very controversial subject will stir the reader's emotions. If reading it makes you angry or dispirited from time to time, if it makes you want to learn more or become more actively involved in the debate, then I will consider that writing the book has been time well spent. Furthermore, I hope that the reader will attempt to read the book with an open mind and a willingness to question the conventional wisdoms, rather than from a desire for the cosiness of consensus, and a sterile re-stating of the platitudes which have been a feature of the debate to date.

If this book helps us to ask better questions, then it will have served a valuable purpose.

John Swarbrooke

Acknowledgements

This book is one that I have wanted to write for some time now. The fact that I have been able to complete it is thanks to a wide variety of people, including:

(i)   the authors whose detailed studies of aspects of sustainable tourism or particular destinations or companies have provided much of the substance of the book

(ii)   those students who have allowed me to try out my ideas on them and have given me their valuable, honest opinions on my views.

Whatever strengths the book has are largely due to these two groups while the weaknesses are all mine.

However, this book could not have been written without the selfless support offered by my wife, Susan Horner. It would not have been typed were it not for Judy Mitchell, the only person in the world who can read my hand-writing. Finally, it would have taken over my life had it not been for our son John, who convinced me that reading comics, playing tennis in the yard, and listening to music is more important than writing books.

I must also place on record the eternal debt of gratitude I owe my parents who made sacrifices for me and encouraged me to always ask questions.

Part One

Introduction

This section sets the scene for the rest of the book and provides valuable background for the reader.

The four chapters in this part of the book cover:

(i)   the history of the whole concept of sustainable development
(ii)   the nature and scope of sustainable tourism
(iii)   a critique of current thinking on issues and techniques in sustainable tourism
(iv)   the author's ideas on the principles which should underpin the practice of sustainable tourism.

1

Historical Background

The History of the Concept of Sustainable Development

The debate over the concept of sustainable tourism is a phenomenon of the 1990s. However, its origins lie in the wider concept of sustainable development which has been with us for many centuries.

By sustainable, we generally mean development which meets our needs today without compromising the ability of people in the future to meet their needs. It is thus about taking a longer term perspective than is usual in human decision-making and implies a need for intervention and planning. The concept of sustainability clearly embraces the environment, people and economic systems.

While the term 'sustainable' has only begun to be used explicitly in the past 20 or 30 years, the ideas which underpin it date back to the earliest examples of city planning, for example. Perhaps, therefore, some of the earliest attempts to achieve sustainable development were the towns and cities which were planned and developed by the Romans.

Likewise, many traditional agricultural systems were based on the principle of sustainability. Farming was carried out in ways which preserved rather than destroyed the productive capacity of the land so that it would still be able to support food production in the longer term.

However, over time, technological inventions, population pressures, together with social and economic change, led to the growth of industry and urbanization. This in turn put pressure on farmers to maximize food production in the short term. These developments led to problems which in turn led to private and state initiatives as we can see if we look at the case of urbanization in the UK.

Industrialization in the UK transformed the economy and society as well as the natural environment. There was a recognition that if it were not controlled, the process could destroy the physical environment, and lead to a very poor quality of life for the population. This resulted in the growth of 'model' settlements, built by paternalistic industrialists who attempted to provide good living conditions, such as New Lanark, Saltaire and Port Sunlight. At the same time some industrialists developed parks to ensure that future generations would have some green space to enjoy in the heart of industrial cities.

Most of these were initiatives taken by affluent, powerful business men. However, as industrialization led to urban sprawl and a decline in public health, governments and local councils began to take action to safeguard the long-term future of towns and cities, as well as ameliorating short-term problems. This trend was at the heart of the development of the first statutory town planning systems in Europe, which dated from the end of the last century and the beginning of this century.

The desire to safeguard the environment and provide social equity also stimulated the rise of the Garden City movement in the UK which was formed in 1898.

The Second World War gave a new impetus to all forms of planning, with the idea that a new world order had to be built once the war ended. This resulted in a plethora of plans that were all related to the concept of sustainable development. Leading planners like Abercrombie were preparing blueprints for the future development of whole regions such as Greater London. Strategies were being developed to systematically exploit social and economic resources in ways which reduced disparities between regions. Plans were being laid to create national parks across Europe.

Also in the postwar period, the first major planning legislation was introduced in many European countries, most notably in the UK. Slowly, across the developed world, bureaucratic systems of land-use planning developed between 1945 and the 1970s.

However, some commentators would argue that planning has failed to help us achieve sustainable development. There is growing cynicism about the ability of planners to manage development effectively in the interests of sustainability. Indeed, writers such as Beckerman would even argue that state intervention probably impedes the move towards sustainable development by distorting the free market system. The argument being that the market, if left alone, will ultimately lead to sustainable development. However, this author feels it his duty to point out to any reader who is relatively new to the sustainable tourism debate, that this is a position held by a minority of commentators. The conventional wisdom appears to be, rightly or wrongly, that sustainable tourism requires intervention and planning.

From the 1960s the question of sustainable development also became a major issue in the so-called 'Third World'. As the countries of Asia and Africa gained their independence, they were intent on closing the wealth gap between themselves and the developed countries. Some of them took a purely short-term view and set out to exploit their natural resources for short-term gain. Others tried to take a longer term view and there was much debate about how development could take place in a more sustainable manner.

At the same time, there was a growing recognition in some developed countries that the emphasis on materialism and the 'consumer society' was taking too heavy a toll on the world's resources. For example, in 1960, the US marketing guru, Vance Packard, published *The Waste Makers*, a critique of the 'throw-away society'.

In 1972, Danella and Dennis Meadows published 'The Limits to Growth', a report on the impact of economic growth on the future of the world. The Massachusetts-based team used computer simulations to show that the world could not cope with the level of resource use and pollution that economic growth was creating. They used a systems approach to analyse the problem and suggest that the economic system had to be modified to achieve a 'state of global equilibrium'.

Numerous reports also warned that the earth's future was under threat because the global population was growing too rapidly, and was not sustainable in relation to the Earth's resources. One of the first reports to talk openly about the concept of sustainable development was the 'World Conservation Strategy' which was published in 1980 by the International Union for the Conservation of Nature and Natural Resources. Then in 1987 the World Commission on Environment and Development published 'Our Common Future', otherwise known as the Brundtland Report. This

> placed the concept of sustainable
> development centre stage and promoted it
> as a vehicle for deliverance (Murphy, 1994)

This report was based on the well-established idea that:

> we do not inherit the Earth from our
> forefathers, but borrow it from our children
> (Murphy, 1995)

Table 1.1. Sustainable development components. Source: adapted from Murphy (1995) based upon the Brundtland Report 1987.

Establishing ecological limits and more equitable standards	'. . . requires the promotion of values that encourage consumption standards that are within the bounds of the ecological possible and to which all can reasonably aspire'
Redistribution of economic activity and reallocation of resources	'Meeting essential needs depends in part on achieving full growth potential and sustainable development clearly requires economic growth in places where such needs are not being met'
Population control	'Though the issue is not merely one of population size but of the distribution of resources, sustainable development can only be pursued if demographic developments are in harmony with the changing productive potential of the ecosystem'
Conservation of basic resources	'. . . sustainable development must not endanger the natural systems that support life on Earth: the atmosphere, the waters, the soils, and the living beings'
More equitable access to resources	'Growth has no set limits in terms of population or resource use beyond which lies ecological disaster . . . But ultimate limits there are, and sustainability requires that long before these are reached efforts are made to ensure more equitable access to resources . . .'
Carrying capacity and sustainable yield	'. . . most renewable resources are part of a complex and interlinked ecosystem, and maximum sustainable yield must be defined after taking into account system-wide effects of exploitation'
Retention of resources	'Sustainable development requires that the rate of depletion of non-renewable resources foreclose as few future options as possible'
Diversification of the species	'. . . sustainable development requires the conservation of plant and animal species'
Minimize adverse impacts	'Sustainable development requires that the adverse impacts on the quality of air, water, and other natural elements are minimised so as to sustain the ecosystem's overall integrity'
Community control	'. . . community control over development decisions affecting local ecosystems'
Broad national/international policy framework	'. . . biosphere is the common home of all human-kind and joint management of the biosphere is prerequisite for global political security'
Economic viability	'. . . communities must pursue economic well-being while recognising that [government] policies may set limits to material growth'
Environmental quality	'Corporate environmental policy is an extension of total quality management'
Environmental audit	'An effective environmental audit system is at the heart of good environmental management'

It was based on the idea that economic growth had to take place in a more ecologically sound and socially equitable manner.

Table 1.1 outlines the main components of sustainable development, as defined largely by the Brundtland Report, interpreted by Murphy. The emphasis is clearly primarily on the environment. As we will see, as the book develops, this emphasis on the environmental dimension to sustain-ability rather than the economic and social dimensions, is a real problem in the debate on sustainability and sustainable tourism.

Since 1987 the growing interest in sus-tainable development has been fuelled by:

- the Rio Summit in 1992 and Agenda 21
- environmental problems such as 'global warming' and the 'smog' which affected South-East Asia in Autumn 1997.

In 1997, Hunter produced a valuable list of the key issues which are wrapped up in the sustainable tourism debate. This list is

Box 1.1. Major issues in interpreting sustainable development. Source: Hunter (1997).

- The role of economic growth in promoting human well-being
- The impact and importance of human population growth
- The effective existence of environmental limits to growth
- The substitutability of natural resources (capital) with human-made capital created through economic growth and technical innovation
- The differential interpretation of the criticality of various components of the natural resource base and, therefore, the potential for substitution
- The ability of technologies (including management methods such as environmental impact assessment and environmental auditing) to decouple economic growth and unwanted environmental side-effects
- The meaning of the value attributed to the natural world and the rights of non-human species, sentient or otherwise
- The degree to which a systems (ecosystems) perspective should be adopted and the importance of maintaining the functional integrity of ecosystems

reproduced in Box 1.1. The inclusion of such disparate issues clearly helps to explain the breadth and lack of focus which typifies much of the sustainability debate.

The Sustainable Development Spectrum

In the same article, Hunter went on to adapt the earlier work of Turner, Pearce and Bate-man, to argue that sustainable development is not a single absolute standard. Instead there is, as Table 1.2 suggests, a wide spec-trum of attitudes, and levels of commitment, towards sustainable development. This spectrum is also seen in terms of consumer interest in sustainability as we will see later in the book when we look at the concept of 'shades of green consumer'.

Sustainable Development and Ethical Business

Since the 1980s, there has been a growing interest in the ethical standards of busines-ses. This has been a response to numerous scandals relating to unethical or irresponsi-ble actions on behalf of companies. Public and political pressure has been growing for companies to behave more ethically in rela-tion to a range of issues, some of which are illustrated in Fig. 1.1.

The concept of sustainable development fits readily into this trend. Companies are being encouraged to take their responsibili-ties towards the environment most seriously, because:

- if they destroy environmental resources on which their business depends, then the future of their business will be in jeopardy
- if they do not act voluntarily, govern-ments may need to regulate their activities
- they have broader responsibilities to society, to be 'good neighbours'.

As a result, more and more companies are seeking to make their activities more sus-tainable through:

- pollution and waste reduction meas-ures
- energy conservation initiatives

Table 1.2. A simplified description of the sustainable development spectrum. Source: Hunter (1997), adapted from Turner *et al.* (1994).

Sustainability position	Defining characteristics
Very weak	Anthropocentric and utilitarian; growth oriented and resource exploitative; natural resources utilized at economically optimal rates through unfettered free markets operating to satisfy individual consumer choice; infinite substitution possible between natural and human-made capital; continued well-being assured through economic growth and technical innovation
Weak	Anthropocentric and utilitarian; resource conservationist; growth is managed and modified; concern for distribution of development costs and benefits through intra- and intergenerational equity; rejection of infinite substitution between natural and human-made capital with recognition of some aspects of natural world as critical capital (e.g. ozone layer, some natural ecosystems); human-made plus natural capital constant or rising through time; decoupling of negative environmental impacts from economic growth
Strong	(Eco)systems perspective; resource preservationist; recognizes primary value of maintaining the functional integrity of ecosystems over and above secondary value through human resource utilization; interests of the collective given more weight than those of the individual consumer; adherence to intra- and intergenerational equity; decoupling important but alongside a belief in a steady-state economy as a consequence of following the constant natural assets rule; zero economic and human population growth
Very strong	Bioethical and ecocentric; resource preservationist to the point where utilization of natural resources is minimized; nature's rights or intrinsic value in nature encompassing non-human living organisms and even abiotic elements under a literal interpretation of Gaianism; anti-economic growth and reduced human population

- the use of recyclable materials
- improved recruitment and training procedures.

Companies are trying to prove that in the debate over sustainable development, they can be part of the solution rather than the problem.

For many organizations, this is part of a wider campaign to be seen as ethical, by their actions, in the belief that this might improve their competitive position in the market. The link between sustainable tourism and ethics in business will be explored in more detail in Chapter 34.

Throughout this book, the author will argue that we need to take a very broad view of sustainable tourism; that means that we should consider all of the issues outlined in Fig. 1.1 as being part of sustainable tourism.

The Early Origins of Sustainable Tourism

Clearly, the debate about sustainable tourism is partly influenced by the general concept of sustainable development discussed above. At the same time, there has been a parallel debate going on for several decades that has led to the widespread acceptance of the concept of sustainable tourism. Figure 1.2 illustrates the process by which the debate in tourism has developed.

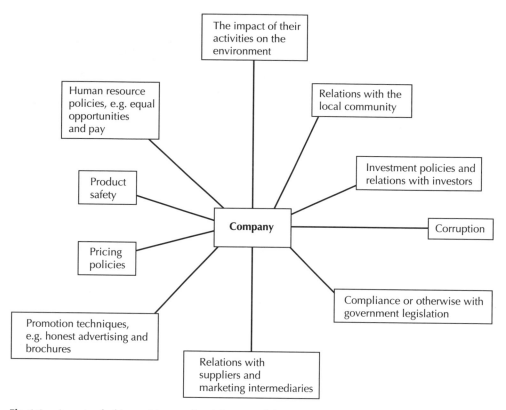

Fig. 1.1. Aspects of ethics and issues of social responsibility.

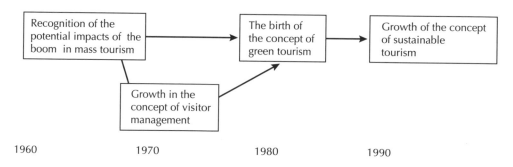

Fig. 1.2. The chronological development of the concept of sustainable tourism.

A number of key books have paved the way towards the concept of sustainable tourism, since mass tourism became a phenomenon from the 1960s onwards.

- In 1965, Michael Dowers' report, 'Fourth Wave – The Challenge of Leisure' aler-

ted society to the potential impact of the massive impending growth in leisure time and leisure activity.

- Young's book *Tourism: Blessing or Blight?* published in 1973, also drew attention to the negative potential impacts of tourism.

- *Tourism: Passport to Development*, published in 1979 by De Kadt discussed the role of tourism in the economies of developing countries.
- In 1982, the highly influential text *Tourism: Economic, Physical, and Social Impacts*, written by Mathieson and Wall, spelt out the worldwide impacts of tourism.
- The relationship between tourism and the host community was first discussed in detail by Peter Murphy in *Tourism: a Community Approach*, released in 1985.
- The Swiss writer Jost Krippendorf, looked at tourism and its impact from the point of view of the tourist in his work *The Holiday Makers*, published in 1987.

Several popular books were published in the early 1990s which attempted to influence directly the behaviour of tourists by making them aware of the negative impacts of some forms of tourism. Two of the most important such books were:

- *The Good Tourist* by Wood and House which dates from 1991
- *Holidays that Don't Cost the Earth* by Elkington and Hailes, published in 1992.

As the negative impacts of tourism were recognized, a series of initiatives were taken by public sector bodies to try to manage tourism through visitor management techniques. In general, tourism management initiatives were designed to ameliorate the worst excesses of tourism in the short term. They were generally small scale and did not seek to change the nature of tourism as a whole.

The term 'sustainable tourism' began to be used from the late 1980s, when tourism academics and practitioners began to consider the implications of the Brundtland Report for their own industry. However, the terms 'green issues' and 'green tourism' were at that time used more commonly. A major conference in Leeds in 1990 on what would now be termed sustainable tourism,

for example, was called 'Shades of Green'. The use of the term 'green tourism' reflected the rise of interest in environmental issues in the late 1980s and the growth of 'green politics' in the UK, Germany and France.

Green tourism was all about reducing the environmental costs, and maximizing the environmental benefits of tourism. This concept was highly influential in government circles. For example, in 1991, the English Tourist Board published its report 'Tourism and the Environment: Maintaining the Balance'. This was a set of guidelines for developing tourism in more environmentally friendly ways.

Since the early 1990s the term 'sustainable tourism' has become more commonly used. It encompasses an approach to tourism which recognizes the importance of the host community, the way staff are treated and the desire to maximize the economic benefits of tourism, for the host community. This concept was recognized in the Green Paper on Tourism published in 1995 by the European Union.

In 1997 Clarke suggested that the development of the concept of sustainable tourism involved four approaches which are, in largely chronological order, as follows:

- **Polar opposites**, whereby sustainable tourism and mass tourism were seen as polar opposites. We had to renounce mass tourism if we hoped to develop sustainable tourism.
- **A continuum**, whereby sustainable tourism and mass tourism were no longer seen as polar opposites, but rather it was acknowledged that there were different shades of sustainable and mass tourism, which would merge at some point in the middle.
- **Movement**, an approach which suggested that positive action could make mass tourism more sustainable.
- **Convergence**, is the idea that all types of tourism can strive to be sustainable.

The author agrees with the idea of 'convergence' but it is clear that much of what is said today is still based implicitly on the idea of 'polar opposites'.

The Rationale for Sustainable Tourism

Few people seem to think about a rationale for sustainable tourism, preferring instead simply to see it as a good idea. However, at the Globe '90 conference, in Vancouver, a list of the benefits of sustainable tourism was compiled as follows:

- Sustainable tourism encourages an understanding of the impacts of tourism on the natural, cultural and human environments.
- Sustainable tourism ensures a fair distribution of benefits and costs.
- Tourism generates local employment, both directly in the tourism sector, and in various support and resources management sectors.
- Tourism stimulates profitable domestic industries – hotels and other lodging facilities, restaurants and other food services, transportation systems, handicrafts and guide services.
- Tourism generates foreign exchange for the country, and injects capital and new money into the local economy.
- Tourism diversifies the local economy, particularly in rural areas where agricultural employment may be sporadic or insufficient.
- Sustainable tourism seeks decision-making among all segments of the society, including local populations, so that tourism and other resource users can coexist. It incorporates planning and zoning which ensure tourism development appropriate to the carrying capacity of the ecosystem.
- Tourism stimulates improvements to local transportation, communications and other basic community infrastructures.
- Tourism creates recreational facilities which can be used by local communities as well as domestic and international visitors. It also encourages

and helps pay for preservation of archaeological sites, and historic buildings and districts.
- Nature tourism encourages productive use of lands which are marginal for agriculture, enabling large tracts to remain covered in natural vegetation.
- Cultural tourism enhances local community esteem and provides the opportunity for greater understanding and communication among peoples of diverse backgrounds.
- Environmentally sustainable tourism demonstrates the importance of natural and cultural resources to a community's economic and social well being and can help to preserve them.
- Sustainable tourism monitors, assesses and manages the impacts of tourism, develops reliable methods of environmental accountability, and counters any negative effect.

The Tourism Industry and Sustainable Tourism

Since the 1980s the tourism industry has begun to take green issues and the idea of sustainable tourism seriously. The hospitality industry has been at the forefront of the development of environmentally friendly operations management. Following work particularly by the Inter-Continental chain, the International Hotels Environmental Initiative was set up. This industry-sponsored organization provides advice for hoteliers on how to make their operations greener including energy conservation measures, recycling and waste reduction. All of these measures tend to also reduce the hotels costs. As yet, the industry has shown little real interest in the social side of sustainability in terms of their human resource management policies, for example.

Transport operators have also focused on the environmental side of sustainability. Airlines, for example, have sought to introduce quieter, more fuel-efficient aircraft as part of an industry-wide agreement on environmental practices. While most visitor attractions have also focused on the environmental dimension, some have also considered their local community. For instance, they may try to purchase supplies from small local businesses wherever possible.

Some tour operators, particularly the specialist ones, have taken a broader view of sustainable tourism than businesses in any other sector of tourism. They have endeavoured to develop products which minimize the negative socioeconomic impacts of tourism, and maximize the economic benefits for the host community. A number of destinations have also sought to attract more sustainable forms of tourism that minimize the costs and maximize the benefits of tourism for the local population. These have been stimulated either by the public sector or local community groups.

The apparent growing interest of tourism organizations in sustainable tourism has been fuelled by the advocacy of:

- professional bodies
- pressure groups such as Tourism Concern, Green Flag and the Campaign for Environmentally Responsible Tourism
- the media.

Tourists and Sustainable Tourism

There has been little evidence to date that tourists are very interested in the concept of sustainable tourism, beyond natural concern over the quality of the environment in their own holiday resort. There have been no boycotts of environmentally unfriendly air travel or demands for hotels to pay higher wages. Perhaps, tourists who may take sustainable development seriously in their everyday lives, believe that their annual vacation is the only time when they can behave hedonistically, without the need to be responsible. Why should tourists seeking to escape from their everyday routine take an interest in sustainable tourism?

Sustainable Tourism and Sustainable Development

So far we have separated sustainable development from sustainable tourism. Yet, in recent years, we have seen government bodies trying to make use of tourism to help achieve the sustainable development of geographical areas. For example:

- In the USA and the UK, tourism has been used to try to regenerate old industrial cities and provide them with a new direction for the future. This has been seen particularly in places such as Baltimore and Liverpool, for example.
- The use of rural-based tourism to help achieve the sustainability of the rural economies and societies, and compensate for the decline of traditional agriculture. This phenomenon has been seen clearly in the countryside of France, Italy, Spain and Portugal.
- Attempts have been made to utilize tourism as a way to facilitate the sustainable development of economies in the developing world, particularly where other possible mechanisms for achieving the same end are limited. This is illustrated by Cuba, where tourism is being used as an alternative now that Cuba no longer receives aid from the former Soviet Union, and impoverished countries like Vietnam, Cambodia and Laos.

At the same time, the challenge in many traditional resort areas is to find more sustainable forms of tourism, as the traditional 'bucket and spade' holiday declines. In those resorts where tourism is now the dominant element in the local economy, failure to do this will probably mean that the community has little or no future.

Conclusions

We have seen that the concept of sustainable development has been around for several decades at least, but that sustainable tourism is a more recently accepted term. Perhaps this reflects the fact that tourism is a relatively new industry. At the same time, it is clear that while sustainability has environmental, social and economic dimensions, it is the former that has dominated in the debates about both sustainable development and sustainable tourism until now.

Having looked at the historical development of the concepts of sustainable development and sustainable tourism, we will now move on, in the next two chapters, to:

- outline what sustainable tourism means today
- offer a critique of current thinking about sustainable tourism.

referred to in this chapter. How do each of them relate to today's debate about sustainable tourism?

3. Discuss the reasons why levels of interest in sustainable tourism may vary between different countries.

4. Evaluate the nature of the links between sustainable development and sustainable tourism.

Discussion Points and Exercise Questions

1. Discuss the potential benefits and costs of sustainable development.
2. Choose any *two* of the books by Young, Mathieson and Wall, Murphy, Krippendorf, Wood and House which were

Exercise

Identify the implications of the 14 'sustainable development components' identified in Table 1.1 for tourism. Which ones are most relevant for tourism organizations and which are of little or no relevance to tourism?

2

The Nature and Scope of Sustainable Tourism

Towards a Definition of Sustainable Tourism

There is no widely accepted definition of sustainable tourism. It could, of course, be suggested that sustainable tourism should simply be about applying the Brundtland Report definition of sustainability to tourism. This could lead to a definition such as:

> Forms of tourism which meet the needs of tourists, the tourism industry, and host communities today without compromising the ability of future generations to meet their own needs.

It is usually thought vital that any definition of sustainable tourism emphasizes the environmental, social and economic elements of the tourism system. This might lead to a definition that sustainable tourism:

> means tourism which is economically viable but does not destroy the resources on which the future of tourism will depend, notably the physical environment and the social fabric of the host community.

Some commentators feel that trying to produce definitions of sustainable tourism is dangerous because:

> [general definitions] can give the impression of simplicity in what is a complex area. Tight definitions might also

limit the range of issues to be covered under the heading of sustainable tourism ... Definitions tend to be irrelevant, misleading, and ever-changing. (Richards in Bramwell *et al.*, 1996)

Conversely, the lack of widely known and accepted definitions can lead to some confusion over what sustainable tourism means. Richards, in a report about sustainable tourism education on an ATLAS project funded by the European Union, offered several examples of this phenomenon. The report contained examples of definitions offered by tourism academics and practitioners in Europe, including the following:

> Sustainable tourism is tourism which develops as quickly as possible, taking account of current accommodation capacity, the local population and the environment... The development of tourism and new investment in the tourism sector should not detract from tourism itself... New tourism facilities should be integrated with the environment. (Richards in Bramwell *et al.*, 1996)

The same report also noted some other interesting difficulties involved in defining sustainable tourism, notably:

- it is not a 'concrete' enough concept for practitioners; it sounds too scientific and technocratic

Fig. 2.1. The relationship between sustainable tourism and other terms.

- many languages, notably French, do not have an appropriate phrase that summarizes the concept of sustainable tourism.

At the same time, the existence of other words which are often deemed as acronyms for sustainable tourism are an added complication. While they are all related to sustainable tourism in some way, none of them are synonymous with it. Some of these terms are identified in Fig. 2.1.

The Principles of Sustainable Tourism Management

If we cannot easily define sustainable tourism, it is perhaps possible to propose a set of principles that should underpin any approach to sustainable tourism management. One set of some principles is illustrated in Box 2.1. While such principles are very useful, it is important to recognize that they are concerned largely with processes rather than outcomes. They say relatively little about what sustainable tourism might actually look like 'on the ground', in reality, in particular locations. They relate to how sustainable tourism might be achieved and what the implications of sustainable tourism could be, without necessarily focusing on what would distinguish sustainable from non-sustainable tourism.

Table 2.1 contrasts sustainable with non-sustainable tourism development based on the work of a number of authors. This approach includes the tourist in the equation, something which many definitions and approaches to sustainable tourism often fail to do. If they do consider the tourist they are

Box 2.1. Principles behind sustainable tourism management. Source: Bramwell *et al.* (1996).

- The approach sees policy, planning and management as appropriate, and, indeed essential responses to the problems of natural and human resource misuse in tourism
- The approach is generally not anti-growth, but it emphasizes that there are limitations to growth and that tourism must be managed within these limits
- Long-term rather than short-term thinking is necessary
- The concerns of sustainable tourism management are not just environmental, but are also economic, social, cultural, political and managerial
- The approach emphasizes the importance of satisfying human needs and aspirations, which entails a prominent concern for equity and fairness
- All stakeholders need to be consulted and empowered in tourism decision-making, and they also need to be informed about sustainable development issues
- While sustainable development should be a goal for all policies and actions, putting the ideas of sustainable tourism into practice means recognizing that in reality there are often limits to what will be achieved in the short and medium term
- An understanding of how market economies operate, of the cultures and management procedures of private sector businesses and of public and voluntary sector organizations, and of the values and attitudes of the public is necessary in order to turn good intentions into practical measures
- There are frequently conflicts of interest over the use of resources, which means that in practice trade-offs and compromises may be necessary
- The balancing of costs and benefits in decisions on different courses of action must extend to considering how much different individuals and groups will gain or lose

Table 2.1. Sustainable versus non-sustainable tourism development. Adapted from Krippendorf (1982), Lane (1989, 1990) and Godfrey (1996).

Sustainable	Non-sustainable
General concepts	
Slow development	Rapid development
Controlled development	Uncontrolled development
Appropriate scale	Inappropriate scale
Long term	Short term
Qualitative	Quantitative
Local control	Remote control
Development strategies	
Plan, then develop	Develop without planning
Concept-led schemes	Project-led schemes
All five landscapes concerned	Concentrating on 'honey-pots'
Pressure and benefits diffused	Increase capacity
Local developers	Outside developers
Locals employed	Imported labour
Vernacular architecture	Non-vernacular architecture
Tourist behaviour	
Low value	High value
Some mental preparation	Little or no mental preparation
Learning local language	No learning of local language
Tactful and sensitive	Intensive and insensitive
Quiet	Loud
Repeat visits	Unlikely to return

usually seen as the problem, because of the impact they have. Many commentators talk about the responsibility which tourists should have but not their rights as paying customers.

Conversely, such an approach also polarizes the debate so that there are only sustainable (good) and non-sustainable (bad) forms of tourism. However, we know that in reality things are rarely black and white, but rather various shades of grey. Nevertheless, this table is valuable because it represents much mainstream thinking in the sustainable tourism debate.

It is also important to recognize that there are many subjective value judgements implicit in the table, about the value of vernacular architecture and the learning of local languages by tourists for example.

The Scope of Sustainable Tourism

Sustainable tourism is clearly a broad, ill-defined area that encompasses many of the elements of the tourism system. This breadth is illustrated in Fig. 2.2.

In the rest of this chapter, we will look at a number of aspects of sustainable tourism, including:

- the stakeholders of sustainable tourism
- sustainable tourism and different types of environment
- different types of tourism and sustainable tourism
- sustainable tourism and different types of tourism organizations
- different sectors of tourism and sustainability

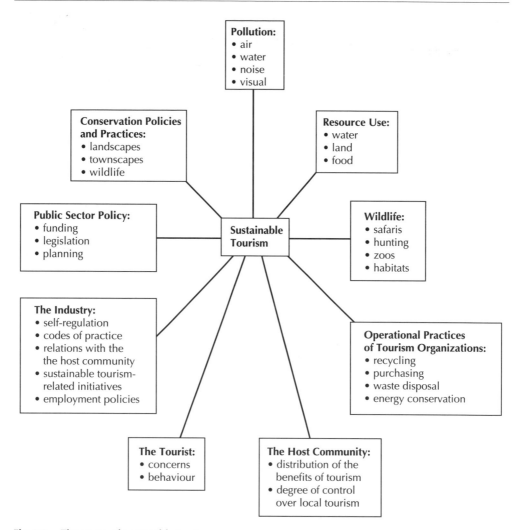

Fig. 2.2. The scope of sustainable tourism.

- sustainable tourism and functional management
- differences between regions of the world in relation to the idea of sustainable tourism

Each of these issues will be taken up in later chapters.

Sustainable Tourism – the Key Stakeholders

There are many stakeholders in the field of sustainable tourism. The major areas are illustrated in Fig. 2.3. With such a complex web of stakeholders, it is not surprising that it is difficult to reach a consensus on what sustainable tourism means and how it can be achieved. The issue of the stakeholders is covered fully in Part 3 of this book.

Sustainable Tourism and Different Types of Environment

The debate over sustainable tourism tends to revolve around five types of environment. In other words, we talk about sustainable tourism development, and:

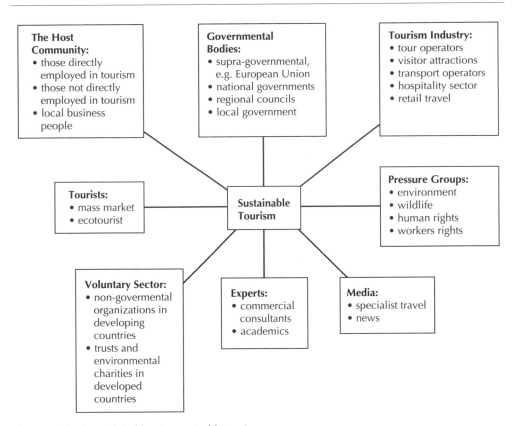

Fig. 2.3. The key stakeholders in sustainable tourism.

- coastal tourism
- tourism on islands
- tourism in the countryside
- mountain region tourism
- urban tourism.

Each type of environment has its own distinctive characteristics and their own tourism management problems.

In recent years we have also seen the growth of a sixth type of environment, marine tourism, namely tourism which takes place at sea such as whale-watching.

In all six types of environment, the emphasis in relation to sustainable tourism is often on managing existing tourism demand in established destinations, and balancing its negative and positive impacts. Alternatively, it involves learning lessons from established destinations that might be applied to new, emerging destinations. These types of environment are covered in Part 4 of this book.

Sustainable Tourism and Different Types of Tourism

In the debate over sustainable tourism, it appears that certain types of tourism are viewed as being inherently more sustainable than others.

There appears to be a commonly held view that mass market coastal-based tourism is not compatible with the concept of sustainable tourism. At the same time, the growing phenomenon of ecotourism is seen by many commentators as being more in keeping with the idea of sustainable tourism. Table 2.2 illustrates the perceived differences between the two types of tourism which may lead to this perception, although we need to recognize that these are perceptions and are therefore subjective and do not necessarily reflect reality. The apparent distinction between 'good' alternative tourism and 'bad' mass tourism is also illustrated in

Chapter 2

Table 2.2. Mass market coastal tourism versus ecotourism.

	Mass market coastal tourism	Ecotourism
Scale	• Large scale, inappropriate to location	• Small scale, in keeping with ability of destination to absorb tourists without damage
Impact on the physical environment	• New, aesthetic unattractive buildings • Over-building of the infrastructure leading to pollution and traffic congestion	• Little new building • Little extra demand on infrastructure
Host community relations	• Formalized relations • Little contact with local people who are not involved in the tourism industry	• Informal contact • Interaction with all types of local people
Sociocultural impact	• Transforms local culture • Immigration of labour from outside the area	• Minor impact on host culture • Labour needs are wholly met from the local community
Economic impact	• Much tourism income is lost to enterprises based outside the destination • Tourism becomes the dominant economic activity	• Most tourist income is retained in the local economy • Additional income from tourism complements traditional economic activities
The importance of the location	• Can take place anywhere with sea and good weather • The specific location is not important	• The specific location offers a unique experience that cannot be found elsewhere
Quality of the experience for the tourist	• Short-term relaxation and sun tan	• Learning about places brings long-term understanding of where and how other people live
Tourist behaviour	• Insensitive to local culture and traditions • Indifference to life of local people • Hedonistic	• Sensitive to local culture and traditions • Interested in life of local people • Responsible

Table 2.3. However, in both cases, such distinctions are based on subjective judgements rather than empirical evidence.

As we will see in Chapter 3, the view of ecotourism is over-rosy and is perhaps just a function of the fact that it is a new phenomenon. If it grows to a mass scale, as it has in Kenya with the safari business, then it may start to exhibit many of the characteristics of mass market coastal tourism. In other words, ecotourism is not, perhaps, inherently more sustainable than other forms of tourism.

Nevertheless, there are still apparently generally held views that some forms of tourism are more sustainable than others. Some of these currently held principles are outlined in Table 2.4. However, this is clearly a very simplistic view that is not based on facts, but rather on subjective judgements. Nevertheless, these ideas combined in Table 2.4 do reflect what is written in many texts on sustainable tourism.

This idea that some forms of tourism are inevitably more sustainable than others is a major issue in the sustainable tourism debate. It may make those who offer those

Table 2.3. Attributes of mass and alternative tourism. Source: Hunter and Green (1994), adapted from Himmetoglu (1992).

	Mass tourism	Alternative tourism
General features	Rapid development Maximizes Uncontrolled Short term Sectoral	Slow development Optimizes Controlled Long term Holistic
Tourist behaviour	Large groups Fixed programme Tourists directed Comfortable and passive No foreign language Nosy Loud	Singles, families Spontaneous decisions Tourists decide Demanding and active Language learning Tactful Quiet
Basic requirements	Holiday peaks Untrained labour Publicity clichés Hard selling	Staggered holidays Trained labour force Tourist education Heart selling
Development strategies	Unplanned Project-led New buildings Outside developers	Planned Concept-led Re-use of existing buildings Local developers

Table 2.4. Sustainable tourism and different types of tourism.

Types of tourism which are highly compatible with the concept of sustainable tourism	Types of tourism which are largely incompatible with the concept of sustainable tourism
• Ecotourism (see Table 2.2) • Cultural tourism which involves visitors learning about the history and culture of an area • Urban attractions which provide new uses for derelict sites • Small-scale rural 'agro-tourism' which brings income to farmers • Conservation holidays where tourists do conservation work during their vacations	• Mass market coastal tourism (see Table 2.2) • Activity holidays which have a negative impact on the physical environment such as skiing, off-road vehicle driving and mountain biking • Sex tourism which leads to the spread of infection such as HIV and other sexually transmitted diseases • Hunting and fishing holidays, particularly where the activity is unregulated • Visiting very fragile environments such as rain forests and the Antarctic

types of tourism which are perceived to be more sustainable, complacent, while it may at the same time discourage those who offer less sustainable forms of tourism from doing anything because they may believe they cannot succeed. Perhaps we need, therefore, to think that *all* forms of tourism can be made sustainable, or at least more sustainable.

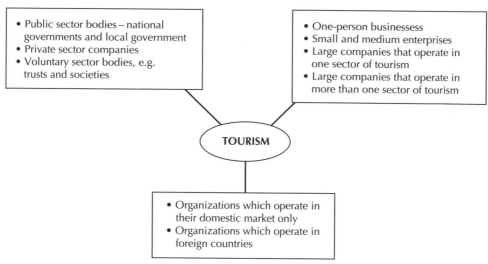

Fig. 2.4. Different types of organizations in tourism.

Sustainable Tourism and Different Types of Tourism Organizations

Tourism involves a range of types of organization as can be seen from Fig. 2.4. The existence of these different types of organizations in tourism has various implications in terms of sustainable tourism, including the following:

- public sector bodies tend to be those which develop tourism strategies for destinations but it is the private sector organizations which are responsible for most of the tourism products which tourists buy. In other words, those who set the strategies must try to persuade those who dominate the supply side of tourism to go along with their plans
- it is large organizations, often based outside the destination, which are seen to be the villains in the sustainable tourism debate. They are accused of showing little long-term commitment to any destination for they can simply move elsewhere if things get difficult. Conversely, most one-person businesses, and small- and medium-sized enterprises, are locally owned and have a long-term commitment to the destination which is also their home area
- transnational enterprises that sell their products in foreign countries must take into account sustainable tourism issues in each of these countries, not just in their own country.

It is therefore important for the future of the concept of sustainable tourism to recognize the growth in tourism of large-scale, transnational companies.

Sustainable Tourism and the Different Sectors of Tourism

Each sector of tourism has its own issues in relation to sustainable tourism, as illustrated in Fig. 2.5. There is also the question of business tourism and sustainable tourism. Business tourists, who generally travel more frequently than leisure tourists, clearly have a greater impact than the average pleasure tourist. The business tourism sector will be looked at in greater detail in Chapter 32. In the meantime, the roles of the different sectors of tourism are covered in Chapters 24–28.

Sustainable Tourism and Functional Management

Every area of functional management has a role to play in the search for more sustain-

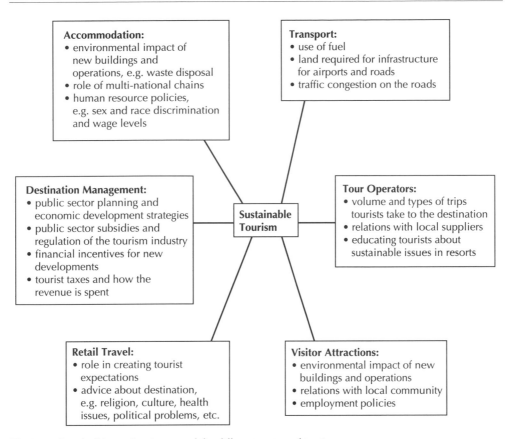

Fig. 2.5. Sustainable tourism issues and the different sectors of tourism.

able forms of tourism. The links between the different types of functional management namely marketing, human resources, finance and operations, are illustrated in Fig. 2.6. In other words, sustainable tourism should rightly be the concern of every person in an organization, regardless of their job title or department. The issue of functional management and sustainable tourism is the subject of Part 5 of this book.

The Concept of Sustainable Tourism in the Different Regions of the World

Interest in the idea of sustainable tourism is greatest in those countries where there is a high level of interest in sustainable development in general, notably Germany and Scandinavia. There is also above average interest in Canada, while in the USA, there

is a similar debate although it is often debated as if ecotourism and sustainable tourism were one and the same thing.

The UK has been a leading player in the development of the concept of sustainable tourism, through both academics and pressure groups such as Tourism Concern.

It is interesting to note that, in general, interest in sustainable tourism has been higher in these developed countries which have traditionally been generators, rather than receivers, of international tourism trips.

To date, there has been little tangible interest in, or action about, sustainable tourism in the less developed countries of the Mediterranean, Eastern Europe and Asia. Here the priority has been short-term economic development, rather than longer term resource conservation. However, slowly, the issue is becoming a major point of debate

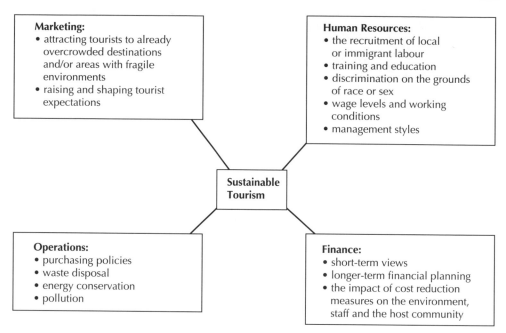

Fig. 2.6. Sustainable tourism and functional management.

worldwide, largely as a result of the work of supra-governmental bodies such as the World Tourism Organisation.

Conclusions

In this chapter, we have looked at the nature and scope of sustainable tourism. We have looked at difficulties in sustainable tourism and seen how difficult it is to find any simple, single definition which works. At the same time, we have identified the stakeholders in the sustainable tourism debate. We have also looked at the links between sustainable tourism and:

● different forms of tourism
● different types of tourism organization
● different sections of tourism
● the various areas of functional management.

However, as Pigram states:

Sustainable tourism has the potential to become a tangible expression of sustainable tourism development. Yet it runs the risk of remaining irrelevant and inept as a feasible policy for the real world of tourism development, without the development of effective means of translating the idea into action. (Pigram, 1990)

In Chapter 3, we will critically evaluate current theory and practice in sustainable tourism to help explain why the situation outlined by Pigram has arisen.

Discussion Points and Essay Questions

1. Discuss the relationship between sustainable tourism and the other terms outlined in Fig. 2.1.
2. Critically evaluate the principles of sustainable tourism management featured in Box 2.1.
3. Evaluate the extent to which cultural tourism trips and activity holidays can be sustainable forms of tourism.

Exercise

Carry out a small survey to test public perceptions of the concept of sustainable tourism, in terms of:

- what 'sustainable tourism' means

- the level of public awareness of the concept of sustainable tourism.

Your findings should be presented in the form of a report. The report should also note the problems experienced in carrying out the survey.

3

A Critique of Current Thinking in Sustainable Tourism Management

We saw in Chapter 2 that sustainable tourism is a broad, complex subject which has very blurred edges. Nevertheless, in recent years, a number of ideas have developed which are often seen as pre-requisites for sustainable tourism such as community involvement. Likewise, a range of techniques have been developed as tools for helping to achieve sustainable tourism, like carrying capacity.

While little empirical data exists to support any of these ideas and techniques, they appear to have become part of conventional wisdom in tourism, and are rarely questioned.

A number of these ideas and techniques are illustrated in Fig. 3.1. The author believes that the apparently unquestioning acceptance of ideas, in a field which is still at a very early level of development, is not desirable. It has created

- 'sacred cows', in other words ideas which are apparently so widely accepted that they are rarely questioned
- 'cash cows' where the label of 'sustainable' or 'green' is being used to simply boost profit margins or attract new market segments
- 'mad cows', a rather strong term for ideas which appear to be either unrealistic or which would bring problems

with their implementation which would be worse than the situation they are intended to alleviate.

In this chapter we will look at each of the issues outlined in Fig. 3.1 and critically evaluate them. The aim is not to denigrate these ideas and those who propose them, but rather to show that there are no easy answers and that the subject is more complex than it might at first appear. Hopefully this will stimulate debate and further research that will help to refine the concepts and techniques, which in turn will increase the likelihood of developing more sustainable forms of tourism. Let us now consider each issue in turn.

Value Judgements and the Lack of Factual Evidence

The whole sustainable tourism debate often appears to be based more on value judgements than on empirical research or other factual evidence. For example, two of the most influential books on the subject in the UK in the early 1980s are entitled *The Good Tourist* (Wood and House, 1991) and *Holidays That Don't Cost the Earth* (Elkington and Hailes, 1992), both heavily value-laden phrases. Inside they are packed with judge-

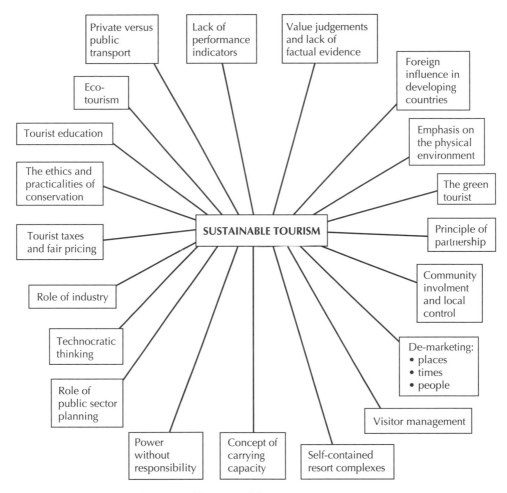

Fig. 3.1. The key issues in the sustainable tourism debate.

ments that appear to have little hard evidence underpinning them.

Commentators have written as if certain opinions and attitudes are proven facts. For example, there seems to be an implicit belief that:

- large high-rise coastal resorts around the Mediterranean represent a less sustainable form of tourism than ecotourism holidays in Central America
- independent travel is more sustainable than package holiday tourism
- small-scale tourism is always better than mass tourism
- cultural tourism is more sustainable than hedonistic tourism.

Yet there appears to be little if any evidence that these are true. Indeed, it could be argued that, providing it is well managed and the infrastructure is adequate, mass seaside resort tourism is a very sustainable form of tourism. It:

- provides jobs for a large number of people
- satisfies the needs of a large number of tourists so that they do not take trips to more fragile environments, further afield

- does not cause the negative sociocultural impacts that tourists mixing with local people can cause because there is little contact between both groups, and there are often relatively few indigenous local people living in the resort.

Perhaps, therefore, what is happening is that commentators are supporting those forms of tourism that they themselves prefer. The educated middle classes who comprise the majority of such commentators often seem to prefer cultural holidays to sun, sand, sea and sex trips, and they tend to make up a large part of the independent travel market. Thus a significant proportion of the literature that has appeared may be at least partly instigated by a desire to justify the author's own behaviour and that of their peer group.

The lack of empirical evidence in the sustainable tourism field is also making it difficult for us to evaluate the scale of some of the problems with the negative environmental impacts of tourism. Furthermore, the combination of this and the value judgements of commentators who have a partisan view on the subject, may be resulting in us getting some problems out of proportion. Two examples will illustrate this point, as follows:

- the pollution caused by coastal tourism in the Mediterranean is probably only a minor cause of the problems being experienced in that sea, compared to manufacturing industry, agriculture and the waste produced by residents
- rural planners are greatly concerned by footpath erosion at a time when British upland areas are suffering agricultural decline, rural poverty and unemployment that threaten their long-term survival.

Finally, given that sustainability is about the future, we seem rather arrogantly willing to feel that in spite of the lack of hard evidence, we know what is best not only for today, but also for tomorrow.

The Green Tourist

Much discussion on sustainable tourism seems to be based on what is described as the 'rise of the green tourist'. Yet there appears little evidence of the rise of this tourist as a real force in the tourism market. Unlike the consumer boycott of products containing CFCs (chlorofluorocarbons) seen in the late 1980s there seems to be no such consumer action in the tourism field. There is little evidence that tourists are:

- switching from the use of private cars to public transport for their holiday trips
- demonstrating against the environmental impacts of new theme parks
- insisting that hotels recycle their waste.

It is perhaps better therefore to talk in terms of 'shades of green' tourists, in other words the fact that the market is divided into groups which vary from being very dark green to not being green at all. The differences between these different shades of tourist opinion are illustrated in Fig. 3.2. It is clear from this argument that dark green/totally green tourists are a small niche only, in the UK at least.

Some argue that the situation is different in other countries, like Germany, where consumers seem to be far more concerned with environmental issues. Certainly a BAT-Leisure Research Institute report of 1993 claimed that, "of ten criteria for a quality holiday listed by consumers, seven related to the environment" (Horner and Swarbrooke, 1996). However, on closer examination it appears to be more about the vested interests of these consumers in the environment as a key determinant in the quality of their holiday experience, than their concern with the environmental impacts of tourism in general.

Even these limited examples of environmental concerns on the part of tourists, are not typical of the world as a whole. In some of the more recently economically developed regions of the world, even a modest

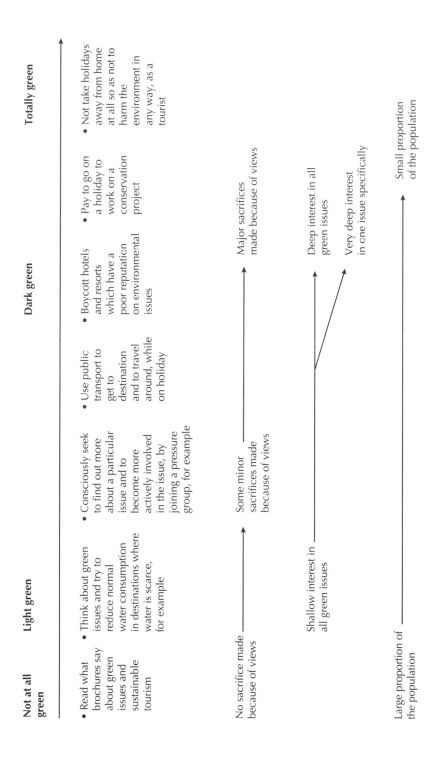

	Not at all green	Light green	Dark green	Totally green
	• Read what brochures say about green issues and sustainable tourism	• Think about green issues and try to reduce normal water consumption in destinations where water is scarce, for example	• Use public transport to get to destination and to travel around, while on holiday	• Not take holidays away from home at all so as not to harm the environment in any way, as a tourist
		• Consciously seek to find out more about a particular issue and to become more actively involved in the issue, by joining a pressure group, for example	• Boycott hotels and resorts which have a poor reputation on environmental issues	• Pay to go on a holiday to work on a conservation project

No sacrifice made because of views

Some minor sacrifices made because of views

Major sacrifices made because of views

Shallow interest in all green issues

Deep interest in all green issues

Very deep interest in one issue specifically

Large proportion of the population

Small proportion of the population

Fig. 3.2. "Shades of green" tourist.

level of concern appears to be largely absent. Indeed there appears to be evidence that interest in the environment amongst tourists is low, and may even be falling, at least in the UK.

Research conducted by MORI (Martin, 1997) has indicated that:

- In 1996, 21% of consumers believed too much 'fuss' was being made about the environment, compared to 11% in 1992.
- In the UK only 3% of people felt the environment was the most important problem facing the UK in 1996, whereas the equivalent figure in 1992 was 11%.
- Only 11% of tourists questioned in the mid-1990s said environmental problems in a destination would make them decide to not to return to the destination.
- In 1995, just 16% of tourists said it was very important for them to deal with a tourist organization that took environmental issues into account, while 18% said it was not at all important.
- Only 6% of people questioned in 1995 believed tourism caused major damage to the environment while 30% thought it caused no damage or involved no damage.

So far we have focused on the 'green tourist' who one would expect to be concerned with purely environmental issues. There is even less evidence of the existence of a 'sustainable tourist' who is also concerned about the long-term social and economic impacts of tourism. Few tourists appear to be demanding to pay a higher price to provide more economic benefits to host communities. Likewise there seems to be no evidence of tourists demanding better pay and working conditions for tourism and hospitality industry employees.

If one believes in the concept of customer-led, market-led marketing, then the tourism industry should not be taking much interest in the concept of sustainable tourism.

Ecotourism

The rise of ecotourism has been a controversial issue in the context of the debate over sustainable tourism. This was well summed up by the book edited by Cater and Lowman, *Ecotourism: a Sustainable Option?*, which was published in 1994.

The tourism industry clearly wants clients to feel that ecotourism is less harmful and more sustainable than mainstream mass tourism, perhaps because it thinks that this will make tourists feel good about buying such products. This argument is seen time and again in brochures for a range of holidays, including:

- treks in the Himalayan range
- expeditions in the jungles of Central America
- whale-watching holidays from California to the Arctic
- sledge tours in Lapland
- river trips by canoe in South-East Asia.

The claim of such ecotourism products to be sustainable is usually based on the following characteristics:

- the desire of participants to learn more about their destination than the average tourist
- the attempt to maximize contact with indigenous people
- the small size of most groups.

Nevertheless, it is arguable whether ecotourism can be viewed as sustainable tourism. The ecotourists are not primarily motivated by a desire to protect the environment but rather by a desire to see the native ecosystem at first hand.

Likewise if 100 people buy and enjoy an ecotourism product this year, and tell their friends, this could rise to several thousands in 3 years. Certainly, some ecotourism tour operators have grown in recent years to become medium-sized operations. It is therefore not inherently small scale.

If ecotourism were to grow in an area, without regulation, it could easily become as harmful as other forms of mainstream tourism. Indeed because it tends to take place in areas with rare and fragile ecosystems, it could be even more harmful. This is particularly true because ecotourists are always looking for new destinations ever more off the beaten track than the last one, whereas many mainstream tourists are happy to holiday in established resorts. Thus, ecotourists may not be content until they have visited – and brought the mixed blessings of tourism – to every area of the world.

The Concept of Carrying Capacity

The concept of carrying capacity is a common one in the sustainable tourism literature. There are several types of carrying capacity, including:

- **physical** capacity, the number of tourists a place can physically accommodate
- **environmental** or **ecological** capacity, the number of tourists that can be accommodated before damage begins to be caused to the environment or ecosystem
- **economic** capacity, the number of tourists that can be welcomed before the local community start to suffer economic problems, e.g. increased housing values and land prices
- **social** capacity, the number of people beyond which social disruption or irrevocable cultural damage will occur
- **perceptual** capacity, the number of people a place can welcome before the quality of the tourist experience begins to be adversely affected.
- **infrastructure** capacity, the number of tourists that can be accommodated by the destination infrastructure.

However, in terms of developing sustainable tourism, all six types share one criticism, namely, even if you can measure the capacity, how do you put it into practice? Elsewhere in this chapter we will see that one means of implementation, de-marketing, is fraught with problems.

Furthermore, some concepts of carrying capacity, such as social and perceptual are very subjective, and no two observers will agree on the actual figure. At the same time, they are generally rather unrealistic in that they suggest that damage will occur at a particular point when a specific number of tourists are present, in a certain place. The process of tourism-related damage is almost certainly slower and less clear cut than this. It is a progressive, rather than a sudden phenomenon.

As each locality is totally different in terms of geography, ecosystem, social structure and economy, it is unlikely that the carrying capacity will be the same in any two places, so its application in any place is very difficult to forecast.

While carrying capacity is a useful concept, it is very problematic to use in a practical way to help develop sustainable tourism. Finally, however, it is clear that carrying capacity can be modified by visitor management schemes, in other words, they are not absolute or inevitable.

De-marketing

Some proponents of sustainable tourism appear to place great faith in the concept of de-marketing. This involves manipulating the marketing mix or 'four Ps' to discourage rather than attract tourists to visit destinations which are thought to be over-visited. While carrying capacity is a useful concept it is very problematic to use in a practical way to help develop sustainable tourism. To date, this has largely meant simply reducing the amount of brochures which are produced to promote certain destinations. For example, the local authority in Cambridge took a decision several years ago to stop printing brochures about the city as a tourist destination.

However, this is clearly a longer term strategy and cities like Cambridge are famous the world over, and even then this

may prove to be ineffective, for the following reasons:

- many tourists become aware of destinations from sources other than
  promotional literature produced by the
  destinations themselves. These other
  sources include:
     friends and relatives
     the media
     the tourism industry such as coach
     operators
- repeat visitors are already aware of the
  destination
- business tourists do not choose their
  destination, it is determined by the
  demands of their jobs, whether it be a
  visit by a sales person to a potential
  client or a lecturer attending a specialist
  conference.

Perhaps, therefore, de-marketing can only
work if a more radical approach is taken that
uses all the four Ps. In the case of Venice, for
instance, demand might be reduced by:

- raising prices. However, for a unique
  product like Venice, higher prices might
  not reduce demand significantly, as
  many people will want to see it once, so
  they will be willing to pay the price. At
  the same time, such a policy could be
  seen as morally unacceptable as it dis-
  criminates against those on lower
  incomes
- only allowing a certain number of people into the city per day through a
  'ticket' system. It would have to be pre-
  booked or else people taking a special
  trip to visit Venice would be very disappointed or angry!

However, these approachs would require an
expensive system of implementation even
in a city like Venice where there are relatively few entry points. Nevertheless, such
limited numbered ticket schemes do operate
successfully at some attractions and in certain American National Parks.

It is likely, though, that in a city like
Venice, where so many people are employed
directly or indirectly in tourism, that any
attempt to reduce visitor numbers would be
unpopular. Thus any attempt to introduce
de-marketing would probably have to come
from external pressure and could be
opposed by local people. This would clearly
make it an ethically questionable course of
action.

Ironically, one of the few ways in which
the industry might divert some demand
from honey-pot destinations is by using new
products and prices to encourage repeat
visitors to a country to visit other areas.
These tourists could be told that other areas
represent the 'real' character of the country
while special interest holidays in these areas
might be offered to help these tourists 'learn
more about the country'.

Before too much time and money is spent
on de-marketing, we need to be sure the
problem merits such drastic action. Often it
is outsiders who think the number of tourists in an area is the problem, as it affects the
quality of their holiday experience, or the
place they have chosen to retire to. But providing that the infrastructure can cope and
the benefits are distributed fairly to local
people, perhaps the problem is not serious
enough to merit such action.

In some cases it is not the total volume of
visitors that a destination receives that is the
problem, but rather when they visit. Most
destinations have clear peak seasons which
can last for just a few weeks each year. In
these cases perhaps, the challenge is to de-
market peak times, not the place as a whole.
This means developing new products and
offering prices that will tempt people to visit
at quieter times of the year instead. However, there are also problems with such an
approach. For example:

- some people are tied to taking their holidays at certain times of the year because
  of their job or their children's school
  holidays
- most destinations have times of the year
  when the weather is not good enough to
  make them attractive to the majority of
  tourists.

One of the main ways of attracting tourists in
the off-peak season is through organizing

special events and festivals or offering themed breaks. In many cases, these will simply attract new customers rather than diverting demand from the peak season. This is particularly true as we see the growth of people taking second or even third holidays each year.

Perhaps it is better to have a quiet season when resorts can be refurbished and local residents can enjoy a more normal life style, albeit for just a few months. Finally, we are seeing the growth of a third form of de-marketing, namely the de-marketing of people. Many destinations increasingly talk of wanting to attract 'quality tourists' which often translates as higher spending, older tourists who are quiet and well-behaved.

Some resorts are consciously trying to de-market the so-called 'lager-louts' to make them more attractive to the 'quality tourist'. This often means changing the physical environment of the destination together with stricter policy and controls on behaviour, for example. However, such a policy will be unpopular with bar owners in these resorts, who make a living from the young 'hedonistic' tourists. The labelling of people as 'quality tourists' or 'lager louts' is also laden with prejudice, and is morally questionable.

We have seen that all three types of de-marketing are problematic in both practical and moral terms. However, even if it were a desirable activity, changing tourist behaviour is a massive challenge that would require an enormous budget. Yet many of the organizations that seek to practise it are public sector organizations with limited budgets.

Tourist Taxes and Fair Pricing

It is sometimes suggested that we should use tourist taxes to help develop sustainable tourism, in two main ways:

- charging tourist taxes that are high enough to discourage some tourists from visiting certain places, thus reducing demand, and the problems which

flow from over-use

- using the funds generated by tourist taxes to help pay for the maintenance and development of the local tourism infrastructure.

Clearly, the first application is more radical and is about influencing demand, while the latter will simply help manage existing demand more effectively. However, implementing the former approach has a number of potential pitfalls, including the following:

- To reduce demand at unique destinations such as Venice or the pyramids in Egypt, would require a high tourist tax, and this could be seen to be discrimination against lower income tourists.
- We would need to know far more than we do currently about tourists' willingness to pay a particular tax levy for a specific resort. Otherwise, the tax could be set too high, and severely reduce a destination's visitor numbers with serious economic costs as a result.
- The mechanism for implementing the tax would be complex and costly. In areas where day-trippers are the majority of the market, it could even involve stopping cars on the road into national parks, as it would not be possible to collect the tax via accommodation establishments. On busy days, in the Peak District National Park in the UK, this could cause horrendous traffic congestion. However, perhaps this fact would discourage people from taking a trip and thus help reduce demand indirectly!
- It assumes that all tourists are equal in terms of their impact and does not encourage responsible behaviour or penalize anti-social behaviour. Instead it simply seeks to reduce overall numbers.
- Given our inadequate understanding of carrying capacities how do we know which ideal visitor number we are aiming for in the first place, when we try to

use taxes on tourists to manipulate demand?

- In a highly seasonal market, we would need to be constantly changing the rate of the tax levied to ensure that we were dampening demand at the times of most overcrowding but not at times when destination capacity was under-utilized.

The second use of tourist taxes is specifically designed to get tourists to pay more of the real costs of meeting their needs, rather than the whole burden falling on the local population. A good existing example of such a tax is the 'Taxe de Séjour' which certain recognized resorts in France are allowed to levy. The product of the tax can be spent on infrastructure which is used by tourists but the tax has three main problems:

- As it is largely only collected in hotels, tourists using other forms of accommodation such as self-catering, cottages and campsites, generally do not pay it, although they still make use of the infrastructure.
- The collection of the tax is often seen as an imposition by the hoteliers and the collection rate often falls well below 100%.
- As the rate is very low, typically 2–5 francs per person, it is not a major source of revenue.

Visitor Management

Over the years great confidence has been placed in the use of 'visitor management' techniques to manage tourism in areas where it is seen to be having a negative impact. This usually involves trying to divert demand away from 'honey-pot' areas, and involves initiatives like:

- using interpretation techniques to try to direct demand to less heavily used areas of the region
- closing roads from time to time and/or siting car parks, so that visitors cannot

drive into already overcrowded or environmentally fragile areas.

The hope is that this inconvenience will dissuade tourists from visiting the site.

Alternatively, visitor management techniques can be used to reduce the negative impacts of the existing level of demand. This could involve re-surfacing footpaths with material that is more resistant to the erosive power of walking boots, or park-and-ride schemes that keep cars out of the heart of villages, town centres, or fragile environments.

Visitor management can be effective, but it is also quite costly. It can also have a negative effect. For example, if a site is well known to tourists, improved interpretation of other less well known sites could simply increase overall demand and result in new pressures being placed on previously little used sites, as well as continuing pressure on the already popular site.

Private versus Public Transport

For several decades, the private car has been seen as the enemy of sustainable tourism, particularly in the countryside and historic cities. Having at first liberated the tourist, it is now seen as a monster that imprisons them in traffic jams, and causes untold harm to the physical environment. Many writers also lament what they see as the negative impact the presence of cars has on the ambience and aesthetic quality of destinations.

The conventional wisdom is that we need to encourage tourists to leave their cars at home and use public transport instead. In spite of the money and effort that has been put into such schemes, particularly in the national parks of the UK, it is clearly a losing battle, because:

- tourists enjoy the flexibility and freedom which using their own car offers
- public transport systems are often inconvenient because of the need to travel to a pick-up point and the fact that consumers have to fit in with the operator's timetables

- in a number of countries, subsidies for public transport have been declining in recent years, which is taking away any price advantage it might have over the private car.

As attempts to encourage tourists to change their preferred mode of transport from the car to public transport have largely been unsuccessful, the only solution may be to forbid the use of cars in certain places. Clearly, this would be a very difficult decision for politicians to take, given the political influence of car owners and the car industry.

It would also have to be managed carefully so as not to inconvenience the host community, who would still need to use their cars for their business and leisure activities.

Before any such action is taken we should also be realistic about some of the negative environmental impacts of public transport, such as its energy consumption, and the pollution it causes. For example, in the UK, de-regulation of bus transport is leading to problems which make bus travel less environmentally friendly, including:

- the fact that competition is in some cases leading to buses travelling with fewer passengers
- more older buses being on the road which are, apparently, worse in terms of pollution than modern buses.

Tourist Education

Some commentators appear to speak blandly about the need to 'educate tourists' to make them more concerned about the environmental impacts of tourism and the principles of sustainable tourism. However, an observer could be forgiven for taking a rather cynical view of this idea, for two main reasons, as follows:

- We are not even sure yet what sustainable tourism is, so how can we provide guidelines that, if followed by tourists, would help develop more sustainable forms of tourism?
- The evidence from other well-meaning education campaigns – such as those relating to sex and drugs – appears to show that their impact is severely limited, unless the audience wants to hear the message.

Even if we did know what sustainable tourism was, it would still not be an easy message to sell to tourists if it involved making any sacrifice on the part of the tourist. In any event, attempting to influence the well-established behaviour patterns of millions of people would be an expensive activity that would take a long time to take effect.

Finally, one could argue that if we are to spend time and money on educating tourists about anything, then we should focus on vitally important issues such as the link between tourism and HIV infection and other sexually transmitted diseases.

Community Involvement and Local Control

One of the most widely accepted principles of sustainable tourism appears to be the idea that tourism can only be sustainable if the local community is involved in tourism planning and management. However, even where attempts have been made to achieve this aim, there have been problems. These include:

- communities rarely, if ever, speak with one voice. There are many interest groups and individual viewpoints and there is no easy way of reconciling these to reach a consensus
- the mechanisms that are used to elicit the views of the community provide an opportunity for a minority of self-appointed community spokespeople, or people with strong views to dominate the process. The views of the so-called 'silent majority' can therefore be ignored
- professionals can sometimes under-

value or even ignore local views that are the opposite of their own. This can particularly occur when 'public participation exercises' are held to legitimize decisions which have already been taken, to some extent

- conflicts that debate causes within communities can be serious and can continue for a long time after the debate ends.

Even if a community could speak with one voice, its ability to control local tourism development would be limited by a number of factors, including:

- the power of the tourism industry. For example, tour operators are largely footloose, and if a destination tries to control their activities they may simply move on to somewhere where they will not face similar constraints
- central government policies and funding may over-rule local preferences. For instance, a community may wish to limit the growth of tourism in an area but the government may want to maximize the attraction of foreign tourists to the destination to help the balance of payments of the country
- externally based organizations may already have a strong voice in the area because of their ownership of local businesses. An example of this would be resort complexes and hotels owned by national hotel chains or transnational companies.

Even if communities could control their local tourism industry, this might not always be a desirable state of affairs. It could lead, for example, to tourism being used as a vehicle for nationalistic aspirations. Tourists of certain nationalities could be excluded from resorts, and heritage attractions could be used to spread propaganda about different nationalities. This could be a problem in certain regions of Eastern Europe for example, where different national groups live in close proximity to each other, with a long history of conflict between them.

Role of Public Sector Planning

Many commentators assume that public sector tourism planning will play a major role in the development of sustainable tourism. Yet, in Europe at least, central state planning appears to be in retreat, for a variety of reasons including the following:

- Scepticism about state planning and its alleged lack of achievements. In the UK for example, there has been urban planning for 50 years yet the country has many examples of dysfunctional and visually unattractive towns and cities.
- The climate of de-regulation and privatization, which has been reinforced by the European Union's attempts to create a Single Market in Europe.
- The dislike of planning in Eastern Europe where it is seen as a reminder of the doctrinaire old communist regimes.
- The growing power of transnational corporations whose area of influence extends beyond the geographical boundaries of any government.

In any event, it is difficult to see what state planning can achieve in the tourism area, given that public sector bodies do not own or control many of the key elements of the tourism product, including:

- accommodation units
- the tour operation function
- visitor attractions except in the heritage sector
- bars, night clubs, taxis and coach operators.

It is for this reason that the concept of partnership has grown in popularity in recent years.

The Role of Industry

Interestingly, as noted earlier in the section on the 'green tourist', industry often appears to be more concerned with sustainable tourism than consumers. It also seems to be doing more in terms of concrete initiatives than governments. The following two brief examples illustrate these points:

- The International Hotels Environmental Initiative, which has sought to encourage hoteliers around the world to make their operational practices 'greener'.
- The sponsorship of sustainable tourism award schemes like the 'Tourism for Tomorrow' award by British Airways.
- Conferences on sustainable tourism organized by local tourism industry bodies such as the 'Ecological Conferences' arranged by the Halkidiki Hotel Association in Greece.
- The 'Thomson Holiday Code', a set of guidelines for clients of the tour operator.

Cynics may argue that this interest by industry is more about marketing hype than an altruistic belief in sustainable tourism. However, this may be unfair given that there appears to be little explicit concern with sustainable tourism on the part of most tourists. Perhaps therefore, we have to look at some more subtle motives for the attitudes of the industry, including:

- convincing governments that the industry is capable of regulating itself to prevent the threat of governments introducing legislation to control the activities of the industry
- taking initiatives that reduce costs, and therefore improve financial performance and competitiveness
- attempting to impress the media given that today, the media plays a vital role in influencing consumer behaviour.

Conversely, a number of small specialist tour operators in tourism, run by individual entrepreneurs, appear to be embracing sustainable tourism as a core element of their business. They try to attract customers, partly at least, through their contention that their product and operations are complementary with the ideas of sustainable tourism, such as being small scale, and encouraging contact with local people. This is true of many of the members of AITO, the Association of Independent Tour Operators for example, in the UK, particularly those which offer ecotourism products.

It could be argued that for these small operators, which focus on a narrow niche market, the emphasis on sustainable tourism helps them to differentiate themselves from the large mass market operators, with which they cannot compete on price. It is likely that the relatively affluent clients who tend to make up the majority of the market for specialist tour operators, will be darker green than the average tourist and will respond well to this message.

However, ironically if the specialist operators do attract customers because of their more sustainable approach to tourism, they may well grow and become more commercial and ultimately, less sustainable!

The Principle of Partnership

There has clearly been a growing recognition that sustainable tourism cannot be achieved by public sector policy alone. Most public bodies lack the budget or expertise to have a significant impact on the tourism industry and its activities. In crucial areas like accommodation and tour operation, the public sector is not a player of any significance. Its only influence comes via regulation and legislation but this tends to be more about preventing worst practice rather than encouraging good practice.

This has resulted in the concept of partnerships in tourism which have taken a number of forms, including:

- The Visitor and Convention Bureaux, funded by both the public and private sectors, that market tourist destinations
- Government encouragement of industry to take the issue of sustainability more seriously, via reports and conferences, for example.

However, in a competitive, commercial market like tourism, industry can only go along with public policy objectives in the tourism field, providing they are not required to do anything that will increase their costs, or otherwise reduce their competitiveness.

One way around this problem has been for governments and pressure groups to persuade the private sector that the sustainable development of tourism resources is a key interest of the tourism industry. The problem with this approach is that the private sector can generally only afford to have a short-term perspective, based on the financial year, and annual marketing plans. It is therefore naive to expect people in industry to take a long-term view.

Perhaps, a final obstacle for the partnership is that both parties often appear to speak different languages! Although progress has been made, there still often seems to be a communication gap, with industry and academics not understanding each other's needs and constraints.

Technocractic Thinking and Jargon

Academics and policy-makers know that achieving sustainable tourism will mean influencing tourists and the industry. Yet, at times, one could be forgiven for thinking that this was not the aim for much of the work of both groups of people tends to:

- be unrealistic in the context of a competitive and largely commercial market
- not take account of the political dimension of sustainable tourism, in terms of who would gain from it and who would pay, and the making of decisions about the resources on which tourism depends
- use jargon which may exclude non-specialists, with the use of terms like carrying capacity, holistic approaches and host communities.

In return, the same two groups also often complain about the fact that, as they see it, the tourism industry does not pay enough attention to their views. However, given that they are trying to sell a set of ideas to the industry, the onus is on these groups to make their message more accessible to the industry.

Power without Responsibility

One of the dangers of the sustainable tourism debate is that it can involve people seeking to have power over the lives of other people, without necessarily having any responsibility towards these same people. For example, some decision-makers or would-be decision-makers want to:

- stop other people visiting particular places without having to offer them any alternative
- force the industry to change its practices in varying ways without having any responsibility for the people who will ultimately pay the price, whether it is the customer or the staff who are made redundant as a consequence of a resulting increase in costs.

This criticism is particularly appropriate, perhaps, for some voluntary sector pressure groups in the UK who seek to change the industry radically yet are elected by no one and have no mandate from the population as a whole.

Self-contained Resort Complexes

One of the most controversial areas of the sustainable tourism debate has been the growth of self-contained resort complexes, from the Caribbean to South-East Asia, South Africa to the UK, with brand names like Sandals, Club Med, Center Parcs and Sun City. The conventional view would normally be critical of such complexes because of the lack of contact between tourists and local people. Indeed, it is true to say that they can actively take away the rights of the local population to use beaches they have used for generations.

Furthermore, the fact that all tourist needs are met on site by the resort operator, means there can be little opportunity for small local businesses to benefit from the presence of visitors through the purchase of meals, souvenirs and taxi services, for example.

They can also be criticized because they are often large and can be aesthetically unattractive. At the same time, they are often owned by outside entrepreneurs or corporations with little commitment to the area.

Conversely, if one believes that tourism can be a form of sociocultural pollution, then the fences around them are protecting local people from such pollution. Some small complexes have even been commended as examples of sustainable development, such as the Center Parcs complexes in the UK. Their design is sensitive, new wildlife habitats have been created during their construction, and supplies are sourced locally wherever possible.

Perhaps, therefore, well-managed self-contained resort complexes could play a positive role in the development of sustainable tourism.

The Ethics and Practicalities of Conservation

It appears to be generally accepted that there is a strong link between conservation and sustainable tourism, for the latter is about conserving current resources so they can support tourism in the future. We therefore, have to ask ourselves some questions about what we are conserving, the ways in which we are conserving it, and the methods used.

In the UK, perhaps, we are too concerned with conserving certain parts of our heritage while we do not do enough to conserve other aspects of our heritage which are also important for the development of sustainable tourism. In the UK, we allocate substantial resources, for instance, for conserving stately homes, industrial heritage and works of art. However, we seem to be doing little to protect our heritage in the areas like food and drink, popular culture and sport. All of these could be key elements in the development of dynamic, popular forms of sustainable tourism in the UK.

At the same time, our planning system, in relation to listed buildings for instance, has been rather negative and perhaps counterproductive. It has stopped aesthetically or architecturally inappropriate changes from being made to these buildings, but has done little to find viable new uses for such buildings. It could also be argued that we are trying to conserve too much of our heritage and that our emphasis on heritage is preventing us from looking to the future. We appear to be giving little attention to developing good quality modern architecture; instead we are conserving past buildings or copying traditional architecture styles. Surely sustainable development means innovation and imagination as well as just conservation.

Emphasis on the Physical Environment

While the concept of sustainable development clearly has social and economic implications, the emphasis in the debate still tends to focus largely on the physical environment. In some ways this is understandable, because the impacts of tourism on the environment are highly visible and we know that the environment is a finite resource. However, it is clear that as the physical environment is shaped by the action of man, any attempt to manage environmental impacts must encompass economic systems and the needs of society in general and individual communities, in particular.

On the positive side, there is now considerable attention being paid to host communities, in terms of the impact of tourism upon them and their role in its management. At the same time, the continued emphasis on the physical environment is preventing enough attention being paid to other aspects of sustainable development, namely:

- the human resource management problems of tourism enterprises in terms of equal opportunities, pay and training, which are vital to both the well-being of employees, and ultimately, the sustainability of the tourism industry
- the economic viability of tourism enterprises

- the needs, opinions and rights of the tourist themselves who are often cast as villains, but whose pleasure-seeking brings income and jobs to communities, as well as problems.

Attempts to develop sustainable tourism must also address the dissatisfaction with their home environment, and everyday lives that fuels the tourist's desire to take holidays in the first place.

Finally, in some cases, it is the balance between the physical environment and the human dimension which appears to be inappropriate. For example, in several British national parks, considerable attention is being paid to footpath erosion while rural communities experience severe levels of poverty which attracts relatively little attention.

Foreign Influences in Developing Countries

The concept of sustainable tourism has probably increased the power and influence of the developed countries over the so-called developing countries, in several ways:

- Environmental and sustainable tourism pressure groups in the northern hemisphere are often involved in lecturing governments and people in developing countries on how they treat their wildlife. However, these groups may, of course, have little idea of the true situation in these countries.
- Foreign tour operators are pressuring governments and businesses in developing countries to take action to placate the views of their clients, but are not usually keen to increase the overall price of the product, as a result.
- Most of the academics and consultants who are active in the sustainable tourism field come from the northern hemisphere, but much of their work is in the developing countries.

There is a clear issue of self-interest here.

People in developing countries could be forgiven for thinking that the concern of foreigners about sustainability in their country is just about enhancing the quality of holiday experience for tourists from the northern hemisphere. A cynical observer might say that those from the developing countries having failed to manage their own tourism industry particularly well, are not in a strong position to lecture others.

Lack of Performance Indicators

As we have seen, there are no clearly accepted definitions of what forms of tourism are the most sustainable. Given this fact it is therefore impossible to identify performance indicators and targets that will allow the industry to monitor its success or otherwise, in moving forward becoming more sustainable in its activities. This is a problem because experience shows us that for any strategy to be successfully implemented organizations need measurable targets to keep them on course.

At the same time, unlike the field of environmental management, there are no accepted official standards either. The broader, less measurable field of sustainable tourism has no equivalent of BS 7750, for example. The absence of such a standard has two main drawbacks:

- it makes it difficult for organizations to act, because there are no guidelines and no blueprint for them to work towards
- organizations may feel that unless there is official accreditation of achievements, which they can use for marketing purposes, they cannot afford to expend time and money on sustainable tourism.

Relationships between Different Key Concepts and Techniques in Sustainable Tourism

Given the author's scepticism about some of the key concepts and techniques in the sustainable tourism debate, there is a further

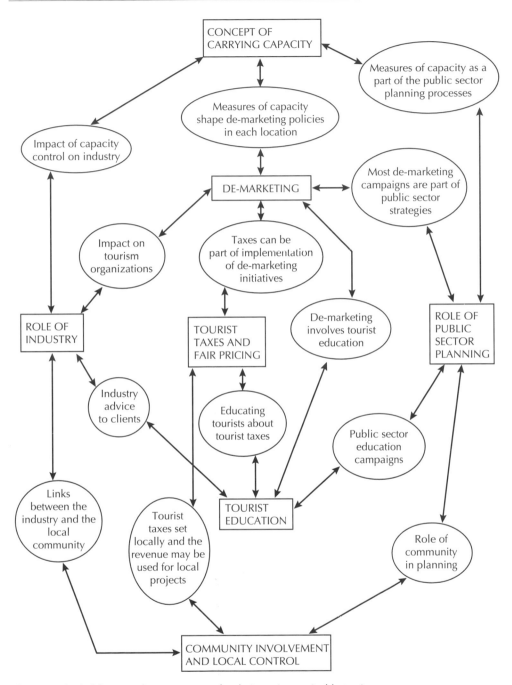

Fig. 3.3.   The link between key concepts and techniques in sustainable tourism.

complication in that many of them are inter-related, as can be seen from Fig. 3.3. This fact makes sustainable tourism management an even more complex task.

Tourism is Not an Island

As the final section of this chapter, the author would like to join other authors who have expressed concern at the parochiality of the sustainable tourism debate. Too often tourism is seen as a self-contained world in its own right. However, as we have seen when discussing the issue of sustainable development, tourism is just part of the wider sustainability debate. We need to recognize and study the links between tourism and other industries and activities if we are to fully understand sustainable tourism.

Conclusions

This chapter has highlighted some of the author's concerns over current thinking on sustainable tourism. Many of the ideas and techniques discussed clearly have a role to play in sustainable tourism management. However, the problems we have identified will need to be resolved or ameliorated before they can make a full contribution to managing tourism in a more sustainable manner. Many of these ideas and techniques are therefore examined in more detail later in the book to see how they might be refined and further developed. In the meantime, we will move on to look at some of the principles we should perhaps adopt to guide our approaches to sustainable tourism, based upon the critique of current thinking in this chapter.

Discussion Points and Essay Questions

1. Discuss the practical and moral problems involved in implementing the concept of de-marketing.
2. Critically evaluate the advantages and disadvantages of self-contained resort complexes for destinations which wish to develop more sustainable forms of tourism.
3. Discuss the factors which will determine whether or not the 'dark green tourist' market segment will grow or decline in the future.

Exercise

Choose a destination with which you are familiar, and imagine you have been employed as a consultant. Your brief is to devise a workable scheme for a tourist tax for all visitors to the destination. You are required to:

- outline the scheme you are proposing
- suggest the benefits the destination would gain from the introduction of your scheme
- highlight difficulties that might be experienced in trying to implement your scheme
- suggest how the tax revenue might be spent.

4

Towards a New Approach to Sustainable Tourism Management

Following on from the critique of current thinking in Chapter 3, some principles are now put forward that could constitute a new approach to sustainable tourism management. These principles are briefly outlined below but many of them will be considered in more detail later in this book.

- There is a need to recognize that **sustainable tourism is, perhaps, an impossible dream**, and the best we can hope for is to develop more sustainable forms of tourism. This may be because tourism is inherently non-sustainable or may be due to the fact that unforeseen future political, economic, social and technological change may make current approaches to sustainable tourism management obsolete.
- We must **endeavour to introduce more objectivity into the sustainable tourism** debate. It is the author's belief that too much current thinking is judgemental and prejudiced about certain forms of tourism, with little real firm evidence to support these judgements and prejudices. The polarization of tourism into 'good' and 'bad' is divisive and unhelpful.
- It is important for us to recognize that **sustainable tourism is an overtly political subject**, in that it is about the distribution of resources, now and in

the future. The fact that some people will gain and some people will lose as a result of sustainable tourism means that it is inherently political. Technocratic solutions will fail if they ignore the political dimension.

- The political nature of the sustainable tourism debate means that **sustainable tourism is about who has the power** – host communities, governments, the industry and tourists – and how they use the power. We need to recognize that definitions of sustainable tourism and devising strategies to try to achieve it will normally reflect who has the power in any particular situation.
- This brings us to the idea that **sustainable tourism is about stakeholders** whose interests have to be balanced.
- We should accept that the idea of **community involvement as a cornerstone of sustainable tourism is fraught with problems**. It is necessary for us to recognize that:
  (i) communities are rarely homogeneous, taking a single homogeneous view on any issue. There is a need to develop mechanisms for arbitrating the conflicting views that will emerge over tourism in any community
  (ii) tourism management should not

allow articulate minorities to dominate the process to the exclusion of other citizens

(iii) in some instances, the community may wish to pursue policies which are anti-sustainable tourism. We cannot assume, therefore, that community involvement will automatically ensure more sustainable forms of tourism.

- The **emphasis needs to shift from strategy generation to implementation** for there are many sustainable tourism strategies in destinations, but as yet few examples of successful initiatives.

- Accepting that in most countries **while public sectors can help facilitate the growth of more sustainable forms of tourism in many ways, ultimately, the key determinants of what happens will be the market**, in other words, tourist demand and industry responds to this demand. This means that **public sector policy must focus on developing partnerships** with both tourists and the industry, based on an understanding of how the tourism marketing actually works.

- Instead of concentrating on the tourism industry **the emphasis should be on the tourist**, for it is their desires, choices and behaviour which ultimately determine the impact which the tourist has on the world.

- At the same time we need to **recognize that tourists have rights too**. They spend their hard earned money on vacations to destinations which have often worked hard to persuade them to go there. They are there as invited guests not invaders.

- We need to acknowledge that **well-managed tourism can bring great social, economic and environmental benefits** as well as being the cause of problems if it is poorly managed.

- It is also important that we always remember that **sustainable tourism is not just about the environment**, it is also about social equity, and economic viability.

- We have to be **careful to avoid the temptation to introduce draconian measures that are out of proportion to the scale of the problem**. In an era when freedom of movement is accepted as a basic human right we must only ever consider restricting access to sites and places as an absolute last resort.

- We should **accept that there are 'shades of green' tourism** and that currently very few tourists are dark green.

- There is a need to **clarify the relationship between ecotourism and sustainable tourism** and be clear that they are not the same thing.

- Future **research on carrying capacities should involve consideration of how the results can be represented**. There is little point in learning that a woodland can only accommodate 500 tourists per square kilometre at any one time if we cannot then introduce measures to restrict usage to this level or below.

- While the concept of **de-marketing does have great potential in relation to sustainable tourism, we have to recognize that it has limitations**. For example:

(i) changing established behaviour patterns in tourism is a very sophisticated marketing challenge that will take time to achieve and will require huge budgets

(ii) de-marketing will rarely reduce overall demand, instead it will merely channel it in another direction

(iii) de-marketing is highly political because it may reduce income from businesses in some destinations and it is a form of social engineering, seeking to manipulate tourist behaviour.

- **Tourists should pay a fair price for their holiday experience.** They should not be subsidised by local people who do not gain financially from tourism.

- The **most sustainable forms of tourism may be those where tourism is 'fair traded'**, in other words, where local communities sell directly to the tourist, cutting out the tour operator and travel agent in between. This may mean more of the tourists' spending will go to the local community. However, given the power of the tourism industry and the high cost of entering the tourism destination network, this may be as difficult to achieve in tourism as it has been in relation to commodities such as coffee and tea.

- **For destinations, particularly those in developing countries, to gain a fair share of the benefits of tourism, they will probably need to work together** to increase their joint power *vis-à-vis* the tourism industry in developed countries which are the generators of most international tourist trips. However, such an approach could be seen as a cartel and anti-competitive in an era when free trade and de-regulation is the order of the day.
- There will almost certainly have to be **more restrictions on the use of private car transport** for in many developed and newly developed countries, the car has gone from being the liberator of the tourist to being the tourist's jailer, preventing tourist mobility through congestion. Voluntary experimental schemes for encouraging people to leave their car behind and use public transport have generally not worked, even on the limited scale on which they have been attempted.
- We **should not place too much faith in 'educating tourists'** until we are sure of what the educational message should be at a time when we are still rather vague about what sustainable tourism means.
- **If we want the industry to behave in a more sustainable way, we must accept that it may do so for commercial motivations rather than altruistic reasons.** Provided that their activities are positive, we should not, perhaps, worry too much about the motives of the companies.
- **At a time when there is a growing number of pressure groups in the sustainable tourism field, we should not let them have power without responsibility.** If such groups influence

tourism policy they may affect other people's lives, e.g. causing a reduction in their income, yet they are not currently asked to take responsibility for their actions, which is unfair.
- We could also perhaps adopt the slogan, **'sustainable tourism begins at home'**. In other words, commentators from developed countries should focus on their own country and the behaviour of its own tourists, rather than telling people in developing countries how they should manage their tourism.
- **There is a need for more clear thinking in relation to what we seek to conserve, and how we conserve it.** If we try to conserve too much we retard the evolution of new building styles, landscapes and life styles. This could result in fossilization; sustainability should be about managed change, not stopping change.
- There is a **need for us to develop good performance indicators** for sustainable tourism so that we can monitor our progress and recognize where we are failing.
- It would also be helpful if a **system of official standards or sustainable tourism labels** could be developed to help those consumers who wish to purchase more sustainable tourism products.
- **We have to recognize that sustainable tourism is inextricably linked with the question of sustainable development in general, and other industries such as agriculture.**

The Need for More Research

All of these points imply a much greater role for research and the wider dissemination of research findings. This should include:

- comparable work on the impacts of tourism that helps us to develop standard common ways of assessing these impacts
- research on the workings of the tourism industry that increases our understanding of how it might be managed to achieve desired outcomes

- more empirical work on the behaviour of tourists so we gain a better understanding of their motivations and the processes through which they make decisions
- longitudinal studies of both tourism in individual destinations, and the behaviour of the market segments.

The results of this research must be disseminated widely in a readily understandable form so that it can illuminate the whole sustainable tourism debate. If we cannot find funding for such research, it does not augur well for our ability to develop more sustainable forms of tourism.

Changes in the Concept of Sustainable Tourism Over Time

We have to accept that the concept of sustainable tourism will change over time. We can, therefore, never allow our ideas of sustainable tourism to become too fixed, so that they cannot be changed as the world and social attitudes change. If we look at the debate over sustainable development in general, as we did in Chapter 1, we can see that the nature of public concern has changed over time from:

- urban living conditions in northern European cities in the 19th century *to*
- Third World development in the 1960s *to*
- over-population and pollution in the developed world in the 1970s *to*
- global warming in the 1980s and 1990s.

The sustainable tourism debate has also moved on from the concern with the environment and 'green issues' to the wider subject of sustainable tourism. It is likely, therefore, that our level of interest in sustainable tourism, and the issues which concern us in relation to tourism, will be very different in 10, 20 or 30 years from now.

Ironically, given the definition of sustainable development, we must ensure that we do not do things today which mean that future governments do not have the freedom to tackle sustainability in the best way for them at the time.

Conclusions

This chapter suggests a set of guidelines that might underpin a new approach to sustainable tourism management, building on the critique offered in Chapter 3. We have now set the scene for the rest of the book which will concentrate on how we might put the principles of sustainable tourism into practice.

Discussion Points and Essay Questions

1. Discuss the contention that, 'sustainable tourism is, perhaps, an impossible dream'.
2. Evaluate what the concept of 'fair trading' in tourism might mean for tourists, the tourism industry and the host community.
3. Critically evaluate the idea that, 'sustainable tourism is an overtly political subject'.

Exercise

Select a book *or* major article on sustainable tourism, with which you are familiar. Compare what they say about sustainable tourism with what the author has said in this chapter. Identify and discuss any differences between the views of the different authors.

Conclusions to Part One

In Part One the scene has been set for the rest of the book.

We have seen that sustainable tourism is simply an extension of the concept of sustainable development, and that this concept is far from new. The idea that urban development, for example, should be sustainable dates back many centuries. However, sustainability has only become a major issue in recent years in relation to industry in general, and tourism specifically.

In Chapter 2, we noted that the term, 'sustainable tourism' is a broad and ill-defined concept, that is open to a number of interpretations. We are still not certain that we know which forms of tourism are the most sustainable.

In Chapter 3 the author offered a critique of current thinking in sustainable tourism that criticised conventional ideas on the grounds of both their feasibility as well as their desirability.

Finally, in Chapter 4, a number of guidelines were suggested that should underpin what the author described as a new approach towards sustainable tourism management.

Part Two

The Three Dimensions of Sustainable Tourism

In Part Two, we look at the three dimensions of sustainable tourism, namely:

- the environment, both natural and built
- the economic life of communities and companies
- social aspects of tourism, in terms of its impact on host cultures and tourists, and the way in which those employed in tourism are treated.

While it is the former element – the environment – which usually receives most attention, it is the author's contention that all three are equally important. It is also the author's belief that sustainable tourism management can only be successful if the inter-relationships between all three dimensions are fully recognized.

5

The Environmental Dimension

To many people sustainability is about the environment, primarily the natural, physical environment, and its protection. However, as we will see in this chapter, there is far more to the environment than just the natural landscape. The author will argue that the development of more sustainable forms of tourism will require us to:

- think in terms of ecosystems rather than 'the environment', and recognize that man is an important and valid element within the ecosystem
- take a far more critical view of the concept and practice of conservation, and accept that conservation can lead to fossilization and prevent the natural evolution which has given us those townscapes and landscapes which we treasure and seek to conserve today.

But firstly, we need to identify just what we mean by the environment. Figure 5.1 illustrates the scope of the term in relation to tourism. We know, of course, that whilst useful, this distinction is partly artificial, and that there are strong links between them. For example inshore coastal waters can be transformed by the creation of fish farms, and agricultural systems tend to dictate the pattern of human settlement and the form of villages.

We also need to recognize that the environment, all five types of environment, are currently changing, as are our perceptions of them. It is also important to understand that:

> an important characteristic of the interaction between tourism and the environment is the existence of strong feedback mechanisms: tourism often has adverse effects on the quantity – and quality – of natural and cultural resources, but it is also affected by the decline in quality and quantity of such resources. (Coccossis, 1996)

Let us now move on to look at the five aspects of the environment.

The Natural Resources

Tourism makes use of a range of natural resources, and in many cases, the core attraction of a destination's product may be natural resources, such as:

- clean, pure mountain air
- land
- the mineral waters which have healing properties and are the focus of spa development
- the water in lakes and seas, if it is relatively warm and clean, and therefore suitable for bathing.

Yet, while tourism can provide an economic rationale for protecting such resources, it

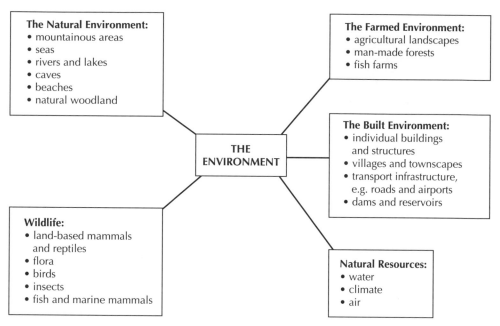

Fig. 5.1. The scope of the concept of the environment.

can also be a threat to their survival. Tourists make great use of water resources for their baths and swimming pools and their sewage can pollute the seas if not adequately treated.

The easiest way to think about the impact of tourism on natural resources is to think about the growth of a new resort complex on the coast in an arid coastal region. The development could:

- divert water from the local community to fill the swimming pool, provide showers and irrigate the golf course
- pollute the sea with sewage and fuel from the boats in the marina
- mean building on land, thus destroying the vegetation and disrupting the wildlife which was previously found on the site.

The Natural Environment

We need to recognize that:

- there are few 'natural' landscapes or

wilderness areas left in the world. Almost all 'natural' landscapes have been affected to some extent, by the actions of man through the centuries

- tourism is only one industry or activity which changes landscapes, and it is probably less significant in its impact than other industries, such as agriculture and forestry, and mining and quarrying, for example
- the natural landscape represents the core of the tourism product in many areas including:
  (i)   natural forests like the Amazonian rain forest
  (ii) regions which attract tourists because of their rivers and lakes such as the Rhine in Germany, and the Lake District in the UK
  (iii) mountains which are perceived to be particularly beautiful such as the Alps and the Rockies
- the natural landscape can also be an obstacle to the development of tourism. For instance, hills behind a resort can stop it growing or can force it to develop vertically through high rise buildings.

Table 5.1. Some major potential impacts of tourism on the natural environment. Source: Hunter and Green (1996).

Impact aspect	Potential consequence
Floral and faunal species composition	• Disruption of breeding habits • Killing of animals through hunting • Killing of animals in order to supply goods for the souvenir trade • Inward or outward migration of animals • Trampling and damage of vegetation by feet and vehicles • Destruction of vegetation through the gathering of wood or plants • Change in extent and/or nature of vegetation cover through clearance or planning to accommodate tourist facilities • Creation of a wildlife reserve/sanctuary or habitat restoration
Pollution	• Water pollution through discharges of sewage, spillages of oil/petrol • Air pollution from vehicle emissions, combustion of fuels for heating and lighting • Noise pollution from tourist transportation and activities
Erosion	• Compaction of solid causing increased surface run-off and erosion • Change in risk of occurrence of land slips/slides • Change in risk of avalanche occurrence • Damage to geological features (e.g. tors, caves) • Damage to river banks
Natural resources	• Depletion of ground and surface water supplies • Depletion of fossil fuels to generate energy for tourist activity • Change in risk of occurrence of fire • Depletion of mineral resources for building materials • Over-exploitation of biological resources (e.g. overfishing) • Change in hydrological patterns • Change in land used for primary production
Visual impact	• Facilities (e.g. buildings, chairlift, car park) • Litter • Sewage, algal blooms

Tourism and the Sustainability of the Natural Environment: Friends or Foes?

In many regions of the world we have seen that tourism can be an enemy of the natural environment, as illustrated in Table 5.1.

At the same time, tourism can be beneficial to the natural environment by providing a motivation for environmental conservation. Without the financial incentive for conservation which tourism represents, many public sector bodies would probably pay less attention to the protection of the natural environment.

Mathieson and Wall, in their seminal work on the impact of tourism, suggested that:

> Tourism can also be credited with extending environmental appreciation. (Mathieson and Wall, 1982)

It has made people more knowledgeable about the environment. Nevertheless, overall, it is difficult not to come to the conclusion that tourism generally has a negative impact on the natural environment.

The Farmed Environment

The farmed environment can cover a diverse range of agricultural systems, including, for example:

- intensive crop-rearing such as the grain-growing areas of eastern England, and the Mid-West of the USA and the rice fields of South-East Asia
- traditional mixed farming such as that seen in the Mediterranean region with the wine, citrus fruits and olives being cultivated alongside the grazing of sheep and goats
- monocultural cash crops such as the vines of the Herault area of France, and bananas of some Caribbean islands
- nomadic communities of people engaged in livestock-raising such as the Maasai people in Africa
- areas where timber is farmed such as northern Scandinavia, South-East Asia and parts of Canada.

In this era of the growth of 'pisciculture' we should also add to our list the fish farm, which contributes its own distinct structures to the shores around Ireland and Scotland, for example.

It is generally held that tourism has a negative impact on the farmed environment, including the following:

- tourists can trample crops, or light fires in woodland that get out of control
- new tourism developments eat up farmland and use water that is required for agriculture
- the jobs offered in tourism may tempt young people to give up farming.

However, it is also important to recognize that tourism can also be beneficial to the farmed environment. Tourist spending on farm-based accommodation, for example, can help maintain the viability of marginal farms. In France, the government has used gîtes and fermes-auberges deliberately as part of a tourism policy designed to provide extra revenue and social benefits for farmers.

Wildlife

In the context of this chapter, the issue of wildlife has a number of dimensions, as follows:

- Areas where wildlife is a major attraction for tourists, including:
  (i)   the big game of Kenya, Tanzania and Botswana
  (ii) the bird life of the Danube Delta, or Ireland and Cyprus in the winter
  (iii) natural woodland and unusual flora, in the Amazon Basin
  (iv) unusual creatures such as the giant turtles of the Galapagos Islands.
- Marine life which attracts tourists to take trips on the sea to view it, such as the whales of New England, Iceland and New Zealand.
- Tourism which is based on hunting wildlife including fishing trips.
- Visitor attractions such as zoos, wildlife and aquaria, where creatures in captivity are a major draw for tourists.
- Traditional events which tourists are invited to attend which involve wildlife, notably bull-fighting in Spain.
- The exploitation of animals to 'entertain' tourists like the 'dancing bears' of Turkey.

Tourism can clearly be very harmful to wildlife through:

- the destruction of habitats
- affecting feeding habits
- disrupting breeding patterns
- fires in woodlands
- people picking rare plants.

Conversely, tourism can benefit wildlife by giving it an economic value, which in turn provides a motivation for its conservation. There is little doubt that without tourists there would now be fewer lions or elephants in the world.

However, conserving wildlife for the benefit of tourists brings its own problems. There are ethical dilemmas, notably:

- Is it right for us to 'play God' and interfere in the process of 'evolution'?
- Should we affect the livelihoods of some humans to protect animals?
- Could it not be argued that preserving species so they can be viewed by tourists is simply self-indulgent exploitation?

The Built Environment

The built environment exists at no less than three levels:

- individual buildings and structures
- small-scale settlements such as villages
- large-scale settlements, e.g. towns and cities.

We also need to recognize that, in terms of tourism, there are also several dimensions to the built environment as follows:

- Those historic villages, towns and cities where the built environment is, in terms of its age, aesthetic appearance and historical interest, a major attraction for tourists, and is the core of the tourism product. This category includes a wide variety of settlements from the honey-coloured villages of the Cotswolds in the UK, through the hill towns of Tuscany, to whole cities like Venice and Jerusalem.
- Individual historic buildings which are major attractions for tourists, within otherwise rather unspectacular townscapes like the Taj Mahal in Agra.
- Historic townscapes which have been conserved in their entirety, almost as museums, such as Colonial Williamsburg in the USA.
- Spectacular examples of modern architecture such as Gaudi's 'cathedral' in Barcelona and the Antigone development in the French city of Montpellier.
- The conversion of old buildings or areas which were not built for the purpose of tourism. For example, the old docklands of New York, San Francisco and Liverpool being turned into visitor attractions, and the conversion into hotels of the Paradores in Spain.
- Modern purpose-built tourist resorts like Ayia Napa and Protaras in Cyprus.
- Individual buildings and structures, particularly accommodation establishments and visitor attractions.
- Tourism infrastructure, notably airports.

As can be seen from Table 5.2, tourism development can have a major impact, both negative and positive, on the built environment.

The Five Aspects of the Environment: Some General Comments

It is clear that tourism can be very harmful to any aspect of the environment. Conversely, we have seen that it can also be a positive force in relation to the environment. It can:

- provide a motivation for governments to conserve the natural environment and wildlife because of its value as a tourism resource. Without this motivation, particularly in developing countries, even more damage might be done to the environment and wildlife by industrial and residential development
- raise tourist awareness of environmental issues and lead them to campaign for environmental protection based on what they have learned while on holiday
- keep farms viable by providing a vital extra income for agriculturists, thus preventing the 'desertification' of farmed rural landscapes
- provide new uses for derelict buildings in towns and cities, through the development of new visitor attractions.

Towards a More Sustainable Relationship between Tourism and the Environment

Tourism and the environment are inextricably linked and interdependent. If tourism

Table 5.2. Some major potential impacts of tourism on the built environment. Source: Hunter and Green (1996).

Impact aspect	Potential consequences
Urban form	• Change in character of built area through urban expansion or redevelopment • Change in residential, retail or industrial land uses (e.g. move from private homes to hotels/boarding houses) • Changes to the urban fabric (e.g. roads, pavements, street furniture) • Emergence of contrasts between urban areas developed for the tourist population and those for the host population
Infrastructure	• Overload of infrastructure (e.g. roads, railways, car parking, electricity grid, communications systems, waste disposal, buildings, water supply) • Provision of new infrastructure or upgrading of existing infrastructure • Environmental management to adapt areas for tourist use (e.g. sea walls, land reclamation)
Visual impact	• Growth of the built-up area • New architectural styles • Litter • Beautification
Restoration	• Re-use of disused buildings • Restoration and preservation of historic buildings and sites • Restoration of derelict buildings as second homes
Erosion	• Damage to built assets from feet and vehicular traffic (including vibration effects)
Pollution	• Air pollution from tourists and tourist traffic • Air pollution from non-tourist sources causing damage to built assets

continues to grow, we have to find ways of improving the relationship between the two and making it more sustainable. This might involve the following.

Holistic Thinking: the Concept of Ecosystems

Too often, in tourism, we fall into the trap of thinking about the environment in terms of self-contained compartments such as wildlife or rain forests, or mountains. However, the environment is a complex phenomenon, made up of a set of inter-relationships between the physical environment and flora and fauna species, and human beings are one of those species. To manage the link between tourism and the environment more effectively, we need to recognize this concept of 'ecosystems' and plan accordingly.

Regulation of the Negative Impacts

There is a clear need for legislation and a system of land-use planning and building control to reduce the negative impact of tourism on the environment. However, we must recognize that while regulation can help prevent negative outcomes, it can do little to stimulate the creation of positive outcomes.

Encouraging Good Practice

It is more pro-active and positive to encourage good practice rather than merely preventing bad practice. In relation to the built environment this could mean, for example, ensuring that all new development is:

• built on an appropriate site, in terms of the existence of on-site services and infrastructure
• of a suitable scale for the site and locality
• constructed of recycled and locally sourced materials, wherever possible

- designed to be energy-efficient
- developed in a way that minimizes the use of resources like water, and the disruption of wildlife habitats.

Keeping a Sense of Proportion

We need to ensure that our level of concern and action is in proportion to the scale of the problem. There is no point in taking draconian, expensive measures to tackle a problem which is not very serious. For instance, minor footpath erosion is not a big enough problem to merit widespread closure of footpaths and/or expensive visitor management techniques.

Raising Awareness amongst Tourists and the Industry

Some of the damage caused to the environment by tourism is not unavoidable while much of it is not deliberate. Better knowledge on the part of the industry and tourists would help reduce some of the negative environmental aspects of tourism.

Paying a Price that Covers the Environmental Costs of Tourism

Tourism causes environmental problems which cost money to ameliorate or solve. The prices paid by the industry for services they buy, and the tourists for their holiday, must be high enough to ensure that money is available to cover the environmental costs of tourism. Otherwise either the local population will have to subsidize the tourist or the environmental problems will not be tackled.

Maintaining a Balance Between Conservation and Development

We need to find a balance between conserving the environment as it is today and the development which is needed to provide jobs and social benefits.

The Dangers of Conservation

It is important to recognize that conservation is a relatively modern phenomenon.

Only in recent years have widespread attempts been made to conserve landcapes, buildings and wildlife, across the world.

Conservation has been most in evidence in developed countries where the pace of economic and social change has led to great changes in the environment. This has stimulated attempts to conserve – or 'preserve' – the status quo, almost out of a sense of nostalgia.

There is a clear link between tourism and conservation, for:

- the destruction of the environment caused by large-scale tourism has often stimulated demands for conservation
- the recognition that the environment is a major attraction of tourists has given an economic motivation for conservation
- many conservation projects are wholly or partly funded by income from tourism.

Conservation is now evident throughout the areas visited by tourists and is generally seen to be a very positive concept. Yet, the author believes that it involves dangers which are not always recognized, and which in themselves, threaten the long-term sustainability, of both tourism and host communities. These include:

- The tendency to believe that everything old is worthy of conserving or 'saving' or 'preserving'. This can lead to us spreading resources too thinly to be effective as we try to conserve everything.
- Sometimes we place the conservation of wildlife or landscapes above the welfare of humans, particularly those who lack political power. Nomadic people in East Africa are therefore having their traditional life styles disrupted to protect the wildlife on which the local tourism industry depends. Nearer to home, local young people in the national parks of the UK suffer a lack of job opportunities, partly at least, because of planning policies which are unsympathetic to industrial development.

- The apparent obsession with conserving all old buildings means there is a danger that new building styles will not be developed or valued. If imaginative modern architecture is not encouraged to develop, what will people in the future choose to conserve as symbols of our age?
- Tastes and preferences change over time so the next generation may not appreciate the results of today's efforts to preserve life styles and environments. Instead of seeing it as an asset it may see the results of our conservation as an unwanted liability.

We have to accept that most landscapes and buildings have been developed by mankind to fulfil a specific purpose. If we try to keep them after their original purpose has disappeared it will simply be preservation, and will leave us with buildings and landscapes which are as dead as fossils. Conservation is often a reaction to changes which are perceived to be negative such as industrial farming or modern architecture. It is a last resort. Perhaps we should instead focus on the forces which shape these changes which we see as undesirable and try to influence those so that conservation becomes unnecessary.

In the spirit of sustainability, we perhaps need to be more selective and careful to ensure that our conservation activity today does not impose unwanted burdens on future generations.

Conclusions

This chapter has been, by necessity, rather short, simplistic and superficial. Nevertheless, it has highlighted some key issues, including the following:

- the environment has five elements

- tourism can have both negative and positive impacts on the environment, but on balance it has a negative impact on the environment
- there is a set of principles that might make tourism more environmentally friendly
- environmental conservation has some inherent dangers.

A range of issues relating to the environmental dimension of the sustainable tourism debate have been briefly discussed. Many of these issues will be re-visited later in the book, for they underpin many of the key aspects of the concept of sustainable tourism.

Discussion Points and Essay Questions

1. Critically evaluate the idea that tourism and the environment are enemies rather than allies.
2. Discuss the extent to which legislation and regulation can safeguard the environment from the negative impacts of tourism.
3. Discuss the advantages and disadvantages of attempting to conserve one of the following:

- traditional landscapes
- historic buildings
- indigenous wildlife.

Exercise

Select a tourist destination with which you are familiar, or one for which you can gather data without too much difficulty. For your chosen destination, you should produce a report which highlights the problems and benefits which tourism has brought to the local environment.

Case Study: the Environmental Impact of Declining Levels of Tourism in UK Seaside Resorts

Most studies of the environmental impact of tourism focus upon the impacts of tourism on the environment in new and developing destinations. However, given that there are now many established resorts which are experiencing decline, we must also look at the environmental effect of decline in resorts.

Cooper, in 1997, published an interesting study of the environmental consequences of decline in UK seaside resorts. Cooper identified the following problems:

- the traditional, and often attractive, features of the resort townscape have either deteriorated or disappeared altogether. This includes the grand old hotels and Victorian piers, together with theatres and promenades. They have often been replaced by poor quality amusement arcades and fast food outlets
- poor levels of maintenance of open spaces
- neglect of maintenance in small- and medium-sized accommodation establishments
- many accommodation units have been either converted to other uses, or, in some cases, have become derelict
- townscapes have been blighted by the construction of new roads and by car and coach parking facilities.

The English Tourist Board noted in 1991, that:

> The environmental consequences of long-term market decline in the resorts has produced a spiral of decline which has put in jeopardy the quality of life of those who live, work, and holiday in resorts ... Market shifts have produced a negative cycle of falling product quality, lower profitability, lack of investment even for refurbishment, and further decline in the quality of the experience provided in resorts. (English Tourist Board, 1991 quoted in Cooper, 1997)

Resort decline is clearly a threat to sustainability so sustainable tourism also means re-juvenating and re-generating existing resorts as well as simply ensuring the new resorts are planned with sustainability in mind.

Case Study: the Environmental Impact of Uncontrolled Small-scale Tourism Development in Malaysia

Hamzah has shown that even small-scale tourism development can have negative environmental impact if it is not adequately controlled. He explained that small-scale tourism in Malaysia grew around picturesque fishing villages near beaches or on offshore islands. In the early days, the tourism involved informal tourism with drifters or 'hippies' spending long periods in the villages.

However, between the 1970s and the 1990s these small-scale resorts developed dramatically. Many settlements experienced a growth in accommodation of up to 2000% between 1970 and 1990. On one island alone accommodation increased by 500% over just 2 years between 1988 and 1990 (Hamzah, 1997).

The small resorts have grown in an unplanned manner. As a result Hamzah was able to identify several negative impacts as follows:

- Conflict over limited resources, such as water, grazing land, and rights of way.
- The depletion of marine habitats and ecosystems. As Hamzah noted:

> Uncontrolled development has mainly caused the depletion of corals and the deterioration in water quality, and, to a lesser extent, the depletion of mangroves. In 1984, more than half of the corals at Pulau Tioman were found to be damaged by boat anchors (Ridzwan, 1994). In 1995, between 20% and 40% dead corals were found in the waters fronting the popular tourist spots on the island, mainly due to sediment (World-wide Fund for Nature, Malaysia, 1995). Also, the *E. coli* content in the coastal water exceeded the prescribed standard by 92 times (Voon, 1994). (Hamzah, 1997)

- Environmental damage has been caused by the construction of new accommodation units, including the process of site clearing and back filling which was carried out on such a scale that resulted in the killing of many of the mature trees on the sites.

Hamzah summarized that there is a need for tourism planning and for statutory local plans which should provide strict guidelines for future tourism development. He also suggested the need for a planning manual that would give positive advice on the sensitive development of sites so as to minimize the negative environmental impacts of such development.

However, in common with a number of developing countries, Hamzah recognized that the expertise needed for effective tourism planning was not available in the local authorities concerned.

Malaysia is also a good example of the link between socio-economic and environmental impacts of tourism development through the role of local entrepreneurs, and the lack of benefits from tourism for most members of the community.

In relation to both environmental and socio-economic impacts, therefore, it appears that the priority should be planning for the public good rather than allowing private gain to be the main motivator of development.

6

The Economic Dimension

In the debate over sustainable tourism, the economic dimension is often given relatively scant attention compared to the environmental issues. Yet tourism is an economic phenomenon of great potency worldwide. It:

- is the major industry and foreign currency earner in many developing countries
- is the basis of the growth of many transnational corporations
- accounts for a significant proportion of the annual disposable income of many people in the so-called developed countries
- swallows up billions of pounds every year in public sector infrastructure investment.

This chapter looks at a range of issues relating to the economics of tourism in terms of sustainability.

The Economic Impacts of Tourism

Figure 6.1 illustrates the economic impact of tourist spending, based on a model discussed by Murphy and modified by Page. It originally related to urban areas but the principles apply in any geographical context. This diagram shows the complexity of the economic impacts of tourism in a particular locality.

The Economic Costs and Benefits of Tourism

As we can see from Table 6.1, tourism brings both economic benefits and economic costs.

Cost–Benefit Analysis

When evaluating the economic costs and benefits of particular projects or events, use is often made of cost–benefit analysis. This technique seeks to identify, if possible, all the associated costs and benefits so that a rational decision can be made. While useful, cost–benefit analysis does have certain limitations. For example, it is:

- difficult to quantify social costs and benefits which arise from tourism developments such as crime, social alienation and the erosion of traditional cultures
- not always easy to evaluate short-term versus longer term impacts
- not usually sophisticated enough to take account of the fact that the costs and benefits are different for different people.

A project may benefit the region as a whole but may bring great costs to a small section of the community. Nevertheless, cost–benefit analysis can be a valuable tool in

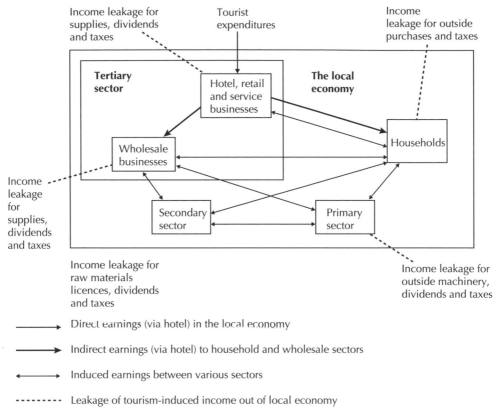

Income leakage for supplies, dividends and taxes

Tourist expenditures

Income leakage for outside purchases and taxes

Tertiary sector

Hotel, retail and service businesses

The local economy

Households

Wholesale businesses

Income leakage for supplies, dividends and taxes

Secondary sector

Primary sector

Income leakage for raw materials licences, dividends and taxes

Income leakage for outside machinery, dividends and taxes

──────▶ Direct earnings (via hotel) in the local economy

──────▶ Indirect earnings (via hotel) to household and wholesale sectors

◀─────▶ Induced earnings between various sectors

--------- Leakage of tourism-induced income out of local economy

Fig. 6.1.   The economic impact of tourist spending.

helping make decisions on tourism development project proposals.

Types of Economies in Tourist Areas

When looking at the costs and benefits of tourism, we have to be aware that the economic impact of tourism is dependent partly on the nature of the economy in question. Some of the commonest types of local economy found in tourist destinations are illustrated in Fig. 6.2.

The economic impact of tourism will vary significantly between these different types of economies, in terms of levels of tourist spending, who will be employed in tourism, wage rates and the degree of leakage of tourism income from the local community. This issue of leakage now leads us on to a brief discussion of the multiplier effect.

The Multiplier Effect

When considering the costs and benefits of tourism to the local economy, much attention is paid to the principle of the 'multiplier effect'. This means the idea that every pound, dollar or mark spent by the tourist circulates around the local economy in a series of waves.

Figure 6.3 offers a simplified clear view of the concept of the multiplier effect. In terms of sustainable tourism, the aims are to maximize tourist spending and then to minimize the leakages of tourism income from the local economy. It is important to recognize that the multiplier effect varies between different economies, as can be seen in the case study on the multiplier effect at the end of this chapter.

The type of economy influences the level of the tourism multiplier and the extent to

Table 6.1. The economic benefits and costs of tourism.

Benefits	Costs
● Job creation ● Injection of income into the local economy through the multiplier effect ● Helping keep local businesses viable ● Regeneration and restructuring of the economies of towns and cities where other industrial activities are in decline ● Stimulates inward and industrial investment	● Many jobs are low paid and/or seasonal ● Opportunity costs, i.e. money invested in tourism that cannot then be used for other purposes ● Congestion ● The need to invest in expensive infrastructure which may only be required for part of the year ● Over-dependence on tourism which makes the host economy vulnerable to changes in the tourism market

which leakage will take place. Leakage is high, for example, in those economies where local suppliers cannot, do not or are not allowed to meet the needs of the tourist, so that their needs are met by externally based organizations.

Table 6.2 illustrates, in general terms, which types of economy are likely to experience high and low leakage of tourism income. While basically sound, this is a very simplified picture and ignores the impact of factors such as state intervention and the role of major foreign tour operators in established destinations.

The Consumption of Resources

Tourism makes great demands on resources as we can see from Table 6.3. Tourism also clearly makes demands on fragile natural resources such as beaches and wildlife. It also exploits intangible resources such as an area's cultural heritage. As we will see in the next section, the tourism industry and the tourist do not pay the full cost of the resources they consume. This is clearly unfair and at odds with the concept of sustainable tourism.

Towards a Fair Price for the Tourism Product

Given the social equity dimension of sustainable tourism it is important to ensure

that tourists pay a fair price for their holiday experience. At the moment many tourists pay less than the true cost of their holiday because:

● the perishability of the tourism product leads to last minute discounting by tourism organizations so that late purchasers pay an unrealistically low price
● central government may subsidize transport infrastructure and state-owned visitor attractions
● local government and local taxpayers fund the cost of local tourism-related infrastructure.

These latter two naturally lead us to a consideration of the role of the public sector in tourism development, and the economic impact of this involvement.

The Ethics of Government Support for the Tourism Industry

There are many reasons why public sector bodies become involved in tourism for the sake of society as a whole. Tourism can:

● contribute to improving a country's balance of payments situation
● provide employment
● bring income to local communities

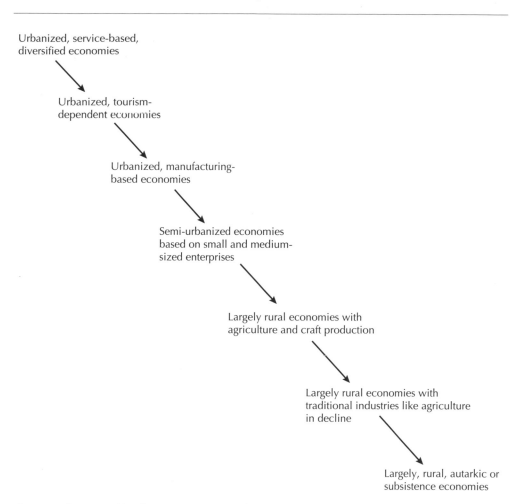

Fig. 6.2.   The range of local economies in tourist destinations.

- generate tax revenue for public sector bodies
- stimulate rural and regional development, regenerate urban areas, and diversify local economies.

Public sector organizations intervene in tourism in a number of ways which have an economic impact. These ways are illustrated in Fig. 6.4.

The active involvement of the public sector raises several ethical issues:

- The idea that it is wrong for taxpayers as a whole in an area or country to be asked to pay for destination marketing activities when it is the private sector which

gains from such activities. When a local council promotes weekend breaks using public money, the main economic benefits go to the local hotels. Most residents who have paid for the promotion of the short breaks usually gain little or nothing from the tourist's expenditure.

- State subsidy of certain tourism organizations can create unfair competition. On a large scale they can involve state-owned, subsidized airlines being given an unfair advantage over smaller, non-subsidized privately owned airlines. On a smaller scale it may be a case of publicly owned subsidized visitor attractions being unfair competition for privately owned attractions. While

Tourists spend for:	Second round of expenditures:	Ultimate beneficiaries (a partial list)
Lodging	Wages and salaries	Accountants
		Appliance repair persons
Food	Tips and gratuities	Architects
		Artisans and crafts people
Beverages	Payroll taxes	Arts and crafts suppliers
		Athletes
Entertainment	Commissions	Attorneys
		Auto service persons
		Bakers
Clothing	Music and entertainment	Bank workers
		Butchers
Gifts and souvenirs	Administrative and	Carpenters
	general expenses	Cashiers
		Charities
Personal care,	Professional services	Cinema and video
medicines,		makers/distributors
cosmetics		Clerks
	Purchases of food and	Clothing manufacturers
	beverage supplies	Cooks
Photography		Cultural organizations
		Dairies
Recreation	Purchase of goods for resale	Dentists
		Department store
		owners/workers
Tours, sightseeing,	Purchase of materials	Doctors
guides and local	and supplies	Education providers
transportation		Electricians
	Repairs and maintenance	Engineers
Miscellaneous		Farmers
	Advertising, promotion	Fisherpersons
	and publicity	Freight forwarders
		Furniture makers
		Gardeners
	Utilities	Gift shop operators
		Government workers
	Transportation	Grocers
		Health care providers
	Licences	Housekeeping staff
		Insurance workers
		Laundry service providers
	Insurance premiums	Manufacturing workers
		Office equipment suppliers
	Rental of facilities	Painters
	and equipment	Petrol stations
		Plumbers
		Porters
	Interest and principal	Printers and publishers
	payments of borrowed funds	Recreation equipment,
		sales/rental
	Income and other taxes	Resort owners, operators
		and workers
	Replacement of capital assets	Restaurant owners, operators
		Road maintenance workers
	Return to government	Sign makers
		Transportation workers
		Utilities, providers of and
		repairpersons
		Waiters and waitresses
		Wholesale suppliers

Leakage: When the private or public sector purchases goods or services from sources outside the community, that money is no longer subject to the multiplier effect and the economic benefits leak out of the community

Fig. 6.3. The multiplier effect in tourism.

Table 6.2. Differences in leakages between different types of economy.

High leakage	Low leakage
Areas in developing countries with economies based largely on primary production such as agriculture, where tourism is a relatively new phenomenon	Well-established major tourist destinations in developed countries

persuasive arguments can be advanced to support the use of subsidies in some cases, overall one is left with a feeling that too often they are unfair and act against the ultimate interest of consumers.

- The money spent by the public sector on tourism represents an opportunity cost. In other words, this money could be spent on other things like education and health, which could bring benefits to more people in the country concerned.

Having looked at how government action can be in conflict with the principles of sustainability and fairness let us look at one way in which it could act that may be more complementary to sustainable tourism: the role of tourist taxes.

Tourist Taxes

We saw in Chapter 3 that there are many problems with the way tourist taxes are being used at the moment. However, instead

of using tourist taxes just to manage demand, or alleviate some of the burdens of tourism on local people, perhaps we should instead start thinking in terms of fair pricing of the tourism product, from the beginning. In other words, we should try to ensure that whoever gains must pay more and vice versa. The implications of this are far-reaching and might include:

- An end to the use of public money to subsidize private sector tourism interests, such as the use of public money to promote weekend breaks in cities where the bulk of tourist money goes on privately owned hotels, restaurants and shops. Surely it is fair for the private sector to fund such campaigns wholly. Unless they do, local tax payers, even those who do not gain at all from tourism, are subsidizing private businesses.
- Tour operators may have to be forced to pay a fair price to their suppliers, such as hotels, to ensure that the latter can pay good wages to their staff.
- We need to do far more research on the hidden economic costs and benefits of

Table 6.3. Resources called on by travel and tourism. Source: Bull (1996).

In generating areas	In destination areas
• Consumer incomes • Consumer time • Labour for selling/marketing/transport • Capital: investment in transport equipment • Fixed capital investment • Business travel time/expenditure • Selling enterprise	• Land • Property/buildings • Labour for lodging/destination services • Foodstuffs • Marketing expenditure • Lodging and operational enterprise

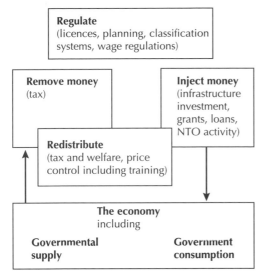

Fig. 6.4. The roles of government in tourism.

Seasonality and Sustainability

In terms of the effective use of resources the seasonality of the tourism market can be viewed as either negative or positive. Depending on one's view, seasonality can either:

- lead to the under-use of infrastructure which is economically inefficient or
- allow over-used resources a period of time during which they can recover before the next season.

More detailed research is required to allow us to decide which view is the nearest to reality.

Economic Trends – Friend or Foe?

The problem for sustainable tourism is that several current economic trends are not compatible with the concept of sustainability, including:

- The trend towards globalization which is leading to product standardization and a reduction in the influence of national, regional and local cultural and geographical differences. This is threatening the diversity which is implicit in the concept of sustainability.
- The rise of multi-national enterprises (MNEs) is also a potential threat to the idea of sustainability in tourism. Based on the work of Dunning and McQueen in 1982, Bull (1995) has identified five possible areas of concern for local host economies from the growth of MNEs. They are as follows:
  (i) control over the structure and development of the tourism industry, or particular subsections of the industry
  (ii) control over tourist markets and tourist flows
  (iii) prices obtained for host economy tourism products
  (iv) the destination of factor and input payments
  (v) competition with locally owned

tourism so we can know what a holiday really costs.
- We need to recognize that some people in a destination gain considerably from tourism while for others it is a net cost. Should this not be reflected in some way in terms of taxation?

Perhaps what we need is a universal tourist tax everywhere, applied to all tourists, to ensure that they pay the full cost of their tourist trip. Or better still, and certainly less bureaucratic, we might make the tourism industry responsible for managing its own impacts to an officially approved standard. It would then have to pass on the cost to its customers or bear the costs itself. The former may well be the most appropriate as it is the consumers' demands which create the problem, and local people would probably suffer job losses and wage cuts if the latter approach were to be adopted.

Conversely, the second idea is more appealing than the tourist tax in that the tax would be a bureaucratic nightmare to collect. Such a tax could also tempt governments to divert the product of the tax to non-tourism-related spending priorities, so that the local community and local industry would not benefit from the revenue.

enterprises and the demonstration effects of production techniques.

In the case of both trends the fundamental issue is the loss of local control, something which is often seen as one of the guiding principles of sustainable tourism.

Towards More Economically Viable Forms of Tourism

Developing more sustainable forms of tourism will involve several main priorities in economic terms:

- developing forms of tourism which optimize the economic benefits of tourism while minimizing its economic costs
- ensuring that the benefits of tourism are spread as widely as possible throughout the host community, particularly amongst the most economically disadvantaged sections of the local population
- making sure that the tourist pays a fair price for their holiday experience
- taking action to share the costs of attracting and meeting the needs of tourists fairly between the tourism industry and the government agencies in the destination
- protecting local businesses from unfair competition from larger, externally owned enterprises which have little commitment to the destination
- reducing leakages from the local economy.

However, it is important that in seeking to implement these ideas we do not go too far. Too extreme an application of these ideas could lead to protectionism and a near monopoly which would give too much power to local businesses *vis-à-vis* the tourist. This could result in poor service and high prices and ultimately a reduction in tourist numbers. There is clearly, therefore, a balance to be struck between local control, a free market and consumer choice.

Conclusions

We have seen that tourism can bring both economic benefits and costs, the exact nature of which varies between different destinations. The main economic issues in relation to sustainability, the author believes, involve whether or not the price tourists pay is a fair reflection of the cost of their holiday, and the extent to which the tourism industry is subsidized by the public sector. We have also seen that the economic trends of globalization and the rise of MNEs are both a threat to sustainable tourism. Clearly, there are obvious links between the economic dimension of tourism and its social impacts. It is therefore appropriate that we should now move on to the social dimension of sustainable tourism in the next chapter.

Discussion Points and Essay Questions

1. Critically evaluate the extent to which globalization is a threat to the development of more sustainable forms of tourism.
2. Discuss the relevance of the concept of the 'multiplier effect' to sustainable tourism.
3. Discuss the contention that tourists do not currently pay a fair price for their holiday.

Exercise

Select a holiday package at random from the brochure of a leading tour operator. For your chosen holiday, identify *all* the occasions when the tourist could be said to be being subsidized by public sector agencies. Finally, estimate what the cost of the holiday might be if no such subsidies existed.

Case Study: the Multiplier Effect

As we saw in the chapter, the concept of the multiplier is based on the idea that:

> Money spent by the tourists is re-spent by the tourism operators on suppliers and labour, who in turn spend their income on other items. Hence the tourist dollar is being turned over several times as it ripples through the economy. (Oppermann and Chon, 1997)

In Exhibit 1 are estimates of the multiplier effect for a number of selected destinations based on the work of a range of authors. These figures, while they are only estimates, indicate that the multiplier effects are closely linked with the rate of leakages. Where leakage is high, particularly on small islands, the multiplier effect is much lower than that of larger islands and mainland countries with lower leakage rates.

These figures focus upon the income multiplier but there is also an employment multiplier, which measures the employment created by tourism spending. Oppermann and Chon discussed the study by Archer and Fletcher in 1995, conducted on the Seychelles, which showed that:

> Tourists from different origin countries have a varying employment multiplier effect although their income multipliers differed only slightly. (Oppermann and Chon, 1997)

Exhibit 1. The income multiplier effects in selected developing countries. Source: various authors quoted in Oppermann and Chon (1997).

Country	Income multipier
Turkey	1.96
Egypt	1.23
Jamaica	1.23
Dominican Republic	1.20
Cyprus	1.14
Hong Kong	1.02
Mauritius	0.96
Seychelles	0.88
Bahamas	0.79
Vanuatu	0.86
Tonga	0.42
Nieu	0.35

Case Study: the Economic Impact of Tourists in Two UK Rural Tourism Destinations

In 1997, Slee, Far and Snowdon published a paper on the economic impact of tourism on two rural destinations in the UK: Exmoor in south-west England and Strathspey in Scotland. The survey was conducted in summer 1994. The authors' findings were as follows:

- In Strathspey the income generated by tourists staying in farm- or forest-based accommodation was higher than that in commercial accommodation with ten or more units. However, in Exmoor the figures were similar for both types of accommodation.
- Tourism in both destinations created between 2.6 and 4.8 full-time equivalent jobs per £100,000 of tourist expenditure.
- The income multiplier effect in Exmoor and Strathspey varied between 0.20 and 0.27.
- The employment multiplier, in terms of direct employment varied in the destinations between 2.2 and 2.9 while that for indirect employment ranged between 0.7 and 1.3.
- It was estimated that in the 'core areas' of both destinations the following amounts were spent by tourists:
  (i)   in Strathspey, around 107,000 tourists spent approximately £3.8 million
  (ii)   in Exmoor, a little over 68,000 tourists spent approximately £1.9 million.
- The total number of jobs resulting from tourism in the core areas amounted to 614 in Strathspey and 289 in Exmoor.

The authors also found that 'soft' (farm- or forest-based tourism accommodation) businesses were often more beneficial than 'hard' (commercial non-farm or forest-based accommodation) enterprises, because they:

- employed more people per unit of visitor spending
- generated more income per 100,000 days of visitor spending.

As Slee *et al.* concluded:

> The promotion of small-scale soft rural tourism may thus constitute a legitimate element of agency actions to support the more integrated development of rural economies and to provide an alternative source of well-being for households that are likely to experience diminishing returns from their land-based activities (such as farming or forestry). (Slee *et al.*, in Stabler, 1997)

7

The Social Dimension

The social dimension of tourism has been given less attention in the sustainable tourism debate, than the environmental impact of tourism. Perhaps this is because the socio-cultural impacts of tourism usually occur slowly over time in an unspectacular fashion. They are also largely invisible and intangible. Yet the social impact of tourism is usually permanent with little or no opportunity to reverse the change once it has taken place.

When the social impact of sustainable tourism has been considered the focus has normally been upon the 'host community'. There has been an almost paternalistic desire to 'protect' host communities from the excesses and negative effects of tourism. This issue is dealt with in more detail in Chapter 11.

However, the author believes that we need to take a broader view of the social aspects of sustainable tourism. Furthermore, we need to acknowledge that *all* the stakeholders in tourism have both rights and responsibilities that need to be recognized.

At the same time, it is also the author's contention that any discussion of such issues in tourism must also become more 'political', reflecting the overtly political nature of tourism planning and development.

Figure 7.1 shows a model of what the author considers to be the scope of the social dimension of sustainable tourism. These issues are taken up in more detail in Part 3 of this book and in Chapter 24. They are all clearly inter-related, and indeed, interdependent. This is clearly a very simplistic model but it does illustrate the range of issues involved and the complex inter-relationship of the key stakeholders in the social aspects of sustainable tourism in relation to international tourist flows.

We can perhaps best sum up the social dimension of the drive to develop more sustainable forms of tourism by talking about implementing the four Es:

- **Equity**, ensuring that all stakeholders in tourism are treated fairly
- **Equal opportunities**, for both the employees involved in the tourism industry and the people who want to be tourists
- **Ethics**, in other words, the tourism industry being honest with tourists and ethical in its dealings with its suppliers, and destination governments being ethical towards their host population and tourists
- **Equal partners**, namely, tourists treating those who serve them as equal partners not as inferiors.

The author argues that sustainable tourism must be socially equitable for all the players and suggests that we need to develop a concept of **'fair trade'** in tourism, which was

---

THE TOURIST

- who can, and cannot, afford a holiday
- paying a fair price for the holiday
- the legitimacy or otherwise of the benefits gained from tourism, from relaxation to having sex with children
- visiting destinations with poor human rights records
- the need to feel safe and secure
- interactions and relations with fellow tourists and the host community
- attitudes towards staff
- exploiting low wage-earners to enjoy a cheap holiday

FOREIGN TOUR OPERATORS

- relations with the local tourism industry and the host community
- exploiting low cost economies to reduce their costs
- images and expectations created by their promotional activities
- doing business with destinations with poor human rights records
- doing business with entrepreneurs who may have a poor record as employers
- lack of long-term commitment to local communities

DESTINATION GOVERNMENT

- restrictions on, and harassment of tourists from particular countries and cultures
- devoting resources to tourism that could otherwise be allocated to other priorities such as health and education
- subsidizing the cost of holidays for tourists
- creating images of the destination for tourists through their promotional activities
- deciding how tax revenues from tourists will be used
- degree and nature of regulation of the tourism industry
- attitudes to traditional cultures and indigenous people in the destination

---

LOCAL TOURISM INDUSTRY

- human resource issues including pay, working conditions and promotion opportunities
- influence with government decision-makers
- value for money, or otherwise, offered to tourists
- representations of local cultures for tourists

HOST COMMUNITY

- attitudes towards, and relations with, the tourists
- level of involvement and degree of influence on public sector decision-making in relation to tourism
- impact of tourism on the society and culture
- strengths of, and commitment towards, conserving the society and culture

Fig. 7.1. The scope of the social dimension of sustainable tourism.

discussed in more detail in Chapter 6.

In this chapter, we will explore several key issues in relation to the social dimension of sustainable tourism, most of which are discussed further in other chapters.

The Sociocultural Impact of Tourism on the Host Community

The sociocultural impacts have been studied and discussed for several decades and were exposed to a wide audience in the classic 1982 Mathieson and Wall book, *Tourism – the Economic, Physical, and Social Impacts.*

In general, attention has focused on the negative impacts of tourism on host societies and cultures. However, it is important to recognize that the effects can also be positive. Some of the main impacts of tourism in societies and cultures are illustrated in Fig. 7.2. Clearly the judgements that lead to these factors being placed in one column or another are largely subjective but they do appear to reflect the conventional wisdom in the sustainable tourism literature.

There are a number of factors that determine whether or not the balance of sociocultural impacts will be positive or negative in a particular location, including:

- the strength and coherence of the local society and culture
- the nature of tourism in the resort
- the level of economic and social development of the host population in relation to the tourists
- the measures, if any, taken by the public sector in the destination to manage tourism in ways which minimize the sociocultural costs of tourism.

The major problems seem to occur in destinations in developing countries where the majority of tourists are from developed countries, and the government has little say in the development to tourism to local people. It is often even worse when people in the destination are living in areas where the local population is seen by central government as being either:

- relatively backward or
- politically at odds with the government.

The Impact of Tourism on the Tourist

We should not under-estimate the impact of tourism on the tourists themselves. In the past three decades the growth in international holiday-making has changed many people's lives in the developed countries. It has:

- given them an opportunity to see new parts of the world and widen their horizons
- perhaps increased interest in the food of destinations like Greece and the USA
- led to many people buying second homes and retirement homes in tourist destinations so that they can spend part or all of the year, and even the rest of their lives, in a place they have discovered through tourism and which they prefer to their home country.

At the same time, tourism has provided a vital opportunity for people from industrialized, urbanized countries to:

- relax and unwind, as an antidote to the stresses of the modern way of life
- escape from humdrum or monotonous jobs
- get away from their everyday living environment which may be a small apartment in a polluted industrial town in a country where the sky is often grey.

Holidays give many tourists something to look forward to in their everyday lives. They are a chance to be free from the constraints of daily life in one's own home community. Unfortunately, this can mean that tourists may be unwilling to act responsibly in line with the principles of sustainable tourism. They may see their vacation as their one chance of the year to behave irresponsibly. It may be difficult to convince them to curtail

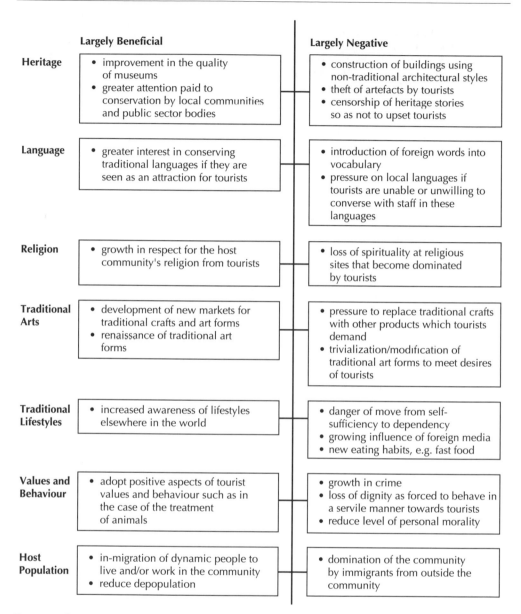

	Largely Beneficial	**Largely Negative**
Heritage	• improvement in the quality of museums • greater attention paid to conservation by local communities and public sector bodies	• construction of buildings using non-traditional architectural styles • theft of artefacts by tourists • censorship of heritage stories so as not to upset tourists
Language	• greater interest in conserving traditional languages if they are seen as an attraction for tourists	• introduction of foreign words into vocabulary • pressure on local languages if tourists are unable or unwilling to converse with staff in these languages
Religion	• growth in respect for the host community's religion from tourists	• loss of spirituality at religious sites that become dominated by tourists
Traditional Arts	• development of new markets for traditional crafts and art forms • renaissance of traditional art forms	• pressure to replace traditional crafts with other products which tourists demand • trivialization/modification of traditional art forms to meet desires of tourists
Traditional Lifestyles	• increased awareness of lifestyles elsewhere in the world	• danger of move from self-sufficiency to dependency • growing influence of foreign media • new eating habits, e.g. fast food
Values and Behaviour	• adopt positive aspects of tourist values and behaviour such as in the case of the treatment of animals	• growth in crime • loss of dignity as forced to behave in a servile manner towards tourists • reduce level of personal morality
Host Population	• in-migration of dynamic people to live and/or work in the community • reduce depopulation	• domination of the community by immigrants from outside the community

Fig. 7.2. The main potential impacts of tourism on host cultures and societies.

their natural desire for escapism, to behave sensibly for the sake of the rather abstract concept of sustainability.

The other issue in relation to the tourist in terms of the social dimension of sustainable tourism is the fact that not everyone is able to enjoy the benefits of tourism which are highlighted above. International tourism is still a luxury beyond the reach of many people on the planet in Africa, South America and southern Asia. However, the number of participants in the tourism market is increasing, as travel opportunities become more available to the people of the relatively industrialized countries of South-East Asia.

This is creating one of the great dilemmas of sustainable tourism which is how we allow those who have not been tourists before to enjoy the benefits of tourism that we have taken for granted for years, at a time when many destinations are already perceived as over-crowded. Similarly, we cannot deny these opportunities to be 'new' tourists but we must manage the implications of this development.

Host–Guest Relationships – Key to Success or Disaster?

The key to the sociocultural impacts of tourism appears to be the relationship between hosts and guests. At this stage we will just deal with the key issues briefly as this subject is covered further in Chapters 11 and 24.

According to Mathieson and Wall, writing in 1982, the relationship between tourists and local people has five major features as follows:

- It is transitory or short term, in that each tourist is generally only around from between a day or two and a couple of weeks. By definition any relationships that develop tend to be superficial. A deeper relationship will only develop where the tourist returns to the same resort and accommodation frequently.
- Tourists are under pressure to enjoy a wide variety of experiences in a short time period which may make them very irritated if any delays occur. This fact may also lead to residents exploiting these time pressures under which tourists operate.
- Tourists are often segregated from local people and spend most of their time in and around tourism facilities with other tourists. They may rarely meet any local people other than those who are employed in the tourism industry.
- Host–tourist relations tend to lack spontaneity, they are often formalized and planned.
- Host–guest relations are often unequal and unbalanced in nature, in terms of both material inequality and differences in power. The tourist is in control and has the power to generally impose their

will on the hosts, who are seen as servers.

All of these characteristics can be seen as negative impacts in relation to the concept of sustainable tourism.

There is also a view that the quality of the relationship between hosts and guests worsens as tourism develops and the number of tourists rises. This idea is the basis of Doxey's influential Irridex model which is covered in detail elsewhere in this book.

We will now look in a little more depth at two important aspects of the relationship between hosts and guests, namely:

- the demonstration effect
- relative deprivation.

The Demonstration Effect

The demonstration effect is a broad concept which revolves around the idea that the presence of tourists and the exposure of local people to tourist life styles has an impact on the expectations and life styles of local people. In 1982, Mathieson and Wall stated that:

> The demonstration effect can be advantageous if it encourages [local] people to adapt or work for things they lack. More commonly, it is detrimental and most authors indicate concern for the effects on foreign destinations of the industry and the impacts of tourists who parade symbols of their affluence to interested hosts. Alien commodities are rarely desired prior to their introduction into host communities and for most residents of destination areas in the developing world, such commodities remain painstakingly beyond reach. As a result discontent grows among the hosts. (Mathieson and Wall, 1982)

Therefore, particularly in developing countries, tourism can raise expectations that cannot be met for most residents which results in resentment of tourists.

However, there can also be problems when tourists misinterpret the life style of tourists, because they come from a different culture. For example, Rivers noted that:

> ... young Spaniards [became] convinced

that all female tourists were easy conquests. (Rivers, 1973 quoted by Mathieson and Wall, 1982)

Likewise, Cohen in 1971 reported that:

> ... fair-headed girls from Scandinavia were thought to be seeking sexual adventures in their travels and were sought by his study group of Arab boys. (Cohen, 1971 quoted in Mathieson and Wall, 1982)

The way in which the demonstration effect can undermine traditional values was highlighted by UNESCO in 1976 and reported by Mathieson and Wall in 1982, as follows:

> The hosts quickly perceive the desire of tourists to spend money lavishly to gain experiences and acquire souvenirs of their stay ... At the outset hosts may develop an inferiority complex which sets off a process of imitation. The weaknesses of the tourists are quickly perceived and are subsequently exploited. A dual pricing system often develops. (Mathieson and Wall, 1982)

However, we must also recognize that the demonstration effect works in both directions. Many tourists are deeply affected by what they see on holiday and this can result in them:

- becoming interested in particular cultures and wanting to learn more about them
- developing romanticized views of the local population that become stereotypical such as the idea of the 'simple' life in Ireland or the Greek Islands
- looking to some cultures such as the Hindus of India and the Buddhists of Thailand, for spiritual enlightenment that they cannot get in their own country.

As more and more residents of so-called developed countries become ever more discontented with their everyday lives, this aspect of the demonstration effect may grow. Tourists will want to imitate the life styles, or perceived life styles, of the host communities in destinations, to try to enrich their own lives. This could either be a meaningful development in the quest for sustainable tourism, or it could prove to be superficial and may open the tourist up to further exploitation by the hosts.

Relative Deprivation

One of the major elements in the resentment factor of some hosts is the concept of relative deprivation. This has been defined as:

> Feelings of deprivation relative to a group with which an individual compares himself or herself ... the theory holds that how people evaluate their circumstances depends upon whom they compare themselves to. (Giddens, 1993 quoted in Seaton, 1996)

In a very interesting study, Seaton has applied the concept of relative deprivation to different aspects of society. His conclusions are outlined in Table 7.1.

Sex Tourism

This is perhaps the most controversial and condemned aspect of tourism. Traditionally sex tourism has meant men buying sex from female prostitutes; however, modern sex tourism is a more complex matter than this, as can be seen in Fig. 7.3.

In terms of sustainable tourism, where do we draw the line between 'acceptable' and 'unacceptable' sex tourism? All of these forms of sex tourism have disadvantages in relation to sustainable tourism, ranging from the risk of sexually transmitted diseases to the oppression and exploitation of powerless children.

To most people, sex with children is the most morally repugnant form of sex tourism yet control is difficult. Foreign governments have sometimes legislated to outlaw trips abroad by their citizens where the motivation is the desire to have sex with children. However, sometimes the demand for such experiences is domestic rather than just foreign.

Often, though, sex tourism is merely a new form of colonial-style exploitation.

Table 7.1. Intensity and effects of different kinds of relative deprivation (RD1, RD2, RD3) in four kinds of society. Source: Seaton, in Robinson *et al.* (1996).

Type of society	RD1	RD2	RD3
Developed socialist	Little or mild RD if tourists are seen as not much richer than hosts	Strong RD if state-provided privileges for tourist exist, since privilege conflicts with ideology of equality. Political dissent	Little RD if tourist employment is not seen as better paid than other kinds of employment
Developed non-socialist	No/little RD: Tourists not seen as very much richer, if at all, than hosts. Some crime against tourists by poor, subordinate groups within rich host countries	No RD because no special provision exists for use of tourists, denied to rest of population	No RD since tourism employment is not seen as better, but less well paid, than other employment
Less developed non-socialist	Strong RD because of highly visible contrast between wealth of tourists and hosts. Crime against tourists. RD not a political issue because system never promised equality. Some emulation since system encourages it	Medium RD. Special provision for tourists may be envied (e.g. luxury hotels) but seen as creation of market, rather than government. It may be fatalistically accepted as one of many inequalities deriving from economic 'realities', not political factors	Low/medium RD where tourism employment only seen as slightly better paid than other occupations, if at all
Less developed socialist	Strong RD because of highly visible contrast between wealth of tourists and hosts, but crime against tourists may be limited. Hostility to state. Little emulation	Acute RD. Special treatment of tourists seen as illegitimate in contrast to scarcity in host country. May provoke political dissent or even terrorism	Acute RD where tourism employment seen as better rewarded than other occupations. Political dissent. Attempted emulation in 'black' tourism economy

Tourists travel abroad to exploit the desperation of poor people in other countries to do things that are not available, or are illegal, in their own country.

In terms of sustainable tourism, sex tourism is a major challenge for such regions of the world as South-East Asia. We must, for instance, recognize that attacks on sex tourism will have major implications for the economies of these countries, for as Michael Hall has noted:

> Tourism-oriented prostitution has become an integral part of the economic base in several regions of south-east Asia ... Banning prostitution may be counter-

productive and may create even greater hardship for those who engage in it. (Hall, 1992)

We also need to finish by noting the growth of another variation in sex tourism, that is the rise of men from the West seeking brides amongst Asian women. According to the Philippine Women's Research Collective in 1985:

> Promoted as meek, docile, submissive, home oriented and having tremendous capacities in bed, Filipino women have been sought by many Australian men through pen-pal links and mail-order bride

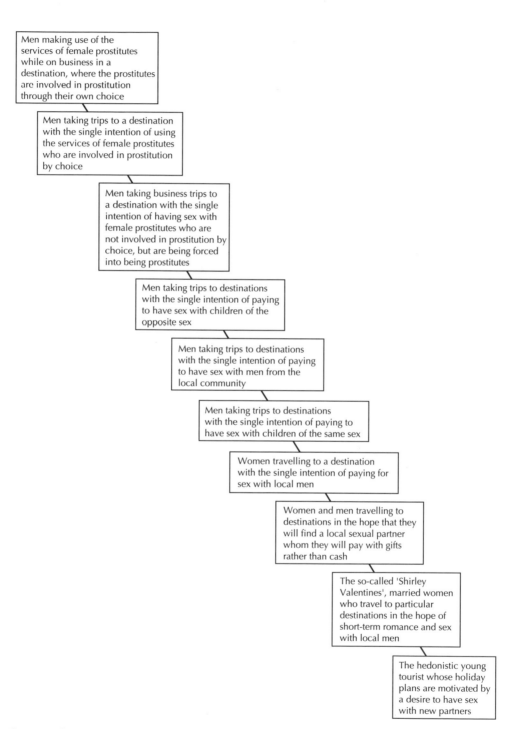

Fig. 7.3.   The nature and scope of sex tourism.

business. (Philippine Women's Research Collective, 1985)

Often men travel to the Philippines to meet potential wives they have selected from brochures. This activity is also being seen in the former Soviet Union, and will be one of the future challenges, albeit a rather marginal one, of the social dimension of sustainable tourism.

Animal Rights versus Human Rights

In Chapter 6 we looked at the issue of wildlife conservation and the impact it could have upon the rights of host communities. It is important for us to recognize that sometimes the protection of wildlife can have a massive social impact on indigenous peoples. Governments and developers who recognize the economic value of wildlife as a tourist asset are often willing to ride roughshod over local people who are seen to be of less value than the wildlife.

A special issue of *Tourism Concern* in 1997 gave two powerful examples of this phenomenon, in Myanmar and Tanzania.

Myanmar

In Myanmar (formerly Burma) the army has been clearing the Karen area, allegedly razing villages and killing people to help clear the way for the development of the largest nature reserve of its kind in the world. The government hopes it will attract millions of tourists, as it is meant to signal to the developed world the government's commitment to environmental conservation. When challenged on their apparent involvement in Myanmar, the Smithsonian Institute spokesperson stated that: 'We are there to do important conservation work. We may disagree with a regime but it is not our place to challenge it' (*The Observer*, 23 March 1997). A WWF spokesperson also stated that: 'Sometimes we have to deal with repulsive regimes. We have to weigh up whether the conservation benefit is worth the risk of being seen, directly or indirectly, to be supporting these regimes' (*The Observer*, 23

March 1997).

This separation of conservation and human rights appears, to the author, to be wholly unacceptable, in terms of sustainability. We cannot say host communities are all important, but ignore them if there is also wildlife in the area which outsiders say is very important, apparently more important than the rights of the indigenous population.

Tanzania

The Maasai people of Tanzania have been progressively moved off their traditional lands so that nature reserves could be developed, largely for the benefit of tourists. The irony is that the Maasai themselves lived alongside the animals and their activities and were no threat to the future of the wildlife. Few conservation bodies consulted the Maasai before making decisions that affected their lives. Officials often told the Maasai that their camps were unsightly to tourists while at the same time they were sanctioning the construction of unsuitably designed new lodges to accommodate tourists.

It is clearly not morally right to move powerless tribespeople off their lands to accommodate the demands of tourists who want to see wild animals. Perhaps the solution is for the Maasai to be permitted to become more actively involved in tourism so that they can gain more benefits from tourism as follows:

> Some of the Maasai would like to organise walking safaris for tourists. These would not only allow them to see the wild animals in a new and more environmentally-friendly way, but might also lead the Maasai and the tourists to a better understanding of each other's point of view. (*Tourism Concern*, Spring 1997)

Conversely, perhaps we should think the unthinkable and suggest that the Maasai should come before animals and tourists, and we should

- remove 'natural reserve' status from the Maasai's traditional areas

- ask tourists to either not visit these areas or invite them to meet the Maasai rather than the animals.

Towards More Socially Equitable Tourism

It is the author's contention that sustainable tourism means tourism which is socially equitable. Sustainable tourism cannot exist if we protect the environment but ignore the social needs of tourists and hosts. It can also not truly exist if the environment can only be protected by denying the human rights of groups of people. Sustainable tourism, therefore, means fairness which in tourism implies:

- all stakeholders in tourism being given fair treatment
- employees having equal opportunities irrespective of their age, sex, race or disability
- increasing the opportunities for everyone in the world who wants to take a holiday to be able to do so
- local people and staff being treated as equals rather than inferiors and servants in relation to the tourists
- managing tourism so the local people can maintain their dignity and sense of pride in themselves and their communities
- boycotting tourism in those countries where the local population is denied human rights
- the development of the concept of 'fair trade' in tourism, where tourists are required to pay a fair price for the holiday they take, and where the benefits of tourism are widely distributed around the host community.

These all require action by destination governments, tourists, the host community and the tourism industry. It also implies that host communities need more power to allow them to exert their rights in the tourism planning and development process.

Conclusions

We have seen that the social dimension is crucial to sustainable tourism, particularly in relation to the sociocultural impacts of tourism and host–guest relations. The author has also suggested that we must recognize the beneficial effects of tourism upon the tourist and the rights of indigenous people as well as the rights of wildlife. It has been suggested that sustainable tourism means socially fair tourism and that this involves the four Es, namely: equity, equal opportunities, ethics and tourists and hosts being equal partners. There is a need to integrate the social dimension of tourism with the environmental and economic dimensions to allow us to take an holistic view of sustainable tourism.

Discussion Points and Essay Questions

1. Evaluate the measures that can be taken by tourism planners to minimize the negative sociocultural effects, and maximize the positive sociocultural impacts, of tourism, on the host community.
2. Discuss the relationship between the 'demonstration effect' and sustainable tourism.
3. Discuss the implications of the nature and scope of sex tourism outlined in Fig. 7.3 for the development of more sustainable forms of tourism.

Exercise

Conduct a survey of a small number of people who have taken a foreign holiday in the past few months, to ascertain the effect their holiday had on them. You should look at:

- why they took the holiday
- what they hoped to gain from the holiday
- if, and how, they felt better after their holiday
- to what extent, if at all, they are looking forward to their next holiday and how this anticipation helps to enhance their quality of life.

Case Study: Southern Tunisia

In 1996, Bleasdale and Tapsell produced a study of the sociocultural aspects of tourism in the Tozeur region of southern Tunisia, an Islamic country. The research on which the study was based involved observing tourism over 5 years and interviews with local residents and public sector representatives.

The authors found that the national government in Tunisia had sought actively to develop tourism in the region since 1987 through a variety of means, including the building of a new airport. By 1994 the area was receiving 722,017 visitors with an average stay of 1.2 nights. The 62 local hotels had occupancy levels of around 35%.

The main results of the research indicated that tourism was having the following sociocultural impacts:

- Tourism had created around 1600 jobs between 1988 and 1994 in terms of direct employment and a further 4600 jobs through indirect employment. The higher paid jobs were filled by men while women were employed in lower paid jobs as cleaners and chambermaids. Unlike on the coast of Tunisia women were not found working on reception desks which may reflect stricter religious standards in the Tozeur area. Many of the industry jobs were in self-employment but the opportunities were almost inevitably taken by men.
- The authors found that the 'demonstration effect' was in evidence but largely only in relation to the people who had direct contact with tourists, who were mainly younger men. In the case of these young men, they adopted Western dress and habits.
- Many local people, particularly women, found the dress of tourists – shorts in particular – somewhat offensive.
- Local traders developed the ability to converse with tourists in a range of languages. They also seemed to view different nationalities of tourists as having different attitudes and spending potential.
- In general, restaurants were not willing to serve alcohol although the tourists' hotels did serve alcohol to tourists.
- Revenue from tourism has helped the town re-build its mosque that was damaged by flooding in 1988/1989. At the same time money from tourism had led to the restoration of many houses in the town.
- A visitor attraction was developed on the 'Arabian Nights' theme which was rather like a themed amusement park and was clearly aimed at tourists. It seems to have little to do with Tunisian culture and is therefore questionable in relation to the concept of sustainable tourism.
- While tourism has increased sales of locally produced crafts, the demand of tourists has led to a modification of traditional styles and designs. New colours have been added to woven products and camel designs have been added to the traditional symbolic, abstract designs.
- The authors found evidence of 'staged authenticity' in the Tozeur area. Hotels were offering shows featuring belly dancers and snake charmers as well as 'Bedouin feasts' and 'wedding feasts'. These events have little to do with Tunisian culture.
- The wealth accruing from tourism is giving young males more status in the community than they would have had traditionally. This is causing tension between older residents and the young men. Conversely, it appears that the role of young women had been little affected by tourism.

It will be interesting to see how these impacts may change over the next decade as tourism in the region develops.

Case Study: Goa

Wilson, in 1997, produced a study that looked at lessons from Goa in relation to sustainable tourism, based on work carried out in 1996. He found that:

> ... international tourism in Goa has emerged as an unplanned *ad hoc* response to growing numbers of arrivals, and is at present undergoing rapid transformation into a major package holiday destination ... The state government has encouraged the expansion of up-market tourism as Goa acquires a reputation as the Riviera of the Indian sub-continent. There is a well-organized local anti-tourism lobby which argues that a more appropriate comparison is Benidorm. (Wilson in Stabler, 1997)

This lobby has also ensured that the negative aspects of tourism in Goa have been well publicized. According to critics, tourism in Goa has:

- led to hotels being given preference over local residents for scarce water resources
- restricted access to beaches for local people
- resulted in villagers being intimidated into leaving their homes by developers
- involved some low-cost budget travelling backpackers holding moonlight parties with drugs
- led to a growth of prostitution and paedophile activity
- corrupted local values.

However, there is a feeling that this criticism has both:

> exaggerated these problems whilst ignoring other issues, such as government and police corruption, and the impact of domestic tourism, which has been estimated to account for 90% of the tourists. (Wilson in Stabler, 1997)

This raises the important point that tourists are often easy targets to blame for unpopular social change which is not wholly due to the tourist.

Tourism has led to several conflicts within the community in Goa, including:

- A dispute between local taxi drivers and coaches hired by the tour operators over business which had been traditionally taken by taxis but is increasingly being serviced by the coaches such as excursions and airport transfers. The coaches were guaranteed by the government that their rights to this business would not be removed which has left the large – too large – number of taxis with less business.
- Conflict between the government and enterprises over the 'shacks' which offer food and drink to tourists. The former wants to get rid of the latter and has even passed legislation to try to have them removed.

Goa offers a good example of the different problems associated with two distinctly different types of tourism, low-budget backpackers and upmarket hotel-based tourism. Any attempts by the government to reduce the former in favour of the latter will have serious consequences for those villages which rely on the budget tourist.

Wilson also draws attention to the importance of local perceptions of the value of tourism to their country when we are considering the impacts of tourism in local culture and societies:

For tourism to be sustainable in the social and cultural sense, it must be wanted by
the local inhabitants and it must be perceived as benefiting the majority of local
people, not just an elite handful. It must be something which provides employment
for the skilled as well as the unskilled and which generates opportunities for social
and economic advancement. The jobs up-market tourism provides in Goa are mainly
for menial low-paid jobs, such as waiters, room boys and ground staff, which do not
allow local people to participate as petty entrepreneurs, establish their own
competitive businesses and profit directly from the tourist dollar. Unlike in the
Seychelles, up-market tourism in Goa is not wanted by many local people, not just the
environmentalists, and this is another reason why continued large scale expansion of
this sector would be unsuitable. (Wilson in Stabler, 1997)

The work of Wilson suggests that the conventional view that up-market tourism is
more beneficial than low-spending tourism may well be wrong.

Conclusions to Part Two

In Part Two, we have seen that tourism has environmental, economic and social impacts. Sustainable tourism is about maximizing the impacts which are positive and minimizing the negative ones.

On balance, it appears that the environmental impacts are negative, the economic effects positive, and the social impacts a combination of both. However, it is also important to recognize that there are clear links between the three aspects of tourism – the environmental, economic, and social dimensions – and these are illustrated below.

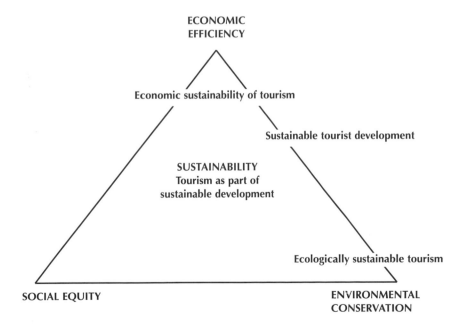

Part Three

The Key Actors in Sustainable Tourism

In this section of the book, we will look at the six key sets of actors involved in sustainable tourism, namely:

(i)   the public sector, including supra-governmental bodies such as the European Union, national governments, local authorities, and quasi-governmental organizations
(ii) the tourism industry
(iii) voluntary sector organizations, notably pressure groups and professional bodies
(iv) the host community
(v)   the media
(vi) the tourist.

We will also look at the links between all six, and how they can work together in partnership.

8

The Public Sector

Most commentators seem to believe that the public sector has a major role to play in the development of more sustainable forms of tourism. In this chapter we will explore the nature of this role.

However, first we must define what we mean by the public sector. This term refers to those bodies which are intended to represent the whole community/public interest, and which are supposed to act on behalf of the total population. They are not commercial organizations trying to make a profit. Instead they spend the revenue from taxation to implement policies and projects which benefit the whole population over which the authority has jurisdiction.

Normally, it is assumed that public sector bodies will be run by democratically elected representatives of the people, although they may be run by dictators or totalitarian systems.

It is important to know that there are different types of public sector organizations and that there are different geographical levels at which public sector bodies operate. This is illustrated in Figs 8.1 and 8.2. This makes both destination planning and destination marketing a complex task.

The Rationale for Public Sector Involvement in Tourism Planning and Management

There are a number of reasons why it is thought appropriate that the public sector should play a leading role in trying to develop more sustainable forms of tourism. These include the following:

- The public sector usually has a mandate to represent the whole population not just particular interest groups or stakeholders.
- The public sector is seen to be impartial with no commercial axe to grind or interest to protect.
- Because it is not constrained by short-term financial objectives the public sector is seen to be able to take a longer term view.

Public Sector Policy and Sustainable Tourism

The public sector influences tourism in a number of ways, and can play a role in the development of sustainable tourism by a variety of means, including:

- legislation and regulation
- funding and fiscal incentives
- land use planning

- Supra-governmental bodies involving cooperation between two or more countries, such as the European Union

- Government Departments and Ministries

- QUANGOs: Quasi non-governmental organizations which are publicly funded agencies that work on behalf of government but are managed semi-autonomously, such as the British Tourist Authority

- Nationalized organizations such as state railways like SNCF in France

Fig. 8.1. Different types of public sector organization.

- development and building control, including the role of Environmental Impact Assessments (EIAs)
- the provision of infrastructure
- the example the public sector can set through its role as an active player in the tourism industry
- official standards
- the designation of particular areas for special protection
- government control over tourist numbers.

Shortly, we will look at each of these issues in a little more detail. However it is important to know that to be successful, public sector policy has to be coordinated effectively, between:

- different departments in the local government
- different government agencies in one country
- different governments in supra-governmental bodies.

Legislation and Regulation

Public sector bodies could do a great deal to make tourism more sustainable through legislation and regulation.

In 1987 the World Commission on the Environment and Development (WCED) better known as the Brundtland Report suggested a framework for the legislative control of sustainable development in general, which is also applicable for tourism. This framework is reproduced in Table 8.1.

However, while many national governments have policies that relate to sustainability and sustainable tourism few yet seem to have legislated to make them a reality. The only relevant legislation that tends to exist is that which controls building development in general. There also tends to be legislation on certain environmental issues such as pollution.

There is little if any legislation that relates directly to sustainable tourism, such as the statutory regulation of:

- tourist behaviour
- tourism industry employees' working conditions, wages and rights
- the social and cultural impacts of tourism
- the impact of tourism on wildlife
- the use of the private car in tourism.

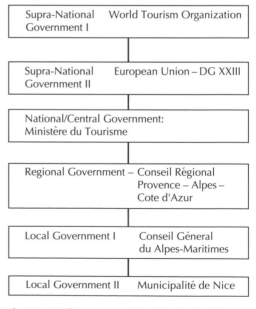

Fig. 8.2. Different geographical levels of public sector organizations which have an interest in tourism in Nice, France.

Table 8.1. A summary of the goals and legal principles of sustainable development, as proposed by the World Commission on Environment and Development (WCED, 1987).

Goals	Legal principles
• A political system that secures effective participation in decision-making • An economic system that is able to generate surpluses and technical knowledge on a self-reliant and sustained basis • A social system that provides for solutions for the tensions arising from disharmonious development • A production system that respects the obligation to preserve the ecological base for development • A technological system that can search continuously for new solutions • An international system that fosters sustainable patterns of trade and finance • An administrative system that is flexible and has the capacity for self-correction	• All human beings have the fundamental right to an environment adequate for their health and well-being • States shall conserve and use the environment and natural resources for the benefits of present and future generations • States shall maintain ecosystems and ecological processes essential for the functioning of the biosphere, preserve biological diversity, and observe the principle of optimum sustainable yield in the use of living natural resources and ecosystems • States shall establish adequate environmental protection standards and monitor changes in and publish relevant data on environmental quality and resource use • States shall make or require prior environmental assessments of proposed activities which may significantly affect the environment or use of a natural resource • States shall inform in a timely manner all persons likely to be significantly affected by a planned activity and to grant them equal access and due process in administrative and judicial proceedings • States shall ensure that conservation is treated as an integral part of the planning and implementation of development activities and provide assistance to other states, especially to developing countries, in support of environmental protection and sustainable development • States shall co-operate in good faith with other states in implementing the preceding rights and obligations

Conversely, there are some positive developments in relation to legislation in the field of sustainable tourism. For example, an increasing number of governments are introducing legislation that makes it a legal offence for their residents to go on sex tourism trips.

However, as usual, the problem with legislation is how can it be implemented and the sex tourism laws are no exception. It is not only controlling tourist behaviour that is difficult to legislate for, controlling the tourism industry is also problematic. This is particularly true in the case of those transnational corporations which operate across national boundaries and are more powerful than some small state governments.

Perhaps that is why many public bodies have seemed to rely instead on industry self-regulation and a belief in educating the tourist to behave more responsibly. However, if this approach continues to achieve only modest success there may be a need in the future to risk the implementation problems and legislate for sustainable tourism.

Funding and Fiscal Incentives and Controls

The public sector can intervene in tourism in financial terms, in several ways to help make tourism more sustainable. These means include:

- providing grants, interest-free loans and other fiscal incentives for sustainable tourism projects
- levying taxes on less sustainable activities such as the use of private cars to make tourist trips
- introducing tourist taxes which represent a fixed sum paid by tourists when using a destination with the revenue generated being ploughed back into making tourism more sustainable in the destination.

As yet none of these methods have been widely used in tourism. For example, to date, little if any attempt has been made to apply the concept of 'the polluter pays' to tourism. Furthermore, as we saw in Chapter 6, the state subsidies of tourism where they exist, tend to ensure the tourists do not pay the true full cost of their holiday which makes the development of sustainable tourism even less likely to occur.

Land-use Planning

Most writers on sustainable tourism place great faith in land-use planning as a tool for achieving more sustainable tourism development. The main principles of a model land-use planning structure are outlined in Table 8.2.

The classic approach to land-use planning is based on the following system:

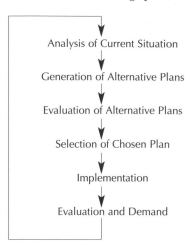

In terms of sustainable tourism, the analysis phase should include an assessment of:

- current development in terms of land-use conflicts
- infrastructure capacity
- the carrying capacity of the area
- possible future threats and opportunities
- the resources of both the area and the public sector.

The evaluation of alternative plans and the selection of the final strategy should clearly involve the host community. More detail on this issue can be found in Chapter 11.

In 1991 Inskeep published a matrix which he suggested might help with the evaluation of alternative plans. Most land-use plans are based on the concept of zoning, in other words, the allocation of specific areas for particular land uses. This is designed to separate uses that might bring conflict if they existed side by side in the same area.

Within an area this zoning in relation to tourism could have two dimensions within destination regions, as follows:

- Zoning of tourism uses away from other land uses such as industry and housing given that the presence of heavy industry could put tourists off visiting a place

Table 8.2.   A model land use planning structure. Source: Hunter and Green (1996).

Policy level	Function
Supra-national policies	Provide guidance on policy directions
National plans and policies	Establish national goals, develop policy and broad strategies for implementation
Regional plans and strategies	Formulate general policies and plans for socio-economic and physical development
Development plans/local plans	District-wide land use plans which may include detailed development proposals or zoning of land
Development controls	The coordination and approval of individual development proposals

while tourists could cause great nuisance for residents.

- Zoning to separate different types of tourism or tourists who may not be compatible, such as different nationalities or young people and older people.

Zoning is also widely used in national parks to separate conflicting recreational uses of land.

It can also be used within relatively small geographical areas as part of a site management strategy, an example of which is outlined below in relation to the Borobodur National Archaeological Park in Java, Indonesia:

> The land use planning approach [used] was that of establishing zones for various types and intensities of land use around the monument. Five zones were established (Inskeep, 1991)

- Zone 1 – Area for protection of the immediate environment of the monument with no development allowed except for landscaping.
- Zone 2 – Area for development of facilities for visitor use, park operation and archaeological conservation activities.
- Zone 3 – Area including the access road and smaller monuments within which land uses are strictly controlled to be compatible with the park concept.
- Zone 4 – Area for maintenance of the historical scenery.
- Zone 5 – Area for undertaking archaeological surveys and protection of unexcavated archaeological sites.

Development and Building Control

In many countries, a system of development and building control exists, at least in theory, to help implement the land-use plans. Development control seeks to regulate the location of new development and issues like access, and the existence of adequate infrastructure to support the development. Conversely, building control focuses specifically on the building itself in relation to materials and the actual construction.

Development and building control is a negative measure in that it prevents poor quality or inappropriate development. It does little to positively encourage good quality new development, as it is reactive rather than pro-active.

However, development and building control can be made more positive and pro-active by the use of 'development briefs' which promote particular sites and provide guidelines of what would be acceptable development for prospective developers.

Conversely, it is important to note that in many countries which are important tourist destinations either:

Table 8.3.   Sample evaluation matrix for alternative plans. Source: Inskeep (1991).

Evaluation Factor	Evaluation ranking			
	Alternative 1	Alternative 2	Alternative 3	Comments
Satisfies overall tourism development objectives				
Reflects overall national/regional development policy				
Reflects tourism development policy				
Optimizes overall economic benefits at reasonable cost				
Provides substantial employment and increased income				
Provides substantial net foreign exchange earnings				
Helps develop economically depressed areas				
Does not pre-empt other important resources areas				
Minimizes negative sociocultural impacts				
Helps achieve archaeological/historic preservation				
Helps revitalize traditional arts and handicrafts				
Is not disruptive to present land use and settlement patterns				
Minimizes negative environmental impacts				
Reinforces environmental conservation and park development				
Makes maximum use of existing infrastructure				
Makes maximum multi-purpose use of new infrastructure				
Provides opportunity for staging development				

Notes
1.   This list of evaluation factors is only an example of the type which could be used, and the evaluation factors actually used will depend on the specific planning situation. If the plan objectives are complete and specific they can sometimes be used directly as the factors.
2.   The evaluation ranking can be done on a scale of 1–5 or 1–10 with the upper end of the scale indicating the higher achievement level. The more important factors can be given a greater numerical weighting. The comments column is important for noting special situations. For example, substantial employment may be provided by the plan but considerable migration of workers may be required to provide the employment.

Table 8.4. Sample evaluation of tourism for environmental impact assessment. Source: Inskeep (1991).

Type of impact	Evaluation of impact				
	No impact	Minor impact	Moderate impact	Serious impact	Comments
Air quality					
Surface water quality					
Groundwater quality					
Road traffic					
Noise levels					
Solid waste disposal system					
Archaeological and historic sites					
Visual amenity					
Natural vegetation					
Wild animal life • Ground animals • Birds and insects					

Note: This list of types of impacts is only a sampling. There may be additional or different factors in an actual environmental analysis.

- no legal system of development and building control exists, *or*
- even where it does exist it is not rigorously enforced and there is a great deal of illegal building.

Environmental Impact Assessment

A tool which is being used increasingly in development control is the Environmental Impact Assessment (EIA). According to Middleton and Hawkins, an EIA is designed to:

> Prevent environmental degradation by giving decision-makers better information about likely consequences that development actions could have on the environment. (Middleton and Hawkins, 1998)

It thus informs planning decisions, and ensures that decision-makers take environmental issues into account when making development control decisions.

The assessment will usually be undertaken by planners working for the relevant public sector body. However, part of it usually includes the Environmental Impact Statement (EIS) which is a statement produced by the developer concerning their view of the likely environmental effects of their proposals.

Table 8.4 offers a simple model of what a hypothetical EIA might look like in relation to a tourism development proposal.

Changing Approaches to Land-use Planning

Land-use planning dates back several decades and over that time lessons have been learned and approaches have been modified

Table 8.5. The evolution of local government attitudes to planning and development control, in the UK. Source: Middleton and Hawkins (1998).

	1950s Control and regulation	1970s Economic regeneration and facilitation	1990s Sustainable development and private sector partnerships
Primary objectives	Enforcement of regulations for land use, buildings and infrastructures. Development control focus	Identification of *ad hoc* opportunities for economic development, including planning support and financial incentives where possible	Clearer focus on overall area development plans and mission statements, incorporating quality of life and a sustainable environment for residents
Focus for action	Specific controls for protection of health and safety including water, waste, pollution and air quality. Land use and building controls	Concern for securing employment and protecting the physical environment. Greater concern for public access and recreational use of the physical environment	Wider concerns for sustainable development, AGENDA 21 and achieving economic growth while reducing the impacts. Growing recognition of heritage, culture and tourism as an economic sector
Principal procedures	Control of businesses through enforcement of regulations operated by local government staff. Public sector planned redevelopment schemes such as town centres	Targeting of business activities, creation of support packages with the commercial sector, indicative planning and better information for decisions. Urban regeneration schemes led by development corporations	Partnership development procedures emerging rapidly, drawing on public sector agencies and the private sector. Increasing use of EIAs, multi-funding investment packages and joint planning procedures
Ethos	Essentially reactive, protective, defensive with relatively inflexible local plans. Clear separation between public and private sector	More proactive, seeking specific growth opportunities with more flexible concepts of structure and local plans and more private sector involvement	Proactive and innovative, developing new forms of public/private sector partnership in which local government is more enabler/facilitator than provider

to reflect changes in thinking. Table 8.5 illustrates some of the ways in which local councils who are the planning authorities in the UK, have changed their approach to land-use planning.

We will now look at three ways in which the public sector can pro-actively influence the development of sustainable tourism.

The Provision of Infrastructure

Public sector bodies are the main developers and operators of the infrastructure of the tourism industry such as roads, airports and sewage plants. There is clearly scope for the public sector to develop the infrastructure in more sustainable ways. In the case of sewage this might mean using biological treatment plants and ensuring that raw sewage is not pumped out into the sea near the beaches in seaside resorts.

The public sector can also help by trying to use other measures to reduce the need for new infrastructure. For instance, it might use taxation and regulation to reduce the use of private cars so there is less need for new infrastructure like roads. This is not only more sustainable but it also reduces the need for public expenditure on new roads.

The Public Sector as an Active Player in the Tourism Industry

The public sector can also set a good example through its role as an active player in the tourism industry, in terms of:

- state-owned visitor attractions such as museums and historic buildings
- state-owned airlines and railways
- the role of national and regional tourist bodies.

It has to be said that as yet there are few real examples of public sector organizations like these playing a particularly pro-active role in making tourism more sustainable.

Although the public sector only owns and controls a minority of the tourism product it could nevertheless use those it does control as role models for the private sector. If it does not then the public sector will have little moral authority when putting forward formal policies on sustainable tourism.

Designated Areas for Protection and Development

The public sector can also play a positive role by designating areas where the landscapes and/or communities will be protected from tourism and other potential threats. These protected areas might include:

- national parks

- regional nature parks
- nature reserves
- building conservation areas.

At the same time, areas can be designated for development where tourism will be particularly welcome as a way to help overcome existing social and economic problems.

However, both of these forms of intervention are difficult to implement and can cost a great deal of money to try to put into practice, with no guarantee of success.

Official Standards and Labelling

Another valuable role for the public sector is establishing official standards for sustainability that would allow tourists to identify the most environmentally friendly and sustainable products.

There are already official standards for environmental management systems within organizations for which tourism organizations will be eligible. For example, there is ISO 14001 operated by the International Standards Organization. However, whilst there is product labelling in relation to vegetarian foods for example, there is as yet no similar label for environmentally friendly or sustainable tourism products.

While it would be difficult to devise such standards or labels, it is difficult to see how sustainable tourism can be developed without them. It is no good teaching tourists about the need to buy more sustainable holidays if there is no official standard or label to help them choose the most sustainable product.

Government Controls on Tourist Numbers

Many destinations today would like to be in a position to control the quality and quantity of tourists they receive, with most wanting a moderate number of high spending tourists distributed evenly throughout the year. However, very few destinations are in a position to actually control their tourism to this extent. One such destination is the Himalayan Kingdom of Bhutan. Bhutan sets limits for foreign tourist arrivals in the country. In 1992, 4000 foreign tourists only were granted entry visas while in 1996 the figure was 6000.

Furthermore, all foreign tourists went on pre-arranged, all-inclusive tours. No individual travel is allowed and tourists must spend at least US$200 per day. While this seems a sensible way of protecting Bhutan, it does smack of exclusivity and elitism, and is at odds with the concept of equality which should be implicit in sustainable tourism.

The Growing Role of Supra-governmental Action

In recent years treaties and regulations as a result of intergovernmental cooperation between countries has played an ever greater role in environmental protection, including the following (adapted from Middleton and Hawkins, 1998):

●   the United Nations Environmental Convention on Climate Change
●   the Montreal Protocol on Ozone Depleting Substances
●   the United Nations Framework on Biological Activity
●   the Convention on International Trade in Endangered Species
●   the United Nations Framework Convention on Desertification
●   International Civil Aviation Organization Chapter 3, Aircraft Regulations
●   the European Union Bathing Water Quality Directive
●   UNESCO Convention concerning the Protection of World Cultural and National Heritage.

Clearly, all of these treaties and regulations have implications for the tourism industry in general, and sustainable tourism specifically. One particular international convention that has great implications for tourism is AGENDA 21.

AGENDA 21 and the Travel and Tourism Industry

In February 1997 the WTTC/WTO/Earth Council published a press release which outlined how AGENDA 21 might be applied to the travel and tourism industry. It included the following sections:

●   Assessing the capacity of the existing regulations, economic and voluntary frameworks to bring about sustainable tourism.
●   Assessing the economic, social, cultural and environmental implications of tourism industry operations.
●   Training, education and public awareness.
●   Planning for sustainable tourism development.
●   Facilitating the exchange of information, skills and technology relating to sustainable tourism between developed and developing countries.
●   Providing for the participation of all sections of society.
●   Designing new tourism products with sustainability at their core as an integral part of the tourism development process.
●   Measuring progress in achieving sustainable development at local level.
●   Partnerships for sustainable development.

According to Middleton and Hawkins this list 'summarises the AGENDA 21 action identified for the public sector' (Middleton and Hawkins, 1998). At a time when tourism is becoming increasingly dominated by major transnational corporations intergovernment cooperation is especially important in developing more sustainable forms of tourism. Only by working together can governments counter the power of the tourism industry.

Perhaps in future we will see intergovernmental cooperation to prevent tour operators, for example, from playing one country off against another. Like the OPEC organization in relation to oil, developing and newly developed destination countries may combine to fix the price of holidays so that tour operators cannot exploit poverty and low wages to provide low cost holidays for tourists. This may be the only effective chance for us to develop 'fair trade' in tourism.

The Politics of Sustainable Tourism

While, as we have seen, the public sector has a valuable potential role to play in sustainable tourism, we have to accept that there is a strong political dimension to sustainable tourism. In any tourism plan or policy there are winners and losers and this makes public sector tourism policy a political issue. It is also a political issue because tourists are also voters and any attempt to control tourist behaviour or limit choice for tourists may result in a backlash from voters who are also tourists.

Tourism has powerful vested interests that will seek to influence the political process such as transport operators and hoteliers. These groups may also oppose measures to make tourism more sustainable.

At the same time we must recognize that local communities and governments will take tourism decisions often for political reasons rather than just on the merits of the case from a tourism point of view.

Obstacles to the Role of the Public Sector in Sustainable Tourism

There are a number of obstacles that will limit the role of the public sector in tourism planning and development as follows:

- In many countries, tourism is only a low priority for the public sector and there seems to be a lack of political will to develop sustainable tourism.
- The concepts of public sector planning and regulation are out of fashion at the moment in an era of privatization. It is particularly out of favour in the former communist countries of Eastern Europe.

- Many public sector bodies lack the financial resources required to play a major role in tourism planning and development.
- There is a lack of staff expertise in tourism in most public sector organizations around the world.
- The cycle of elections affects the willingness of politicians to make the kind of long-term decisions on which sustainable tourism depends.
- Many public sector planning systems are slow and cumbersome and incapable of responding to the rapid rate of change in the tourism industry.
- In general, the public sector is only a minor player in the tourism industry, with little real control over most of the tourism product.
- In a number of places, central and local government corruption limits the potential role of the public sector in development of more ethical, sustainable tourism.

Conclusions

We have seen that the main potential role of the public sector in sustainable tourism is largely negative in terms of regulation and planning controls. However, it is also clear that the public sector can play a positive, pro-active role too. There is also a trend towards supra-governmental cooperation and action in general that could play a greater role in sustainable tourism in the future. Yet there are also factors, as we saw at the end of the chapter, that may limit the role of the public sector in the quest for sustainable tourism.

Discussion Points and Essay Questions

1. Discuss the potential contribution of legislation and regulation to the development of sustainable tourism.

2. Evaluate the ways in which the public sector might use fiscal incentives and controls to further the cause of sustainable tourism.
3. Discuss the likely future role of supragovernmental action in the sphere of sustainable tourism.

Exercise

Choose a country with which you are familiar and for which you can obtain information. Evaluate the current role of central and local government in that country in relation to sustainable tourism.

Case Study: Tourism Policy in Bermuda

In 1996 Conlin published a study of tourism policy in Bermuda. He identified several characteristics of Bermuda's tourism industry in the early 1990s, saying it:

- had experienced rapid growth, from 55,000 arrivals in 1949 to 631,000 in 1987
- had then seen a decline in tourist numbers between 1987 and 1992
- had conservative tourism policies with a moratorium on new hotel development, and timeshare developments, for example, and restrictions on the number of cruise passengers
- attracted a narrow market niche, consisting largely of older, better educated tourists from the USA.

In 1992 a Commission on Competitiveness was established to focus on the island's two main economic activities; tourism and international trade. The Commission had a Tourism Policy Committee which was given the duty of the island's tourism industry. The Committee considered it important for its strategy to enjoy community support.

The planning process is outlined in Exhibit 1. In terms of trying to make Bermuda tourism more sustainable, the Tourism Planning Committee reached a number of conclusions including the following:

- the island's economy and quality of life were dependent upon tourism
- many of the factors which Bermuda was experiencing were global factors which were beyond its control
- Bermuda was heavily dependent on the American market
- tourism enterprises such as hotels in Bermuda were losing business
- the cruise ship visitor could not match the staying visitor in terms of economic benefits for the host community
- seasonality was still a problem
- some island residents were not aware of the importance of tourism for the island
- business profitability was being adversely affected by labour disputes
- there were deficiencies in the product which in any event was overpriced.

The Committee made several recommendations, as follows:

- more emphasis must be placed upon product development
- the Government's Department of Tourism should widen its role from promotion to strategic planning and product policy
- the creation of a Tourism Education Council to coordinate education and training
- the development of partnerships with organizations such as the Bermuda Chamber of Commerce to help enhance the quality of the product
- developing a Task Force on Employment to improve labour–employer relations
- lengthening the season
- offering tourists more value for money.

Interestingly, the government did not act immediately on the recommendations of the Tourism Planning Committee. As Conlin noted:

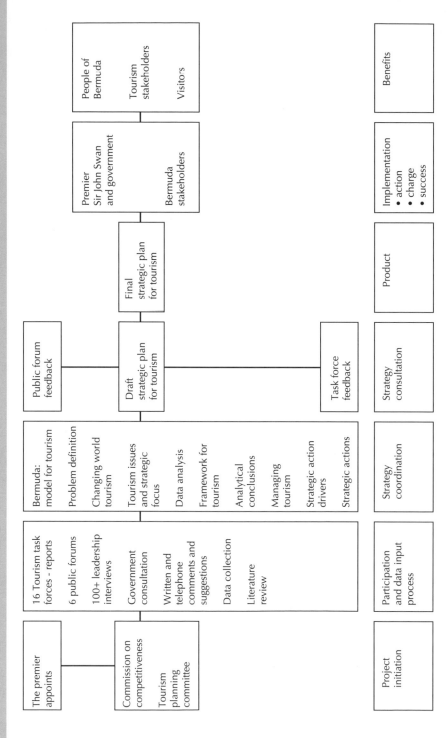

Exhibit 1. Bermuda tourism: strategic reassessment planning process. Source: LDR International Commission on Competitiveness Final Report (1994); Conlin (1996).

In a small island community like Bermuda, wide-ranging recommendations that would create fundamental changes in how the tourism industry is planned and managed would encounter political opposition. (Conlin in Harrison and Husbands, 1996)

At the same time, there has been an apparent upturn in the fortunes of the Bermuda tourism industry which again reduced pressure on the government to implement the suggestions of the Tourism Planning Committee.

The truth is that the Bermudan government has initiated little action in response to the Committee's report and the tourism industry is not really being particularly innovative.

Case Study: the Role of the European Union in Sustainable Tourism

In recent years the European Union has become increasingly involved in tourism.

Overall, the aim of its intervention has been to sustain the tourism industry and maintain Europe's position as the region of the world that attracts more international tourist trips than any other.

However, its activities in a number of areas also have implications for sustainable tourism, including the following:

- The pro-active stance taken on regional policy and the substantial funds allocated to stimulating development in economically disadvantaged regions have done much to aid the growth of tourism in rural areas and those cities where traditional industries have declined.
- Schemes for training and education under the European Social Fund have helped improve the quality of the workforce in the industry in those areas which are eligible for this programme.
- Rural tourism has also been helped by funding under the European Agricultural Guidance and Guarantee Fund.
- The Envireg programme supports schemes which aim to protect the ecosystem in areas where tourism is being developed, in Mediterranean areas, for example.
- The Leader programme which has helped fund several hundred rural development schemes in disadvantaged or under-developed regions. Many of these programmes have involved tourism projects.
- The Regis programme that aims to aid development, including tourism, in the remotest regions of the European Union such as Madeira and the Canary Islands.
- The Resider and Rechar programmes helps fund industrial heritage projects in areas where heavy industry is in decline.

There is no doubt that all of the schemes have helped develop tourism in the less favoured regions of Europe. However, it remains to be seen if the grant-aided projects will prove viable in the longer term.

The European Union is also involved in measures that are related to sustainable tourism, notably:

- Its Social Chapter which increases the rights of part-time visitors and seeks to limit working hours, although many tourism organizations are likely to be exempt from the latter.
- The Package Travel Directive which has increased the rights of tourists as consumers and has forced the tourism industry to market its products more honestly.

However, some European Union policies also represent a potential threat to the concept of sustainable tourism in the broadest sense of the term. For example:

- Airline liberalization may force smaller airlines out of business, thus reducing consumer choice. It also means that airlines cut costs, leading to redundancies in many countries in Europe.
- The Single Market is encouraging the growth of large transnational corporations and is thus reinforcing the trend towards the standardization of the

tourism product within Europe. While this may be good news for customers, it is helping reduce the uniqueness of each area of Europe. This uniqueness is the core of each area's appeal, particularly to non-European tourists.

Nevertheless, overall, the impact of the European Union in respect of tourism appears to be quite positive. However, the concern now is what will happen as the European Union grows in the years to come, bringing in many new, generally poor, countries, including established tourist destinations such as Malta, Cyprus and also the Czech Republic and Hungary.

The worry is that funds will be diverted to those new member countries at the expense of the least well off tourist destinations of the existing European Union such as Portugal, Greece and Ireland. At the same time, the inclusion of these new members in the European Union will increase competition within the Union for both funds and tourists. This will come at a time when the main threat to tourism in Europe probably comes from non-European competitors such as the USA and South-East Asia.

9

The Industry

Many commentators see the tourism industry as the villain in the sustainable tourism melodrama. Tourism enterprises are often portrayed, rightly or wrongly, as being narrowly concerned solely with their profits and with short-term perspectives. However, if the industry is a major cause of the negative impacts of tourism, it is obvious that the industry must also play a major role in any attempt to create more sustainable forms of tourism.

In this chapter, we will look at a number of issues in relation to the tourism industry, and sustainability, including

- voluntary actions by the industry and the idea of self-regulation
- the issue of local ownership versus externally based enterprises and between SMEs and large transnational corporations
- the relationship between the industry and the tourist and industry codes of conduct for the tourist
- the motivators for tourism enterprises to take an interest in sustainable tourism
- sustainable tourism and competitive advantage

However, we need to begin by reminding ourselves of what we mean by the tourism industry. It is a complex phenomenon which has a number of dimensions. Figure 9.1 illustrates the range of sectors in tourism

and the geographical aspects of the tourism industry.

It is important to note at this stage that some of the players are public sector rather than private sector. As we have already considered the public sector in Chapter 8, we will, in this chapter, focus upon the private sector.

Figure 9.2 shows the range of size and types of organizations found in the tourism industry. Clearly, as we shall see later, this range of types of organization, is very relevant to the idea of sustainable tourism.

A Critique of the Tourism Industry in Respect of Sustainable Tourism

The tourism industry is often criticized in relation to sustainable tourism in terms of both:

- how it develops the physical, tangible elements of its product such as new hotels or airports
- how it operates in terms of everything from energy consumption to policies, from wage levels and working conditions to the exploitation of wildlife.

In general terms, the criticisms focus on the accusations that the tourism industry is:

- too concerned with short-term profits

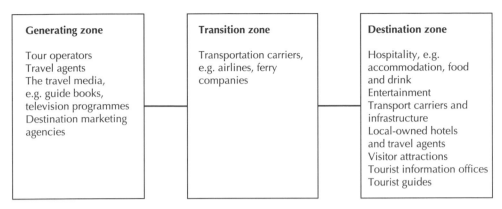

Fig. 9.1. The sectors of tourism and the geographical aspects of the tourism industry.

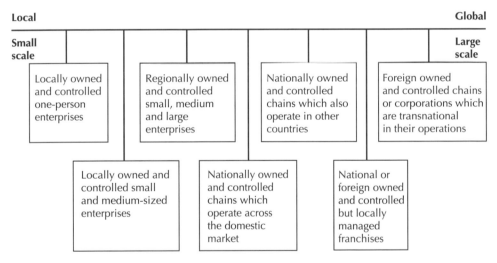

Fig. 9.2. The types of tourism organizations.

rather than with long-term sustainability

- about exploiting the environment and local populations rather than conserving them
- relatively footloose and shows relatively little commitment to particular destinations
- being increasingly controlled by large transnational corporations who are disinterested in individual destinations
- not doing enough to raise tourist awareness of sustainability
- only jumping on the sustainable tourism 'bandwagon' when there is a prospect of achieving good publicity and reducing costs by so doing.

In the light of such criticism and perhaps with the final point in mind, some tourism organizations have taken voluntary action on sustainable tourism in recent years.

Voluntary Industry Action

The tourism industry now has a number of well-known initiatives that respect voluntary action in sustainable tourism issues, notably:

- the International Hotels Environmental Initiative
- the actions of the German tour operator, TUI
- the activities of British Airways in respect of sustainable tourism such as the sponsorship of the Tourism for Tomorrow Awards, and the donation of free travel to those involved in conservation projects.

The first of these initiatives is featured in a case study at the end of this chapter, while the other two are dealt with in later chapters on the tour operation and transport sectors, respectively.

In the hotel sector, action has tended to focus on the environment and on operational issues that can also help reduce costs. Many hotels have become involved in measures which:

- reduce energy consumption
- allow the recycling of waste
- reduce waste.

When it comes to the environment, transport operators like airlines are often under statutory obligations to minimize air and noise pollution, for example, and also to reduce fuel spillage. Here, therefore, the scope for voluntary action is more limited.

A number of tour operators have, however, taken an interest in sustainable tourism, given their pivotal role in taking tourists to destinations. A survey of 36 operators, reported in the *Practice Makes Perfect* publication showed that the tour operators contacted claimed to be involved in the following activities (% of sample of 36):

- 'Ecotips' and advice in brochures (37%)
- Donations to local charities and schools (37%)

- Sponsoring research into impacts and management of tourism (26%)
- Promotion of specialist 'green' holidays (22%)
- Lobbying of host government tourist offices to improve infrastructure of destinations, etc. (22%)
- Recycling brochures (22%)
- Careful selection of tour guides from local communities (19%)
- 'Sympathy leaflets' (17%)
- Partnerships with local groups over waste management (17%).

These are all worthwhile initiatives but they do not seem to be attacking the issue of sustainable tourism across a broad front.

The people who conducted the survey also suggested that some of these claims were rather exaggerated and that the reality was somewhat less positive than these figures would seem to indicate.

It appears that most industry action is designed, at least in part, out of a desire to prove that the industry can regulate its own behaviour so that governments will not initiate statutory control on tourism. Voluntary self-regulation is seen as being preferable to imposed legislation, from an industry point of view.

Industry Codes of Conduct

Some industry bodies have taken the concept of self-regulation further by devising voluntary codes of conduct for the industry as a whole or specific sections. Middleton and Hawkins have identified several codes of conduct that have been devised by tourism industry bodies. These include:

- Pacific Asia Travel Association – Code for Environmentally Responsible Tourism
- World Travel and Tourism Council – Environmental Guidelines
- European Tour Operators – Environmental Guidelines.

Table 9.1. The advantages and disadvantages of small locally owned enterprises.

Advantages	Disadvantages
• Should be sensitive to local situation in terms of the ecosystem and the culture • Should have high levels of commitment to the future of the area • Should retain a large proportion of revenue generated within local community • Often concerned not with profit maximization at all costs but with earning enough to enjoy a reasonable living standard	• May lack financial resources to implement sustainable tourism initiatives • May be unaware of what is happening in the wider world in relation to sustainable tourism • The need to survive in a competitive market may force the enterprise into cost cutting including offering poor salaries and working conditions

A Critique of Industry Initiatives

However, the voluntary industry actions can be criticized on a number of fronts. For example, they:

- are almost totally concerned with the environment and take little account of the social and economic climate, whether this be staff wages, local sourcing of supplies or the rights of the local community
- are generally either low cost or may even reduce the organization's expenditure. Very few initiatives involve significant investment on the part of the tourism organizations themselves
- are sometimes rather cosmetic, and are perhaps designed more to give tourists a 'feel good' factor than to make a significant difference in terms of sustainable tourism.

Nevertheless, anything which raises awareness of sustainable tourism and makes a positive contribution, no matter how small, is probably welcome and should not be criticized too greatly.

Conversely, perhaps such voluntary action is a smokescreen which stops us seeing that what is really needed is statutory action on sustainable tourism.

Small and Local or Large and Foreign?

We saw in Fig. 9.2 that the tourism industry contains many different sizes and types of enterprise. In the sustainable tourism debate the conventional wisdom appears to be that small locally owned enterprises are best, and large externally based enterprises worst. However, the picture is undoubtedly more complex as we can see from Tables 9.1 and 9.2 which highlight, in general, the advantages and disadvantages of both types of organization.

However, the features listed in the tables are generalizations. Local entrepreneurs could equally be ignorant or disinterested in the area and simply be trying to earn enough from tourism as quickly as possible to allow them to move away or retire.

In general, therefore, the advantages and disadvantages are mirror images of each other. However, this is clearly a simplistic view which also assumes that locally owned enterprises will, by definition, be small scale, but many local enterprises develop their businesses successfully to become major large-scale enterprises in their home area. This in turn can lead to problems of local monopolies and can result in small local businesses being squeezed out not by foreign enterprises, but by a large locally owned enterprise.

Table 9.2. The advantages and disadvantages of large externally owned enterprises.

Advantages	Disadvantages
• Should have the financial resources to devote to sustainable tourism initiatives and to provide good salaries and working conditions for its staff • Should be able to adapt models of good practice from other parts of the world where it operates	• May lack commitment to the destination and the host population • May not understand the local ecosystem or culture • May export most of the revenue generated in the destination to the home area or company of the organization • May concentrate on short-term profit maximization

We must also recognize the added complication that often the tourism product is the outcome of a relationship between an externally based large-scale tour operator, and a small locally owned hotel. In this case the issue of large versus small enterprise becomes impossible as the large operator may impose a deal on the hotelier which quickly reduces the economic benefits of tourism for the hotel. Alternatively, the operator may insist on the hotel adopting more sustainable practices than it might wish to do otherwise.

One very important implication of the rise of multi-nationals in the tourism industry is that some tourism organizations are now so powerful that they can flout the wishes and even the regulatory framework of some of the small-scale destination governments.

The Tourism Industry and the Tourist

In an era of consumer-led marketing the perceived wisdom is that organizations will only succeed if they meet the demands of their target markets. Yet, as we will see later in the chapters on 'The Tourist', there appears to be little real tourist interest in sustainability.

Nevertheless the industry is seeking, albeit gently and on a modest scale, to raise tourist awareness of the issues and encourage them to behave on holiday in a more sustainable manner. As we will see later in this chapter, these actions have sometimes led to the creation of codes of conduct or behaviour for tourists.

However, in this respect the industry has to walk a tightrope. If it is too critical of tourism impacts it may lose business. The aim, generally, therefore, appears to be to attempt to ameliorate the negative impacts of tourist behaviour and give the tourist a 'feel good' factor when they heed the industry's advice.

Codes of Conduct

Conscious of the fact that it is the activities of tourists which actively cause the harmful effects of tourism, some tourism organizations have devised codes of conduct to guide tourists towards more sustainable forms of development. Such codes also make the tourist feel involved in making the environment better. One example of a code of conduct, that of the UK tour operator, Thomson, lists the following advice on 'keeping the holiday code':

KEEP THE HOLIDAY CODE
While here on holiday, you can help protect the environment and conserve natural resources by following our holiday code:

DON'T LITTER
– discarded litter can be an eyesore, so please put yours in a bin

SAVE WATER
– please use sparingly, and turn off taps after use

SAVE ENERGY
– always switch off lights and electrical or gas appliances when not in use

FIRE KILLS
– so don't light picnic fires and please ensure cigarettes are properly extinguished

QUIET PLEASE
– loud noise can be annoying, so please keep it down

PROTECT WILDLIFE
– many animals are protected by law. Please don't buy souvenirs made of turtle shell, ivory, reptile skins, furs or exotic feathers

FOLLOW THE THOMSON HOLIDAY CODE: TAKE NOTHING AWAY. LEAVE NOTHING BEHIND. AND, NATURALLY, HAVE A GREAT TIME

Source: Thomson Literature.

While all the points made are sound they could be accused of being rather tokenistic and do not really tackle the social dimension of sustainable tourism. Like many such industry initiatives it is solely concerned with the environment.

Industry Motivators, Sustainability and Competitive Advantage

It is important to ask the question at this stage, why should the tourism industry and individual tourism organizations take the issue of sustainable tourism seriously? Why should it spend money on projects and seek to influence the behaviour of its customers, risking alienating them by its exhortations? The simple answer is perhaps 'enlightened self interest'. In other words sustainable tourism:

- makes good business sense by protecting the resources or assets on which tourism depends, not only today, but in the future
- can help improve the short-term financial performance of an organization by reducing costs.

At the same time there is a view amongst some organizations that sustainable tourism can actually help them to achieve a competitive advantage in the market place, or make them seem to be more ethical, simply because of the enhanced price tourists might be prepared to pay for a more sustainable product.

For instance, the survey of 36 tour operators quoted earlier found that:

> 23% [of operators] sold 'green' holidays as a value-added niche product ... 40% [of operators] saw that 'responsible tourism' was also 'quality tourism' and hence could reasonably demand a higher price tag ... three of the largest operators saw a commercial advantage in improving their environmental performance. (*Practice Makes Perfect*)

Perhaps the key to sustainable tourism lies in creating a climate of consumer opinion and government policy where organizations will compete on the basis of who acts in the most sustainable manner. This way the most sustainable forms of tourism develop while organizations will also be able to meet their corporate objectives. However, they will require action to ensure that there is substance to what organizations do rather than simply marketing hype. This may involve some form of eco or sustainable tourism-labelling of products to ensure consumers are not misled.

Limits to the Potential Role of Industry in Developing Sustainable Tourism

It is important to recognize that there are limits and obstacles to the consideration which industry in general, and individual

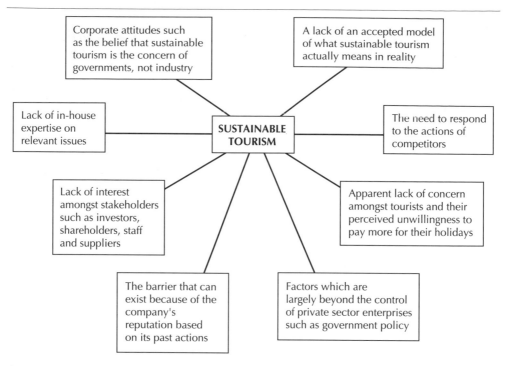

Fig. 9.3. The limitations on tourism industry action in sustainable tourism.

enterprises in particular, can achieve in rela-tion to sustainable tourism. These are both internal and external and are illustrated in Fig. 9.3.

Globalization and Sustainable Tourism

Before we conclude this chapter, we should recognize that the move towards sustainable tourism is affected by trends in industries other than tourism. It is particularly suscep-tible to the trend towards transnational operations and global consumer brands. As if we know that many tourists are attracted to destinations because they are different to their home area, then this phenomenon is a potential threat. The process of globaliza-tion is leading slowly but steadily to a situation where many of the high street retail and catering outlets are the same ones in Birmingham, Barcelona, Bangkok or Bris-bane. Likewise, the growth of international brands in everything from footwear to music, drinks to sunglasses means that

increasingly people in Manchester, Marra-kech, Manila and Melbourne are wearing similar clothes, listening to the same music and drinking the same beverages. This is particularly true of younger people and the business people visiting each place.

If places become increasingly alike due to this process, the tourists who want to visit somewhere different may turn their back on places where this trend is most advanced. These destinations may thus lose revenue and employment as a result and become less sustainable as communities.

Conclusions

We began by suggesting that if we are to achieve more sustainable forms of tourism it will require the support and cooperation of the private sector tourism industry. Then we went on to evaluate voluntary industry action to date, finding much of it to be rather cosmetic and only concerned with the envi-ronmental dimension of sustainable tourism. It seems clear that if industry is to do more about sustainable tourism, it will probably require pressure from governments and/or greater sincere interest in sustainable tourism on the part of tourists. There is little evidence that either development is likely to take place in the near future.

Discussion Points and Essay Questions

1. Discuss the contention that sustainable tourism is not the responsibility of private sector tourism organizations, but is instead the responsibility of destination governments.
2. Critically evaluate the advantages and disadvantages of industry self-regulation and government statutory regulation, in the sustainable tourism field.
3. Discuss the value of the Thomson Code of Conduct, outlined above, in the development of more sustainable forms of tourism in destinations.

Exercise

Choose a destination with which you are familiar, and then select two small locally owned enterprises and two externally owned enterprises. Compare your organization to the advantages and disadvantages of each type of organization outlined in Tables 9.1 and 9.2. Critically evaluate the accuracy of Tables 9.1 and 9.2 in the light of your findings.

Case Study: International Hotels Environmental Initiative (IHEI)

The IHEI is perhaps the largest scale and best known voluntary industry initiative in tourism. It grew out of the work of the Inter-Continental chain and is now a worldwide organization, although it is actually part of the UK-based Business Leaders Forum.

The IHEI claims to be:

> a network of hotel companies and industry partners, which encourages improvement in the environmental performance of the international hotel industry. (IHEI Literature)

Its members include major players in the global hotel market including: Accor, Hilton International, Inter-Continental, Mandarin Oriental, Marriott, Radisson SAS, ITT Sheraton and the Taj Group. It publishes a highly influential guide to good environmental practice in the hotel sector. The second edition of this guide, published in 1996 at the price of £100 included sections on:

- introducing an environmental culture into your hotel
- waste management
- energy and water conservation
- water quality
- printing
- air emissions
- noise
- stored fuel
- pesticides.

It also included examples of hotels which had successfully introduced environmental management policies. The IHEI publishes videos and wallboards to help hoteliers green their operations. In 1995 they launched a quarterly magazine, *Green Hotelier* which highlights 'success stories' from hotels around the world.

The organization also sponsors conferences on environmental issues, sometimes in partnership with other industry bodies. For example, in June 1997 the IHEI organized a joint event on 'Greening the Hospitality Curriculum: Training, Education, and the Environment', with the Hotel, Catering and Institutional Management Association (the HCIMA).

However, while its work is undoubtedly valuable, the IHEI can be criticized for:

- Taking too narrow a view of sustainability by just focusing on the environment. It should, perhaps, instead also be looking at the employees in the industry in terms of their wages, working conditions, and equal opportunities, given the sector's generally poor record in these areas. Environmentally friendly hotels that exploit their staff are clearly not in keeping with the spirit of sustainable tourism
- Concentrating just on operations management rather than also looking at how hotel units are developed. Many of the operational problems of hotels in relation to the environment stem from poor design in the first place.

Case Study: the Role of Tour Guides

A key aspect of the tourist experience is the tour guide, the person who accompanies tourists on their itinerary and interprets the destination for them. Therefore the attitudes, knowledge and skills of the guide can play a significant role in the implementation of sustainable tourism.

Exhibit 1. The less sustainable and more sustainable tour guide.

Less sustainable	More sustainable
Born and lives outside the destination	Born and lives within the destination
Does not speak the local language	Speaks the local language
No local friends or acquaintances	Well-developed network of local friends and acquaintances
Lacks up-to-date knowledge of destination	Has up-to-date knowledge of destination
Concentrates on historic and natural sites – does not cover modern life of the people in the destination	Focuses on modern image of local people as well as historic and natural sites
Takes tourists to shops, bars and markets in return for payment from the owners	Does not take money from local shop keepers, bars, etc.

Exhibit 1 illustrates what may be termed the less sustainable and the more sustainable guide.

A special issue of the Tourism Concern newsletter in summer 1997 highlighted several cases of approaches to tour guiding which show a sensitivity towards the concept of sustainable tourism in the broadest sense of the term. They included:

- One World Tours, an Australian-based tour operator whose tour leaders are bi-cultural and bi-lingual and have a good knowledge of the destination. Its guides are not paid but their travel, accommodation and food are all paid for. Part of their job involves setting up opportunities for tourists to meet local people.
- The Near East Tourist Agency in Jerusalem, a Palestinian-owned organization, and the views of one of its guides, Anwar Shomaly who wants to use tour-guiding as a way of developing mutual respect amongst the three religions – Islam, Christianity and Judaism – for whom Jerusalem is a holy city.

However, the tourist may sometimes reject the idea of seeing how people really live in a destination, preferring instead to focus on the past glories of the destination. A story told by guide Connie Attwood illustrates the point as follows:

> Even in the case of 'up-market' tourism, such as study tours accompanied by guest lecturers, the group members don't necessarily want to discover what the country and the people are really like – they often have a pre-conceived idea, which they want to

have confirmed. During the course of an Art Study Tour of China, I organized visits to factories and agricultural communes, thinking that the group members would be interested in seeing some of the contemporary life of China, not just art galleries, museums and temples. However, several group members said afterwards that if they had known they were going to have to visit a commune, they would not have come on the tour! Furthermore, they said, they didn't like modern China – it was a vast series of allotments with ugly concrete buildings. The country they had come to see, apparently, was the China of classical arts and antiquities and scroll-painting landscapes. (Source: Tourism Concern, summer 1997.)

The guide can only help develop sustainable tourism, it appears, if the tourist is prepared to let them.

10

The Voluntary Sector

The voluntary sector, in this context, is taken to consist of four groups:

- public pressure groups, such as Tourism Concern, in the UK, which lobby government and the industry in support of the concept of sustainable tourism
- professional bodies, such as the Association of Independent Tour Operators (AITO), and the Hotel, Catering and Institutional Management Association (HCIMA) which have taken an interest in aspects of sustainability in tourism
- industry pressure groups such as the Campaign for Environmentally Responsible Tourism, and the World Travel and Tourism Council
- voluntary trusts, groups of private citizens, who get together to achieve a particular purpose, with no individual making a profit from their activities. A good example is the National Trust in the UK which is involved in conserving the UK's heritage landscapes and historic buildings.

We will look briefly at the role of each of these in this chapter.

Pressure Groups

A number of public pressure groups, which operate independently of the tourism industry, are playing a role in the development of more sustainable forms of tourism. They fall into four distinct types:

- tourism-specific groups whose main focus is sustainable tourism such as Tourism Concern
- general environmental groups which also take an interest in tourism such as Friends of the Earth
- groups, largely religious-based organizations, which are particularly concerned with the social impacts of tourism, such as sex tourism
- organizations which are concerned with particular countries or regions of the world, which take an interest in tourism issues in that country, such as ACTSA, Action for Southern Africa.

Tourism Concern

Tourism Concern is perhaps the highest profile pressure group in sustainable tourism in the UK. Table 10.1 illustrates the objectives and activities of the organization. Tourism Concern emphasizes the social and economic side of tourism. This is made clear in their literature. One brochure claims:

> Tourism Concern looks past the cosmetic 'green' issues such as recycling and energy conservation to the way that tourism affects the *people* living in destination areas, their communities, and their environment. (Tourism Concern, 1997)

Table 10.1.   Tourism Concern. Source: 'In Focus', Tourism Concern, 1998.

Tourism Concern takes the view that all sectors involved in tourism – governments, industry, media, educators and holiday makers themselves – have contributed to its negative impacts and must all be involved in challenging and changing it. Membership reflects this broad base and is drawn from all sectors

What is Tourism Concern?
- A membership network set up in 1989 to bring together British people with an active concern for tourism's impact on community and environment, both in the UK and worldwide
- A unique information resource – through its membership network, global contacts and resource collection. Tourism Concern is an important centre of advice and information on tourism's impact
- A catalyst for positive change – Tourism Concern is already influencing and informing decision makers in government, industry and education. It is recognized as an independent voice working for the principles of justice and sustainability in tourism

What does Tourism Concern stand for?
Tourism concern advocates:
- Tourism that is *just*, yielding benefits that are fairly distributed
- Tourism that is *participatory*, recognizing the rights of residents to be involved in its development and management
- Tourism that is *sustainable*, putting the long-term social and environmental health of holiday areas before short-term gain

What is Tourism Concern doing?
- *Campaigning* to raise issues of injustice because of tourism, like the displacement of people, and the abuse of children in sex tourism; to see that sustainable tourism is recognized by governments, development agencies and the tourism industry as a key issue
- *Networking* globally to exchange information on a broad range of tourism-related issues; bringing people together working on local and global projects, such as small-scale enterprises in the Gambia, and formulating a Himalayan Trekking Code with Himalayan groups and overseas tour operators
- *Informing* the public, mounting exhibitions and producing literature to heighten awareness of tourism issues; providing speakers, information for the press, broadcasts and conferences
- *Developing* a library of information on tourism issues
- *Educating* by publishing and distributing teaching resources on tourism's impacts and exploring new ways to integrate tourism issues into education

In Focus magazine
- **In Focus**, Tourism Concern's quarterly magazine takes an in-depth look at a different tourism-related topic each issue. Topics covered so far include: ecotourism, displaced people, women, water and many more

Their social concerns are reflected in their campaigns which include:

- lobbying tour operators which use hotels that usurp local rights to water and land
- the issue of fair trade in tourism
- the displacement of local people so that golf courses can be developed
- the forced eviction of people to make way for tourism developments in Myanmar and East Africa.

Tourism Concern enjoys strong support amongst academics and students but its effectiveness is limited by the fact that only a modest number of tourism industry figures are members. Nevertheless, it has been very active in raising awareness amongst students, the industry managers of the future.

Pressure Groups – Friend or Foe?

Pressure groups clearly aid the course of sustainable tourism by raising awareness of issues and campaigning for change. However, they can sometimes be accused of being a self-appointed 'elite', or of taking an over-simplistic view of problems. Often they are made up of people who live outside the destination in question so there are questions about the right of outsiders to seek to influence what happens in an area. Conversely, where local people have little or no political power, these external influences may be very important.

Professional Bodies

In recent years, with the perceived growing interest of consumers in environmental issues and sustainability, professional bodies have taken an increasing interest in the subject. Two examples from the UK will serve to illustrate this point:

- the HCIMA in the UK has been at the forefront of the development of environmental institutions in the hospitality industry
- the Association of Independent Tour Operators which represents many smaller specialist tour operators. Its main involvement in the sustainable tourism context is its commitment to:
  (i)   ensuring that its members act in as environmentally friendly a manner as possible
  (ii) quality holidays and high standards of honesty and integrity on the part of member tour operators
  (iii) selling via independent travel agencies which are not owned by the large tour operators.

Limitations on the Role of Professional Bodies

Professional bodies could play a major role in sustainable tourism influencing industry-wide strategies and practice. Peer pressure, even in competitive markets, can be an effective influence on corporate behaviour. These bodies represent the industry and after all it is the industry which largely has

the power to make tourism more sustainable or not. However, the contribution of professional bodies is limited by two factors:

- most professional bodies have only limited financial resources to fund sustainable tourism initiatives
- the bodies rarely have the power to insist that members undertake particular initiatives.

Most professional bodies that have become involved in the sustainability issue in tourism could be seen to be motivated largely by the desire to prove industry can regulate itself to prevent the introduction of statutory regulation by governments. Or they could be accused of trying to simply enhance the industry's reputation with consumers, largely on the basis of rather cosmetic action?

Industry Pressure Groups

Unlike the public pressure groups we looked at earlier, there are also pressure groups which are either made up exclusively of industry representatives or are directly involved in the industry.

An example of the former type of pressure group is the World Travel and Tourism Council (WTTC) which is supported by major tourism companies. This body lobbies on behalf of the interests of the tourism industry. It has, in recent years, supported a large amount of research on sustainable tourism. While most of this research has been excellent, the organization suffers from the perception, rightly or wrongly, that it may be primarily concerned with promoting the benefits of tourism.

The second type of industry pressure group will be discussed briefly, through the example of one such body.

The Campaign for Environmentally Responsible Tourism (CERT)

The CERT was created largely by people who were consumers rather than industry

Table 10.2.   The benefits of the Environmental Kitemark for tour operators. Source: Campaign for Environmentally Responsible Tourism (1997).

The Kitemark informs people that the company:
- has a company environmental policy
- ensures staff and customers are aware of the policy
- is making environmental improvements in some of the key activities and operating methods
- actively encourages customers to become more environmentally aware
- makes a financial contribution to CERT's Environmental Projects Scheme
- is committed to CERT's guiding principle to actively involve the travel industry in securing environmentally sustainable travel destinations for local people, wildlife and the travel industry

practitioners. However, from its early days, its aim was to develop a partnership between the industry and the consumers. Its membership largely consisted of tour operators and its aim was to make its tour operator members behave in a more sustainable manner. Set up in 1994, CERT claims that it

> seeks to encourage good environmental practice in the travel and tourism industry by working with tour operators, and communicating the travel industry's commitment to their customers and the public at large ... CERT is unique because it involves the travel industry, the consumer, and conservationists, and seeks to benefit both the environment and the travel industry ... CERT is a positive initiative which firmly believes that the tourism industry can produce long-term sustainable development. (Centre for Environmentally Responsible Tourism, 1997)

CERT is involved in three initiatives designed to further its work:

- an Environmental Kitemark Scheme which gives recognition to organizations which meet minimum standards of environmental practice
- producing a leaflet designed to encourage tourists to be aware of their own responsibilities toward the environment
- the CERT Environmental Project Scheme which encourages and finances environmentally sustainable projects in destinations.

In 1997, 24 tour operators had received the 'Environmental Kitemark' most of them small specialist operators. A CERT leaflet explains the benefits of the scheme for operators, as can be seen from Table 10.2.

As yet, CERT has had relatively little impact on the larger tour operators, and little or none on other sectors of the tourism industry. Nevertheless, it has, at least, undertaken practical projects that have actually affected the behaviour of a number of smaller operators.

Furthermore, in the past year or so, the organization has deliberately set out to widen its membership to include individual consumers as well as companies in sectors other than tour operations. This is part of a conscious effort to increase the influence of CERT in the wider tourism industry, and amongst consumers.

However, it would be fair to say that given its stated objective of "communicating the travel industry's commitment to good environmental practice to their customers", it still has a relatively low profile amongst tourists and is unknown to most consumers.

Voluntary Trusts

Voluntary trusts may play a positive role in the development of more sustainable forms of tourism. Their contribution may include:

- providing voluntary labour to help with conservation projects

- conserving valuable heritage sites and developing them as visitor attractions, using the revenue generated to further their conservation work on the site
- raising money to support conservation projects.

The Problems with Voluntary Trusts

While generally helpful, few voluntary trusts have the power to make a major contribution to sustainable tourism. An exception to this rule is the National Trust in the UK. At the same time, voluntary trusts can sometimes be criticized for being either rather amateurish or too narrow, concerning themselves with one single issue only.

Conclusions

We have seen that the four different types of voluntary organizations we have considered can all play a positive role in sustainable tourism. However, we have also noted that each type of organization has factors which limit its potential contribution.

Discussions Points and Essay Questions

1. Evaluate the objectives and activities of Tourism Concern in terms of how they might contribute to the development of more sustainable forms of tourism.
2. Critically evaluate the idea that professional bodies are simply trying to pre-empt the need for government regulation in the sustainable tourism field.
3. Discuss the contribution which the CERT Environmental Kitemark Scheme might make to sustainable tourism.

Exercise

Select a voluntary trust which operates in tourism in your area. Assess the extent to which its activities are compatible with the principles of sustainable tourism.

Case Study: the Role of Voluntary Trusts in the UK

Voluntary, charitable trusts in the UK play a major role in the tourism industry, particularly in the visitor attraction sector. Their activities are also often in line with the principles of sustainable tourism. Voluntary trusts contribute to sustainability in several ways, as follows:

- The National Trust, one of the world's largest voluntary sector organizations conserves historic landscapes and buildings and provides public access to them. It uses the income generated from visitors to further its conservation activities.
- Small voluntary groups of enthusiasts play a considerable role in the UK in the conservation, or at least the preservation of:
  (i)   steam railways
  (ii)   industrial archaeology sites
  (iii) wildlife conservation sites.
- Voluntary trusts have often taken over and rejuvenated museums, owned and operated by local authorities, that would otherwise have been forced to close.
- Voluntary bodies have pioneered some of the most innovative approaches to tourism in the UK. For example, the Jorvik Viking Centre in York was established by a voluntary sector archaeological trust.

Voluntary trusts have the twin advantages of having access to:

- voluntary labour
- sources of funding which are not available to either public sector bodies or private sector companies.

However, voluntary groups also occasionally face criticism relating to the concept of sustainability. For example, the National Trust has been criticized for its:

- perceived elitism and preference for rural scenery and stately houses rather than urban townscapes and industrial heritage
- unwillingness to ban fox-hunting on its land
- policy of charging relatively high prices for admission to the properties it owns.

Nevertheless, there is little doubt that, in the UK at least, voluntary trusts play a positive role in respect of sustainable tourism.

Case Study: Pressure Groups – Action for Southern Africa

Action for Southern Africa (ACTSA) is the successor to the Anti-Apartheid Movement. It campaigns for the international support vital to fulfil the hopes of change in Southern Africa (ACTSA leaflet).

It has taken an interest in tourism in Southern Africa, as one can see from the following examples from one of their leaflets.

Exhibit 1. Raising awareness of tourism-related issues in Southern Africa. Source: ACTSA literature, no date given.

Put people in the picture

For you, holidays are an escape from everyday routine. But for people across southern Africa, struggling against the poverty left by apartheid, they provide the basics of life.

Tourism can bring much-needed funds for schools, clinics or safe water – especially to far-flung rural communities most in need. In South Africa, where one in three is jobless, tourism could create two million jobs by the end of the decade.

With prices in the doldrums for traditional exports like copper and coffee, debt-strapped and war-scarred southern African economies are looking to tourism to boost resources for rebuilding. Tourists to the region have doubled since 1990. Many of these come from Britain.

> 'It seems to us that the West cares more for elephants than it does for people'. (Game warden, Zimbabwe)

Holiday money

Despite this rapid growth, the bulk of the profits go to big travel companies in rich countries like Britain. The poorer countries of southern Africa which host the tourists are often short-changed.

Across southern Africa, local communities, unions and governments are working for a fairer deal from tourism. But they need your support.

With travel companies all chasing you as a potential holiday-maker, you can wield your consumer power to demand tourism which puts people first.

Check in to act

Sign ACTSA's people-first traveller's cheque below. **Return it to us today**. ACTSA will present it to the travel industry as evidence of consumer demand for a better deal for the people of southern Africa.

And **please give** what you can to the campaign on the slip overleaf.

Dream holiday

People-first tourism initiatives are now springing up across southern Africa. The Tsholotsho community in Zimbabwe receives the proceeds from tourists who visit the game reserve on their land. With these, the community has built a clinic, so mothers no longer have to walk 10 miles for medical help. A new well is providing clean water and the local school has new desks.

> 'With the participation of affected communities . . . and with respect for the natural environment, then tourism will be a vital force for the sustainable development of our country'. (**President Nelson Mandela**)

As a consumer, you can press the British travel industry to give greater support to such initiatives by signing ACTSA's people-first traveller's cheque inside.

Clearly ACTSA is focusing on trying to persuade British tourists to put pressure on the UK tourism industry to make it more sensitive to the needs of the host population in Southern Africa.

This organization focuses attention on several key issues in relation to sustainable tourism. It:

- shows the link between tourism and the wider issues of sustainable development
- highlights the political dimension of tourism
- recognizes the relative powerlessness of the host population through the fact that it has to appeal to the tourist's conscience to try to achieve its aims
- brings into sharp focus the issue of human rights versus animal rights.

11

The Host Community

The concept of the host community is at the heart of most sustainable tourism literature. Most commentators seem to agree that the most important aspect of tourism policy is the 'protection' of the host community and its environment. One of the cornerstones of sustainable tourism is the idea that the host community should be actively involved in tourism planning and should perhaps control the local tourism industry and its activities.

Yet, the idea of the host community is a difficult concept to define. It is even more difficult to find effective mechanisms for involving the community as a whole in the tourism development process.

In this chapter we will critically evaluate the concept of the 'host community' and its place in the sustainable tourism debate. Most of this chapter looks at community involvement in public sector decision-making but at the end we will also look at a more radical way in which the local population can become involved in influencing the commercial development of tourism in their area.

The Definition of Host Communities

This simple term, which suggests homogeneity, in fact covers a very diverse topic. The suggestion seems to be that the host community is all those people who live within a tourist destination. However, Fig. 11.1 highlights some of the complexities involved in any discussions of the host community.

We will now consider each of these points in a little more detail.

The Geographical Area Issue

Imagine a family taking a touring holiday in the Provence region of France; who is the host community? Presumably it is all the people who live in every town or village they stay in or visit during their vacation.

However, it could also be argued that the concept should also be taken to include:

- the residents of everywhere else in Provence they do not visit
- every resident in the country of France.

The reason for these two suggestions is that these people pay taxes which will be used in some small way to pay for the services used by our tourists. They also elect the regional and national governments that make policies that affect our tourists' holiday. Maybe therefore they should be seen as part of the 'host community'.

Indigenous People versus In-Migrants

Perhaps, morally, the main influence should be in the hands of those who were born and

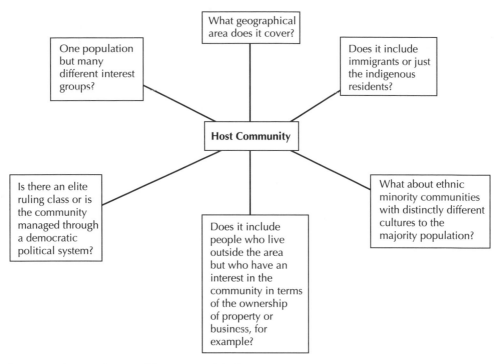

Fig. 11.1. The complexities of the concept of the host community.

bred in a community. However, in many communities often the most vocal critics of tourism can come from those who have moved into the community, including:

- people who have purchased second homes in the region
- those who have retired to the destination
- immigrant workers.

There is a big question mark over the morality of immigrants seeking to restrict tourism when they themselves are not locally born people.

Majority and Minority Communities

Many destination communities now contain minority communities whose culture, and language, may be different to that of the majority community. The interests of these ethnic minority communities may be at odds with the majority community.

External Residents with an Interest in the Community

There are people who, while they do not live in a particular area, could legitimately claim to have a right to a say in what happens in a community. This group could include those who:

- own property in the area
- are the proprietors of tourism-related and non tourism-related enterprises in the area
- were born in the area, have moved away, but still have relations in the area.

Whether or not they do have a right to a say and how big a say they should have, is again a sensitive and, at times, a controversial subject.

Elite and Democratic Systems

The idea of a community seems to imply an element of democracy and an expectation that decisions affecting the community will be taken democratically. However, we know that in many communities around the world, this is not the case. In some communities decisions are taken by an elected economic and political elite, or they may even be taken by self-appointed elites and dictators who were never elected and who have no democratic mandate.

One Population, but Many Different Interest Groups

There is an idea implicit in the concept of community involvement that host populations will tend to have a shared set of interests. However, within any community there is likely to be a range of groups with very different interests, who will take different stances on the issue of tourism. These might include:

- those who own tourism enterprises
- those employed in the local tourism industry
- those entrepreneurs who are not involved in the tourism business
- those who are not employed in the tourism industry and are generally unaffected by the industry
- those whose life is adversely affected by tourism in terms of noise, for example.

The Myths of Community and Consensus

The idea of community is a cosy, comfortable idea, where people living in an area share a sense of purpose and identity. It suggests stability and consensus, an appealing concept in a world where change and conflict are perhaps more common.

However, if we are to make progress with the concept of sustainable tourism we need to recognize that there is generally no such thing as a community. Figure 11.1 showed the diversity of dimensions to the 'community' in any area that means that in reality there are always several host communities rather than a single host community. The community could be divided in terms of:

- elites and the rest of the population
- indigenous residents and immigrants
- those involved in the tourism industry and those who are not
- property owners and property renters
- younger people and older people
- employers and employees or the self-employed
- those with private cars and those who are reliant on public transport
- affluent and less well off residents
- majority communities and ethnic minority communities.

These differences create different interest groups and some of them imply conflict in themselves such as the tensions between the tastes of younger and older people and between employers and employees.

If we add to these the personalities of each individual resident and the history of what has happened between them over the years, conflict is far more likely than consensus. Consensus may only exist as an artificially imposed concept where there is a dominant elite which can impose its will on others. This was seen clearly in the old Soviet Union where the State repressed conflict between ethnic groups and portrayed the image of harmony between Armenians and Azerbaijanis, for instance. However, once the centralized state collapsed, conflict broke out between the two communities. This is an extreme example but it illustrates the point.

In most communities there is a history of conflict over all kinds of events ranging from who bought a particular piece of land to new building developments to neighbour disputes. It is not surprising, therefore, that tourism in general and tourism development in particular, usually leads to conflict. Part of the conflict relates to tourism but it is often also a continuation of conflicts which date back to other issues and times.

Finally, we need also to be wary of the idea that communities are represented by, and spoken for by, 'community leaders', many of whom are self-appointed or represent a small section of the community only. Policy-makers need to be aware that while the idea of being able to gain the views of a population from one or two community leaders is attractive it can lead to the views of the substantial population of the community not being heard.

The Rationale for Community Involvement

Implicitly, the rationale for community involvement in tourism planning is that it is believed to:

- be in keeping with the concept of democracy
- give a voice to those who are most affected by tourism
- make use of local knowledge to make sure that decisions made are well informed
- reduce potential conflict between tourists and the host community by involving the latter in shaping the way in which tourism develops.

There is also an idea that, somehow, it is the fair and right thing to do. Yet, there appears to be very little concrete evidence that community involvement ensures better quality tourism development or less conflict between hosts and guests.

The Scope of Community Involvement

Policy-makers need to carefully consider where the community can be involved in tourism. For example, they might be involved:

- only in the generation of statutory, formal tourism strategies, responding to options proposed by professionals
- only when specific proposals are received for developments on particular sites.

This is a reactive approach, for the community could also be involved more pro-actively, by for example:

(i) deciding which messages about the area should be included in destination brochures

(ii) choosing which heritage themes will be developed in new museums

(iii) suggesting what the 'Acceptable Limits to Change' are for their community.

The Level of Influence of the Community

The same policy-makers must also know what level of influence the community will have. Figure 11.2 illustrates this, in terms of what might be called the 'Ladder of Community Influence'.

Clearly, there is also a major issue here of the rights of a local community against those of the wider national community, and even the world's population as a whole. For example:

- Should rural communities whose farms and services are often subsidized by urban taxpayers be able to restrict access to the countryside for those same urban dwellers?

Communities have total control of strategic policy and tactical decisions in relation to tourism in the area
Communities have a veto on all tourism policies and decisions that are in the hands of public sector bodies
Communities set the priorities and parameters for public sector policy and/or decisions
Communities are permitted to select a policy or strategy from a small number of options all of which have been generated by public sector policy-makers
Community views are used to help justify decisions taken by public sector bodies
The community is consulted but its views do not significantly influence public sector policy

Fig. 11.2. The ladder of community influence.

- Should a majority community be able to discriminate against ethnic minority groups?
- Should a small local community be able to hold up or defy national economic strategies, designed to benefit the population as a whole, and drawn up by a democratically elected government?

The Timing of Community Involvement

It seems sensible that community involvement should take place as early as possible in the planning and development of tourism in areas to try to reduce the likelihood of destinations experiencing Doxey's Irridex response to tourism, moving from euphoria to antagonism. Community involvement may help by both:

- reducing the negative impacts of tourism which are due to inappropriate development and the attraction of unsuitable forms of tourism, and
- increasing community tolerance of tourism and tourist behaviour.

Community Involvement Mechanisms

The concept of community participation in public sector decision-making is not new. In the area of town and country planning, for example, it has a history which dates back several decades. Indeed, it was a highly fashionable idea in the 1960s and 1970s.

In the UK, 1969 saw the publication of the Skeffington Report on 'People and Planning' which defined participation as

the act of sharing in the formulation of policies and proposals. (Skeffington Report, 1969)

The report suggested that there was unanimous enthusiasm for the idea and a willingness on the part of authorities and the public to work together.

In 1969 Arnstein devised his ladder of citizenship participation which classified eight forms of participation mechanisms:

- manipulation
- therapy
- informing
- consultation
- placation
- partnership
- delegated power
- citizen control.

Wall has suggested that:

Because of the importance of the resources under their care, the managers of protected areas may have an opportunity to demonstrate a leadership role in addressing such issues. Certainly it is in their best long-term interests to do so ... The bottom rungs on the ladder were regarded as non-participation, those further up were viewed as types of tokenism, whereas those at the top were considered to represent varying degrees of citizen power ... Recognition of the necessary involvement of aboriginal peoples in decisions which affect their lives can be seen as a specific aspect of the broader issues of public participation, self-determination, and the desire to enable individuals and groups to participate in the taking of decisions which influence their well-being. While the appropriateness of involvement is widely acknowledged, the form which that involvement should take, although tending to move up successive rungs of Arnstein's ladder over time, is far from clear or unanimous and varies from situation to situation both within and between countries. (Wall, 1996)

In the 1970s, guides were produced to allow local people to participate effectively in the planning system. For example, in 1974, the Town and Country Planning Association in the UK published The New Citizen's Guide to Town and Country Planning.

However, even in the 1970s the difficulties did not revolve around the idea of participation but rather how to develop effective mechanisms for implementing the concept in practice. That is also the case today in the field of community involvement in tourism policy and planning.

Traditionally, community involvement in its broadest sense is concerned with electors voting for their democratic representatives. Formal public participation in the decision-making process then tends to involve the gathering of public opinion via public meetings which are of course not attended by all residents. Residents may also be invited to submit written observations or objections.

However, these techniques have drawbacks in that they:

- discriminate against those who are less articulate or have other priorities in their life such as work or family commitments
- tend to involve responses to specific proposals rather than inviting local people to devise their own policies and plans
- rely on information being available to residents.

Often relevant documents will be written in professional jargon which the everyday citizen finds difficult to comprehend.

In many areas, heavy reliance is also placed upon consultation with local organizations such as chambers of commerce and trade unions, even though these bodies may only represent a minority of the local population.

The Negative Side of Community Involvement

Giving great influence to the host community can also have a negative side. It can:

- add greatly to the cost of tourism planning and development
- lengthen the period needed to develop plans or carry out controversial projects
- provide an opportunity for local interest groups to deny opportunities for leisure and employment to people from outside the area, who may be less well off than them
- allow the majority local community to

discriminate against local ethnic minority groups.

The choice of mechanisms is therefore important to minimize these potential problems.

The Host Community in Tourism: a More Radical Approach

Most conventional thinking in sustainable tourism focuses on how the community can influence public sector tourism planning and development control systems. However, if local communities are really going to maximize the benefits they gain from tourism and minimize its costs then a more radical approach is needed.

Instead of relying on public sector regulation of the private sector tourism industry, communities should set out to be more proactive, by becoming active players in the tourism market.

Din, in an essay in Cooper and Wanhill (1997), has showed how the people of Malaysia might attempt to become actively involved in the tourism market. He suggested:

- consortia of local Chambers of Commerce
- cooperatives
- local communities having equity shares in new developments
- the development of tourism via non-profit making trust companies.

In these cases control would be in local hands and profits could be used for the public good rather than for private gain.

Such organizations could play a major role in destinations in terms of:

- visitor attractions such as heritage centres, retail complexes and restaurants
- ground handlers organizing itineraries for inbound tourists
- local transport systems.

These organizations could work together to offset the negotiating power of external and local large-scale tourism enterprises.

For this idea to work, however, there would be a need for:

- training in management and business skills
- start-up, 'pump-priming' funding
- a clear legal structure for these types of organizations.

This approach would also maximize direct control between local people and tourists which is usually seen as desirable in the sustainable tourism literature.

Conclusions

We have noted that while the concept of the community is central to most debates on sustainable tourism, the idea of community is largely a myth. Indeed local populations will normally consist of different interest groups some of whom may be in conflict with each other. It has also been seen that there are different levels of community involvement in tourism planning.

Finally, it has been suggested that instead of simply seeking to influence public sector policy the community should seek to gain influence by becoming an active player in the tourism market through various means.

Discussion Points and Essay Questions

1. Discuss the main issues involved in trying to involve the community in tourism policy in developing countries.
2. Critically evaluate the contents of Fig. 11.1.
3. Discuss the factors which determine the level of influence that communities have on public sector tourism planning and policy, with reference to the 'Ladder of Community Influence' illustrated in Fig. 11.2.

Exercise

Think about your own local area and the people who live there. To what extent is there a homogeneous local community? If the population is heteregeneous, indicate the main subgroups and interest groups which exist within the local population.

Case Studies: Two Examples of Community Involvement from North America

It is no coincidence that both case studies in this chapter are from North America, as this has been the pioneer region and the front runner in this area of community participation in tourism planning.

For example, in his seminal work on the community dimension to sustainable tourism *Tourism: a Community Approach*, Peter Murphy (1985) discussed the way public participation had helped shape the tourism strategy of Greater Victoria in British Columbia, Canada.

This early widespread adoption of the concept of community participation in North America reflects the history and culture of Canada and the USA, and its liberal, relatively de-centralized political system. Community participation is less likely to develop in countries with totalitarian and/or highly centralized political systems.

Let us now look at two detailed examples of community involvement in North America.

Case Study: an Early Example of Community Participation, Canada

As we noted earlier in this chapter, the concept of community participation is not new. Attempts have been made all over the world to put the idea into practice. One early example of such initiatives related to a small village in the Arctic Circle, which was set up in 1981.

Pangnirtung, a small village situated just below the Arctic Circle on Cumberland Sound in Canada's Northwest Territories, is home to about 1200 Inuit [Eskimo]. Known by them as 'place of the big running out' because of the high tides, Cumberland Sound was historically a whaling centre (until about 1910) and fur trading area (into the 1950s). The Inuit still rely heavily on the resources of the sea and land.

In the early 1970s a sport fishing camp and hotel were developed by local non-native interests, and Auyuittug National Park Reserve, which offers world class mountaineering, hiking, photography and nature watching opportunities, was established 30 km north. For the most part, tourism occurred in an unstructured manner with no local control and very few benefits for the community – until 1981 when the Government of the Northwest Territories, through the Canadian Department of Economy, Development and Tourism, initiated a community-based tourism development strategy.

The tourism potential of the area was great, but in order to respect the cultural heritage of the Inuit, community members were encouraged to set the pace and direction of tourism development in a manner consistent with their lifestyles and traditions. The community first had to develop an understanding of what tourism meant as a concept, and then appreciate its consequences before knowing whether to support it as a means for social and economic growth. Concerns about cross-cultural impacts were aired. For instance, some residents were concerned that tourists would walk into local houses and ask too many questions. They were also fearful that 'outsiders' would not understand the Inuit lifestyle of hunting and trapping, and would criticize it.

The Pangnirtung Hamlet Council, consisting of guides, outfitters, and others involved in tourism, took the lead role in directing community discussion, they involved community members, government agencies, and other organizations. Many long meetings took place. What, at the time, seemed like an unproductive process of contemplating concerns and dreams, actually was a necessary part of building community consensus. The process of self-examination continues even today when new issues or plans are considered.

A public information and education programme was a critical factor in the discussion process, and included radio, a newsletter, posters, and community meetings. Throughout the process, community involvement grew from cautious concern, to interest and support, and finally to direct participation. While tourism had and continues to have opponents as well as supporters, this dynamic tension provides the checks and balances necessary to ensure full community involvement in setting the pace of development. Out of this process grew a number of tourism goals and objectives which still provide clear direction to the community today. These include:

- promoting development that is compatible with subsistence and hunting activities, and respects traditional Inuit lifestyles;
- promoting development that provides jobs and reduces dependency on social assistance;
- promoting cultural programmes and facilities which benefit both tourism and local social development;
- encouraging local ownership, decision making, and skill development in managing tourism business;

- encouraging long-term self-sufficiency of the community;
- facilitating cross-cultural learning and providing opportunities where Inuit and non-Inuit can get to know each other, so local people can develop skills in dealing with non-Inuit people;
- development awareness so that residents can make informed decisions regarding tourism development.

The Kekerten and Angmarlik projects did much to catalyse the community's desire to preserve and show their culture. Arriving at the point of commitment led to a collective understanding that the natural, cultural, and archaeological resources must be safeguarded and carefully managed. This commitment, in turn, led to a community decision to develop a small number of specific sites and resources for tourism in order to leave other locations untouched and undisturbed, and elders and hunters agreed to take the time to explain to visitors the importance of the land and sea and the relationship of those resources to the social and economic well-being of the community. In terms of employment and income, this type of controlled tourism growth (not necessarily measured only in visitor numbers) broadens the narrow economic base and can be sustainable and beneficial. The community decides what level of development is acceptable, and will be able to make adjustments at the opportune time. (Paper presented to World Conference on Tourism Development and the Environment, Canary Islands, Spain, 1989 by Gordon Wray, Minister of Economic Development and Tourism, GNWT, Canada quoted in World Tourism Organization, 1993)

This example acknowledges that tensions about tourism, and even approaches to tourism, still exist in the community. But the author argues that this tension helps to ensure that there is a system of checks and balances in relation to tourism development. It seems as if participation was used by the government to try to increase community interest in their own heritage which is an example of social policy objectives being met via community participation in tourism development.

However, it has to be said that active participation in a small, isolated community, with a single-culture population, like this one, is much easier to achieve than trying to do the same in a major city with a multi-cultural population.

Case Study: Community Involvement in the Baffin Region, Canada

Addison has reported on a community project to develop a strategy for a community-based town in the Baffin region in the far north of Canada. The host community in the area was made up largely of 10,000 Inuit people living in 14 communities. The idea was to ensure that tourism development was shaped in response to the wishes of local people. Consultants worked with local government officers with experience of working with these communities, and local interpreters to, firstly, make local people aware of the project. The Consultant

- arranged for radio announcement(s) advising of the arrival of a tourism planner and the AEDO
- distributed the previously prepared newsletters to each household. In some of the smaller communities, these were delivered personally to provide opportunities for any initial questions or comments
- organized one or two phone-in shows on the local radio station to provide listeners with an opportunity to ask questions of the planner and the AEDO, as well as to make comments about tourism and/or the study
- invited residents to a drop-in session at a convenient location to speak with the planner and the AEDO
- held group meetings with, for example, local council, community elders, the hunters and trappers association, the land claims committee, the education society, the recreation committee, arts and crafts groups, the historical society, and senior school classes
- met with individuals who had, or might have had, some connection with the local tourism industry (e.g. elected officials, government representatives, hamlet managers, co-op managers, community leaders, outfitters, hotel owners, transportation operators, educators, church representatives, people with knowledge of local resources). (Addison in Harrison and Husbands, 1996)

The results of this process were as follows:

Most communities were generally in favour of tourism if growth was slow and if residents were able to maintain a high degree of control over numbers of visitors, timing of visits, and the activities of visitors.

- Residents wanted more information about the local benefits of tourism.
- Many experiences with tourists had been negative, and concerns were expressed about the intrusive impact of uncontrolled tourism on existing lifestyles.
- Many residents believed that tourists should not be allowed to access traditional hunting and fishing areas.
- Most communities wanted to control the tourism business and be involved in specific tourism developments.
- Residents wanted tourists to have an Inuit as a guide.
- Residents believed that tourists should know more about the likes and dislikes of the Inuit before coming to the region and should not ask too many questions. (Addison in Harrison and Husbands, 1996)

Eventually a tourism strategy was developed and implemented. Ten years later, a study was undertaken to see what had actually happened. This report was rather negative in its conclusions as can be seen from the following excerpt:

Overall, this type of development has not given the community control over tourism. Rather, it has been a means for greater community involvement in economic development. In the final analysis, government agencies have held financial, and hence political, control over the tourism development in Pangnirtung. Tourism's economic benefits have been significant and appropriate. In particular, local people have been able to supplement their family income by informal, direct sales to tourists. However, training and management skills have not kept pace with capital development. This has presented problems in terms of keeping command over the industry at the local level.

- The goals of community control over tourism had not yet been fulfilled. Tourism development remained largely driven and controlled by EDandT.
- A local Tourism Committee had taken on an advisor role rather than the decision-making and initiating role that had been intended. It had also tended to involve itself primarily in capital projects, neglecting other more general tourism issues such as awareness, training, management, and industry growth. Hence, when the capital projects (largely government-driven) were complete, the Tourism Committee had ceased to function. It was unprepared to take control of the operational phase of development.
- Factors thought to be limiting community participation in the tourism industry included the lack of formal education, business experience and support from lending institutions, insufficient awareness and understanding of tourism industry opportunities, and the activities of government agencies in protecting their own investments and those of established private sector businesses.
- Insufficient training opportunities and an overall under investment in human resource development were repeatedly identified as reasons for limited community participation in the tourism industry. It was also stated that training had not kept pace with the growing demands for quality service in the tourism industry. Moreover, women felt excluded from training opportunities.
- Although the general attitude towards tourists was good, community awareness of tourism had decreased over the years. This was particularly true of Pangnirtung's youth, who did not recognize tourism as a potential career choice and were developing negative attitudes towards tourists.
- Some local residents believed that the historic picture presented to tourists of their culture and history (one which emphasised the whaling period and early postcontact history) presented a rather narrow, one-sided view of Inuit culture and history. It was also widely felt that community elders were not sufficiently involved in cultural interpretation. (Reimer and Dialla, 1992 quoted in Harrison and Husbands, 1996)

This case study illustrates some of the problems involved in turning the idea of community involvement into action.

12

The Media

The media plays a significant role in both shaping tourist behaviour and raising awareness of issues relating to sustainable tourism. It is therefore clear that the media must make a contribution to the development of more sustainable forms of tourism. Fundamentally we can divide the relevant media into two types:

- **travel media**, which are designed to directly influence or advise the tourist
- **non-travel media**, which indirectly influence or advise the tourist, without this being their real purpose.

To help us understand the role of the media better, perhaps we first need to recognize the breadth of the media in this context. Table 12.1 outlines the main types of media.
There is no doubt that:

- in recent years, there has been a growth in the travel media sector
- the non-travel media, particularly with the rise of satellite television channels, has made people all over the world more aware of other places on the planet.

In this chapter we will consider several issues involving the media, both travel media and non-travel media, to the concept of sustainable tourism.

The Negative Side of the Travel Media

The travel media acts against the principles of sustainability in that:

- television programmes, guidebooks or magazine and newspaper features encourage tourists to want to visit 'off the beaten track' places so that the negative impacts of tourism are spread to new areas. They also encourage the idea that independent travel is superior to package travel even though there is no evidence that the former is any more sustainable than the latter
- many television programmes and magazines and newspaper features promote destinations which have oppressive political regimes
- most programmes and features are produced as a result of trips by journalists which are paid for by the tourism industry. They are therefore in danger of being seen as not being objective, for presenters are unlikely to offend the companies who have paid for their trip
- few programmes or features ever look at tourism from the point of view of the host community

Table 12.1.   The main types of media relevant to sustainable tourism.

Travel media	Non-travel media
<ul><li>Guide books</li><li>Television and radio programmes with a tourism theme</li><li>Specialist travel magazines</li><li>Travel features in newspapers and journals</li><li>Travel literature, i.e. the memoirs and experiences of travellers</li><li>Travel-related Internet pages</li></ul>	<ul><li>News programmes on TV, the radio, and in newspapers</li><li>Special interest programmes, notably about wildlife</li><li>Consumer 'watchdog' programmes that cover tourism-related issues</li><li>Popular culture which features particular, identifiable locations such as films and television series</li></ul>

- sometimes best-selling travel books like Peter Mayle's *A Year in Provence* lead to the saturation of the area by 'literary' tourists.

The Negative Side of the Non-travel Media

The effects of the non-travel media are more diverse reflecting the breadth of types of non-travel media. The main negative aspects of the non-travel media in respect of sustainable tourism are as follows:

- News programmes which report civil disturbances, crime, political instability or national disasters in a country may cause a short-term reduction in demand for the destination. This costs the host community money and jobs. Yet often the reports are based on occurrences in one locality only, but the way they are reported may affect the whole country or region. While no one would suggest censoring news, the news media should recognize their responsibility to report news accurately and without sensationalizing it.
- Wildlife programmes on the television can lead to an upsurge in demand for destinations with fragile ecosystems which is not helpful.
- The 'consumer watchdog' programmes and features clearly have a role to play in protecting the rights of consumers.

However, they may sometimes encourage tourists to believe that they are entitled to more than the price they have paid merits. They also talk about tourist's rights but rarely acknowledge that these rights also bring with them responsibilities.

- When tourists learn where television programmes or films are made it can lead to visitor pressure which cannot easily be sustained by the local community. An unreasonable burden can be placed on the local environment and the infrastructure.

Media Interest in Sustainable Tourism: Only 'Sexy' Issues Need Apply

Since the early 1990s, the media has shown a growing interest in the concept of sustainable tourism although the level of interest is still relatively low. Figure 12.1 illustrates the apparent level of media interest in different aspects of sustainable tourism.

The emphasis is clearly therefore on the tourist and the environment rather than on social and economic issues and the host community. More balance is needed if the media is to play a positive role in making tourism more sustainable.

Where the media is interested in a topic it can also be rather over-simplistic or superficial in its coverage and tends to look for heroes and villains rather than recognizing

High Media Interest — Wildlife conservation
Conservation of the earth's
  resources
Landscape conservation
Industry responsibilites
Tourist rights and consumer protection

The environmental impact
of tourism

Government responsibilities

Social impacts of tourism
The rights of the host community

The rights of employees in the
  tourism industry
The economic impact of tourism
The human rights records of destination
  governments
Low Media Interest — Tourist responsibilities

Fig. 12.1. Media interest in the different aspects of sustainable tourism.

the fact that the issues tend to be more grey than black or white.

Traditional and Alternative Guide Books

Traditional guide books – Michelin, Baedeker, Blue Guides, Fodors, Frommers – have tended to focus purely on those issues relating directly to the tourist's own holiday experience, including hotel accommodation, restaurants and cultural and natural sights. They tend to be aimed at the middle to higher level market. They have generally said little that is critical of the destination preferring instead to focus on the positive or exclude places about which they find it difficult to be positive. In any event they have invariably focused on those areas which were clearly on the 'tourist map'.

In recent years we have seen the rise of what might be termed 'alternative guides' such as the Lonely Planet and Rough Guide series. These differ from the traditional guide in several respects, notably:

- they cover most of the country, not just the established tourist spots
- they are willing to criticize as well as praise

- they draw tourist's attention to ethical issues such as local environmental policies or government human rights records.

It could easily be argued that these new guide books are more in tune with the concept of sustainable tourism than the traditional guides.

A case study that compares both types of guides can be found at the end of this chapter.

Film and Television Tourism

Film and television tourism is the modern extension of the literary tourism which is at the core of the appeal of destinations like Stratford-upon-Avon.

The locations where films are shot and popular television programmes made are now popular attractions for large numbers of tourists. This has led to ironic situations such as in the case of the film, 'Braveheart'. The film is set in Scotland and depicts a key character in Scottish history. However, the film was shot in Ireland and it is the Irish locations which have benefited from increased numbers of tourists.

The power of film- and television-related tourism is being increasingly recognized by places which want to get on the tourist map who are pro-actively going out of their way to attract film and television companies to use their areas as locations. They know that any film and television series made in their area will lead to an influx of tourists keen to see the locations where they are set. Considerable income and employment can be created in this way in places which would otherwise struggle to attract tourists or other forms of economic development. In this respect it can be seen to be highly compatible with the concept of sustainability.

Conversely, it can lead to a sudden increase in visitors with no time for preparations to be made for the services they require. Likewise once the series ends or the film goes out of circulation, the volume of visitors can fall dramatically. Clearly, in these two respects, film and television tourism is in conflict with the idea of sustainable tourism.

Consumer Protection or Consumer Insulation

The non-travel media has developed an interest in consumer protection in tourism, through consumer 'watchdog' programmes. These programmes take up cases where tourists feel aggrieved by holiday experiences which have failed to live up to their expectations. Often the complaints involve:

- becoming ill on holiday
- delays to journeys
- alterations to itineraries.

Often, particularly in developing countries, these are unavoidable results of the low level of economic development in the countries concerned. In most cases, the inconveniences of the tourists are less than those felt by local people. The problem appears to be that the industry has raised unrealistic expectations of developing destinations in the minds of tourists and has not made them aware of potential hazards.

Likewise the tourists want the low cost holidays offered by such destinations but do not want the problems that go with holidaying in the destinations. The tourist wants to be insulated from the realities of life in these destinations. This is clearly not compatible with the idea of sustainability.

There is a danger, therefore, that consumer protection programmes can reinforce the unreasonable and unrealistic expectations of tourists.

Wildlife Programmes and Ecotourism

Given the huge success of television programmes about wildlife in developed countries, there seems little doubt that they have played a role in the growth of ecotourism. This is particularly the case in the rain forests of Central America and the rise of whale-watching.

These programmes and their makers must recognize their influence more and consciously seek to be more responsible. Perhaps programmes should be made in those places where the inevitable resulting influx of tourists is either desirable or at least manageable.

Likewise it is not helpful for wildlife programmes to stress the fact that particular species are dying out or vegetation disappearing rapidly. This simply encourages people to visit now while there is still something to see, and in doing so simply hastens the demise of the wildlife in question.

Towards a More Positive Role for the Media

Firstly, we have to recognize that there is no real reason why the media should wish to play a more positive role in the sustainable tourism debate. There is not enough consumer pressure yet in the travel media to make them take the issue seriously while most of the non-travel media could say it is simply too peripheral to their core activities to merit any in-depth attention.

It is, therefore, more appropriate, perhaps to talk about the media adopting a more ethical approach to their coverage of tourism issues. This means not siding too closely with either the industry or the tourist and showing more interest in the rights of the host population in foreign countries.

The media could if it wanted to, play a major role in developing more sustainable forms of tourism for it clearly has great influence on tourist behaviour, particularly the travel media. It could, for example:

- give tourists objective advice about problems in destinations
- raise awareness of social problems and government policies in destination areas.

As the role of the media grows in tourism it could almost be argued that the idea of sustainable tourism will fail unless it can harness the power of the media.

Conclusions

We have seen that both the travel media and the non-travel media often are against the interests of sustainable tourism. It is clear from this chapter that the rise of 'alternative' guide books, consumer watchdog programmes, film and television tourism, and wildlife programmes, all have implications

for sustainable tourism. Finally, it has been seen that the media could play a positive role in the sustainable tourism debate but it is not clear why they should wish to do so.

Discussion Points and Essay Questions

1. Discuss the role which the media might play in the development of more sustainable forms of tourism.
2. Examine the reasons why the media may be more interested in tourist's rights and wildlife than host communities and employee's rights.
3. Evaluate the advantages and disadvantages of film- and television-related tourism in relation to the concept of sustainable tourism.

Exercise

Select a destination and obtain a range of recent guide books covering your chosen destination. Analyse the content of each guide book to see to what extent they raise awareness of issues relating to sustainable tourism. Finally, you should suggest what more such guide books could do to further the cause of sustainable tourism.

Case Study: Traditional versus Alternative Guide Books – Baedeker meets the Rough Guide in Cyprus and Majorca

An analysis of the 'traditional' Baedeker and 'alternative' Rough Guide books on Cyprus and Majorca illustrates the differences in approach, outlined in the chapter itself. We can best illustrate this point if we look at the treatment of issues in each guide which relate to the wider concept of sustainability. The main differences are illustrated in Exhibit 1 (Cyprus) and Exhibit 2 (Majorca).

It is clear from these two examples that the new 'alternative' guide books do, perhaps, tend to take a more pro-active stance on sustainability issues, than their traditional rivals.

Exhibit 1.   The coverage of issues in Cyprus.

Issue	Baedeker	Rough Guide
Environmental problems	• No specific section • Occasional references to individual issues	• A chapter on wildlife which takes a strongly conservation-oriented approach to the subject • Sections on specific issues such as the loggerhead turtles, building developments in inappropriate locations and the environmental damage caused by the building of golf courses
The Turkish invasion and its implications	• Around two pages on the invasion and its implications	• Nine pages on the invasion and its implications • Further sections on specific issues such as the Kokkina Enclave, and the identity of the Turkish Cypriots
Encouraging tourists to try to learn and speak a little of the language	• A three-page long list of key words in Greek and two pages of Turkish words	• A four-page guide to Greek • A three-page guide to Turkish • A list of phrase books, dictionaries and 'teach yourself' language courses tourists may wish to purchase

Exhibit 2. The coverage of issues in Majorca.

Issue	Baedeker	Rough Guide
Environmental problems	• Very occasional brief references to individual issues • Brief mention of need to contain further tourism development	• Three pages on wildlife including some information on local conservation campaigns
The existence of the local Mallorcan language/dialect	• Recognizes local dialects and gives a one page guide to it • No translation of words into local dialect	• Mentions local dialect and offers two pages of words in the local dialect of Catalan
Encouragement to cycle rather than use private cars or public transport	• One sentence on bicycle hire	• A third of a page guide to cycling

13

The Tourist

Often the only mention of the tourist in the sustainable tourism literature is as the cause of the 'problem', in terms of the environmental, economic and social impacts of their activities. It is as if the tourist were an unwelcome intruder rather than an invited guest, spending their hard-earned money visiting a place.

If we are to develop more sustainable forms of tourism, the author believes that we must both place more emphasis on the role of the tourist and adopt a more even-handed attitude towards the tourist. This means:

- recognizing that unless tourists begin to take a genuine interest in, and show a commitment towards, sustainable tourism, then little will be achieved by either government action or industry initiatives
- accepting that tourists have rights as well as responsibilities
- promoting forms of potentially sustainable tourism that will be attractive to tourists and will enhance their holiday experience
- critically evaluating the idea of 'educating tourists' and asking who has the right to educate tourists and what the messages should actually be
- exploring the relationship between tourist behaviour and demand and the response of the tourism industry in terms of new product development and operational problems
- criticizing some of the subjective, moralistic ideas such as the 'good tourist' that have dogged the sustainable tourism debate.

The author believes that sustainable tourism cannot be achieved by regulation or by 'lecturing' tourists. Instead it will involve developing forms of tourism which give tourists a 'feel good' feeling, and which reflect trends in social values and consumer tastes, in general, while maximizing the benefits and reducing the costs of tourism.

Finally, when considering the tourist and sustainable tourism, we also have to address two other related issues which are as follows:

- how destinations which are heavily reliant on tourism can sustain the interest of tourists who are, we are told, becoming ever more sophisticated and demanding
- how tourism can help to sustain the tourist as a human being with a reasonable quality of life.

The Responsibilities of the Tourist

In every aspect of our life we have responsibilities, to ourselves, our friends and family, our work colleagues, and society as a whole.

Box 13.1. Basic responsibilities of the tourist.

- The responsibility for obeying local laws and regulations
- The responsibility for not taking part in activities which while not illegal, or where the laws are not enforced by the local authorities, are nevertheless, widely condemned by society, such as sex with children
- The responsibility for not deliberately offending local religious beliefs or cultural norms of behaviour
- The responsibility for not deliberately harming the local physical environment
- The responsibility to minimize the use of scarce local resources

Box 13.2. Extra responsibilities of tourists in relation to sustainable tourism.

- The responsibility not to visit destinations which have a poor record on human rights
- The responsibility to find out about the destination before the holiday and try to learn a few words of the local language, at least
- The responsibility to try to meet local people, learn about their life styles, and establish friendships
- The responsibility to protect the natural wildlife by not buying souvenirs made from living creatures, for example
- The responsibility to abide by all local religious beliefs and cultural values, even those with which the tourist personally disagrees
- The responsibility to boycott local businesses which pay their staff poor wages, or provide bad working conditions for their employees
- The responsibility to behave sensibly, so as not to spread infections such as HIV and hepatitis B
- The responsibility to contribute as much as possible to the local economy

Often these responsibilities are reflected in laws and accepted codes of behaviour. Whether it is because of the relatively recent rise of mass tourism or its nature, tourism has no such widely accepted set of responsibilities yet.

The author believes that the responsibilities which tourists might have, can be divided into two groups as follows:

- basic responsibilities, which we should expect of anyone who is a resident in another country, albeit temporary. These are outlined in Box 13.1
- more contentious responsibilities relating specifically to sustainable tourism.

The Rights of the Tourist

It is clearly accepted that tourists have responsibilities. However, the concept of sustainability, particularly in relation to its implicit idea of social equity and justice suggests that tourists should also have a set of rights. These rights imply responsibilities towards the tourist on the part of the host community, government agencies and the tourism industry. These rights and responsibilities are outlined in Table 13.1.

It has to be said that in many popular tourist destinations these rights are largely absent or poorly recognized.

As ever, in the case of rights and responsibilities, tourists should be entitled to these rights if they accept the responsibilities outlined in Boxes 13.1 and 13.2. Likewise, tourists can only be expected to accept the responsibilities if they are granted the rights identified in Table 13.1.

Responsible Tourism: a Contradiction in Terms?

The preceding section was on the basis that tourists will wish to behave in a responsible

Table 13.1. The rights of tourists and the responsibilities of the host community, government agencies and the tourism industry.

The rights of the tourist	Those who are responsible for protecting these rights
The right to be safe and secure from crime, terrorism and disease	• The host community • Government agencies, e.g. security services and health authorities
The right not to be discriminated against on the grounds of race, sex or disability	• The host community • The tourism industry • Government agencies, e.g. immigration departments
The right not to be exploited by local businesses and individuals	• The tourism industry • The host community • Government agencies, e.g. police
The right to the fair marketing of products through honest travel brochures and advertisements	• The tourism industry • Government agencies, e.g. the advertising regulators
The right to a safe, clean, physical environment	• The host community • The tourism industry • Government agencies, e.g. environmental bodies and policy departments
The right to free and unrestricted movement providing that they cause no damage	• Government agencies, e.g. security services
The right to meet local people freely	• Government agencies, e.g. security services
The right to courteous and competent service	• The host community • The tourism industry

way, accepting that they have responsibilities, and that they will behave sensibly.

However, there is a strong argument that most tourists see their annual vacation as an escape from their everyday responsibilities. One of the major attractions of a vacation is that for the duration of the trip there is no need to be sensible. Holidays are seen as a time to be carefree. Indeed some types of holiday are the apparent antitheses of the idea of responsible tourism. For example:

• the demand for 'hedonistic' tourism, or the 'sea, sand, sun, sex and sangria' type holiday which can involve casual unprotected sex and alcohol-related damage and annoyance for local people
• activities which harm the environment such as skiing, hunting and off-road bicycling and driving

• all-inclusive holidays which minimize the local economic benefits of tourism, and which minimize informal contact with local people.

Nevertheless, we can encourage more responsible tourist behaviour in two ways:

• by raising awareness of the issues involved in sustainable tourism in imaginative and effective ways
• by showing that the impacts of sustainable tourism can also lead to more satisfying vacations.

Awareness-Raising rather than Tourist Education?

Experience tells us that formal consumer education campaigns tend to have limited impacts, even in the case of activities like smoking, where the dangers are well known and the answers clear. Such education in sustainable tourism is a far more complex matter if only because:

- the scale of the 'danger' is largely unknown
- the solutions are still unclear.

There is also a major issue about who has the right to 'educate' the tourist. The distinction between objective education and subjective, value-laden propaganda is a very blurred area in the sustainable tourism area.

Therefore, perhaps, all we can do is raise awareness of the issues and leave tourists to decide for themselves what they should do in relation to sustainable tourism in terms of:

- their behaviour as tourists
- becoming involved in pressure groups and the political process.

The messages about sustainable tourism have clearly still not become widely understood by either tourists or the tourism industry. Even where the phrase is recognized it seems to be normally defined as relating largely to the physical environment.

We need to focus more attention on the sociocultural dimensions of sustainable tourism.

Tourist Satisfaction and Sustainability

In a relatively free, open, competitive market like tourism, we have to satisfy the tourist or no business or destination will be sustainable. Developing more sustainable forms of tourism, therefore, means devising new products and experiences which enhance the tourist experience while meeting the criteria of sustainability.

The main area where this could be achieved, the author believes, is in the social field of increasing host–visitor links. There is much status for tourists in meeting local

people and there is a great deal to be gained by the tourist from developing friendships with local people. It deepens the sense of identity with a destination for the tourist and makes them feel like an 'honorary local' instead of a tourist. It can also commit them to visiting the destination regularly rather than simply flitting from one place to another. Measures are therefore needed to make it easier for tourists to meet local people, particularly those who have no financial stake in tourism.

Conversely, from the point of view of the physical environment, what satisfies the tourism market is often against the interests of sustainable tourism. Satisfaction in this area comes from visiting places other tourists do not go to see rare wildlife. This leads the tourist into fragile environments where they do harm, unintentionally.

Perhaps, therefore, we need to try to persuade tourists to take more interest in people than environments. However, clear safeguards are needed to prevent tourism from swamping individual communities.

Regulation: a Last Resort?

We must accept that a point may well come in individual locations when awareness raising and attempting to match tourist satisfaction with sustainable tourism cannot solve the problems caused by tourism. Here, if the scale of the problem is perceived to be great enough, there may be a case for regulation of the numbers and activities of tourists. This should be seen as a last resort, though, as it involves interfering with a fundamental human right, namely the right to free movement.

The Good Tourist: Subjectivity, Snobbery and Self-righteousness

In 1991 Wood and House published their book *The Good Tourist*. This title explicitly stated what had been implicit for a while in the sustainable tourism debate, namely that there were forms of tourism and tourist behaviour which were intrinsically better than others. The 'good tourist' tends to be seen as someone who:

- travels independently or with small, environmentally sensitive tourism enterprises
- travels to less well known regions
- travels out of season
- learns the local language
- adapts to local culture
- gets to know local people
- enjoys local traditions
- buys locally produced food
- makes relatively little use of the mass market tourism infrastructure
- travels 'off-the-beaten-track'
- takes an interest in seeing wildlife in its natural habitat.

The author has several criticisms of this concept of a 'good tourist' as follows:

- It implies that there is also an evil tourist, someone whose activities are either motivated by malice or at least are inevitably harmful. This is a divisive concept that does not help bring on board the sustainable tourism bandwagon those people who do not easily fit the model of the 'good tourist'.
- The principles of 'good tourism' have not been proved, by empirical evidence, to be more sustainable than other forms of tourism.
- The type of tourism favoured by the 'good tourist' is still a minority, niche market which excludes the vast majority of the market today. It appeals to what in Chapter 3 we called the 'dark green' tourists who are a minority group.
- There is a nagging worry that many of the people writing about 'good' tourism appear to reflect their personal preferences in their definition of what constitutes a good tourist. Perhaps it is a case of self-justification and self-righteousness on the part of these people.
- Such tourism offers little to those established destinations that rely on mass

market coastal tourism, and where tourism employs thousands of people and represents billions of pounds of investment.

Sustaining the Market in Destinations

Another dimension to the use of tourists and sustainability is the need to make sure that destinations evolve to meet the changing nature of tourism demand to ensure they sustain their share of the tourism market. This means modifying the product of traditional destinations to exploit growth tourism such as:

- the desire to take part in activities while on holiday such as watersports
- the growing interest in health such as thalassotherapy and alternative medicines
- using vacations as an opportunity to develop a new skill
- the theming of tourism attractions and accommodation units
- heritage
- industrial tourism.

Clearly, it is important to ensure that the exploitation of such trends is carried out in line with the principles of sustainable tourism.

One trend in consumer behaviour is directly beneficial to the promotion of sustainable tourism, namely the growth of conservation and volunteer holidays where people spend their holidays working on conservation or aid projects.

Sustaining the Tourist

In their everyday lives today the people who are tourists for only a few weeks every year are living extremely stressful lives, in ever more characterless neighbourhoods. For these people, tourism is performing more and more of a service by improving physical and mental health.

To the author, the social justice dimension of sustainable tourism demands that:

- we use tourism wherever possible to sustain and enhance the quality of life of tourists
- we develop tourism products that help sustain destinations and meet the needs of the tourist for physical relaxation and mental stimulation and escapism.

Thus we can see that sustainable tourism in the future might involve providing:

- all aspects of health tourism, from health 'farms' to specialist spas
- study holidays
- spiritual holidays such as visits to monastic retreats like Mount Athos in Greece
- fantasy virtual reality experiences.

At the same time, the idea of social justice implicit in sustainable tourism also implies more resources being devoted to so-called social tourism which opens up holiday opportunities for the disadvantaged in society whose need for a break is probably greater than anyone else's.

Conclusions

We have seen that the simplistic view that tourists are simply the cause of the problems which lead to the need for sustainable tourism, is not helpful. It is clear that tourists bring benefits as well as problems and that

as well as responsibilities, they should also have rights. The author has also criticized the concept of the 'good tourist' and has argued that the sustainable tourism debate should also embrace the issues of sustaining the market in destinations and the quality of life of tourists.

At the end of this chapter, the author wishes to reiterate his view that sustainable tourism cannot be achieved without the active support of tourists. We must therefore focus more attention on tourists in the sustainable tourism debate.

Discussion Points and Essay Questions

1. Discuss the contention that it is unreasonable to expect tourists to behave responsibly while on holiday.
2. Critically evaluate the range of proposed rights for tourists outlined in Table 13.1.
3. Discuss the arguments for and against the concept of the 'good tourist'.

Exercise

Carry out a brief survey of tourists to see to what extent they believe that tourists should accept the responsibilities outlined in Boxes 13.1 and 13.2.

Case Study: the Rights and Responsibilities of Tourists

According to the World Tourism Organization

In 1985 the General Assembly of the World Tourism Organization (WTO) set out the principles it felt should underpin a proposed **Tourism Bill of Rights and Tourist Code**.

The participants at this event re-stated the:

> fundamental right of everyone, as guaranteed by the Universal Declaration of Human Rights, to rest, leisure, and periodic holidays with pay, and to use them for holiday purposes, to travel freely for education and pleasure.

Other sections of the Tourism Bill of Rights speak of the need to:

- facilitate contact between visitors and host communities with a view to their mutual understanding and betterment
- ensure the safety of visitors
- afford the best possible conditions of hygiene
- not allow any discriminatory measures in regard to tourists
- receive tourists with the greatest possible honesty, and respect.

The WTO also devised a Tourist Code which includes the following sections.

Article X

Tourists should, by their behaviour, foster understanding and friendly relations among peoples, at both the national and international levels, and thus contribute to lasting peace.

Article XI

- At places of transit and sojourn, tourists must respect the established political, social, moral and religious order and comply with the legislation and regulations in force.
- In these places, tourists must also:
  (i)   show the greatest understanding for the customs, beliefs, and behaviour of the host communities, and the greatest respect for their natural and cultural heritage;
  (ii)   refrain from accentuating the economic, social and cultural differences between themselves and the local population;
  (iii) be receptive to the culture of the host communities, which is an integral part of the common human heritage;
  (iv) refrain from exploiting others for prostitution purposes; and
  (v)   refrain from trafficking in, carrying or using narcotics and/or other prohibited drugs.

Article XII

During their travel from one country to another and within the host country, tourists should be able, by appropriate government measures, to benefit from:

- relaxation of administrative and financial controls; and
- the best possible conditions of transport and sojourn that can be offered by suppliers of tourism services.

Article XIII

- Tourists should be afforded free access, both within and outside their countries, to sites and places of tourist interest, and, subject to existing regulations and limitations, freedom of movement in places of transit and sojourn.
- On access to sites and places of tourist interest and throughout their transit and sojourn, tourists should be able to benefit from:
  (i)   objective, precise, and complete information on conditions and facilities provided during their travel and sojourn by official tourism bodies and suppliers of tourism services;
  (ii)   safety of their persons, security of their belongings and protection of their rights as consumers;
  (iii) satisfactory public hygiene, particularly so far as accommodation, catering and transport are concerned, information on the effective prevention of communicable diseases and accidents and ready access to health services;
  (iv)   access to swift and efficient public communications, both internal and external;
  (v)   administrative and legal procedures and guarantees necessary for the protection of their rights; and
  (vi)   the practice of their own religion and the use of existing facilities for that purpose.

Article XIV

Everyone is entitled to make his needs known to legislative representatives and public authorities so that he may exercise his right to rest and leisure in order to enjoy the benefits of tourism under the most favourable conditions and, where appropriate and to the extent consistent with law, associate with others for that purpose.

Conclusions to Part Three

In Part Three we have seen that there are many stakeholders in sustainable tourism, many of whom have conflicting interests and motivations.

However the trend is towards the idea of partnership as we can see from the following model, showing some of these stakeholders:

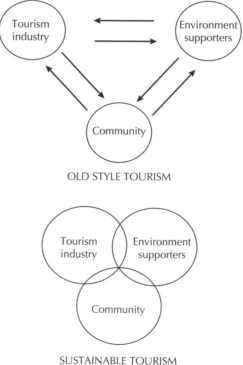

(World Tourism Organisation, 1993)

Interestingly, this model does not specifically refer to tourists as a group of stakeholders. It also excludes the public sector as a key stakeholder. According to Part Three of this book there should be more than three circles in these models, to represent the different stake-holders, notably:

- the public sector
- the tourism industry
- the voluntary sector
- the host community
- the media
- the tourist

We have noted that each of these stakeholders has a number of rights and responsibilities. This is a particularly important idea given that in general:

- there is much talk about the responsibilities of tourists but little about their rights
- host communities are often assumed to have rights but not necessarily responsibilities.

In an ideal world, of course, the aim would be to have not three or six interlocking circles, but rather, one circle which contains all the stakeholders.

Part Four

Sustainable Tourism and Different Geographical Milieux

The six chapters in Part Four explore the concept of sustainable tourism in relation to different geographical milieux, as follows:

(i)   coastal areas and marine environments
(ii) rural areas
(iii) urban areas
(iv) mountainous areas
(v)   islands
(vi) developing countries.

We will see how in some of these milieux, the emphasis is on managing the pressures caused by large-scale tourism, while in others, the focus is on developing tourism and helping it grow. At the same time, an attempt will be made to identify similarities and differences in techniques and issues between the six different milieux.

14

Coastal Areas and the Sea

There is little doubt that much of the impetus for the interest in sustainable tourism grew out of the concern felt over the worst excesses of coastal tourism. Many commentators have said that the large-scale development we have seen from Benidorm to Bali is not sustainable. At the same time, many traditional northern European seaside resorts appear to be in decline, unable, it seems, to keep up with changes in consumer tastes.

In this chapter, therefore, we will consider:

- how new coastal resorts can be developed in ways which are more sustainable
- the regeneration of established seaside destinations.

However, we also have to acknowledge that in recent years, tourism has also taken to the open sea in a big way. Not only has the cruise business experienced a renaissance, but tourists are now taking to the sea for diving holidays, sailing trips and whale-watching. This marine tourism has brought its own problems which we will also discuss in this chapter.

Tourists make great use of the coast and the marine environment these days, as part of their vacation, as can be seen from Fig. 14.1.

The Development of New Coastal Resorts

The conventional wisdom appears to be that the resorts of the Spanish coast symbolize the worst aspects of coastal resort development in tourism. It is important, therefore, that we analyse what are perceived to be the main problems with such developments. They include the following:

- developments which are seen to be too large in scale, in other words, their scale is not appropriate to the location
- high-rise styles of architecture which are out of place and at odds with traditional local building styles
- the infrastructure often lags behind the building development with the result that water pollution occurs
- the inflationary effect they have on land prices
- the ways in which they have a major impact on local culture and society.

These effects are even more extreme if the resort is in a developing country. For example, Wall has highlighted the problems caused by unplanned resorts like Kita on Bali. The problems identified by Wall (in Harrison and Husbands, 1996) include:

- traffic congestion
- air pollution

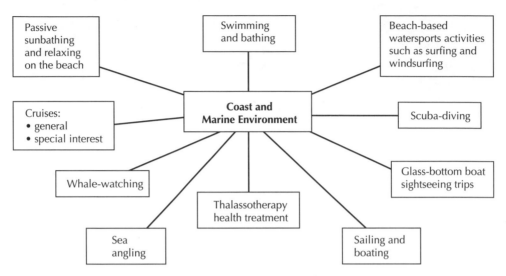

Fig. 14.1. The different uses of the coast and marine environment by tourists.

- noise pollution
- new building which is in conflict with the traditional, religious-based architectural styles of the area
- flooding after rains because of inadequate sewers
- the risk of contamination of the water supply
- beach erosion resulting from the extension of the airport runway.

Wall contrasts Kita in Bali, with the development of the Nusa Dua resort on Bali. Development has been planned by the state-controlled Bali Tourism Development Corporation. As Wall says,

> The resort was built in areas with limited agricultural capabilities and a conscious effort was made to minimise possible adverse effects on Balinese lifestyles by isolating development from the main settlements on the island ... Care was taken to maintain the environment at a high quality. (Wall in Harrison and Husbands, 1996)

However, developments like Nusa Dua also raise questions in relation to the concept of sustainability. They are often

- aimed at the luxury end of the market

rather than accommodating demand at the lower end of the market
- developed in a way which does not allow access to the site for the local community
- designed to offer all-inclusive vacations or at best to keep tourists on site, spending all their money in the resort itself. This can reduce the opportunities for small local enterprises to make a living selling goods and services to tourists
- too large to be accommodated easily within the local environment.

Nevertheless, they do provide employment; and can help stimulate development by leading to improvements in the local transport infrastructure.

Hamzah, in an interesting study of the development of small-scale island resorts in Malaysia (Stabler, 1997), has outlined several useful ideas in terms of how new resort complexes should be developed. Hamzah itemizes the cost of unplanned development as habitat depletion, economic leakage, displacement of the local community, breakdown of traditional values and conflict over limited resources. He goes on to elucidate several principles. These included:

- greater emphasis on tourism in local plans

- the idea that 'small-scale tourism development should not be solely concerned with the provision of accommodation but also with the development of the other intangible aspects of the tourism product, for example, local materials to produce handicrafts and commercial farming to supply fresh [produce] to the islands'
- regular dialogue with the local community
- improving the local community's share in future development, through investment opportunities for local entrepreneurs and joint ventures which bring a share of the benefits for the local community
- improving collaboration between government agencies and local operators.

These points are as relevant in the developing resorts of Turkey, the Caribbean and the Middle East as they are in South-East Asia.

Rejuvenating Existing Coastal Resorts

The other aspect of sustainability in relation to coastal resorts is the need to sustain or rejuvenate existing coastal resorts. Once a resort is developed, it is vital to maintain its position or the result could be dereliction, lost jobs and wasted resources. Sustainable tourism is, therefore, about trying to maintain the appeal of existing resorts to tourists and enhance the quality of both their environment and the tourism they attract.

In recent years, many well-established resorts have apparently reached the saturation and decline stages of the product life cycle. Strenuous efforts have therefore been made to try to rejuvenate or re-launch those resorts. Some examples will serve to illustrate this point, as follows:

- casinos have been built to attract new tourists to resorts such as Atlantic City in the USA, and Scheveningen in The Netherlands
- attempts have been made to develop new markets such as convention tourism in UK resorts like Brighton and Bournemouth.

As can be seen from the case study of Benidorm at the end of this chapter, the key elements in the rejuvenation of traditional, existing resorts are:

- environmental improvement
- attracting new, better quality markets
- new product development.

Indeed, Spain offers an excellent example as a whole, of approaches to rejuvenating resorts which are in danger of decline.

In 1991 Morgan highlighted five problems with Majorca as a destination which could also be said to have applied to other Spanish coastal resorts. They were as follows (Morgan, 1991):

- overdependence on the UK and German markets
- overdependence on the UK inclusive tourism market offering a high volume but low yield
- excess supply (60%) of accommodation in the one to three star categories
- environmental deterioration, particularly as a result of hotel construction, with many developments permitted close to the beach
- a negative image.

However, action was then taken by the public sector in partnership with the tourism industry. Measures included (Hunter-Jones et al. in Stabler, 1997):

- a reduction in bed space capacity through building licenses and hotel inspections (to improve overall quality)
- restrictions on the location and height of new hotel developments
- beach upgrading schemes
- traffic management projects
- development of new markets by diversifying the consumer type and the country of origin
- a range of conservation projects.

Similar schemes were seen across mainland Spain and in the Canary Islands.

It is common now to see the moves towards greater sustainability on the part of established resorts being linked with the idea of quality tourism. This is a useful term which seems to encompass:

- environmental quality
- the quality of tourism policy planning and management
- the quality of the product and service delivery
- the quality of the tourist.

It is this latter issue which is particularly controversial. Quality tourist seems to mean high-spending tourists. Resorts no longer seem to want to encourage visits by low-spending package tourists, yet it was for this market that the resorts were developed. These people will not go away, so who will accommodate these people in the future? We must be careful that sustainability and quality does not become an excuse for discrimination and social segregation.

As time goes on and more of the coast of the world is developed for tourism, the rejuvenation of existing resorts will perhaps become the major concern in relation to coastal tourism.

Marine Tourism

Tourists these days are not content simply to stay on the beach watching the sea. Today they want to make the sea itself their destination through, for example:

- cruises
- sailing and boating holidays
- diving holidays
- sea angling
- whale watching.

In general, it has to be said that tourism and the marine environment are not easy bedfellows – over-use of the sea by tourists can result in:

- pollution by fuel
- disturbance to wildlife and even decimation of particular species

- the theft and destruction of coral and sponges.

Yet, all of the five types of holidays outlined above are growing at the moment.

To date, academics and politicians have paid relatively little attention to marine tourism. It is new, and often no one is responsible for managing the open sea, so it is hard to implement action to achieve more sustainable forms of marine tourism.

One of the greatest areas of concern in marine tourism relates to scuba diving. Davis and Harriott, in 1996, produced an interesting study of the conflict involved in diving holidays in a protected marine environment in eastern Australia. By definition, scuba diving is most popular in marine ecosystems which are rich in flora and fauna and fragile at the same time. It often happens in places which are supposed to be under some form of protection. Yet the major threat to the protection usually comes from the scuba divers themselves.

The authors argued that a range of initiatives might be taken to minimize the damage, as follows (Davis and Harriott in Harrison and Husbands, 1996):

- determining the carrying capacity
- defining the 'limits of acceptable change'
- encouragement of more sensitive practices by divers
- providing mooring buoys for the boats used by divers rather than relying on anchors which damage the coral
- measures to reduce conflict between divers and swimmers
- charging fees, the revenue from which could then be used to fund research and management schemes
- providing an artificial reef and/or alternative site to spread diver pressure.

Cruise Tourism

The cruise is currently going through a period of renaissance with new vessels being launched and sailing to ever more exotic places. Cruise ships are, in effect, floating all-inclusive resort complexes. In sustainability terms, they pose two major problems:

- They may cause environmental change, such as pollution from fuel leaks while cruising in areas of water where the ecosystem is particularly fragile, such as Alaska and Antarctica.
- The fact that they visit each piece of coast for a relatively short time so that tourists can spend only a limited amount of money in the destination. At the same time, they tend to focus on 'honey-pot' ports which can lead to the crowding of anchorages. It also gives passengers little chance to truly discover a place.

Conversely, tax revenue from cruise passengers can be a vital element in the income of governments in small islands and developing countries. It can be estimated for example, that in the mid-1990s taxes paid by cruise passengers contributed around £500,000 to the Treasury of the Island of Aruba, £2.8 million to Jamaica, and up to £20 million for the Bahamas.

We need therefore, to find more sustainable ways of managing cruise tourism in the future.

Sea Angling

Sea angling and game fishing are now a major attraction from Ireland to the Caribbean. On the face of it, this activity would seem to be the antitheses of sustainable tourism, involving as it does the hunting, and usually the death of all kinds of fish, from mackerel to sharks. Yet, at the same time, it brings social and economic benefits, by utilizing fishing boats and providing jobs for fishermen that probably pay more than commercial fishing ever did.

As always, what appears in sustainable tourism to be a simple choice between black and white, turns out to be a case of shades of grey.

Conclusions

The coast has long been an attraction for tourists and still is today. That is why the challenge is to rejuvenate traditional coastal resorts and develop new seaside destinations in ways which show we have learned the lessons from our past experience. It is also clear from this chapter that we have a new and growing challenge, namely the rise of marine tourism. This development will ensure that the coast and the sea continues to be at the forefront of the debate over sustainable tourism.

Discussion Points and Essay Questions

1. Briefly discuss each of the types of tourism outlined in Fig. 14.1 in terms of the extent to which they can be sustainable.
2. Devise a code of conduct for *either* cruise tourism or scuba diving.
3. Discuss the principles which should underpin the development of any new coastal tourism resort.

Exercise

Select an existing seaside resort with which you are familiar that appears to be showing signs of stagnation or decline. Then devise a rejuvenation strategy for your chosen resort which is in line with the principles of sustainable tourism.

Case Study: Benidorm – the Rejuvenation of a Resort

In the late 1980s, many commentators were predicting the demise of Benidorm as a popular resort. It was felt it was out of step with trends in tourist behaviour and would lose out to newer forms of tourism and more sensitively designed resorts. It was felt that Benidorm would attract ever smaller numbers of low-spending, poor quality tourists in a slow process of decline.

However, the reality has been very different. Benidorm is flourishing at the moment because of several factors including the following:

- The public sector has invested considerable sums of money in environmental improvements, particularly beach cleaning and the creation of an attractive new high-quality promenade.
- Many hotels have undergone extensive refurbishment.
- New attractions have been developed such as amusement parks.
- The resort has been very successful in attracting winter-sun holidaymakers from northern Europe.
- Benidorm has also succeeded in obtaining a high share of the European equivalent of the American 'snowbird' market. Large numbers of older northern Europeans now spend the whole winter in Benidorm. Their presence helps hotels open all year round so that jobs can be permanent rather than seasonal.
- The resort has successfully tapped into newly emerging markets such as Russia. It now receives many high-spending Russian tourists who shop and gamble and buy property. In this way it is reducing its dependence on the UK and German markets.
- Marketing Benidorm as a venue for conventions that bring in a different, higher-spending market segment.

In these ways, Benidorm has rejuvenated itself without seeking to exclude those tourists on whom it built its early success.

Benidorm offers its tourists a good deal, and levels of satisfaction are very high. By providing low priced long-stay winter holidays for older northern Europeans it is almost performing a social service. In November 1996, the author interviewed a number of such tourists in Benidorm who said that their time in Benidorm helped them in a number of ways, notably:

- reducing health problems such as arthritis, because of the warmer, drier climate
- providing them with an opportunity to make new friends
- giving them a living environment in which they felt safer than they did in their own country
- reducing their cost of living because of the low cost of the holiday and the fact that they were not paying expensive heating bills as they would have done at home.

We can see, therefore, that the regeneration of Benidorm has benefited tourists as well as the resort. Surely, such mutually beneficial action is in the true spirit of sustainable tourism.

15

Rural Areas

The debate over sustainable tourism in rural areas seems to focus on two alternative scenarios:

- those areas which already receive large numbers of tourists. Here the emphasis is on managing tourism pressure to prevent irreparable harm being done to the environment and the host community
- those areas where the traditional rural economy and society is declining due to factors such as agricultural change and de-population. Here, tourism is seen as a potential saviour, providing jobs and extra income for farmers and locals.

The Importance of Rural Areas

In many countries, rural areas hold a special place in the culture of the country and the psyche of its people. This is hardly surprising given that it is the countryside which has traditionally provided the most basic human need, food. Furthermore, every economy and society, no matter how sophisticated and urbanized they have become, began as an agrarian rural society. Rurality is the seed from which all civilizations have grown.

However, the countryside is viewed in different ways in different countries. In heavily industrialized, urbanized countries, rural areas are viewed as lost worlds where life was simple and idyllic, which now provide playgrounds where urban dwellers can seek an antidote to the ills of modern urban living. They may be seen as timeless places where any change is to be resisted and the main priority is the protection of the physical environment.

To people in rural or recently industrialized countries, the countryside is part of their roots for they may still live in a rural area, or if they are urban dwellers, they may well have been born in the countryside. Rurality is linked to their family history and the countryside is seen as a place to live and work, where the physical environment is merely a setting for these activities. Their view is based on the reality of modern rural life which they may have experienced at first hand. They may have been forced to leave the countryside, or have chosen to leave, because of the lack of employment, housing or social opportunities.

For such people, healthy rural areas might mean ones which are alive with economic and social activity, rather than ones which are physically well preserved, but which lack dynamism, and are more like museums.

Having talked in general terms, we shall now focus on Europe, with particular reference to the French experience.

The Rural Crisis in Europe

Rural regions in Europe are under perhaps unprecedented pressure from a wide range of sources that are bringing change on a massive scale. These pressures are leading to a critical situation in some rural regions where commentators fear that we may be witnessing the death of certain areas of countryside altogether, particularly in the remoter regions.

These pressures are numerous but particularly include:

- continued de-population, particularly amongst the younger, better educated and the economically active
- changes in state and European Union policies on agriculture and agricultural subsidies
- developments in agricultural technology
- the increasing power of food manufacturers and retailers
- the influx of urban dwellers into the countryside, either as permanent immigrants or as second home owners.

The Role of Tourism in Rural Areas in Europe

Tourism developed in the rural regions of northern Europe, in particular, largely as a result of the desire of urban dwellers for countryside recreation. However, in due course, tourism also came to be seen by governments as a potentially valuable tool for rural development in many European countries. Therefore, for many years, rural tourism in Europe has been shaped by two different sets of forces, namely the wishes of individual private citizens and the actions of the public sector acting in the interest of the wider public good.

Depending on the situation in a specific country, tourism policy tends to take two major forms:

- a focus on visitor management in areas where tourist numbers are great, with the aim of protecting the physical environment from the negative impacts of over-use by tourists
- a concentration on developing tourism and attracting more tourists to increase the economic benefits that tourism can bring to rural areas, particularly those with serious social and economic problems.

Managing Tourist Pressure in Rural Areas

In those rural areas where tourism is already on a large scale, the challenge is to manage the process. Tourism can clearly cause major problems in rural areas that threaten the concept of sustainable tourism.

Social and Economic Problems: the Case of France

In rural tourism in those areas of France which are the most visited, notably the Dordogne and Provence, social and economic problems have emerged including the following.

Geographical Concentration

Visitors to rural France are not evenly distributed across the country. Instead they are highly concentrated in small geographical areas, notably the Perigord and Quercy provinces and Provence, while adjacent areas welcome far fewer tourists. This geographical concentration is particularly true of foreign tourists. This concentration causes congestion and makes everyday life much more difficult for local people and puts great pressure on infrastructure and valuable resources, such as water. And in terms of rural development and regeneration, the heaviest concentrations of rural tourism tend not to be in the areas which are most in need of the economic benefits that tourism can bring, but rather are in the relatively prosperous rural regions generally.

Temporal Concentration

Most tourists visit the countryside in the peak summer months, particularly French visitors. Thus for a brief period, rural communities are swamped by tourists and then hardly any tourists are seen for the next 10 months. This means that for much of the year, infrastructure which has to be built to accommodate tourists' needs is under-used. Such seasonality also prevents the creation of permanent jobs in tourism which limits the social and economic benefits which tourism can bring to rural communities.

Lack of Local Control and the Leakage of Benefits

As the market for holidays in rural France has grown, tour operators based outside the rural regions, and perhaps outside the country, have become increasingly involved. This has often resulted in a loss of local control and the leakage of potential benefits away from the host community.

Gaps between Supply and Demand

As demand has grown for rural self-catering accommodation and consumer expectations have risen, gîtes have not kept pace, either in terms of quantity or quality. They are too simple for the tastes of many modern tourists who want more luxury, even though this is hardly compatible with the idea of enjoying the simple rural life. In a survey carried out in June 1994, by the author and Meg Wild, many British tour operators claimed that gîtes were not of a high enough standard for the British market. And even if they are acceptable on quality grounds, there are not enough of them. Therefore, many tourists are renting cottages owned by people who do not live in the host community so that the rent they pay is largely lost to the local economy.

Lack of Interaction between Hosts and Visitors

Many visitors appear to see rural France as a leisure resource to be enjoyed, but make few attempts to interact with the local community. They remain outsiders who exploit the local area for their pleasure, rather than looking at what they can contribute to the local community in return for their pleasure.

Foreign-owned Second Homes and Foreign In-migrants

Literally tens of thousands of foreigners have bought second homes in the French countryside, or have moved permanently to rural France. Whilst in many cases these people have been a positive force, they can also cause problems. Some have antagonized the host community by using people from their own country to help them buy their property and renovate it, rather than using local professionals and trades people. They may have refurbished their property in ways which are not in keeping with vernacular architectural traditions. In some cases, these people are either unwilling, or unable because of a lack of language skills, to become integrated into the local community. Finally, the fact that foreigners tend to congregate in small geographical areas means that local indigenous residents in these areas begin to feel that they are being squeezed out of their own community by these newcomers. For example, there are perhaps 5000 Britons alone living in the Dordogne, while several villages in the Lot probably have enough foreign residents to be able to elect a British or Dutch mayor.

Visitors' Unrealistic Perceptions of Rural France

Many tourists appear to have unrealistic and over-romantic views of modern rural France. These are reinforced by media images of the French countryside and the images conveyed in brochures produced by tourism organizations. Thus, visitors do not understand the problems of rural France, nor the impact which their presence has on the French countryside. Unless tourists are conscious of such issues, it is hard to see how they can ever contribute towards the development of sustainable rural tourism.

Environmental Problems: the Peak District, UK

As arguably the world's most visited national park, with well over 20 million visits per year, it is not surprising that the Peak District exhibits a range of environmental problems as a result of its heavy use by tourists. These problems include:

- footpath erosion caused by people, horses and mountain bikes, notably the Pennine Way which has had to be re-surfaced and where alternative routes have had to be provided
- traffic congestion and pollution due to the fact that the vast majority of visitors to villages like Castleton, use their car
- damage to delicate ecosystems such as the peat moorlands
- fire damage to the vegetation, partic-ularly as a result of camping and vandalism
- damage to rockfaces from the activities of the rock climbers who use artificial aids
- the trampling of vegetation to the pick-ing of flowers Such issues as these are seen in most rural areas that are heavily visited by tourists.

However, the author believes that in some cases the problems outlined above are not always seen in proportion. In the Peak Dis-trict, footpath erosion is seen as a major problem for the National Park Authority. At the same time, the area is blighted by mas-sive quarries, many people are unemployed and farms are going bankrupt. Given these problems, footpath erosion does not seem, or should not be seen, as a high priority.

A Lost Cause?

At the same time, the author argues that often there is little or nothing that can be done to solve these problems. They are the result of factors which no tourism or national park agency can reverse. For example,

- some of the villages in France are in terminal decline and, without tourism, will simply become empty and the farm-land will go through the process of 'desertification' and become wasteland. While some argue that returning the land to a wild state would be a good

idea, it is likely that the rural commu-nities would not agree with such a view
- the use of private cars in the Peak Dis-trict has not declined – instead it has increased – in spite of numerous traffic management and public transport inno-vations which have been in place for nearly 30 years.

Perhaps, therefore, we should accept that while we may wish to ameliorate the prob-lems outlined above, our main emphasis should be on developing tourism in areas which are not currently visited but which need the economic benefits which tourism can bring.

Sustainable Tourism as a Development Tool for Rural Areas

Tourism can play a positive role in diversi-fying and developing the economy of rural areas where traditional activities like agri-culture are in decline, salaries are low and depopulation rife. Again France offers excellent examples of this phenomenon.

Successful Rural Tourism Initiatives in France

The French government has long recognized the value of tourism as a means of develop-ing and regenerating rural regions. Since the 1950s it has taken a pro-active approach to the development of rural tourism. Many of its initiatives have been in sympathy with the principles of sustainable tourism.

There are a number of well-established examples of successful, public sector inspired, rural tourism initiatives which include the following.

Gîtes

These are generally redundant farm build-ings, which are converted to offer simple self-catering accommodation for tourists and provide an additional source of income for farmers and other rural dwellers. In some areas, revenue from letting just one gîte can contribute up to a third of household income. Public sector bodies provide grant aid for the conversion of gîtes, providing they are refurbished in a manner which respects the architectural traditions of the locality. The gîtes are marketed by governmental agencies in France, and abroad. Specialist gîtes have been developed for horse-riders, walkers, skiers or even children taking holidays separately from their parents. Although there are more than 40,000 gîtes in France, demand exceeds supply so that many are booked a year in advance, and few are available by Christmas for the following summer season.

Logis de France

This concept was developed by the government in 1949, with the aim of creating a chain of Logis, good quality small rural hotels, that reflected the character of the local area. Prices were meant to be modest and the restaurants were supposed to be based on the gastronomic tradition of the area. There are now more than 4300 Logis, all controlled by a national quality charter, and they are marketed throughout the world.

Chambres d'Hôtes

Farmers and other rural residents are encouraged to open up their homes to provide accommodation for tourists along the lines of British 'bed and breakfast' establishments. This provides a valuable source of additional income for the household, while public sector grants are available for converting parts of people's houses to create guest bedrooms.

Fermes-Auberges

Farmers are being persuaded to provide meals for tourists in their homes, offering traditional local dishes made from fresh local ingredients. As well as providing an extra source of income for farm households, it provides a market for farm produce and conserves the distinctive gastronomic traditions of the area.

Food and Drink as Heritage

In many areas, traditional foods and drink are exploited as a tourist attraction, through visits to farms and themed trails. These are often linked to direct selling from the producer to the customer. In this way, sales are often increased, and the image of the product, and brand loyalty to it, are enhanced.

Crafts

Traditional crafts are used as an attraction for tourists through groups of crafts people who run cooperative marketing campaigns. These crafts can be diverse and may range from distilling to pottery and from cheese-making to basket-making.

Ecomusées

These are museums where the emphasis is on interpreting local heritage in an authentic manner. They tend to either focus on a specific area of the countryside or follow a particular theme such as the textile industry or agriculture.

Loisirs Accueil

Many local authorities (Conseils Génerals) have set up booking services so that visitors can book special interest and activity holidays, as well as accommodation. They are linked to each other by computer reservation systems and are connected to the Amadeus network, giving them access to over 3300 point-of-sale outlets.

These initiatives are largely a result of the efforts of government agencies and statutory bodies. However, voluntary groups have also played a part in the development of the rural tourism product, particularly in terms of special events. Perhaps the best example is the Cinéscénie at the Puy du Fou, in the Vendée, in the west of France, where most evenings in the summer, 650 local people recreate scenes from the history of the area in a spectacular show. The income generated by the event is then used to fund projects which benefit from the local community such as the financing of a local radio station and providing funding for local students who wish to study in colleges outside the area.

The lessons of the French experience are influencing the development of rural tourism in other regions of Europe which are seeking to use sustainable tourism as a rural development tool, including:

- Spain, notably the La Rioja region, where a LEADER programme to develop more rural tourism was discussed by Zarza (in Bramwell *et al.*, 1996)
- Northern Portugal particularly in the Alto Minho area
- Eastern Europe, particularly Poland, Hungary and the Czech Republic
- Islands such as Majorca and Cyprus.

The latter has been discussed by Godfrey in *Practising Responsible Tourism*, edited by Harrison and Husbands (1996), and is the subject of a case study at the end of this chapter.

Understanding the Consumer – the Key to Success

Wherever attempts are made to develop sustainable forms of rural tourism which in turn stimulates sustainable rural development, the approach will be consumer-led. Too often rural tourism development in the past has been resisted by planners and public sector agencies with little real knowledge of tourism. Tourism has often been seen as a problem and the tourist is the core of this problem. Now that many areas are trying to attract tourists for the social or economic benefits they can bring, there is a need for a change of attitude. Tourism needs to be encouraged and the tourist valued and their needs respected, or they will simply go elsewhere. The first stage of the process involves finding out what tourists want and recognizing that there are different market segments. For example:

- those who may see the countryside as a setting for physical exercise and a healthy life style
- people whose main interest is learning more about the culture and history of an area

- those who wish to feel that, temporarily, they become an accepted part of a rural community
- tourists whose main reason for visiting a specific rural area is that they have been invited to stay with friends and relatives who live there or own a second home there
- people who enjoy trying new experiences while on holiday in rural regions, and are seeking a holiday experience that is in stark contrast with their lives at home.

However, understanding these consumers is not as easy to do as one might think, because of some complications including:

- the fact that marketing research is quite poorly developed in rural tourism and we do not fully understand the complex reasons why tourists behave in a particular way
- tourists can often be apparently contradictory in what they say motivates them, while their behaviour seems to contradict this
- the attitudes and desires of tourists change and develop over time
- consumer behaviour is not the result simply of individuals following their desires, for all purchasing decisions are a compromise. Firstly, there are the compromises that have to be made between different people taking holidays together where the individual may need to modify their intentions to fit in with the wishes of other people in the group. Secondly, there is the fact that all purchasing decisions are a compromise between motivators and determinants such as available money and time.

The Marketing Mix

Once we understand the consumer, we can begin to look at how the 'marketing mix' may be manipulated to meet the desires of the tourists, and the objectives of achieving rural development and regeneration through tourism.

The rural tourism product is made up of a wide variety of elements which can be combined in a myriad of ways. Some of the main elements are as follows:

- types of attraction: natural features, man-made buildings and structures, special events, culture and life style
- types of accommodation: serviced (hotels, farmhouses, bed and breakfast, rural inns and guest houses), non-serviced/privately owned (second homes, caravans and tents), commercial non-serviced (cottages, holiday villages and villas)
- types of holiday: general or special interest, single centre or touring, passive or active
- types of transport: private car, ferry and private car, air and hire car, rail and car hire, rail and bike hire, bus and coach
- types of organization: organized package – group/individual independent travel.

These elements need to be combined in a way which leads to products that are attractive to consumers while being in keeping with the overall aims of sustainability and rural development and regeneration.

'Discover the Real Countryside' Holidays

One type of such a product might be what could loosely be termed, 'Discover the Real Countryside' holidays. The main components would be as follows:

- Visiting rural workplaces such as craft centres, farms and small factories to see how people in rural areas earn a living. This might in time develop to a point where visitors could participate more actively, perhaps, for example, by trying to make simple craft products themselves. In any event opportunities should exist to sell products direct to visitors.
- Taking part in everyday leisure activities in the countryside, such as traditional games, or more controversially but equally authentic, hunting and fishing.

- Trying local food and drink products and perhaps learning how to cook some traditional dishes.
- Listening to older people talking about what it was like to live in the area in the past, and talking to residents about what rural life is about today. It would be important for visitors to meet people whose main livelihood does not come from the tourism industry.
- As far as possible, eating and sleeping in people's homes, as a guest of families, and living as local people live. The emphasis should be on the needs of tourists being met by local small businesses or non-commercial establishments.
- Travelling as far as possible by greener forms of transport (bicycle, foot, horse, canal boat) so that the tourists do not worsen the environment any more than is absolutely necessary.

For this product to meet the broader objectives, it would have to follow some simple rules or guidelines including:

- Generally, the product should be created, managed and marketed by local people, who would decide what to show visitors. Local people must mean a cross-section of the community rather than just a few community leaders.
- Numbers of visitors on each holiday should be limited to maintain the exclusivity and status value of the product for customers and to protect the host community from the problem of over-crowding.
- The product should be authentic, rather than being specifically created for the tourist.
- Communities in areas where the need for tourism is greatest and current levels of tourism are relatively low, should be particularly encouraged to develop such products, for tourists who might not normally go to an area would go to it to enjoy this 'unique' product.
- The product needs to be consciously different in each community and local differences need to be made a major

selling point. Otherwise if customers go to one such holiday, they will not see the point of going on another as they think the product will be the same.

- The relationship between visitor and host should be informal, and not a case of servant and master, otherwise resentment of the tourist will grow.
- As many people as possible should be involved in meeting the tourist and looking after them so that as many people as possible receive some economic benefits from the visitors as well as the social pleasure of meeting new people.
- The duration of trips should be relatively short and should be seen as a second or third annual holiday of perhaps 3 or 4 days duration.
- The organization of the holiday should be like a loose, flexible package so that it does not feel like a 'package' holiday. This product would be in line with current trends in the market and would achieve the wider objectives.

Other types of product in this category might include the following:

- Activity holidays that utilize the area's physical environment but which build in education for visitors and good practice on how to conserve this environment while at the same time enjoying it.
- Special interest holidays including language courses, painting and cooking holidays for example. Again these should be of a broader type than is normal with more commercial products, so that visitors learn more about the area in depth.
- Touring holidays that make use of public transport or non-polluting forms of transport and take visitors to less touristy areas where the need for the economic benefits of tourist are the greatest.

A number of general points could be made about the pre-requisites of success for any of these products. Firstly, quality is all important and quality will be defined by customers as how far they feel they really have been shown the 'real' countryside. In addition, they will highly value informal contact with local people whose life style is substantially different to their own. Secondly, the product will need to develop a clear brand image that is recognized by the target market. This means, thirdly, that the target market for each product must be defined and identified.

Fourthly, service must not be like in the major tourism corporations. It must not be formalized and sloganized as in the mechanical and ubiquitous phrases 'Have a nice day!' and 'How may I help you?' It should be friendly and personal and visitors should be encouraged to join in, like a member of a family, so that they serve themselves. Lastly, but perhaps most importantly, the product must be as unique as possible, so that it is not available anywhere else.

In addition to these combined package holiday products, there is a need to focus on product development within the individual elements of the tourism product. It is particularly important to develop businesses which are locally managed and controlled, to supply the services which visitors require to reduce the leakage of benefit to organizations based outside the area. This might mean trying to develop the following elements of the product in many rural areas:

- attractions which interpret heritage themes and which charge for entry, so that income is generated for the local community
- local integrated transport networks that link the mode or modes of transport used to travel from the tourists' home to the rural region, with the mode of transport used within the region
- the development of communally owned accommodation for visitors, perhaps on the model of the Edda hotels in Iceland or the communal gîtes in France. The first type ensures that school premises are used in the summer vacations while the other provides an income for the municipality
- retail outlets for local products, possibly organized on a cooperative basis.

These are just a few examples of possible product developments. Many of these ideas are not new but looking at them as part of an integrated, holistic, approach is rather novel.

Conclusions

In this chapter we have focused on rural tourism in Europe where this form of tourism is particularly highly developed. The issues and ideas we have discussed are also applicable, with appropriate modifications to allow for national and cultural differences, to other developed countries such as the USA, Canada and Australia.

The situation in developing or recently developed countries is somewhat different, as we will see in Chapter 19.

In many cases the problems caused by mass rural tourism in well-established countryside destinations are either overstated and/or insoluble. Instead, we should focus on those areas where tourism can play a positive role in rural development, providing that a consumer-led approach is adopted.

Discussion Points and Essay Questions

1. Evaluate the difficulties that are likely to be encountered by those destinations seeking to develop more sustainable forms of rural tourism.
2. Discuss the suggestion that the problems caused by rural tourism are often exaggerated.
3. Discuss the advantages and disadvantages of the 'Discover the Real Countryside' holidays concept outlined in this chapter.

Exercise

Choose a rural area with which you are familiar and devise a package, like the 'Discover the Real Countryside' holidays, discussed in this chapter. Your report should detail the marketing mix, i.e. the product, price, distribution and promotion.

Case Study: the Akamas Peninsula, Cyprus

Cyprus is well known as a coastal tourism destination but in 1991 the government's tourism agency, the Cyprus Tourist Organization, launched its rural tourism initiative. This was designed to:

- provide tourist accommodation and facilities in 50 hill settlements
- attract visitors away from the coast
- help stimulate village economies.
  (Godfrey in Harrison and Husbands, 1996)

Clearly, therefore, the aims of this programme were a mixture, trying to solve over-crowding problems at the coast, while diversifying the tourism market and bringing economic benefits to the villages.

One of the projects developed under this initiative was in the remote Akamas Peninsula in north-west Cyprus. This area is rich in wildlife, has a distinctive landscape and a diverse, cultural heritage. It also has nesting sites for the rare loggerhead and green turtles.

After the Turkish invasion in 1974, the area's economy and population declined dramatically. The government has, since then, sought to develop this region. From the late 1980s tourism has been a major element in this policy.

The strategy developed for the Akamas had four main elements:

- the creation of a national park
- fiscal and investment incentives for rural tourism development in the villages
- conservation projects, particularly that at Lara Bay which was designed to protect the green turtle
- the development of new 'mild' forms of tourism, such as the Lara Project which was championed by Friends of the Earth.

However, there is little general agreement on how tourism should develop on the ground. Developers wish to exploit the opportunities while conservationists try to restrict their activities.

In the meantime, a form of ecotourism is threatening this fragile environment. Vehicles with four-wheel drive pour out from Paphos and other resorts to explore the areas, in spite of the poor quality roads.

Those who pioneered the idea of sustainable tourism used to criticize those who spent their whole holiday in concrete resorts, by the swimming pool or on the beach. They encouraged people to go out and explore the area, and find out more about local wildlife and cultures. Now it is exactly this type of activity which is threatening areas like the Akamas Peninsula.

The Akamas Peninsula case also highlights issues involved in centralized planning of sustainable tourism and the 'master planning' approach to sustainable tourism management, which gives little direct influence to local people for whose benefit the projects are supposed to be undertaken.

However, in terms of the role of Friends of the Earth, it also illustrates the dilemma of outside pressure groups seeking to go against the wishes of those in the local community who wish to see tourism developed for its economic and social benefits.

Case Study: Special Interest Tourism in the Gaeltacht areas of Ireland

Since the early days of the Republic of Ireland in the 1920s, the government has been keen to conserve the unique culture of the Irish-speaking, so-called Gaeltacht areas of Ireland. In recent years, tourism has played a role in this strategy to help reduce the pressure for de-population which would threaten the viability of these areas.

In line with the approach taken in Ireland as a whole, the emphasis has been on developing specialist forms of tourism which appeal to affluent niche markets. In the case of the Gaeltacht areas, this strategy has involved the development of products such as:

- crafts and small-scale production of high quality goods where tourists visit the factory and buy the products directly from the manufacturer. Examples include the McKahy pottery in the Dingle Peninsula
- Irish language and culture courses and events or centres such as Scoil Ach in Mayo
- horse-riding holidays which are found all over the Gaeltacht areas
- special interest themed trails such as the Pilgrims Trail which involves trailing on horseback, again in the Dingle Peninsula
- clan reunions, where people whose roots are in the different Gaeltacht areas gather for reunions
- angling packages involving fishing for freshwater, game and sea-water fish
- special interest holidays such as the art and drama run in the winter at the Wild Haven Hotel, in Achill
- literature-related tourism, for example, the 'James Joyce Country' in the Munster province
- environmental issue-related trips such as visiting the peatlands of Connemara, for example
- golfing holidays and day visits to the numerous golf courses which have been developed in the Gaeltacht areas.

In general all of these types of tourism tend to be relatively highly priced with low volumes of visitors.

However, we can perhaps distinguish two forms of product here:

- those products which are concerned with increasing tourist interest in, and knowledge of, the destination
- those products which exploit the areas' resources but involve little or no involvement with the local culture and natural environment, such as golf.

It could be argued that the former is the more sustainable and ethical form of tourism because it is rooted, and place-specific.

More details on tourism in the Gaeltacht is provided in *From the Bottom Up* by Convery *et al.* (1994).

16

Urban Areas

Urban areas receive relatively little attention in the sustainable tourism debate, in comparison to the coast and the countryside. Yet, cities such as Rome and Venice have been attracting tourists for centuries while, every year, new urban destinations try to launch themselves into the international tourism market.

Traditionally, the main concern over sustainable tourism in towns and cities has focused upon the problem of managing the pressure of large tourist numbers in historic cities with fragile built environments. Numerous conferences and reports have sought solutions to the congestion of people and traffic which harms the physical fabric, and destroys the atmosphere in such places.

However, in recent years, the decline of traditional industries in many cities in the developed world has led to government agencies seeking to use tourism to spearhead the regeneration of these cities. New visitor attractions and festivals have been used to try to revive the fortunes of cities from New York and Baltimore to Liverpool and Bradford.

Within this chapter we will also draw attention to two other aspects of sustainable urban tourism, namely the contribution of events and festivals in urban tourism, and the role of business tourism in the regeneration of major towns and cities.

Finally, we will also look at the role of tourism in major cities such as London, Paris and New York in relation to issues such as authenticity and the distribution of the benefits of tourism.

Let us begin by looking at the negative side of urban tourism, namely, its impacts on historic towns and cities.

Managing Tourist Pressures in Historic Towns and Cities

The rise of heritage and cultural tourism has seen ever greater pressure placed on historic towns and cities, particularly in Europe. The rapid growth in tourist numbers in these towns and cities has caused great problems for they are now often trying to cope with more visitors than ever before, and furthermore, the tourists are concentrated in selected parts of the city or town only and on particular days of the year.

This results in a number of problems, including the following:

- damage to buildings caused by the vibration and pollutants coming from cars and tourist coaches
- traffic congestion and the volume of people on pavements delaying local people going about their daily business, thus obstructing the social and economic life of the host community
- the economy becoming heavily depend-

ent on tourism which, together with the resulting traffic congestion may discourage companies from re-locating to such towns, which means they can miss out on new job opportunities

- the city can lose its sense of identity and special places can lose their sense of peace or spirituality or history, in the face of the onslaught of mass tourism
- many tourists in historic towns are day trippers who spend relatively little per head.

Conversely, there is no doubt that, in places like Venice and Bruges, tourism also brings significant benefits, notably jobs. It is cleaner than many other industries and is valuable given that some historic towns and cities have few other geographical advantages to exploit.

Where the pressure of tourist numbers is seen as a problem in historic towns and cities, the measures taken can vary from:

- traffic management initiatives that try to manage rather than reduce traffic flows
- attempts to encourage tourists to walk or use public transport to move around the city or town
- attempts to reduce peak periods visiting and promote off-peak visits
- large-scale de-marketing, such as the decision by the City of Cambridge to produce no more brochures promoting the city.

However, in general, it appears that most of these measures have had only limited success, and that they have focused on trying to ameliorate the first two problems we identified above. They have done little to attack the problems of over-dependency and the loss of the identity, or the issue of low spending per head. For these problems to be overcome other initiatives are required. These include:

- devising 'alternative tourism routes, ... that is networks of attractions, sustained by complementary tourism facilities ... [which] are used to spread demand to other areas of the town or city'. (Van der

Borg in Department of Leisure Studies/ WORC Research Unit, 1995)

- measures to direct tourists from overcrowded historic towns and cities to cultural cities and towns which are keen to receive more visitors.

It is also important to try to maximize the length of stay and spending of tourists. If tourists are going to visit anyway they may at least maximize the benefits of tourism for the host community. This may include developing:

- large-scale attractions which take more than one day to visit, in order that the visitors can see everything, thus necessitating an overnight stay
- special events and festivals
- short break packages, with a theme such as opera, art or particular periods in history.

It might also involve promoting the historic city as a touring centre. That way, the tourists will be elsewhere when the bulk of day trippers are visiting the city but they will be able to enjoy the city in the evening when the day trippers have gone home.

Tourism and Urban Regeneration

In recent years, rapid social and economic change has transformed the economy of many cities in the developed world. Often this has resulted in the decline of the traditional industries on which these cities relied. Examples of this include:

- ports and shipbuilding cities such as Baltimore and Liverpool
- textile producing cities for example, Lowell and Manchester in the USA, and Bradford in the UK
- steel and coal-mining areas like Sheffield in the UK, and the French city of Lille.

This has led to government bodies seeking new sources of jobs and economic prosperity. Given that many of these cities lack the

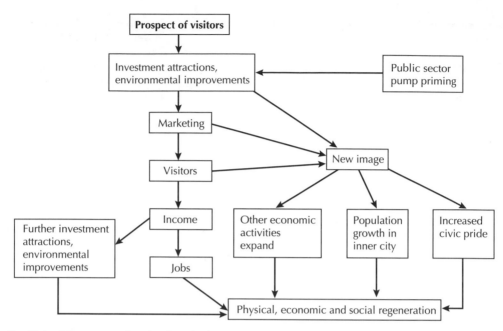

Fig. 16.1. The process of tourism-based urban regeneration.

potential to develop other industries, tourism has been the preferred route in many cases. Tourism-based urban regeneration has become a major phenomenon in the past two decades.

This has led to many cities following the process outlined in Fig. 16.1. Most cities have used one or more of the following approaches to achieving urban regeneration through tourism:

- a **visitor attraction-led strategy** where new physical attractions are used to attract visitors. This could involve building a new state-of-the-art museum, an aquarium or a waterfront development

- using **cultural attractions** such as a theatre or major concert venue to attract tourists

- developing an **events-led strategy** which involves creating new festivals, or attracting existing events such as the Olympics. This approach has been used by Barcelona

- exploiting the growth of interest in **leisure shopping** by developing new shopping complexes, like those which have been built in Minneapolis, and Sheffield in the UK

- promoting the city as a venue for **conferences and exhibitions**, an approach which has been followed in the UK by Birmingham

- selling the night-life of a city to attract tourists, particularly younger tourists. The concept of the **'24 hour a day city'** is part of this attempt to use night-life as a way of attracting tourists to cities as diverse as Leeds in the UK, Copenhagen and Barcelona

- attracting tourists to **visit workplaces** and retail outlets related to local traditional industries such as pottery in Stoke-on-Trent, UK, and glass in Waterford, Ireland

- exploiting **food and drink** as an attraction such as Asian food in Birmingham and Bradford, and even coffee in Seattle.

Figure 16.2 shows how the US City of Baltimore has used physical developments to put history on the tourist map.

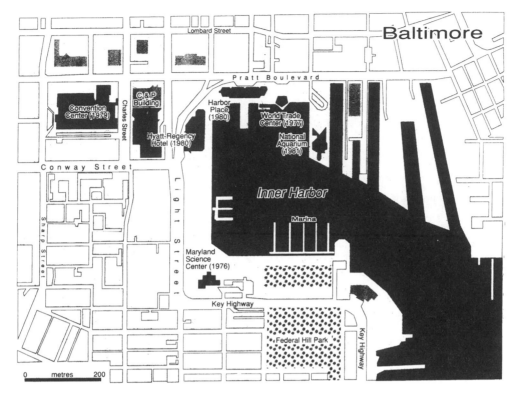

Fig. 16.2. Major visitor-related developments in Baltimore. Source: Law (1993).

Most towns and cities like the idea of tourism as a regeneration tool because it:

- is a growing industry so the future prospects look good
- is a labour-intensive industry that tends to produce a relatively large number of jobs
- creates facilities and services which can also be used by local people and it also helps keep existing services and facilities which are used by local people viable
- often provides new uses for derelict sites which are an eyesore
- can improve the morale of the local population
- improves the external image of the town or city which can help it attract new industries.

However, there are also several contentious aspects to tourism as an urban regeneration tool, notably:

- Public investment in tourism in cities represents an opportunity cost. The money spent on tourism could otherwise have been used, it is argued, for more deserving causes such as health and education. However, this is only partly true, because:
  (i) in many cases the money used is grant aid which can only be used for tourism purposes, or it is money in budgets which can only be used for tourism projects
  (ii) it is argued that investment in tourism today will bring income that can be invested in health and education tomorrow.
- The issue of who benefits from public investment in tourism. The main beneficiaries are often the owners of tourism businesses and their employees, but many local people will receive few

financial benefits from tourism development.
- Many of the jobs are low paid.
- Many of the jobs require skills that are
  not possessed by those who have been
  made redundant by traditional industries like mining or shipbuilding.

The Role of Events and Festivals

Events and festivals have always attracted
tourists, and many of those that are popular
with tourists today have been welcoming
tourists for decades, or even centuries,
including religious festivals and arts
events.

In the case of some traditional events and
festivals, the challenge of sustainability is
the question of maintaining the balance
between the needs of local people and tourists, and not allowing tourists to 'take over'
the event.

For cities and towns seeking to develop
and regenerate themselves via tourism, the
creation of new themed events and festivals
is a good strategy. A themed event attracts
people who are interested in the theme.
They will visit the event wherever it is held,
even in a town or city which is not a recognized tourist destination, or a place which
appears to have little intrinsic tourist
appeal. Once they have visited this town or
city for the event, they may like it and come
again for the place rather than because it is
the location for an event. Events and festivals also often require relatively little
capital investment and are thus a less expensive alternative than the building of
museums for example. Conversely, their
effect does not last as long as a museum.
They only bring tourists to a town or city for
a few days or months, rather than the whole
year round.

Nevertheless, there are notable examples
of the successful use of events and festivals
to put cities on the tourist map in recent
years, including:

- the Edinburgh Festival, in Scotland
- the Oyster Festival in Galway, Ireland
- the Street Theatre Festival in Aurillac,

France
- the Whale Festival at Husavik in northern Iceland.

The Contribution of Business Tourism in Urban Areas

Business tourism is a very attractive form of
tourism for cities trying to use tourism as an
urban regeneration strategy for two main
reasons. Firstly, it is a high-spending form of
tourism which also spreads its benefits more
widely than leisure tourism, because it
makes use of a range of services such as
florists, audio-visual companies and secretarial agencies, which are not used by
leisure tourists.

Secondly, it brings senior managers and
shareholders of companies in a range of
industries to the city for conferences, exhibitions and training courses. The idea then is
that if they like what they see of the city,
they may choose to invest in the city with
new branch factories or offices.

These two benefits may explain why the
UK city of Birmingham chose business tourism, some 20 years ago, as the core of its
urban regeneration strategy. The city has
become a major venue for international
events through both the National Exhibition
Centre and the more recently built National
Convention Centre. It has now, arguably,
eclipsed London as the UK's top business
tourism event destination. However, while
the potential benefits of business tourism are
great, so is the capital investment that is
required. The local authority in Birmingham
has invested many millions of pounds in
building the exhibition and convention centres, together with improvements to the
local airport and the creation of a dedicated
rail terminal at the National Exhibition
Centre.

Business tourism can also, indirectly,
lead to an increase in crime, for business
tourists are a popular target for prostitutes
and muggers. Nevertheless, overall, business tourism is an attractive tool for urban
regeneration, but it is a very competitive
market where it is difficult to stay ahead of
competition.

Alternative Tourism in Major Cities

In major cities like London, New York and Paris, the vast array of tourists tend to visit a relatively small area of the city and see mainly historic sites, shops, restaurants and theatres. The tourist sees little of the everyday life of the people who live in the city or the neighbourhoods, where they live. In this way, the tourist misses out on what could be an interesting experience of seeing the 'authentic' city and the local people lose out on the potential benefits of tourism.

The veteran travel writer, Arthur Frommer, has suggested a number of new approaches to visiting cities like London and New York, that would overcome these problems, and would, furthermore, prove very popular with the new breed of 'alternative experience-seeking' tourist. In London, he suggests that tourists should:

- attend adult education classes, and public lectures at local universities
- visit unusual religious centres such as the St James Centre
- become involved in conservation projects, such as those organized by the British Trust for Conservation Volunteers
- go to meetings and rallies by pressure groups and minor political parties
- explore the 'New Age' side of the city including psychic phenomena, acupuncture and different therapy centres
- attend 'fringe' theatre performances.

In New York, he also promotes the idea of going folk-dancing at Columbia University or attending acting classes. He also suggests people take a walking tour rather than just sitting on a coach, insulated from the world outside. Many such walks are now available in the outer areas of New York such as the Bronx, Harlem, Brooklyn and Queens. Furthermore, New York already actively promotes attractions which aim to increase understanding of the various ethnic groups within the city, such as the Jews and Afro-Americans.

Conclusions

In this chapter we have seen that sustainable tourism is an issue in both historic cities that are crowded with tourists, and in old industrial cities that want to attract more tourists. In both cases it is a matter of using sustainable tourism to sustain communities. We have seen that some of the key issues are:

- the opportunity costs involved in tourism projects
- the fact that some people gain much more from tourism in urban areas than other people
- urban tourism often involves centrally planned initiatives with little local community participation in the decision-making process
- measures to control tourism in historic cities in historic towns and cities have, to date, been relatively unsuccessful in comparison to the initiatives that have been taken to develop tourism in 'new' urban destinations.

As more and more countries in the developing and recently developed world become urbanized, urban tourism will become an ever more important part of tourism and the sustainable tourism debate specifically.

Discussion Points and Essay Questions

1. Discuss the problems which might arise when trying to follow the process of tourism-based urban regeneration outlined in Fig. 16.1.
2. Examine the main problems which mass tourism can cause in historic cities and evaluate the techniques which are currently used to try to solve these problems.
3. Discuss the advantages and disadvantages of a tourism strategy based on events and festivals, which is designed to regenerate a city where traditional industries are in decline.

Exercise

Select a town or city with which you are familiar that has, in recent years, sought to develop tourism as part of an urban regeneration strategy. You should then evaluate the implementation of the strategy in terms of:

- the type of approach which has been adopted, e.g. attraction-led, shopping-led, events-led, and so on
- how successful the approach(es) has(have) been
- who has benefited most and least from the strategy
- the extent to which the local community has been involved in decision-making.

Case Study: 'European Cities of Culture'

The European Union has played a major role in trying to develop cultural tourism in European cities through its 'European City of Culture' programme. This programme is also intended to attract non-European markets to Europe to help maintain the continent's share of the global tourism market.

Since the late 1980s, each year a city in a European Union country has been designated as 'European City of Culture' for the year. It has to be said that in almost every case, even where the city has been the national capital, the cities have generally not been widely recognized as being in the top league of cultural cities.

European Union funds, national government money and private sector sponsorship have then been used in each city to create a one year 'spectacular' of cultural events, from concerts to exhibitions, both mainstream and more 'fringe' activities.

Some of the most successful Cities of Culture have been:

- Glasgow, where the designation came at the end of a period when the city had been successfully regenerating itself
- Dublin, where its period as European City of Culture coincided with a time when Irish culture was going through a renaissance particularly in the fields of film and popular music
- Madrid in 1992, which was the same year as Spain hosted the Olympic Games in Barcelona, and Expo '92 in Seville.

Others have been rather more low key, such as Lisbon in 1995 and Copenhagen in 1996, while Thessalonika in 1997 experienced problems with meeting deadlines and keeping within budget. The 1998 European City of Culture was Stockholm.

In terms of the concept of sustainability, the European City of Culture idea has three drawbacks, as follows:

- the programme tends to be centrally planned with little local community control over decision making
- because the aim is to attract foreign tourists there can be an emphasis on international performers and elitist events rather than community activities
- the major challenge is how to keep the motivation going and prevent the following year being rather an anti-climax.

Nevertheless, this European Union initiative has focused attention on the cultural heritage of Europe and on some lesser known European cities.

Case Study: Tourism, Waterfront Developments and Urban Regeneration in the UK

In the 1980s and early 1990s, waterfront developments were at the forefront of tourism strategies in the old ports and industrial cities of the UK. While Bristol pioneered this approach in the UK, the original inspiration for these developments came from the experience of such projects in American cities, notably the South Street Seaport in New York, Baltimore, San Francisco and Boston.

The waterfront developments in the UK were found wherever there was any stretch of water, including:

- the coastal ports of Liverpool and Hull
- inland ports like London, Salford and Glasgow
- canalside industrial buildings in Wigan and Burnley, for instance.

In general, these developments have been mixed use developments, featuring visitor attractions, offices, leisure shopping outlets and, sometimes, housing.

There is little doubt that some of these developments have been very successful, in tourism terms. The Albert Dock complex in Liverpool is now one of the UK's most visited 'attractions', with well over three million visitors a year. It houses a set of themed museums about The Beatles and maritime history, and the Tate Gallery of the North. However, its impact on the social and economic life of Merseyside has, perhaps, been more limited than expected. The shops have found it difficult to survive and some of them are existing businesses which re-located from other parts of the city, rather than new enterprises. Few of the new jobs created by the development appear to have been taken up by people who were formerly unemployed.

The project has also taken attention away from the city centre, from which it is some distance, and it does not explicitly encourage visitors to also spend time in the rest of the area. It has also had some very controversial aspects, such as the development of the Tate Gallery of the North. This gallery is closely linked to the sugar refiners, Tate and Lyle, who closed a sugar refining plant in Merseyside employing hundreds of people, in the same decade that the new gallery opened. Many felt this was no compensation for all the jobs lost at the sugar refinery. Nevertheless, the Albert Dock has helped attract new tourists and income to the Liverpool area. It also helped to find new uses for derelict but historically important buildings.

However, waterfront developments have been a very expensive way of regenerating old industrial areas and these benefits have tended not to be spread very widely amongst the community. Many of these developments were spear-headed by government agencies, notably Development Corporations, which were non-elected and not answerable to the local community. This brings into focus the common dilemma of local control which can mean slow, piecemeal development that is too small to solve massive problems like those found in Liverpool versus fast, integrated, technocratic solutions that ignore the views of local people.

Case Study: Sports Events and Urban Tourism: Sheffield and Sydney

A number of cities around the world have looked to sporting events to change their image and put themselves even more firmly on the tourist map.

In 1991 Sheffield hosted the World Student Games. This event made a loss of over £10 million (Bramwell *et al.*, 1996) and was very unpopular with local people, who made their feelings known in local election results. However, the £147 million (Bramwell *et al.*, 1996) worth of sports facilities, built for the games, has allowed Sheffield to develop a sports-led urban regeneration strategy. This has involved:

- attracting high profile sports events which bring people in to the city as spectators
- providing a venue for new successful local sports teams such as the Sheffield Sharks (basketball), Sheffield Eagles (rugby league) and Sheffield Steelers (ice hockey). Watching these teams has provided leisure opportunities for local people and their success has raised the profile of the city nationally and internationally
- getting the city recognized as the UK's first 'City of Sport'
- winning the competition to be designated as the venue for Britain's prestigious new UK Sports Institute.

The sports facilities have also been used to put Sheffield on the map as a major venue for rock concerts which can be held in the sports stadia.

The local council in Sheffield has taken the leading role in Sheffield's sports-led regeneration strategy and attempts have been made to involve local people in the implementation of the strategy.

As far as the community is concerned, the sports strategy has been a mixed blessing. Some old declining areas that previously lacked leisure facilities have had new facilities located in their neighbourhood. Conversely, the cost of building the facilities did lead to the closure of some local neighbourhood-based facilities.

The city has recognized the danger of relying on just one area of tourism and has therefore also been promoting cultural tourism through its Cultural Industries Quarter, and the new National Centre for Popular Music.

So far, the strategy seems to be working in putting Sheffield on the map, repositioning it in people's minds and developing its economy. It is ironic, therefore, to note that the strategy would probably have not come about if there had been a referendum of the local community about it first. This raises the question of whether or not the local community is always right and should always be given the final say on tourism strategies.

In recent years the battle to host the Olympic Games has become even more intense as cities have recognized the enormous role it can play in improving their image and generating income. Barcelona, in 1992, undoubtedly gained greatly in terms of urban regeneration and its tourism industry by hosting the Games. However, the experience of Atlanta in 1996 showed that poor organization can also have the opposite effect. Bidding for, and hosting the Olympic Games, is therefore, a high cost, high risk, high potential gain strategy. Because tight deadlines have to be met and the stakes are high, Michael Hall has argued that:

> Given the sense of 'crisis' supporters of hallmark events often generate, the events are sometimes developed in an environment in which public debate is stifled and opponents are labelled 'unpatriotic' ... The planning of large-scale events often circumvents traditional planning procedures because the event is fast-tracked through

the system ... Therefore, the planning process and the media often remains closed to expressions of opposition to hosting events. (Hall in Harrison and Husbands, 1996)

Hall argues that this is what is happening in the case of Sydney which will hold the Games in the Year 2000. This subverting of planning processes and stifling of opposition is clearly at odds with the concept of sustainable development, particularly in relation to a project that will cost Sydney well over A$3 billion at least.

17

Mountainous Regions

Considerable research has been carried out concerning the problems which arise from tourism which takes place in mountainous areas. Most of the work undertaken to date appears to revolve around the issue of the conflict between the ecosystem and the recreational activities carried out by tourists, such as skiing and mountaineering.

In general, most upland areas that attract tourists are sparsely populated although usually there is some form of host community that needs to be considered. Often this community is particularly vulnerable as it may be:

- trying to make a living from farming in areas where agriculture is highly marginal
- declining in size and losing its young people
- politically weak in countries where urban interests dominate the political system
- largely composed of ethnic minority groups whose rights may not be recognized by the central government in the country.

At the same time, the ecosystems of mountain areas are often also very fragile and may represent the last true wilderness areas in a country, a last refuge for endangered wildlife.

Tourism in mountain areas is a rapidly

growing phenomenon, fuelled not just by the increasing interest in activity holidays, but also by the rise of ecotourism and the popularity of long-haul travel. The Himalayas and the Alps have been under pressure from tourism for several decades but international tourists are now visiting new upland destinations such as:

- going to ski in countries like Chile, Japan, Greece and Turkey
- visiting remote tribes in the mountains of Borneo and Papua New Guinea
- exploring the Alto Minho and Picas de Europe national parks in northern Portugal and northern Spain, respectively.

Over the next few years most mountain regions of the world will probably become firmly established on the tourist map.

Before we go on to look at some of the key issues in this area, let us begin by recognizing that there are different types of mountain environments. Table 17.1 illustrates this point.

The Negative Impacts of Tourism on the Environment in the Mountains

As we can see in Table 17.1, there are many different types of mountain environments which makes it very difficult to generalize about the physical impacts of tourism in the

Table 17.1. The different types of mountain environment.

Remote mountain areas	Accessible mountain areas
Mountain areas which are just beginning to attract significant numbers of tourists	Mountain areas with a long history as tourist destinations
Mountain areas with few or no indigenous residents	Mountain areas with significant numbers of indigenous residents
Mountain areas where ecotourism is the main attraction	Mountain areas where recreational activities are the main attraction
Mountain areas which are wildernesses	Mountain areas where agriculture is practised and people live

mountains. In general the problems tends to be of two types:

- impacts associated with particular activities such as hunting or skiing
- impacts that result from the sheer volume of tourists in the mountains, such as litter.

The physical impacts of tourism are many and varied, including:

- soil erosion and footpath erosion
- fire damage, due to both accident and arson
- disruption to wildlife and even the destruction of some species
- damage to vegetation
- water pollution
- noise pollution
- air pollution caused by the transport that takes the tourists into the mountains, such as cars and helicopters.

As many upland areas are national parks or designated areas of national beauty, deemed worthy of conservation because of their physical environment, these impacts are particularly disturbing.

Skiing – the Worst Offender?

Many commentators would argue that skiing is perhaps the greatest threat to the environment of upland areas. The infrastructure needed by the rapidly growing skiing industry clearly causes massive environmental impacts wherever resorts are developed. For example, new ski resort development:

- leads to widespread deforestation to allow for the construction of buildings and the creation of ski slopes
- causes erosion because often topsoil and rock is removed to improve the quality of the pistes
- requires the construction of roads that bring in polluting cars.

At the same time, the management of resorts once they are established also has a negative environmental impact. May, in 1995, noted for instance that:

Poor snowfalls in recent years have promoted the use of snow cannons in many resorts, and by 1991, 110 of the 450 French ski resorts had at least one snow cannon. It takes 200,000 litres of water to produce one hectare of skiing surface. This artificial snow making has a number of negative effects, including a shorter growing season, reduced river currents, affecting fish populations and the destruction of forest cover, leading to greater gullying and soil erosion.

Hotels, restaurants and bars also create waste in great quantities which has to be removed.

His Royal Highness Prince Sadruddin Aga Khan, highlighted in 1994 some of the negative aspects of the 1992 Winter Olympics which were held in Albertville, France, as follows (adapted from HRH Sadruddin Aga Khan, quoted in Cater and Lowman, 1994):

• In Les Saisies rare high mountain marshland was damaged by cross-country skiing and biathlon facilities
• In Les Arcs, ski-runs were carved out of the mountainside, leaving permanent scars
• In Courcheval, a new ski-jump was driven into the mountainside using 300 giant piles
• In La Plagne, villagers were issued with gas masks because of fears of leaks of ammonia from the 'bobsleigh' run.

A number of factors are worsening the situation with regard to skiing and its environmental impacts, as follows:

• skiers are looking to ski all year round and in new places that are off the beaten track. This is leading to a growth in trips to regions that have hitherto been the province of small-scale domestic tourism such as Chile, Bolivia, Japan and India. These tourists increasingly demand the type of infrastructure seen in the Alps and North America
• new variations on skiing are appearing which are very negative in terms of the environment, such as heli-skiing where skiers are taken to the top of a mountain by helicopter and then ski back down.

However, there are initiatives intending to reduce the harmful environmental impacts of tourism in the mountains, particularly skiing. For example, in the Swiss ski resort of **Graubünden** a number of measures have been taken including:

• encouraging tourists to use public transport by offering combined train–bus–lift pass tickets
• energy conservation schemes including the use of solar energy and making use of the heat created by air-conditioning systems to heat water
• recycling everything from ski boots and

even ski passes to rusty cars.

At the same time the village has been seeking to improve the quality of the environment, sustain the local community and enhance the tourist's experience through the 'Breakfast in Davos' initiative. Under this scheme, 35 hotels in the area use only local produce for their guest's breakfast. This reduces the need for transport to bring in externally produced food and increases the income of local farmers.

A paper presented at the Envirotour 1992 Conference in Vienna, outlined steps that are being taken in New Zealand to reduce the problems associated with skiing (Kaspar in Pillman and Predl, 1992). These include:

• retaining land ownership in ski resorts in the hands of national parks and conservation agencies to prevent exploitation by private entrepreneurs
• implementing a ban on heli-skiing
• conducting Environmental Impact Assessments before preventing the creation of new ski areas.

Interestingly, the Department of Conservation which is responsible for the mountain environment receives a percentage of the gross income from the ski field land road tolls to help it with its work.

In a number of countries attempts are also being made to persuade skiers to take up the less damaging activity of cross-country skiing.

Mountain tourism could also be made more sustainable if the development of new resorts was restricted and new design was made more environmentally friendly. Their size also needs to be controlled as some of the large resorts developed with government investment in France, for example, have proved to be particularly negative in terms of their environmental impact.

Conflict, Compatibility and Carrying Capacity: the Three Cs of Sustainable Mountain Tourism

Mountain tourism is about conflict between the environment and different forms of

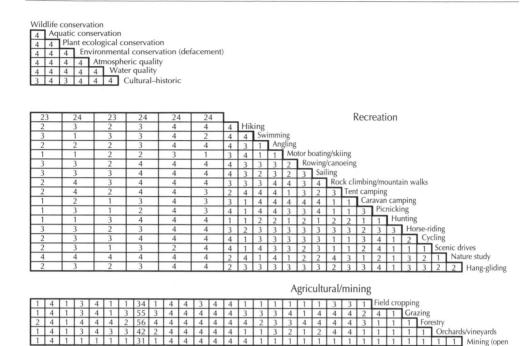

Fig. 17.1. Degree of reciprocal compatibility between conservation, recreation and agriculture.

Key:
1 Clashing/combinations
2 Doubtful/on a limited scale
3 Compatible and/or complementary/control necessary
4 Strong complementary combinations/no contact with one another

recreation, and in some places the relationship of both with agriculture. The degree of compatibility and conflict between different activities also determines the carrying capacity of any mountain area for tourism. Hugo has attempted to explore the nature of the compatibility and conflicts between activities which are often carried out in mountainous areas. His findings are illustrated in Fig. 17.1. From this, Hugo went on to examine conflicts between conservation and recreational land uses. The relationships he found in his study from South Africa, are illustrated in Fig. 17.2.

Clearly such matrices as those found in Figs 17.1 and 17.2 could, theoretically be produced for any mountainous region to help plan upland land use.

The Negative Sociocultural Impacts of Tourism in Mountain Areas

While much attention is focused upon the physical environment in mountain regions, tourism can also have a negative sociocultural impact on upland communities. We have seen in places like Nepal how the influx of foreign tourists from very different countries can lead to the transformation of the values of the host community.

At the same time, tourism can adversely affect the agricultural systems of the highland regions. For example:

- the construction of ski resorts and roads can cause soil erosion and use up valuable, cultivatable land
- tourism can disrupt the traditional pattern of 'transhumance' pasturalism that

Factors that are influenced		1	2	3	4	5	6	7	8	9	10	11	12	13	14	15	16	17	18	19
Wildlife conservation	1	-	0	0	1	0	0	2	0	0	1	1	3	3	3	1	1	2	0	1
Aquatic	2	0	-	0	0	2	2	3	1	1	0	0	0	0	2	0	0	0	0	0
Plant ecological	3	0	0	-	1	0	2	1	0	0	1	2	3	3	0	1	0	1	0	2
NATURE CONSERVATION	subtot				2	2	4	6	1	1	2	3	6	6	5	2	1	3	0	3
Hiking trails	4	2	0	1	-	0	0	1	0	0	0	0	3	3	3	2	3	3	0	0
Swimming	5	0	3	0	0	-	2	3	0	2	0	0	0	0	3	0	0	0	0	0
Angling	6	1	3	0	0	2	-	3	2	2	0	0	0	0	3	0	0	2	0	0
Motor boating	7	0	0	0	0	2	0	-	1	1	0	0	0	0	3	0	0	0	0	0
Rowing/canoeing	8	0	0	0	0	0	0	2	-	2	0	0	0	0	3	0	0	2	0	0
Sailing	9	0	0	0	0	2	0	1	1	-	0	0	0	0	3	0	0	0	0	0
Mountain/rock climing	10	2	0	0	1	0	0	0	0	0	-	0	2	2	3	1	2	3	0	2
Tent camping	11	3	0	0	1	0	0	2	0	0	0	-	3	3	3	2	2	3	0	2
Caravaning	12	1	0	3	0	0	0	0	0	0	0	0	-	1	3	0	0	1	0	0
Picnicking	13	2	0	2	0	0	0	0	0	0	0	0	1	-	3	0	0	0	0	0
Hunting	14	0	0	0	3	2	3	3	3	3	3	3	3	3	-	2	3	3	3	3
Horse-riding	15	1	0	0	0	0	0	0	0	0	0	0	2	2	3	-	1	3	0	0
Cycling	16	2	0	0	0	0	0	0	0	0	0	0	1	0	3	1	-	3	0	0
Scenic drives	17	0	0	2	0	0	0	0	1	0	0	0	0	0	3	1	1	-	0	1
Nature study	18	0	0	0	3	3	2	3	2	2	2	2	2	3	3	2	2	3	-	2
Hang-gliding	19	2	0	1	0	0	0	0	0	0	0	0	0	0	3	0	0	2	0	-

EVALUATION SCALE: 0 = no negative influence 1 = slight negative influence
2 = notable negative influence 3 = strong negative influence

Fig. 17.2. Reciprocal intensity of clashes between conservation and recreational land use.

still persists in many upland areas of the world.

As we saw at the beginning of the chapter, upland communities are often particularly vulnerable and find the pressures of tourism especially difficult to manage.

The Need for Partnership between Tourism and Agriculture

Agriculture is the cornerstone of almost all upland communities so it is vital that forms of upland tourism develop which are compatible with agriculture. Tourism can provide a valuable source of income for farmers through:

- the direct sale to tourists of farm produce which would otherwise have to be transported to a town to be sold at market or via an intermediary
- offering tours of farms for a fee
- offering accommodation and/or meals
- part-time employment for farmers in the tourism industry as ski-lift operators, in the winter.

Tourism can be particularly valuable in helping young women to stay in upland communities, because looking after the needs of tourists:

- provides them with a supplementary income
- reduces their sense of isolation by providing them with an opportunity to meet people from other parts of the world.

In other words, tourism can enhance both the sense of independence and the social life of women in mountainous regions. If young women can be persuaded to stay in rural areas then the male farmers will be able to marry locally and so community life will become sustainable.

The importance of maintaining traditional agriculture and mountain communities was acknowledged by HRH Prince Sadruddin Aga Khan in 1994:

> As long as mountain communities can preserve traditional agriculture in the mountains, they will play a part in stabilising the countryside and help to limit the thoughtless expansion of mass tourism. The farmers' very presence contributed to the struggle against erosion. Their experience in tending the fragile mountain terrain can safeguard against the construction and widening of ski-runs and help to preserve certain slopes from ski-lifts. Their economic and social needs argue against the short-term investment in tourist infrastructure which generally provides few returns for the indigenous populations and often lowers their quality of life through increased traffic and ugly buildings

While this is a rather romanticized view it does contain a fair degree of truth.

Sustainable Tourism and Sustainable Communities in the Mountains

Tourism can also help sustain communities in its own right. Donert and Light in 1996 published a study which shows how a community in the French Alps had sought to regenerate their community and give it a sustainable future by exploiting both its natural beauty and its historic legacy. The community in question was the Alpine town of Argentière La Bessée. Since the 1970s there had been economic and industrial decline in this Alpine town, with factory closures putting hundreds of people out of work in this town with a total population of around 4000 people.

In 1989 a local mayoral candidate suggested the town should use tourism as a regeneration tool and put forward a tourism development plan as one component of an overall regeneration package for the town. He was subsequently elected and the plan was approved in 1990. The main aim was to capitalize on the high volume of tourists who visited the region and who already passed through the town. According to Donert and Light:

> A primary goal was the creation of a distinctive idea for the town. This was to be achieved by providing alternative forms of tourism activity, thereby avoiding direct and intense competition from the more established, local traditional tourist resorts in the area. (Donert and Light in Harrison and Husbands, 1996)

Table 17.2 outlines the main elements of the tourism development plan. The tourism development plan has also led to environmental improvements which have made it possible to attract new industrial investment and residents. The key to the success of tourism in this town, is that it has been part of a coordinated economic regeneration strategy that has seen tourism as part of the solution, not as a panacea for all the town's ills. It is also a good example because:

- it has been based on a diverse, rather than a single, product which reduces the risk of failure if there was over-reliance on one product and the market for that product were to decline
- much of the development is rooted in the history of the community so that it is authentic rather than synthetic tourism.

If tourism is to play a role in sustaining mountain communities then we must also ensure that the benefits of tourism are spread broadly around the community.

We must also recognize that tourism cannot sustain communities on its own although it can provide jobs, income, and social contact, for mountain dwellers who are isolated from the mainstream population. It can also help give people a sense of pride in their community. However, it cannot, or rather should not, employ everyone or the community will simply become a one-industry town or a fossilized settlement.

Table 17.2. Major elements of the tourism development plan for Argentière La Bessée. Source: ACTOUR (1990), quoted in Donert and Light (1996).

Tourism development project	Estimated cost (millions French francs)	Commune's priority for implementation on a scale of 1 (high) to 5 (low)
Renovation of an old industrial building to a multi-use sports hall	5FF	2/3
Extension of hall to provide activity rooms	4FF	3
White water base, including beginner's area, international course, beach area, picnic site and lake, car parks and tourist information point	3FF	1/2
Tennis centre providing five courts next to football stadium	1FF	3/4
Climbing sites providing a range of routes and training sites, picnic areas and toilets	0.3FF	1/2
Fournel Valley Welcome Centre to the national park, woodland trail, cross-country skiing and heritage trail	0.3FF	1/2
Mining and Industrial Traditions Museum, renovation of old water mill into a convention hall	0.5FF	1/2
Discovery trail in Fournel Valley (nature, water and flowers) leading to the Mining Museum and the mine	0.2FF	1/2
Children's Residental Health Centre	6FF	2/3

Dollar exchange rates as of July 1995: 10FF = US$2.10.

Healthy communities are diverse communities with a variety of interest groups, and a range of industries.

Wilderness Tourism, Irresponsible Tourism?

In recent years we have seen a growth in wilderness tourism, the desire of some tourists to visit wild places that few others visit. Most of these are mountainous areas. Often such tourists can give their activities a nice label such as 'ecotourism' or responsible tourism. However, in terms of sustainable tourism it could be argued that it is irresponsible and unethical tourism. Surely man does not have an automatic right to visit places where no human lives, which are the domain of other species only? Clearly, in an environment which has no resident human population, even a small number of tourists, no matter how well intentioned, will have a major impact out of proportion to their numbers.

Even that form of tourism which uses the name 'expedition' and seeks to suggest it is nothing to do with tourism has a negative impact on the environment. The high mountains of the Himalayas for example, are strewn with the debris left behind by climbing groups. One of the worst aspects of wilderness tourism is the use of transport. Most visitors arrive via environmentally unfriendly forms of transport such as fixed wing aircraft or helicopters.

Perhaps we should only take tourists trips to places where man at least has a tradition of habitation, and leave the rest of the planet to other creatures. Surely we must leave some parts of the world for other forms of life. If we do not leave some areas alone we will have no reason to use the gift of imagination which separates us from most other creatures.

Conclusions

Mountainous regions pose some particular challenges in relation to sustainable tourism. They tend to have fragile ecosystems but at the same time they attract forms of tourism which have a high level impact on the environment, such as skiing. The main issue in relation to the environment appears to revolve around the three Cs of compatibility, conflict and carrying capacity. However, we have also seen that tourism can help sustain mountain communities, if properly managed. Finally, we have noted the major ethical objections to the growth of tourism in the wildest, most remote mountain regions.

Discussion Points and Essay Questions

1. Critically evaluate the impact of skiing on mountain environments.
2. Discuss how the results of the research reported in Figs 17.1 and 17.2 could help develop more sustainable forms of upland tourism.
3. Discuss the potential role of tourism in sustaining mountain communities.

Exercise

Choose a mountainous region with which you are familiar, or for which you can obtain information. For your selected region you should provide a report which:

- assesses the negative impacts of tourism in the region
- suggest ways in which the impacts of tourism could be made more positive in the region in the future.

Case Study: the Hohe Tauern National Park, Austria – an Example of Partnership

An interesting discussion of experience of the Hohe Tauern National Park in Austria, published by Stadel in 1996, led the author to suggest that sustainable tourism in the mountains – and perhaps elsewhere – has four main dimensions, as follows:

- Sustainability implies courses of action that do not jeopardise the long-term stability of ecological systems or the survival of key features of the cultural landscape. Achieving sustainability in national park regions that are part of the living space of local populations should be based on a management approach that integrates ecological, economic, social, and cultural parameters and that balances the needs and objectives of both residents and visitors alike.
- Partnerships between park authorities and local communities are critical to addressing the diverse and often conflicting goals and interests of stakeholder groups. Through partnership, public education, and public consultation, the principles of ecorealism may be realised by harmonising ecological and economic imperatives.
- The implementation of national park objectives can be facilitated through a number of strategies geared towards education and guidance of tourists, voluntary limitation of activities, and a respect for nature. The channelling of visitor flows into specific areas and careful management of sites of tourist concentration are critical.
- Careful planned and implemented zoning regulations may prevent conflicts between conservation and the pursuit of economic viability. (Stadel in Harrison and Husbands, 1996)

The Hohe Tauern National Park was developed following an agreement between the three provinces in which it is located. However, it took 11 years from the designation of the park by one of the provinces to when the final province designated its area of the park as a national park. This partly reflected conflict between key interest groups such as the tourism and hydro-electric lobbyists and local communities. The management of the national park as a whole is co-ordinated by the national park authority.

However, there is disagreement in different parts of the park about what the key issues are, ranging from nature conservation in some, to economic regeneration in others. At the same time there are conflicts of interest between different interest groups and land uses.

To resolve this situation, the key stakeholders in the National Park agreed that it should be divided into four zones as follows:

- **The Core Zone (Kernzone).** The main function of this zone of approximately 448 square miles (1147 square kilometres) is nature conservation and minimizing human impacts. It includes the highest and most remote areas outside the zone of permanent settlement and continuous land use. Areas designated as core zones are totally, or largely, preserved in their original state and the natural landscape is protected for scientific or cultural reasons.
- **The Outer Zone (Aussenzone).** The principal objective in this zone of 235 square miles (598 square kilometres) is the maintenance of cultural landscapes (primarily those that have been shaped by mountain farmers over many centuries), the preservation of native plants and animals, and the promotion of environmentally compatible forms of tourism. This zone comprises high mountain pastures and forests. Prohibited, or at least subject to special

approval procedures, are activities or measures that have the potential to persistently or profoundly impair the landscape identity or beauty and/or its recreational and ecological balance.

- **Special Protected Areas (Sonderschutzgebiete).** These areas, which cover only 16 square miles (42 kilometres) include sections that are of outstanding beauty, have special scientific interest, and/or are particularly valuable from an ecological perspective. In these areas, interference with the natural or ecological balance and the impairment of the landscape are prohibited, or are at least subject to special approval.
- **Adjacent Zone (Vorfeldzone).** In addition, a number of communities that are not within the actual boundaries of the national park, but are adjacent to and functionally closely linked to the park, have been designated as being part of a so-called adjacent zone (vorfeldzone).

(Source: Harrison and Husbands, 1996.)

This is a rather conventional approach to national park management, but it does not resolve the underlying conflicts. And within the zones, there will always be anomalies, micro areas or communities which do not fit in with the characteristics of the zone as a whole. Nevertheless, it is a legitimate way to try to ameliorate the conflicts which threaten the future of many national parks. Tourism is only one element in these conflicts but it is often a particularly dynamic, powerful, fluid element. It is therefore rather worrying that in many national parks, the staff of the park authority often include few or even no tourism specialists.

18

Islands

Island tourism tends to face similar challenges in relation to sustainability as tourism on the mainland. However, the geographical isolation of islands and the fact that they are relatively self-contained closed systems brings these issues into sharper focus than on the mainland.

At the same time there is no doubt that islands also hold a particular fascination for tourists. This may be because getting there requires an air and sea journey that might add to the sense of excitement, while their geographical isolation tends to ensure that their cultures are more homogeneous and well preserved than those on the mainland.

Meanwhile many islands are finding themselves being increasingly marginalized in the era of globalization. They also suffer problems, such as higher prices for goods because of the transport costs involved in distributing goods to islands. The problems facing many islands are illustrated in Fig. 18.1 based on a study of the inhabited islands around Ireland. Depopulation and the decline of traditional industries is a common factor in many similar islands today.

Furthermore, many island environments and societies are fragile and susceptible to change from large-scale tourism. It is clear, therefore, that many islands need tourism but have much to fear from badly managed tourism. In this chapter we will examine several issues relating specifically to island-based tourism. At the same time the author would like to stress again that the impacts of tourism and the problems of sustainable tourism are similar on islands to those found elsewhere, they are simply more concentrated.

Our first task, however, is to recognize the diversity of types of island. This is illustrated in Table 18.1. Given this diversity it is very difficult to generalize about island tourism. However, as with all sustainable tourism, the concept of sustainability on islands has several key components, as follows:

- the reduction of the negative impacts of tourism
- the maximization of the positive impacts of tourism
- the sustainable development of tourism in new destinations
- the maintenance of tourism in existing destinations and the sustainability of existing tourism enterprises.

We will now consider several issues which are specifically found on islands.

Peak Season Overcrowding and Small Islands

A major challenge for many small islands is coping with the influx of large numbers of

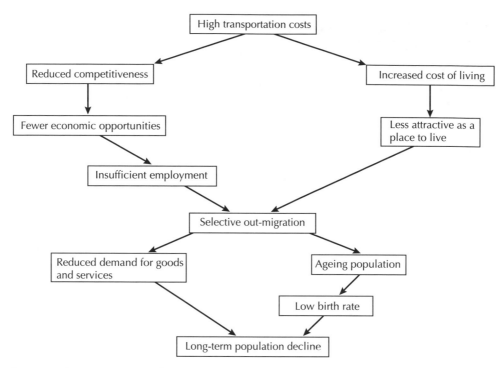

Fig. 18.1. The vicious circle of decline associated with the inhabited islands of Ireland.

tourists over the peak season, when tourists may well greatly outnumber the local population. This can lead to:

- shortages of resources like water
- congestion that makes it difficult for local people to go about their everyday business
- local people feeling like a minority group in their own community
- too much pressure being placed on local infrastructure such as the sewage system and the transport network.

The problem is often worsened by the highly seasonal pattern of demand for many small islands, which reflect:

- climatic factors such as the 'dry' season in places where there is a distinct 'wet' season
- peak periods of demand in the countries from which tourists come, such as school holidays.

This problem of overcrowding is worsened

in some respects by the concentration of tourists in particular areas. In Cyprus, for example, most tourists are concentrated in the resorts of Paphos, Limassol, Ayia Napa and Protaras. However, in some cases this concentration can be beneficial in that it may protect other areas from development, although it often leads to a situation where the rest of the island becomes seen simply as a series of attractions for day trips, usually by coach.

Supply Problems

Seasonal overcrowding, particularly on smaller islands, can lead to problems with supplying the needs of tourists. Many islands, particularly those in tropical regions, have economies which are geared to exporting one or two agricultural products and are not geared to meeting the needs of inbound tourists. This means the food for tourists has to be imported which increases costs and brings logistical problems. Even

Table 18.1. Different types of islands.

Large islands, e.g. Australia	Tiny islands, e.g. Comino, off Malta
Single islands, e.g. Cyprus	Island archipelagos, e.g. Indonesia
Islands located near to the mainland, e.g. the Aran Islands in Ireland	Islands located far from the nearest mainland, e.g. the Azores
Islands which have been tourist destinations for decades, e.g. Capri	Islands where tourism hardly exists, e.g. Jan Mayen Island
Islands which are relatively industrialized and urbanized such as the UK	Islands which are less industrialized and urbanized, e.g. Crete
Islands which are heavily populated, e.g. the UK	Islands which are only lightly populated, e.g. Svalbard
Islands with a growing population, e.g. Java	Islands with a declining population, e.g. some of Scotland's offshore islands
Islands with developed transport links, e.g. Majorca	Islands with poorly developed transport links, e.g. some small Greek islands which have limited ferry services and no direct scheduled flights
Islands with a largely homogeneous population, e.g. Ireland	Islands with a largely heterogeneous population, e.g. Papua New Guinea

where local agriculture is geared to the needs of the tourists, the peak season volume of tourists can lead to problems in meeting demands.

Because of their geographical isolation, small and medium-sized tourism enterprises on islands will often find it difficult and expensive to obtain a whole range of goods and services they need, ranging from staff to sophisticated computer management systems, specialized kitchen equipment to hotel bedroom furniture.

Accessibility Problems

With the growth of long-haul air travel and fast rail services, together with the dominant role of the car as a means of transport, some islands that rely on short flights and ferry journeys from the mainland are beginning to suffer in terms of their tourist numbers. Several examples will serve to illustrate the problems of accessibility faced by some islands as follows:

- Many islands lack a direct air service and journeys have to be completed by boat. While this can make the islands more peaceful it may discourage those who are looking for convenience when they travel on vacation.
- Some ferry and air services are seasonal which is an obstacle to the development of off-peak, high value, low volume special interest tourism.
- In a number of cases, islands are served by rather poor quality ferries that do not encourage tourists to use this form of transport.
- People who are frightened of flying and/ or sea travel will, by definition, not be willing to visit islands.
- Some island airports, in Greece for example, have now exceeded their capacity to cope with the number of travellers they receive which leads to a poor quality experience for tourists.

Many islands find that to sustain or develop their tourism market they need to develop airports and air services, but this clearly brings environmental problems.

Transport Costs and Island Tourism

Travelling to island destinations often seems especially expensive compared to journeys on the mainland. This may be because capacity on ferries and air services is limited, and peak season demand exceeds supply. This not only discourages some tourists from visiting the islands, but it also makes life expensive for those residents of the islands who need to travel to the mainland for business or leisure purposes. The following examples will serve to demonstrate how expensive travelling to islands may be:

- In Spring 1998, the lowest available fare from London to Iceland was twice as expensive as the best deal on offer to Lisbon, a similar distance, and nearly three times more than the cost of the lowest priced flight to Barcelona. It was even more expensive than the lowest cost flights available from London to New York.
- The flights to the three Aran Islands, off the west coast of Ireland, are some of the shortest flights in the world, taking as little as 6 or 7 minutes. In 1998 the cost of taking one of these flights worked out at about £2.50 per minute of flight. If a similar rate was applied to London to New York flights, the return fare would be around £2,000!

The Power of Transport Operators

The reliance of islands on air and sea transport services for their survival gives great power to transport operators. This is particularly true where single operators have a monopoly. For example, many Scottish Islands rely on the ferry services operated by Caledonian McBrayne, while the Isles of Scilly and the Isle of Man are served by only one ferry company.

Where a transport operator has a total or virtual monopoly of services on particular routes to islands, its decisions will have major implications for island communities. Changes to services might:

- lead to job losses
- reduce the volume of tourists
- increase the cost of food and other goods which have to be imported.

The importance of transport services also means that transport operators may have little difficulty in persuading the local population or its political representatives to allow them to build new facilities or increase the number of flights, even where these are detrimental to the environment. In other words, transport operators may be able to use their power to gain favourable treatment from the planning system. This is clearly not in line with the principles of sustainable tourism.

The Role of Transport Gateways in Sustainable Tourism on Islands

So far we have seen the dependence on air and ferry services as a negative point in relation to sustainable tourism. However, there is a positive side in that the tourists can only enter islands through a limited number of transport gateways should make it easier to manage tourism. In other words:

- inbound tourists can be targeted with appropriate messages while entering the country at airports and ferry ports
- de-marketing measures that might curtail visitor numbers are more feasible when there are only a small number of easily controlled entry points.

Taking the first point further, airport or ferry ports are an ideal way to influence tourist behaviour with leaflets, video programmes and face-to-face advice designed to:

- raise awareness of key issues in relation to sustainability on the island
- persuade tourists to stay away from destinations that are already over-crowded

- encourage tourists to buy only locally produced souvenirs and eat traditional local dishes
- give tourists advice on how to use public transport rather than relying on coach tours and self-drive car hire.

Accessible Islands and Low-spending Day Visitors

Islands which are easily accessible from the mainland, or from larger neighbouring islands can find themselves inundated with relatively low-spending day visitors. For example, most visitors to Malta stay on the main island but are encouraged to make day trips to the much smaller islands of Gozo and Comino. As these day visitors do not use accommodation on these smaller islands, their expenditure is relatively low, so that the island gains relatively little from these visitors per head.

On the tiny Irish island of Inis Oírr, Keane *et al.* in 1994 found that around two-thirds of day visitors spent less than IR£10. At the same time nearly two-thirds of short-break visitors spent over IR£30 on their trip, while three-quarters of those taking an extended holiday on the island, spent in excess of IR£50.

The presence of low-spending day trippers may actively adversely affect the appeal of the destination to staying visitors. As Keane *et al.* said of Inis Oírr:

> There is considerable concern amongst the host population that the large numbers of day trippers is rendering the island less attractive to the more lucrative and regular long-stay visitors who value the peace and solitude associated with the traditional lifestyles of small island communities. (Keane *et al.* in Harrison and Husbands, 1996)

The challenge therefore is to:

- encourage day visitors to spend more or de-market to reduce their numbers
- convert day trippers into staying visitors.

The Rise of Exclusive Small Island Resort Complexes

In parts of the world such as the Caribbean, South-East Asia and the Queensland coast of Australia, there has been a dramatic growth in exclusive island resorts. Many tiny islands in these regions have been developed, almost as private islands, with only one accommodation unit on each island. A selection of eight such islands in Australia were included in the 'Jetset Round the World' brochure in 1998, all of them off the Queensland coast. The descriptions of three of these islands give an impression of what these islands are like:

Heron Island – Situated on the Barrier Reef, Heron is a coral bay, rich in natural beauty and wildlife. Life on Heron is very special, stress is replaced by a sense of adventure and your days are filled with discovery. There is a range of watersports to enjoy including snorkelling, reef fishing and scuba diving. Accommodation is offered in three styles, Heron Suites, Reef Suites, and the Turtle Cabin. All restaurant meals (breakfast, lunch and dinner) are included in the tariff.

Brampton Island – Brampton Island provides an ideal environment in which to relax. Superb beaches and small bays ring the island, and there are walking tracks leading to fine lookouts. Many of the activities on the island are free including wind surfing, catamarans, snorkelling, sailboards, watersports instruction, tennis, archery, guided forest walks, a six-hole pitch-and-putt golf course, nightly entertainment and gym equipment. For an additional fee you can also enjoy scuba diving trips and lessons, water-skiing, reef flights and cruises to the Great Barrier Reef and Whit Sunday Islands. Accommodation is offered in Beachfront, Garden and Carlisle Units. Breakfast is included in the tariff.

Bedarra Island – Bedarra is Australia's most exclusive island resort. There are just 16 villas on the island catering for just 32 guests. No day-trippers and no children under 15 years of age are allowed on the island to intrude upon your privacy. Each of the spacious two-level villas are crafted from native timbers and feature separate living areas with private balconies providing ocean views. The island's chefs find new ways to tempt you daily. The open bar is stocked with domestic and imported beers, champagnes, fine vintage reds and whites, spirits and liqueurs. For additional fees you can also enjoy game fishing tours and excursions to the Great Barrier Reef. The tariff includes most activities, all meals and drinks.

Source: 'Jetset Round the World' Brochure, 1998.

Clearly, these island resort complexes raise a range of problems in relation to the concept of sustainable tourism, as follows:

- there are ethical issues about taking tourists to islands that are otherwise uninhabited, as they cannot help but intrude on the wildlife of the area who otherwise would have no contact with man
- the resort's emphasis on watersports will obviously put pressure on the fragile marine environment
- the construction of the units clearly involves destroying woodland and the laying out of tennis courts and golf courses adds to this destruction
- excursions that are offered such as flights over the reefs are not environmentally friendly.

The island resorts are also far from sustainable from another point of view, in that all eight of those described in the Jetset brochure involved travelling by aeroplane, motor launch or helicopter. Only one offered the chance to travel by sailing vessel which would at least not cause fuel pollution of the water, and air pollution, together with disturbance to the wildlife.

These island resorts are also very elitist and are largely only for the privileged few. For example, the three highlighted above cost, in 1998, between £64 and £290 per person per night!

Conclusions

We have recognized that many of the issues facing islands are similar to those in sustainable tourism generally, namely environmental degradation, sociocultural impacts and economic viability. However, it has been seen that islands also have their own problems, many of which revolve around their geographical location and their reliance on air and sea transport. We have also highlighted the potentially problematic rise of exclusive small island resort complexes. Finally, it appears that the issue of sustainable tourism is at its most challenging in small islands, remote from the mainland, with a fragile environment and a declining population.

Discussion Points and Essay Questions

1. Discuss the implications of Fig. 18.1 for the development of sustainable tourism in the inhabited islands of Ireland.
2. Critically evaluate the growth of exclusive small island resort complexes in terms of sustainable tourism.
3. Discuss the relationship between transport and sustainable tourism on islands.

Exercise

Select an island and analyse the current situation in respect of tourism on the island in relation to the principles and practices of sustainable tourism. You should then suggest ways in which tourism on the island could be made more sustainable.

Case Study: Mykonos, Greece

Mykonos is a Greek island renowned for its natural beauty and its unusual traditional architecture. It has an area of a little over 100 square kilometres and has seen a dramatic growth in tourism over the past 25 years. Priestley *et al.* in 1996 showed how tourism on Mykonos had grown in recent years. Between 1971 and 1991 a quarter to a third of the island was taken up with the building of new tourism developments. The accommodation stock has risen dramatically. For example, in 1961 there were 98 beds in hotels while in 1991 there were 4724. Tourist numbers have also risen, growing from around 5150 arrivals at hotels in 1965 to 60,000 in 1995. Likewise hotel bednights have also increased considerably from 34,350 in 1965 to 922,000 in 1995. The island welcomes up to 4000 1-day transfer visitors per day, many of whom are using Mykonos as an intermediate stop on ferry routes or as a day trip destination. The island's population rose too between 1961 and 1991 from 3718 to around 8500, but the rate of growth has been much slower than the rate of growth of tourism on the island.

As Priestley *et al.* noted:

> The island already presents some symptoms of saturation, and undesirable effects on the island's sensitive environments are emerging. These include congestion, lack of parking space, insecurity and water and soil pollution, especially during the peak summer season. Evidence shows that the limited natural resources of the island are insufficient to cope with the competing demands placed on these resources as a result of uncontrolled tourism development. A large proportion of the island's extremely limited land surface has either been absorbed by intensive housing construction, tourism development and its accompanying infrastructure, or left unused for future speculation, thus causing widespread loss of agriculture land. (Priestley *et al.*, 1996)

Furthermore, surveys have indicated that the satisfaction levels for both tourists and residents have fallen as the scale of tourism on Mykonos has grown.

The same authors have also suggested that:

> As a result of the 'cosmopolitan' type of tourism prevalent in the main town (of the island) tourists want to seek the traditional hospitality, spontaneity, honesty of relationships, and the authenticity of the experience in rural areas. (Priestley *et al.*, 1996)

This will ensure that the effects of tourism will also be seen increasingly in the rural areas. Mykonos now faces the difficult task of trying to manage tourism sustainability after so much of the land has already been developed in ways which have not always been sensitive or environmentally friendly.

Case Study: Svalbard, Norway

Svalbard is an archipelago of islands, owned by Norway, which are located high above the Arctic Circle. The main island is Spitzbergen and the total population is around 3000, most of whom are either Russian or Polish. Mining is a major economic activity on Spitzbergen but the islands are attracting a growing number of tourists. However, Svalbard is a remote, wild region where for most of the year temperatures are well below freezing. About 60% of the land mass is covered by ice. The growing season is short but there are nearly 200 species of plant life on the islands. The plant life is vulnerable though and tourists are encouraged to move around carefully for a tourist brochure warns:

> If the vegetation is damaged, the scars on the countryside may be permanent.
> (Svalbard Tourist Board, 1996)

This is because of the climate and particular characteristics of the landscape.

In terms of fauna, Svalbard is home to an amazing variety of bird life together with the Svalbard reindeer and the Arctic fox. The surrounding waters are rich in seals and large numbers of whales visit the islands. Polar bears are also found on the sea ice and islands around the Svalbard archipelago.

Clearly, tourism in such an environment is very specialized. Tourists are offered the following excursions:

- boat trips to Russian settlements
- walks
- barbecue evenings
- snowmobile excursions
- cross-country skiing
- trips with a husky dog team
- visiting a mine.

Obviously, some of these activities raise questions about sustainability. For example, the walks seem to be at odds with what is said about the fragility of plant life on the islands. Furthermore, tourists are permitted, and indeed encouraged, to carry a gun in case of a confrontation with a polar bear. While this is sensible advice, it could lead to the shooting of polar bears who would have been safe if the tourists had not been there in the first place.

Conversely, the authorities are well aware of the potential dangers of tourism and they have elaborate regulations to protect both the natural and the cultural heritage of the islands. In addition, the island's Tourist Board provides a whole page of advice for potential visitors in its main promotional brochure. This page has been reproduced in full in Exhibit 1.

Such control over tourism is possible where the number of visitors is low and tourism has to be highly organized because of the nature of the climate and terrain. At the same time the regulation of tourism in the Svalbard simply reflects the strong stance taken generally on environmental issues by the Norwegian government.

It is difficult, conversely, to see how one can effectively protect other islands:

- which are easily accessible to people from nearby populous countries
- where climate and terrain are both gentle and pose no obstacle to tourism development
- whose governments and populations appear to have little general concern about the quality of their environment.

Exhibit 1. Advice for tourists to Svalbard. Source: Svalbard Tourist Board (1996).

The countryside and environmental conservation. Animal and plant life on Svalbard has adapted to the stringent arctic conditions here, but the countryside is very vulnerable, and even small encroachments can cause permanent damage. Special environmental conservation regulations have therefore been drawn up specifically for Svalbard. We shall outline the most important rules, but we recommend you acquaint yourself thoroughly with these rules before visiting Svalbard.

Nearly 60% of Svalbard consist of conservation areas. These are classified as nature reserves, national parks, bird sanctuaries and plant conservation areas. Regulations applying to these may vary, but common to them all is that no technical or industrial encroachments are permitted. Moreover, you may not

- discard your rubbish
- hunt or disturb birds or animals
- remove plants or fossils
- use cross-country vehicles
- land aircraft
- erect new buildings
- engage in catching or trapping.

This applies to both cultural relics, such as crofts, graves, buildings still standing and installations of any kind whatsoever, as well as loose objects. In addition, the following cultural relics are protected, regardless of age:

- human graves and traces thereof, including crosses, bones, and skeletal remains of humans lying outside their original graves
- skeletal remains on slaughter sites for walrus, toothed whales and polar bears killed by spring guns.

Protection of permanent cultural relics includes an area of 100 metres completely surrounding the relic. You may not set up camp or light fires inside the protected areas or on ground covered by vegetation.

The Act on Cultural Relics determines that:

- protected loose cultural relics may not be removed from the site at which they were found; if there is reason to believe the cultural relic has not been known earlier, its presence must be reported to the sysselmann
- protected cultural relics may not be removed from Svalbard.

Tourism and traffic. Tourism and traffic on Svalbard are subject to regulations intended to protect the natural environment and cultural relics and to safeguard the visitor. Special rules apply to tour organizers and tourist vessels, making the organizer responsible for the safety of their tourists and for ensuring that visitors are informed of and comply with rules and regulations. Moreover, tour organizers must report their programmes to the sysselman before the beginning of each season and must have insurance to cover rescue operations and similar assistance. Individual travellers are duty bound to report their travel plans to parts of Svalbard, and may also be required to take out insurance or submit a bank guarantee for possible rescue operations, etc. Svalbard is a unique piece of Norway in the Arctic. The countryside is different to that found anywhere else in Norway. Several nations live peacefully side by side on Svalbard – no borders or passport controls separate the people, only the enormous distances and the constantly changing weather. On Svalbard, man becomes very small. Nature and the countryside lay down the terms of co-existence, and this is how we want it to remain. With this in mind, we urge you as a visitor to Svalbard to **'Protect Svalbard'**.

One must recognize that Svalbard is unusual and that most islands share one, two or three of the characteristics outlined above. This augurs badly for the development of sustainable tourism on islands, in general.

19

Developing Countrie

In a sense there should not be a need to have a specific chapter on sustainable tourism in developing countries for most of the current thinking and ideas in sustainable tourism are based on Western perceptions of the impacts of tourism in developing countries. The sustainable tourism debate has been influenced by a range of issues relating to tourism in developing countries, including:

- the sociocultural and environmental impact of tourists from industrialized, affluent developed countries visiting developing countries
- the stance taken by governments in developing countries towards tourism such as their encouragement of developments and the involvement, or otherwise of the local community in tourism development
- the role played by powerful, large transnational corporations in the development and management of tourism in developing countries.

In the 1970s, tourism was seen as a tool for development in developing countries. However, concerns about the potential problems of tourism in developing countries are not new. Indeed, as early as 1979, studies were beginning to be produced like that written by De Kadt 'Tourism: Passport to Development' which was a joint UNESCO/World Bank study.

The findings of this study included the following (adapted from De Kadt, 1979):

- tourism can make a substantial contribution to the economic and social development of many countries
- tourism development should be undertaken consciously and methodically and carefully planned as part of the national development effort
- tourism should concentrate on the unique features of the country to reduce the risk of competition from other destinations
- tourism, by giving natural and cultural resources a value, may also play a role in preserving and developing them
- countries have a choice in the types of tourism to be developed, e.g. individual tourism and mass organized tourism
- in regions where many small countries compete in the tourism market there should be coordination and cooperation
- countries should attempt to develop tourism on a scale, and at a rate of growth, and in locations which are consistent with making maximum use of resources without placing undue strain on these resources
- tourism development should bring the greatest possible benefits to the local economy and society
- governments should ensure that regions

...ch as beaches remain in the public domain and that their use for tourism should not indirectly alienate these resources from the people of the country.

These ideals are still relevant today but our experience in the intervening years has shown us that the reality has rarely lived up to these high ideals.

Many believe the issue of development and developing countries is the greatest problem facing the world today:

> The challenge of development in the broadest sense, is to improve the quality of life. Especially in the world's poorest countries, a better quality of life generally calls for higher incomes, but it involves much more. It encompasses, as ends in themselves, better education, higher standards of health and nutrition, less poverty, a cleaner environment, more equality of opportunity, greater individual freedom, and a richer cultural life. (World Bank, 1991 quoted in Oppermann and Chon, 1997)

We have to see tourism development in the context of this general concept of development in developing countries.

While commonly used, the concept of developing countries is a vague one that is open to much argument. However, there are at least three types of developing countries which are quite widely recognized, as follows:

- Less developed countries (LDCs) which have incomes of less than $355 per annum and have low literary rates and low levels of industrial production. According to Oppermann and Chon, there are 42 such countries and they are often known as the Third World to differentiate them from other developing countries.
- Developing countries which have gone beyond the LDC level but which are still relatively poor and non-industrialized.
- Newly industrialized countries (NICs) or 'take-off' countries such as the 'tiger economies' of Taiwan and Korea. Eco-

nomically these are countries which share many characteristics with developed countries but share many social characteristics with developing countries still.

Unlike the first two types of country, the NICs tend increasingly to be major generators of outbound tourism.

The issue of tourism in developing countries has come under increasing focus in recent decades as the number of visitors to them has increased. In 1963 there were just 1.5 million visits to developing countries, representing 19% of all international tourism arrivals worldwide. By 1993 these figures had reached 12.6 million and 25%, respectively.

Tourism as a Tool of National Development

Tourism has great appeal as a development tool, in that it can be developed relatively quickly and is labour-intensive. Unlike agricultural and industrial products when the goods have to be transported to the customer with a leakage of benefits along the way, tourists have to travel to the product. The destination should thus, in theory at least, be able to hold on to the benefits of tourism. Tourism can also provide a motivation for, and resources for, a range of related positive developments such as wildlife conservation, improved training and education, and better hygiene, together with the development of the transport infrastructure.

Tourism Policy in Developing Countries

Governments have tended to dominate the development of tourism in developing countries. While often acting in good faith, their intervention has had a number of largely negative impacts as follows:

- Most governments have focused upon developing resort complexes as highly developed 'oases' of development in 'deserts' of under development. Often these have been largely self-contained with little multiplier effect in the local community and the region.

- The focus has been on encouraging large foreign tour operators and developers in to develop tourism at the expense of smaller local enterprises.
- Much government tourism policy in developing countries has been highly centralized giving local people little say in decisions.
- Some governments have shown little regard for the rights of local people when developing tourism, even resorting to forcible evictions to make way for tourism projects.
- Corruption has often undermined tourism planning in many developing countries leading to inappropriate projects being approved.

For governments, too often, the emphasis has been upon boosting foreign earnings by maximizing visitor numbers and expenditure, rather than how the expenditure is distributed to all sectors of the population. However, even where governments have sought to develop tourism in a sustainable way that contributes to overall national development, they have found it difficult because:

- they often have relatively few resources available for tourism development
- they are highly reliant on transnational corporations which are largely footloose, and over which they have little or no control
- they are having to compete with other developing countries in a highly competitive market.

Sustainable tourism development in developing countries is also a particular problem because often the governments themselves are far from sustainable. Political instability is a major obstacle for sustainable tourism in many developing countries. In recent years, tourism has been harmed by this problem in countries as diverse as Fiji and Gambia,

Egypt and Papua New Guinea, Kenya and Peru.

In developing countries there is always the question of to what extent scarce resources should be devoted to tourism rather than other – perhaps more pressing – problems such as health and education.

Short-term Development versus Long-term Sustainable Development

Observers from developed countries often try to encourage developing countries to take the long-term perspective on tourism development which is inherent in the concept of sustainability. They often lament the 'short-termism' of many governments and enterprises. However, it is easy to see why this should be the case. Imagine the situation in Eastern Europe for example, where to Western observers, tourism 'policy' such as it is, seems unsustainable, consisting as it usually does of:

- giving almost free reign to the private sector to develop tourism as it sees fit, with little or no direct state intervention
- permitting forms of tourism such as hunting, which depletes the rich wildlife
- an apparent lack of concern with the health and safety of tourists

On the other hand, what choice do these governments have? They are often:

- lacking in financial resources
- weak in terms of their influence over their country. In some cases they are not in control of some parts of their countries with rebel groups being more powerful locally
- struggling against major problems such as rising crime, falling industrial production and a decline in the value of wages and pensions.

In this situation, where the longer term future of governments, and even countries, is so uncertain, it is not surprising that there seems to be little interest in sustainable tourism. Similar situations can also be seen around the world, particularly in Africa.

In these situations the best role for developed countries may be, instead of lecturing the developing countries, providing more tangible assistance for them. This might include, more effective aid programmes, writing off some of their debts, more technical assistance to help them, and encouraging them to cooperate together for mutual benefit. This brings us to the topic of the relationship between developing countries and the developed world.

Tourism in Developing Countries: the New Colonialism?

A strong argument could be put forward to the effect that tourism is the new form of colonialism in which tourists from developed countries can be seen as exploiters, using developing countries self-indulgently for their own good. At the same time foreign investors and tour operators often see developing countries as a chance to make money quickly. All these parties know that they are more powerful than the local interests in the developing country and that they will be largely able to do what they like in developing countries. The industry knows it can often exploit the government's desperate need for foreign currency and jobs or the corrupt nature of government to get its own way. Likewise the tourists feel free to behave as they choose. Even those who are poor in their own country can feel rich and powerful in a developing country. In both cases there are shades of empire, reflections of previous colonialism. Let us hope that reason and sensitivity prevail before the populations of these countries feel the need, like their forefathers did, to take up arms against this new form of colonialism.

One Person's Poverty, Another Person's Cheap Holiday

One of the most problematic aspects of tourism in developing countries today is the rapid growth in low-priced holidays to such destinations. The efficiencies of the tourism industry and the great disparities of wealth and living standards between countries have made many long-haul developing country destinations less expensive for tourists from developed countries, than some short-haul developed country destinations. Tourists and society as a whole need to be aware of the fact that these holidays are built primarily upon the poverty and social problems of the indigenous population. This is implicit in all the oft-quoted benefits of holidays in such destinations, such as the following selection, heard by the author in conversations with students and colleagues in summer 1998:

> They could not do enough for us – they always seemed happy to serve us [They perhaps realized that failure to satisfy would result in dismissal and their family becoming destitute in countries with no real social security system]

> Eating out was so cheap, you could get a meal for £3 and clothes were ridiculously cheap [. . . because those who cooked the meal and made the clothes were being paid just a few pence an hour]

> There were almost more staff than guests – they did everything for us, we did not have to lift a finger [Low labour costs mean a high staff to guest ratio]

The callousness of tourists and the industry towards the plight of people in developing countries was clearly visible in spring 1998. In the so-called 'tiger economies' of Asia such as Indonesia, Thailand and Malaysia, people's lives were being devastated by the economic crises in these countries. In developed countries the media made people fully aware of the problems, but there was little public demand for aid to be sent to these countries. Instead legions of tourists rushed to snap up bargain holidays to these places as air fares were slashed and the value of the currencies of these countries crumbled. While a few people may have done this out of a genuine concern to help these countries in some small way, for most tourists, this crisis was a heaven-sent opportunity for a cheap holiday, and no more.

It seems that while consumers in developed countries are concerned about battery hens and fur coats, they are little concerned about the plight of people in developing countries. This does not augur well for the development of sustainable tourism in developing countries.

Indeed the plight of developing countries can make them particularly attractive to some kinds of tourists who are relatively powerless in their own countries. In a poor developing country such people can become powerful, able to order hotel staff around and even obtain sex with children that would not be possible in their own country. This issue is a major challenge in the drive for sustainable tourism development in developing countries.

Towards a More Positive Role for Tourism in Developing Countries

The issues raised in this chapter suggest that changes need to be made if tourism in developing countries is to become more sustainable, and in doing so, is to become a better tool for development in developing countries. Some of these changes are highlighted below:

- We must not consider tourism in isolation from other aspects of development in developing countries. We must integrate tourism policy with other aspects of development policy such as agriculture, education, transport, the creation of locally owned enterprises and health.
- Developing countries need to work together, somewhat like the OPEC countries in the oil industry, to endeavour to counter the power of major transnational corporations and prevent these organizations from playing off one government and country against another for their own ends.
- We need to develop the concept of 'fair trade' in tourism, whereby local communities and developing countries as a whole, gain a fair share of the benefits of tourism. This implies a more direct role for communities and governments in dealing with tourists directly rather than using intermediaries such as foreign tour operators who take a share of the benefits.

- We need to raise the concern of tourists about the plight of the population in the developing countries.
- Moving the emphasis from tourism that is attracted by the low cost of the destination in favour of tourism that is attracted by the unique attractions of the destination. Then when, hopefully, the economy develops, and so too do wage levels, the destination will not suffer the loss of the footloose tourists who would otherwise move on to the next low-cost destination.
- Providing aid for sustainable tourism projects that also contribute to development in developing countries. However, this aid must be channelled effectively to appropriate projects rather than being siphoned off through corruption and bureaucracy.

We also have to recognize that not all of the problems are the fault of tourists and foreigners in general. Local economic elites and politicians must also take responsibility for what happens in destinations.

Furthermore, we must accept that sustainable tourism and development cannot take place unless there is social justice. This takes us back to the four Es identified in Chapter 7.

Conclusions

We have noted that the situation in developing countries has underpinned much of the debate on sustainable tourism over the past 20 years. However, it seems as if sustainable tourism that contributes effectively to development in developing countries is still as elusive as ever. The problems revolve around the weakness of public sector policy, short-term economic and political priorities, and the desire of tourists for inexpensive holidays. However, it is vital for the future stability of the world that the developing countries are helped to develop so that these problems may be overcome.

Discussion Points and Essay Questions

1. Discuss the suggestion that the failure of tourism as a development tool in developing countries has largely been the fault of the governments of those countries.
2. Critically evaluate the links between tourism and other aspects of development policy in developing countries.

3. Discuss the extent to which sustainable tourism and low-cost holidays are incompatible in the context of developing countries.

Exercise

Choose a developing country with which you are familiar and/or for which you can easily gather information. For your selected country produce a report which evaluates government tourism policy in terms of sustainable tourism. Suggest how forms of tourism could be developed that would be more sustainable and could make a greater contribution to national development.

Case Study: an Early Initiative in Developing Country Tourism – the Lower Casamance, Senegal

In response to concerns over the negative aspects of tourism, a new project, 'Tourism for Discovery' was launched in 1971, covering Benin, Mali and Niger as well as Senegal. A full report on this project by Saglio is included in *Tourism: Passport to Development*, which was referred to in the chapter. Eventually, the Lower Casamance region was selected to be the site for the project in Senegal. Saglio described this project in the following terms:

> This project was aimed at exposing tourists to traditional village life, providing for spontaneous interaction between the tourists and residents, dispelling tourists' often erroneous preconceptions about the local environment and culture, and encouraging a sense of cultural pride on the part of residents. The project was designed to bring direct economic benefits to the villagers, including employment for young people to reduce their migration to urban areas. The model called for simple lodgings to be built by the villagers, using traditional materials, methods and styles, and then owned and managed by them. These lodgings are located along the river system, away from established tourist routes, with the village tourists travelling by traditional canoes. With this type of accommodation, the contrast between the quality of tourists' and residents' facilities is lessened and the investment costs are small. Management of the lodgings by the villagers is organized through co-operatives. Local cuisine is served to the tourists. To avoid tourist saturation of the area, the tourist camps are located in villages with at least 1000 inhabitants and accommodation limited from 20 to 30 beds in each camp. Expansion is in the form of developing new camps in different locations and not increasing the size of existing camps. Although there were delays in implementation, the initial camps developed in the 1970s were successful, and the project has expanded substantially throughout the region since then. (Saglio in De Kadt, 1979)

In the event, the project experienced a number of problems, including a drought in 1972 which led to a migration of people and a shortage of labour. There was local opposition to what was seen as a small-scale investment compared to the massive holiday centre projects such as Club Méditerranée and Neckerman. Problems of site selection for camps also developed because of rivalry between villages. Finally, concern grew that tourists might not be prepared to pay to stay in these simple camps with few of the comforts expected usually by international tourists.

In spite of this, accounts showed that in 1974–75 the profits from the scheme amounted to around US$5000 for one village alone. The scheme also proved popular with tourists.

However, in the intervening years, while this project has served as a model for schemes elsewhere, it has never managed to really make a major impact on tourism in Senegal.

Case Study: Tourism in Cuba

In 1996 Seaton published an interesting study of tourism in Cuba, which looked at the issues involved in tourism in developing countries and the political dimension of tourism in developing countries. He used Cuba to test the hypothesis that:

> governments in poor socialist countries which most need tourism to achieve
> economic growth, may be most likely to be subverted by it politically (Seaton, 1996)

Seaton identified several links between tourism and politics in Cuba, as follows:

- Until the revolution of 1958, Cuba was the number one destination in the Caribbean and its tourism industry was largely owned and controlled by US interests and managed for the benefit of American tourists.
- After the revolution one of Castro's political aims was to make tourism available to the domestic market in Cuba.
- In the 1970s and 1980s, visitors to Cuba were those who sympathized with the political regime in Cuba.
- Since the 1980s with the end of financial aid from the former Soviet Union, the economy has suffered and tourism has been encouraged by the government to help fill the gap left by the end of the Soviet aid.

To attract the high spending tourist it requires, Cuba has been forced to develop luxury hotels and guarantee them a supply of top quality foods which are not available to Cubans. Those working in the tourism industry also become better paid than fellow Cubans in spite of them receiving the same official salary, because the tourism industry gives them access to American dollars. Thus the regime's need to develop tourism has led to developments which have undermined the political philosophy on which the government of Cuba has been based for 40 years.

Seaton suggested that tourism was causing a triple form of deprivation as follows:

- a feeling that the tourists who visit from richer countries all have better quality consumer goods than those available to Cubans themselves
- special provision is made so that tourists are able to eat and drink better than the host population
- those who do not work in tourism are resentful of the ability of those who do to become better off because they can get hold of US dollars.

There is a real chance that these problems could undermine the government and de-rail its attempts to develop Cuba as a relatively egalitarian society.

Therefore Seaton concludes by offering five ideas on how the regime might try to overcome the political impacts of tourism in Cuba, as follows:

- Try to reduce the attractiveness of tourism employment through forbidding tipping and clamping down on all forms of black market tourism activity. This would seem repressive and also be hard to enforce.
- Reduce the visibility of the structured inequalities produced by tourism through quarantining tourists into enclaves (a strategy pursued to some extent in Russia and China, and already deployed to some extent in Cuba at Caradero). This is impossible in Havana which is a main tourist attraction and also the main population centre of Cuba.

- Abolish fixed wages and allow a market economy in order to eliminate the advantage enjoyed by tourism employees over others, but this would be the end of the socialist society as envisaged by Castro.
- Abolish special provisions for tourists, but this would have the effect of reducing tourism demand for Cuba among richer nations. Western tourists are attracted to developing countries but few wish to live like them.
- Attempt publicity programmes designed to explain the national economic advantages tourism is designed to achieve and the necessary, if unpalatable, measures of special tourist provision. Such educational campaigns appealing to altruism are difficult to mount successfully.

Case Study: the Dominican Republic – Low Cost Tourism, Low Quality Tourism, Low Sustainability Tourism?

As we saw in the chapter, there has been a growth in low-cost long-haul tourism from developed countries to developing countries. An excellent example of this phenomenon is the Dominican Republic.

In recent years this destination has attracted ever greater numbers of UK tourists, attracted by the low prices and the availability of all-inclusive resort hotels. The Dominican Republic has established itself as a top destination for both beach holidays and weddings.

However, in spring 1998 the media in the UK was full of horror stories and complaints about tourism in the Dominican Republic. The problems generally revolved around health issues such as:

- the poor quality of the water supply
- the high level of incidence of food poisoning and stomach upsets
- the occurrences of diseases such as typhoid and malaria.

Tourists appeared to be shocked at hygiene standards and the poor quality tourism infrastructure of the Dominican Republic.

Yet, as representatives of the government stated, the Dominican Republic is a developing country where standards of hygiene and infrastructure are lower than those in developed countries. These are problems faced every day of their lives by the residents of the country.

The problem is that the tourism industry, keen to sell holidays, has generally not gone out of its way to make tourists aware of the fact that standards in developing countries are not the same as those in developed countries. Thus the tourists tend to have had unrealistically high expectations of the destination.

It is perhaps, nevertheless, unrealistic of tourists to expect high standards or even medium-quality standards in a destination where prices are very low. For example, in April 1998 some sample prices were as follows:

- flight only, London to the Dominican Republic – £99
- 14 nights all-inclusive, including all meals and drinks, flights, entertainment and accommodation in a three-star hotel – £359.

The lessons from this sorry experience appear to be that:

- tourists cannot really expect more than very basic standards when they are visiting developing countries and paying very low prices
- destinations cannot build a sustainable tourism industry unless they develop standards to a satisfactory level before they invite tourists to visit the destination.

The Dominican Republic's tourism industry is now working with foreign tour operators to try to improve standards. However, it will take some time to repair the damage which has been done to this destination's reputation.

Conclusions to Part Four

In Part Four we have examined the impacts of tourism in different types of geographical milieu.

While there are differences between the different types of milieu, in terms of the key issues, there are also similarities. For example, sustainable tourism in all types of destinations, is a matter of both:

(i)   maintaining existing destinations and preventing the onset of decline, and
(ii) managing the development of new destinations in ways which ensure their future sustainability.

It is also clear that sustainable tourism in all geographical milieux means:

- sustainable environments
- sustainable local economies
- sustainable local communities.

Furthermore, the examples we have considered in each of the chapters indicate that sustainable tourism requires:

- pro-active initiatives rather than just reacting to problems
- market-oriented initiatives rather than approaches which fly in the face of trends in tourist behaviour.

Finally, we have noted that perhaps the most intractable problem in sustainable tourism remains the situation in developing countries.

Part Five

Sustainable Tourism and Functional Management

In this section of the book we see what role the following four functional management areas might play in the development of sustainable tourism:

(i)   marketing management, including the use of the Marketing Mix, and de-marketing
(ii) human resource management including recruitment, pay, staff–management relations and staff–guest relations
(iii) operations management, including purchasing policies and environmental practices
(iv) financial management, including investment appraisal techniques and budgeting.

20

Marketing Management

Many people would argue that marketing is the antithesis of sustainable tourism, and that achieving the latter must inevitably involve reducing the power of marketing in tourism. However, the author believes that this view is both unrealistic and incorrect. Marketing is now a very powerful force that influences everyone in every aspect of their lives, and there seems little evidence that this situation will change in the short term, at least. Perhaps in the longer term, there may be a consumer backlash against marketing and consumerism, but until then we need to see if we can use marketing to help advance the cause of sustainable tourism.

We need to begin by making clear what a marketing perspective actually means. Taking a marketing perspective of the issue, sustainable tourism is about being:

- outward-looking, to interpret trends among customer segments, competitors and the overall environment (including the physical, social and cultural environment)
- customer-responsive based on detailed knowledge of current and prospective customers
- forward-looking and innovative in terms of product development and determining added value
- concerned to balance the long-run requirements of sustaining the asset base with short-run needs to satisfy

customers and generate profits. In travel and tourism, the quality of the environment at destinations is a vital part of the asset base

- based primarily on the perceived needs of customer groups or segments rather than on the operational convenience of service providers.

(Adapted from Middleton and Hawkins, 1998)

It is against this positive, modern view of tourism marketing that we will begin our discussion of how marketing techniques may be used to create more sustainable forms of tourism.

The Potential Role of Marketing Techniques in Sustainable Tourism

The classic marketing techniques could be utilized to help achieve more sustainable forms of tourism. Firstly, this means seeking to understand our customers in terms of their motivations and determinants, reflecting the consumer-led concept of modern marketing. You cannot influence a tourist's behaviour unless you understand how they think, what they are looking for and the factors which influence their purchase decisions. There is thus a need for sophisticated marketing research on consumer attitudes towards sustainable tourism.

Then, the organization, be it a destination marketing agency or a tour operator or hotel, needs to scan its business environment for relevant data that might determine the stance it takes towards sustainable tourism. This scanning could involve considering:

- government legislation on environmental issues
- the economic climate
- the level of public concern over the social and environmental impacts of tourism
- the potential influence of technological innovations such as virtual reality.

The organization or destination would then look at itself and its current marketing situation, through a SWOT analysis for example. This should give it a realistic view of both its current situation in relation to sustainable tourism, and future opportunities and threats. It would then be in a position to devise its strategy.

One approach that can be taken by either an individual organization or a destination is to use one of the three forms of generic strategies put forward by Michael Porter. These are as follows.

Cost Leadership

This means producing the product cheaper than competitors so you can either sell at the lowest price and gain more customers because of your price advantage, or sell at a normal price and increase the profit margin. This is the current potential advantage of countries in Eastern Europe over most of those in Western Europe. However, this is often a short-lived advantage as other destinations come on to the market with even lower cost bases. Furthermore, cheapness neither delivers the full potential economic benefits of tourism for the community, or maintains a quality image for the product.

Product Differentiation

In other words, differentiating the product you offer from that offered by others so that people buy it because it is different rather than because of the price. This fits in better with the idea of sustainable tourism and

rural development, through the emphasis on quality rather than price, and on exploiting local uniqueness rather than aiming for standardization which is often the basis of cost leadership.

Market Focus

Here, the focus is on the market rather than the product. So the area or region sets out to become the acknowledged leader in a particular market segment, for example, environmentally sensitive people, those concerned with healthy life styles or those who enjoy particular activities. From our perspective this approach has two advantages. Firstly, people with particular interests like these are often less price sensitive and will pay a premium price for their desired experience. Secondly, once identified they can be targeted quite easily in promotional campaigns, for example, through their readership of specialist journals, hence marketing costs are relatively modest.

Once the strategy is agreed, then the next challenge is to implement it through the manipulation of the four Ps and the marketing mix, namely, product, price, place and promotion.

Product

The product dimension to achieving more sustainable tourism involves both:

- developing products which are more sustainable in nature
- moving away from offering products which are intrinsically not sustainable.

The former category might include:

- conservation holidays
- vacation packages using public transport rather than private cars
- small-scale rural community-based tourism initiatives such as those outlined in the chapter on rural areas.

The latter principle could cover the following:

- hunting trips
- holiday packages to countries with a poor human rights record
- destinations with poor environmental standards where inappropriate development is taking place
- holidays on which tourists consume too many local resources which may be in short supply, such as water.

However, between these two extremes, lie many shades of grey where the aim should be making the various forms of tourism product more sustainable. The complexity of the tourism product makes it difficult to generalize. Readers might like to turn to the chapters on the different sectors of tourism for more detail on this subject.

Price

Traditionally the main emphasis in pricing in tourism has been on low prices to encourage high volume to provide adequate profit levels for enterprises. This low price has often been possible partly because the true cost of the holiday was paid by groups other than the tourists themselves. These might be governments through subsidies or local communities through their funding of tourism infrastructure via their taxes. However, if we are to develop more sustainable tourism, then we must recognize that the price paid by the tourist has to cover the full cost of their holiday. It must also be high enough to:

- ensure a satisfactory experience for the tourist
- provide a satisfactory level of profit for the tourism industry
- generate an appropriate level of benefits for the host community
- cover any costs involved in putting right any damage caused by the tourist to the environment
- pay for the resources consumed by the tourist
- allow for employees to be paid a reasonable salary.

At the same time it is important to make sure that some tourism products are available at prices which can be afforded by the less well off sectors of the community. The quest for 'quality' tourists should not lead to the pricing out of the market of people who are already disadvantaged in everyday life.

The principles of sustainability also mean ensuring that the tourist feels they have received value for money, rather than leaving them with the idea that they have been exploited.

Place

The issue of place, or rather distribution, has two main implications in relation to sustainable tourism, as follows:

- We should perhaps encourage the trend towards direct selling, leaving out the marketing intermediaries, as this often results in a better price for the consumer. It also means that the producer does not lose a proportion of the price paid for the product, to an agent.
- Where an agent is used, action should be taken to ensure that the way they sell a product is ethical and does not raise unrealistic expectations in the minds of the tourists.

Promotion

Promotion is a vital element in creating more sustainable forms of tourism. It is important that the industry, in its brochures and advertisements, does not create expectations that the product cannot live up to. Tourism organizations and destinations can also use literature and advertisements to raise tourist awareness of key issues relating to sustainability.

At the same time, new technologies such as the Internet can allow small tourism organizations to communicate directly, at low cost, with potential customers. This lets them compete on more equal terms with the large national or multinational corporations.

Another way in which smaller, locally owned enterprises can compete with larger organizations is through the setting up of marketing consortia, where resources are pooled to allow more impact to be made in the market, for the mutual benefit of all members of the consortium.

Sustainable Tourism and Competitive Advantage

Having looked at how organizations might use marketing techniques to develop more sustainable forms of tourism, we have to ask ourselves why they should wish to do so. The answer is that as ethical marketing becomes an ever more important subject, there may be competitive advantage for organizations which are seen to take pro-active stances on ethical issues such as sustainable tourism.

Organizations like the Body Shop have increasingly marketed themselves on the basis of their corporate values and their stance on ethical issues. They sell themselves as being in tune with the concept of sustainability, as follows:

- their products are not tested on animals
- the organization supports the concept of fair trade and has invested in aid projects in developing countries.

As yet, there are few such overt examples of this phenomenon in tourism. However, some organizations are edging in that direction. For example:

- Virgin Atlantic Airways is promoting itself, in part, by emphasizing the need for fair competition in the airline industry and emphasizing its commitment to giving the traveller a good deal
- hotel companies like Inter-Continental highlight their good environmental practices.

In the UK, the Association of Independent Tour Operators has tried to link environmental concern and the idea of fair trading to allow its small operator membership to compete with the larger companies.

As yet, however, no tourism organization appears to have taken a pro-active interest in the pay and working conditions of employees in destinations. Instead, most action has focused on the environment and giving tourists a fair deal, presumably reflecting organizations' perceptions of tourists' concerns.

Sustainable Tourism: an Example of Consumer-led Marketing?

In the era of consumer-led marketing, organizations presumably will only take an interest in sustainable tourism if they feel their tourism market is concerned about this issue.

Only limited data are available on this subject but much of that which is available seeks to indicate that most tourists are concerned far more with the environment than with the other aspects of sustainability. Research carried out in 1995 by Dr Peter Aderhold, from Denmark, on tourists in eight European countries, and reported in 1998 by Middleton and Hawkins, showed that

- between 25% and 42% of respondents in the different countries looked for a destination with clean air and water
- between 10% and 27% of respondents claimed to look for an 'unspoilt place'.

There are still issues which are perhaps more about one's own quality of holiday experience rather than reflecting any real concern about broader environmental issues. Research conducted in Germany by BAT Leisure Research Institute in 1993, and quoted by the German tour operator TUI, appears to indicate that seven out of ten characteristics identified by tourists as prerequisites of 'quality tourism' related to the environment in some way. However, this is rather misleading as two of these were a healthy climate and the sun shining! Only three directly related to sustainability namely:

- cleanliness
- very little traffic
- the landscape must be beautiful.

Research carried out in the UK by the MORI organization found that the environment in general had declined as a major concern for British people between 1992 and 1996. In 1992, 11% felt the environment was the major issue facing the UK, but by 1996, this figure had fallen to just 3%. Over the same period, those agreeing with the statement that too much 'fuss' was made about the environment, rose from 11% to 21%. Those questioned did not see tourism as a major cause of environmental damage. Only a quarter felt that tourism caused substantial environmental damage, and of 17 industries, it was placed only 14th in the 'league table' of environmentally unfriendly industries. Respondents were asked to list things about their last holiday which disappointed them. Some of these were related to sustainability such as pollution, over-crowding and hotel environmental practices. However, only 11% felt that such problems were likely to stop them visiting the destination again.

Conversely, a significant proportion of people said that pollution and local disinterest in the quality of the environment could put them off returning to a destination.

In 1997, 20% of respondents said it would be very important for them to deal with a company that 'took account of environmental issues', compared to 30% who said it would be not very or not at all important.

The final question of the sample of 2048 people asked tourists how much extra money they might be prepared to spend to buy the products of companies who were committed to environmental protection. The results were as follows:

- tour operator/travel agent: £7.10
- transport operator: £7.30
- accommodation supplier: £7.80
- tourist attractions: £6.10
- caterers and retailers: £4.80.

The data above are taken from a paper by Andy Martin of MORI presented to the Environment Matters Conference, in Glasgow, on 30 April 1997.

However, there may be some hope of getting tourists more interested in the social dimension of sustainable tourism. German research, conducted as long ago as 1988, and again reported by Middleton and Hawkins, indicates that as tourists become more experienced travellers, their interest in such issues increases. The results of this research are reported in Fig. 20.1.

The evidence overall, however, is that most tourists are not generally very interested in sustainable tourism at present, particularly in the UK. This is reinforced by the fact that most sustainable tourism-related pressure groups have only limited memberships. Perhaps consumer interest is a little greater in countries like The Netherlands and Germany, but it is still only modest.

Therefore, any tourism organization which seeks to gain competitive advantage through taking a pro-active stance on sustainable tourism is not doing it as a result of consumer pressure. However, it may be that if the organization can make tourists 'feel good' about buying what they perceive to be more sustainable products, then it may still work to their advantage.

De-marketing: the Opposite of Consumer-led Marketing?

It is ironic that in the era of consumer-led marketing, many commentators are beginning to suggest that sustainable tourism may mean trying to divert, change or even deny consumer demand, through the concept of de-marketing.

The Concept of De-marketing

De-marketing is a relatively recent phenomenon, hence the almost total lack of any detailed examination of the concept in the tourism literature. Nevertheless, we can say that de-marketing involves manipulating the marketing mix to discourage rather than

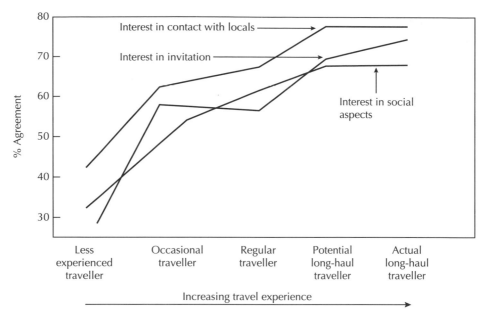

Fig. 20.1. Influence of increasing travel experience on selected attitudes of long-haul tourists (German research, 1988 reported Middleton and Hawkins, 1998).

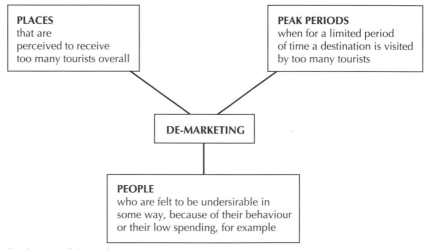

Fig. 20.2. The three Ps of de-marketing.

encourage potential tourists to visit partic-ular destinations. The author argues that in tourism we may seek to de-market in three main ways, as can be seen in Fig. 20.2.

When we discuss de-marketing we are talking largely about the future because, as yet, it has not been adopted as an explicit strategy by many destinations, although the UK city of Cambridge some years ago took

the decision to stop providing brochures promoting the city as a destination.

De-marketing Places: the Example of Venice

It is generally believed that Venice is over-crowded with tourists. Therefore it is an appropriate destination for us to look at in relation to the potential value of de-marketing. Let us look at how the four Ps might be manipulated to achieve the aim of de-marketing Venice.

Product-related

In the most radical solution access to the product could be restricted. For example, Venice might operate a ticket-only system, allowing access to the city to only a certain number of people each day. Clearly this ticket system would have to allow people to pre-book or those who had made a special trip to visit the city would be very disappointed. Such an approach would require an expensive management system to implement it effectively. Furthermore, as in the case of most destinations which lack Venice's unique geographical characteristics it might prove impossible to implement such a scheme. At the same time, seeking to restrict freedom of movement in this way may be seen to be at odds with the concept of free movement implicit in the European Single Market.

Price-related

Economists would argue that the most effective way of reducing overall demand for Venice would be to raise prices. However, this approach has two flaws, one practical, the other ethical. Firstly, Venice is already expensive and as a unique destination it is likely that most tourists would pay a very high price for the privilege of seeing Venice at least once in their lives. Secondly, there are major moral arguments against seeking to price some people out of Venice. It seems unfair that Venice should be the preserve of the rich only. A negative side-effect of raising prices might be a reduction in overnight stays and an increase in day visits. This would reduce the economic benefits of tourism for the host community.

Place-related

The distribution of the Venice destination product could be constrained by restricting the sale of package holidays to Venice, particularly at peak periods.

Promotion-related

We could reduce the amount of literature and advertising that is designed to attract tourists to Venice. However, the fact is that already little direct promotion is undertaken by Venice. As a world-renowned tourist destination, with a very high profile, promotional activity is not really necessary. Even if no more brochures or advertising were to be created by Venice it would still be overcrowded for a long time to come.

These four types of strategy can be seen as negative in nature. Perhaps a more positive way to de-market Venice, or any other place in a similar situation, would be to promote alternative destinations in the Veneto region, where tourism development would be more welcome. While this might not work for the first-time visitor, given most people's desire to see Venice at least once, it could be used with people who have visited Venice before. These people could be sold the other destinations under a 'See the *real* Italy' banner. In other words, status would be accorded to *not* visiting the 'touristy', 'commercialized' city of Venice.

Another positive move could be to try to encourage people to stay in the city overnight rather than just visiting for the day, so that at least they spend more money in the city. Differential pricing could be used in restaurants and museums, for example, to benefit staying visitors. However, this latter approach, while helping maximize the benefits of tourism for the host community, would do little to reduce the overcrowding problem.

De-marketing Peak Periods: the Example of the Peak District National Park

The Peak District National Park in the UK is arguably the world's most visited national park, with over 22 million visitors per annum. However, its main problem is not the overall volume of visitors, but rather their concentration on particular days of the year, notably Sundays in the summer, and

Bank Holidays. De-marketing of the peak periods might involve the following actions.

Product-related

The worst aspect of the peak period in the national park is traffic congestion as most of the visitors arrive by private car. Therefore one approach would be to regulate the use of cars on peak days and insist that visitors use more environmentally friendly rail or bus services, or even horses or cycle transport. However, such restrictions on car owners would be a very controversial issue for politicians, given that car owners are also voters.

Price-related

Currently access to the national parks is free with car-parking being the only charge facing visitors. De-marketing the peak periods could mean either:

- increasing car parking charges to very high rates at peak times, or
- introducing an entrance charge to the park on peak days.

However, this would probably have to be high to have an effect on demand and making people pay a significant price to visit a publicly funded national park would again be a very controversial issue.

Place-related

Action on distribution is not very relevant as visiting the Peak District does not involve pre-booking, or marketing intermediaries.

Promotion-related

Initiatives could involve actively producing brochures or placing advertisements that might publicize the problems of congestion that visitors will face if they visit at peak times. The worry here is the risk that this negative image would also reduce demand at less busy times.

Three more imaginative solutions to de-marketing the peak periods in the Peak District could be as follows:

- Given that most visitors to the park come from the local cities, the park authorities could also encourage the development of attractions on the edge of these cities to divert some people from making trips into the park on peak days. However, if these attractions proved too popular, they might reduce visitor numbers to the park at off-peak periods at great cost to the local economy.
- Attempts to disperse demand at peak times from honey-pot areas to less visited areas which are not overcrowded with tourists, even at peak times. This would at least protect the honey-pots from unacceptably high levels of use on peak days. However, strong magnets would be needed to divert demand to less well known areas. Special events and festivals could be created, for instance, in those places to coincide with the busiest days of the season.
- Incentives could be given for off-peak visits such as discounts at attractions, or free car parking. However, the risk here is that such incentives might simply increase overall visitor numbers to the park rather than reducing peak demand.

An added complication in the de-marketing of the peak periods in the national parks is the relative lack of marketing expertise of those involved in managing tourism in the parks. They also lack the budgets required to change well-established patterns of consumer behaviour.

De-marketing People: the Example of the 'Lager Louts'

Young, badly behaved, heavy-drinking, so-called 'lager louts' have become an unwanted phenomenon in many Mediterranean resorts. While they spend a lot of money in bars, their presence in a resort can blight its image and discourage other market segments from visiting the resort.

De-marketing this particular segment could involve the following approaches:

Product-related

Action could involve trying to re-position the resort to make it less attractive to 'lager louts'. Clubs and bars could be closed and accommodation establishments could introduce rules banning single sex groups of young people.

Price-related

Most 'lager louts' appear to look for cheap, basic accommodation so they can spend as much as possible on drinking and partying. Therefore, they could be de-marketed by raising accommodation prices to the point at which they do not leave the tourist enough money to have a 'good time' in the resort.

Place-related

Certain tour operators which specialize in 'hedonistic' holidays for young people could be discouraged or even prevented from organizing holidays to the destination.

Promotion-related

Promotional activities could be geared to selling messages about the resort that will appeal to other groups and put off the 'lager louts'. This might involve emphasizing cultural attractions rather than night-life and stressing the fact that for most of the year the resort is quiet. The campaign could also stress the resort's desire to be seen as up-market and selective. Brochures and advertisements could feature illustrations of older visitors and families.

However, de-marketing lager louts could cost thousands of jobs across the Mediterranean and it seems morally dubious to single out particular groups of tourists who are willing to spend their money in a resort, as undesirables. Perhaps it would be better to try to educate these young people to simply behave more responsibly while enjoying themselves. Or, more radically, perhaps, a strategy could be devised to develop certain resorts only as resorts primarily for young hedonistic tourists, who are a lucrative market segment for bar and club owners, watersports operators and self-catering apartment owners.

We have seen that in all three cases de-marketing brings difficulties in terms of both its practicality and its desirability. It is also clear that the three types of de-marketing are all interrelated. For example, in the case of Venice, not only does it receive too many visitors overall, but it also receives too many visitors at peak times such as the Carnivale in February, and the summer, and too many low-spending day trippers.

Carrying capacity

De-marketing is also inextricably linked with the concept of **carrying capacity**. We cannot decide on the need to de-market unless we can determine the capacity of a destination.

The concept of carrying capacity is a common one in the sustainable tourism literature. There are several types of carrying capacity, including:

- **physical** capacity, the number of tourists a place can physically accommodate
- **environmental** or **ecological** capacity, the number of tourists that can be accommodated before damage begins to be caused to the environment or ecosystem
- **economic** capacity, the number of tourists that can be welcomed before the local community starts to suffer economic problems, e.g. increased housing values and land prices
- **social** capacity, the number of people beyond which social disruption or irrevocable cultural damage will occur
- **infrastructure** capacity, the number of tourists that can be accommodated by the destination infrastructure
- **perceptual** capacity, the number of people a place can welcome before the quality of the tourist experience begins to be adversely affected.

However, in terms of developing sustainable

tourism, all six types share one criticism, namely, even if you can measure the capacity, how do you put it into practice? Furthermore, some concepts of carrying capacity, such as social and perceptual are very subjective, and no two observers will agree on the actual figure. At the same time, they are generally rather unrealistic in that they suggest that damage will occur at a particular point when a specific number of tourists are present, in a certain place. The process of tourism-related damage is almost certainly less clear cut than this. It is a progressive, rather than a sudden phenomenon.

Finally, as each locality is totally different in terms of geography, ecosystem, social structure and economy, it is unlikely that the carrying capacity will be the same in any two places, so its application in any location is very difficult to forecast. While carrying capacity is a useful concept it is very problematic to use in a practical way to help develop sustainable tourism. The issue of carrying capacity is taken up further, elsewhere in this book.

If de-marketing is to play a valuable role in developing more sustainable forms of tourism, then it must help create tourism which is more environmentally friendly, socially equitable and economically viable. With this in mind we must recognize that there are several key issues in respect of de-marketing as follows:

- There are questions of social equity in relation to ideas such as using price as a de-marketing tool and labelling groups of tourists as 'undesirables' whose presence is not welcome in a destination.
- If de-marketing is too successful it could have a negative impact on the local economy, particularly in resorts where tourism is the dominant industry and there are few alternative industries. It could lead to job losses and locally owned enterprises going out of business.
- There is a danger that sometimes the de-marketing measures may be out of proportion to the scale of the problem. Few destinations are so overcrowded, perhaps, that restrictions on tourists' freedom of movement and large price rises can be justified.

Even where de-marketing is justified we must accept that trying to influence established patterns of tourist behaviour is a very complex and expensive activity.

Furthermore, the tourist is not an unwanted invader but is generally a decent person who has been encouraged to visit the resort as a welcome guest. If resorts are too zealous in their de-marketing they may alienate the tourists whom they rely on for their livelihood. After all tourism can only be sustainable if there are still tourists willing to spend money on visiting destinations. Often de-marketing measures can appear negative and anti-tourist. Instead we need to focus on more positive forms of de-marketing which also enhance the quality of the tourist experience.

Conclusions

In this chapter we have looked at how marketing might contribute to the development of more sustainable forms of tourism, how it might go from being seen as the core of the problem to being part of the solution. We have also noted that de-marketing may be required as well if we are to make tourism more sustainable. This involves manipulating and changing consumer behaviour rather than reflecting demand in the offer. Finally, it has noted that there is little genuine pressure from consumers for the development of sustainable tourism, as yet, and this might explain the apparent lack of interest amongst tourism organizations, currently, in seeking to take a pro-active stance on sustainable tourism to achieve competitive advantage.

Discussion Points and Essay Questions

1. Discuss the extent to which each of Porter's generic strategies are compatible

with the principles and practices of sustainable tourism.

2. Critically evaluate the idea that tourists are only interested in their own holiday experiences, and do not really care about environmental and social issues as a whole.

3. Discuss the practicality *and* the desirability of de-marketing places, peak periods and people.

Exercise

Select a tourism organization with which you are familiar. Analyse the current marketing mix of your chosen organization to see the extent to which it is in line with the principles of sustainable tourism. Then identify ways in which the marketing mix could be improved in relation to the concept of sustainable tourism.

Case Study: Marketing and Sustainable Tourism – the Challenge in Palestine

Palestine offers a fascinating case study of the potential role of marketing in sustainable tourism. The Palestinian Authority is slowly being allowed to take control of the Palestinian territories of the West Bank and Gaza. However, it is still being denied control of the largely Palestinian sector of Jerusalem, East Jerusalem, and Israeli troops continue to be responsible for security in some areas of Palestine. For the first time, Palestinian civil servants and entrepreneurs are responsible for tourism development and marketing in the territories.

The challenge they face is enormous. The West Bank, notably Bethlehem, currently receives large numbers of pilgrims, Christians, Muslims and Jews. This number is expected to rise dramatically when the year 2000 arrives, but often the pilgrims spend very little money while they are in Palestine. Palestine has had to rely on Tel Aviv airport which can be closed to Palestinians and Palestinian-based tourists at any time by the Israeli Government. Arrivals at the new Palestinian airport at Gaza will still be controlled by Israeli security staff. Years of military occupation and under-investment have resulted in a poorly developed tourism infrastructure. New hotels are being built, often with little evidence of real demand.

There are relatively few visitor attractions, restaurants and events which could encourage tourists to spend more money in Palestine. Most tourism in Palestine is controlled by Israeli operators, based outside the Palestinian territories. This reduces the economic benefits of tourism for the host community. Gaza receives very few tourists although it is in great need of the economic benefits which tourism could bring.

Given the political and economic situation in Palestine, there is a great need for the development of sustainable forms of tourism which can in turn sustain the host population. Let us now look at what a sustainable tourism strategy for Palestine might look like. The overall aim should be to increase the income from tourism and distribute it more widely amongst the Palestinian population. To this end, Palestine could, perhaps, try to manipulate the marketing mix, in the following ways.

The Product

In the widest sense of this should mean:

- limiting the building of new hotels until occupancy levels have risen, and developing other forms of accommodation such as self-catering units as well as camp sites, and youth hostels
- giving tourists the opportunity to stay with local families
- attracting new market segments by developing new themed packages including health treatments using Dead Sea mud, riding holidays, painting holidays and archaeological trips
- developing visitor attractions that encourage tourists to spend more money, such as heritage centres based on the important archaeological sites, and leisure parks
- creating themed trails which promote Palestinian culture and products such as traditional foods and farm produce
- ensuring that Palestinian guides are the only people who show tourists around Palestinian sites.

Price

Price is a sensitive issue because Palestine needs to:

- attract high spending tourists who will maximize the economic benefits of tourism for the host population
- recognize that it is important not to be seen to be charging high prices to pilgrims who may not be able to afford them.

At all times the emphasis should be upon quality and giving the visitor, whether they be leisure tourist or pilgrim, good value for money.

Place

Place or distribution means developing the Palestinian travel sector so that it, rather than outside tourism operators and travel agents, distribute the Palestinian product.

Promotion

This is also vitally important given the need to address the negative image which years of adverse media coverage have given Palestine worldwide. At the same time, there is a need to establish a clear brand identity for Palestine. Areas within Palestine also need to be given identities, such as:

- Bethlehem – the Birthplace of Christianity
- Jericho – the ideal winter sun resort
- Ramallah – the *new* Palestine
- Nablus – the *real* Palestine.

As far as promotional media are concerned the Internet is a very attractive option for Palestine. It is inexpensive and cannot be disrupted by border closures.

These ideas may be sound, but the obstacles facing Palestine are enormous. There is the lack of funds, although money is available from foreign 'donor' governments and from the United Nations. Restrictions on the movement of Palestinians between Gaza and the West Bank is a further problem for the development of an integrated Palestinian tourism industry. There are very few experienced tourism marketing or destination management professionals. Finally, the fragile political situation still puts many tourists off visiting Palestine and adversely affects its image.

Palestine needs sustainable tourism to bring economic benefits and jobs for the population. Yet the obstacles it faces are enormous, and it will take a great effort to overcome them, as well as good fortune. It is vital that Palestine succeeds though, not only because it is one of the world's most important cultural tourism destinations, but also for the sake, ultimately, of peace and prosperity in the Middle East.

21

Human Resource Management

Much of the sustainable tourism debate appears to have largely ignored the employees, preferring instead to focus upon the tourist, the host community as a whole and tourism enterprises. Yet, as a service industry, where the service delivered by employees is the core of the product which is offered, customer satisfaction is largely a function of the quality of front-line operational staff rather than managers. Thus such staff are arguably the most important aspect of the organization.

The Importance of Human Resources in Tourism

Staff play a vital role in every aspect of the delivery of the tourism product. If we think about a package holiday from the UK to a Mediterranean island, its quality is heavily dependent upon:

- the competence of the travel agency clerk who finds the right holiday and books it for the tourist
- the attitudes and level of service offered by the cabin crew on the flight to and from the destination
- the ability and commitment to customer service of the tour operator's representative in the resort
- the capabilities of operative staff in the

hotel and the catering establishments where the tourists eat
- the skill and knowledge of tourist guides at historic sites.

For the sake of both the tourists and the future of the tourism industry, it is vital that human resource policies are of the highest standard. Yet, as we will see in the next section, there are problems with the current human resource situation in the tourism industry.

Human Resources and Sustainable Tourism

The relationship between human resources and sustainable tourism has two main dimensions, as follows:

- tourism can only exist if the industry can attract and retain an adequate supply of good quality staff, in other words, if there is a sustainable workforce
- the way in which staff are treated by both managers and tourists given that sustainability is about social equality and justice.

Human Resource Management Challenges in Tourism

While it is difficult to generalize, there are some characteristics of employment within the hospitality and tourism industries which are at odds with the concept of sustainable tourism, in that they are unjust to those who work in the industry. It is the author's contention that not until these characteristics have been changed for the better, we will never be able to develop forms of tourism which are truly more sustainable.

Equal Opportunities and Sustainable Tourism

The industry has traditionally discriminated widely in terms of sex, race and disability.

Women have traditionally been linked to jobs in certain areas only, and have been rarely able to achieve the highest positions in the industry.

> Throughout all sections of tourism where there is customer contact, women predominate – as front office and dining room personnel, activity staff, tourist office personnel, tour guides. However, when it comes to the more senior positions in these same areas, where jobs have less customer contact, but a greater management and decision-making role, the situation is usually reversed. (Sometimes, employers excuse this on the grounds of women's perceived negative traits ... their inability to gain authority and respect, their timidity, and indecisiveness, as barriers to promotion). (Wahl and McKenna, 1990 quoted in Baum, 1995)

While this situation is not confined to tourism, discrimination is perhaps more explicit and embedded in the culture of the industry. Employers frequently reject women applicants who are over a certain age and demand photos of female applicants for jobs.

Likewise, a study of the UK hotel industry by the Commission for Racial Equality in 1991 found that:

> ethnic minorities were disproportionately concentrated in unskilled jobs such as cleaners, washers and packers, with only minimal representation at management levels. (Baum, 1995)

In sectors such as the cruise business the discrimination is virtually institutionalized, with job types being divided on national lines, as we can see from the following example from the Berlitz *Complete Guide to Cruising and Cruise Ships* (1995):

- MV *Americana* – officers: Norwegian
  Dining staff: South American
- MS *Black Prince* – officers: European
  Dining staff: Filipino/Thai
- MS *Crown Dynasty* – officers: Scandinavian
  Dining staff: Filipino
- TSS *Fiesta Marina* – officers: Italian
  Dining staff: Latin American
- MS *Maasdam* – officers: Dutch
  Dining staff: Filipino/Indonesian

The nationality of staff in different positions is clearly perceived to be an important issue given that it is included in such a guide. It also reflects the fact that the dining staff are lower paid than the officers, so that cruise lines are using people from developing countries to fill these posts.

The tourism industry also has a poor record on the employment and promotion of people with disabilities. Conversely, the industry has a better record in relation to age, particularly in the employment and promotion of younger people, in comparison to other industries. However, the industry is often unwilling to take on staff over 40 years of age. At the same time, in some sectors there are upper age limits for the continued employment of staff. For example, a number of Asian airlines have contracts which terminate the contract of front-line female staff when they are in their early 30s.

The existence of discrimination in tourism robs the industry of the services of good staff and means that its workforce does not reflect the composition of its customer base.

Pay and Working Conditions

The tourism industry is renowned for its poor pay and conditions with characteristic problems including the following:

- low hourly rates of pay such that a Department of Employment survey of hotel and catering in 1991, found that full-time earnings in both sectors were over £60 less than the national industrial average

- on many occasions, staff are often expected to work overtime for no extra money or for just the normal hours rate, rather than an enhanced hourly rate
- the reliance on gratuities to supplement wages, and the fact that tips are not passed on to all staff in some enterprises
- long working hours, with working weeks of 50 hours or more being common for hospitality workers and tour representatives, for instance
- some contracts do not guarantee a certain number of hours work each week. Instead staff can be brought into work, at short notice, as much or as little as the employer requires
- many staff do not receive adequate breaks during peak season periods.

It has to be said that these problems tend to be far more rife in the private sector than in the more regulated public sector. They are also a function of the fact that in the majority of the tourism industry, staff are not members of trade unions. Indeed in many companies, trade union membership is not permitted; it is one of the few industries where this is the case.

Seasonality and Casual Labour

Sustainable tourism should mean providing jobs which are permanent so that people can aspire to develop a career and are guaranteed a steady, regular income. However, much of the employment in tourism is seasonal and/or casual. Because jobs are not permanent, local adults with family responsibilities are often not able to take them. They are therefore filled either by local young people or by in-migrant labour. This is particularly the case in the hotel, restaurant and theme park sectors. Such seasonal or casual staff have little or no reason to show commitment to their employer or enthusiasm when serving their clients. In the case of in-migrant staff they may also have problems integrating with the local

community. The seasonality of many tourism jobs also mitigates against the development of a career structure. Promising staff, therefore, will usually move on because they cannot see a clear career path, given that the organization will only be employing a handful of staff, if any, in the off-peak season which can be 4 or 5 months long.

Management Styles

The tourism industry still contains ample evidence of management styles that are not conducive to the development of sustainable human resources and fair treatment of staff. According to Baum, these include:

- *ad hoc*, unplanned recruitment
- high staff turnover being seen as inevitable and desirable
- little or no interest in why staff leave
- recruitment to 'plug gaps' with no preparatory training
- key staff imported from outside rather than being 'grown' or developed from the local workforce
- staff perceived as a cost rather than an asset
- authoritarian, remote management cultures
- inflexible imposition of corporate culture regardless of local culture
- no senior management commitment to training.

These management styles do not encourage loyalty to organizations and their customers or interest in a long-term career in the tourism industry.

Training and Personal Development

The tourism industry has an increasingly well-developed system of vocational training, particularly in the retail travel and hospitality sectors. However, in difficult economic times, training tends to be one of the first areas to be cut. Furthermore, most training is normally related to people's current job. It is rarely concerned with preparing them for possible future roles or developing staff as people rather than operatives. Given that many people in the industry have had little formal education beyond school level, this lack of personal development opportunities is a weakness. Such development could improve the self-image of employers and raise the status of employees in the industry which in turn might reduce turnover.

In many cases there is still too wide a gulf between industry and educational institutions which further reduces training and personal development opportunities.

Job Satisfaction

Many staff are employed in jobs which offer little job satisfaction. For example, many tasks, such as making computer bookings and working theme park rides, are monotonous. At the same time, the continuing process of de-skilling, in restaurant kitchens, for example, has reduced the job satisfaction of staff whose job once gave them scope for creativity. Now they simply tend to be involved in carrying out low-skill, low-interest tasks. Poor levels of job satisfaction contribute to high staff turnover, particularly amongst the more talented, ambitious staff, exactly the type of employees an organization should be seeking to retain.

Staff–Tourist Relations

In relation to the idea of equality and justice implicit within the concept of sustainable tourism, the relationship between staff and tourist is often negative. Tourists often show very little respect towards staff. This may reflect the low status which jobs in tourism have amongst customers. In a survey conducted by Baum in 1991, and reported in his book of 1995, a sample of 384 people were asked to identify the desirability of employment in different sectors of tourism. Jobs in the following sectors were all seen as being desirable by **less** than half of the sample:

- restaurant operation and management jobs – seen by 39% of respondents as desirable
- heritage attractions – 38%
- operational jobs in hotels – 32%
- souvenir shops – 27%
- operational jobs in restaurants – 26%.

The widespread practice of tipping is a negative phenomenon in social equality terms. It is undignified to expect people to rely on what is in effect charity for part of their wage and it also puts too much power in the hands of the tourist.

High Turnover and Sustainability

The characteristics of tourism employment have tended to lead to high turnover, particularly in the hospitality and retail travel sectors. Indeed, amongst many employers, there is an apparent acceptance that people will take jobs in these sectors on a short-term basis until a better opportunity arises. High turnover is very costly in terms of the need for constant training of new staff and the loss of continuity in operations while vacancies are filled. It also makes it very difficult to build sound foundations for the future of the industry.

Human Resource Issues, the Different Sectors of Tourism and the Different Types of Tourism Organizations

Figure 21.1 attempts to identify the sectors of tourism and types of tourism organizations which are the most problematic in terms of the relationship between human resources and sustainable tourism. It is very simplistic but it is a helpful framework for considering this complex issue. It is not always as clear cut as Fig. 21.1 might suggest. For instance, a small, locally owned enterprise may pay lower wages than a transnational corporation.

Examples of Good Practice

However, there are many examples of good practice in the types of organizations and sectors which according to Fig. 21.1 have human resource practices which are not very compatible with the concept of sustainability, such as large transnational enterprises and private organizations in competitive markets like hospitality.

Some notable examples of good practice in tourism include:

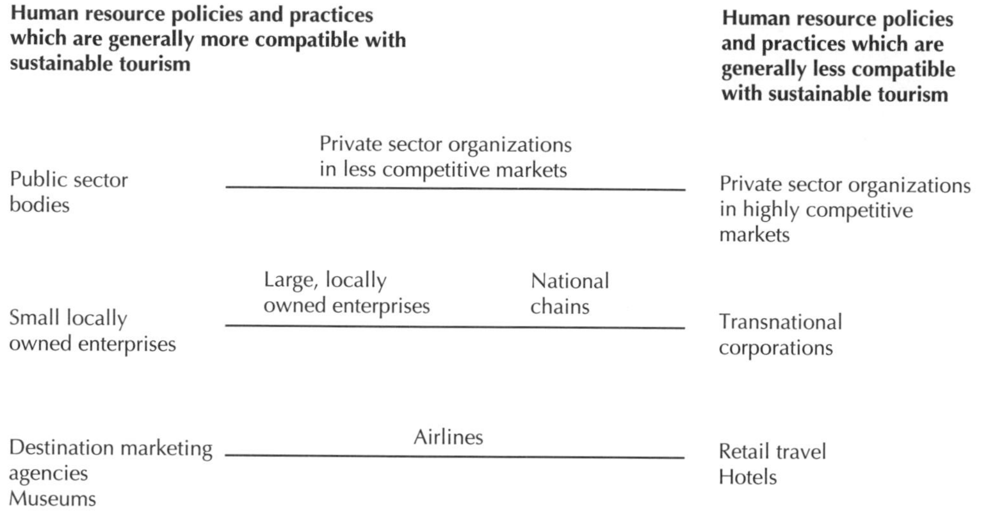

Human resource policies and practices
which are generally more compatible with
sustainable tourism

Human resource policies
and practices which are
generally less compatible
with sustainable tourism

Public sector
bodies

Private sector organizations
in less competitive markets

Private sector organizations
in highly competitive
markets

Small locally
owned enterprises

Large, locally
owned enterprises

National
chains

Transnational
corporations

Destination marketing
agencies
Museums

Airlines

Retail travel
Hotels

Fig. 21.1. Human resources, the sectors of tourism, types of tourism organizations and sustainability.

- the idea of empowerment, where organizations like Accor and Marriott have given staff more power to make decisions in their everyday jobs
- Club Méditerranée which has always tried to break down the barriers between staff and customers by the concept of 'Gentils Membres' (GMs) and 'Gentils Organizateurs' (GOs) and the idea of the organization operating as a club
- the policy of companies like Center Parcs which seek to meet their employment needs through the recruitment of local labour
- the training school near Bremen which is run by Hapag Lloyd, the German retail travel organization.

The Positive Dimension of Tourism Employment

It is also important to recognize that tourism employment does have a positive side in relation to the idea of sustainable tourism. Compared to other industries, tourism employment:

- creates large numbers of jobs at a relatively low cost

- is relatively safe, with little risk from industrial injury or job-related diseases
- provides opportunities for dynamic young people to develop interesting careers
- involves high levels of contact between customers and staff and provides opportunities for staff to meet people from many different countries.

Nevertheless, overall it is fair to say that, currently, human resource management in general in the tourism industry is not very conducive to the development of more sustainable forms of tourism.

Globalization, Multinational Corporations, Human Resources and Sustainability

Tourism is seeing the rise of globalization and the related growth of multinational corporations which are taking an increasing share of the world tourism market. This process carries significant threats for sustainability in relation to human resources, as follows:

- many of the multinational corporations such as McDonald's have grown through standardized products and selling them in a highly regimented environment. This restricts the opportunity for local staff to develop products and service delivery processes which reflect local cultural differences

- these major corporations tend to insist on labour practices which differ from the norm in their host country and can be in conflict with cultural values in the same host country
- multinational corporations feel free to use labour from anywhere in the world and tend to employ those who will work for the lowest wage. Such people may then be used anywhere throughout the company's operations throughout the world, often undercutting local labour.

The Special Case of Developing Countries

Developing countries are in a particularly difficult situation when it comes to developing their human resources with a view to creating more sustainable forms of tourism. They tend to have a poorly trained workforce which may not be used to working in the highly disciplined, but low status jobs found in the tourism industry. Furthermore, because the tourism market is often dominated by in-bound foreign tourists, many businesses are foreign owned and bring in with them their own supervisory and management level staff.

The local people are thus denied the opportunity to move up the career level and gain experience. Local people who show promise may find that their only prospect of developing a management career is to leave their home country and travel abroad to work. Thus their skills are lost to the local industry.

Towards More Sustainable Human Resource Management

Baum, in 1995, highlighted some general principles which he felt would lead to more sustainable human resource management. This is important because sustainable human resource management helps create sustainable tourism and sustainable communities. These principles were as follows:

- Human resource management in tourism should have a strong moral dimension, where pay and conditions are improved, for example, because it is morally the right thing to do.
- Employers must accept a sense of responsibility towards the local community and the people who live within it.
- Organizations should see their employees as an asset and should have faith in the ability of their staff.

He also advocated:

- the need to plan human resources on a long-term basis
- career planning for staff and making the criteria for promotion known to staff
- that key staff be grown and developed locally by the organization
- the operation of equal opportunities policies
- a partnership between staff and employers
- full senior management commitment to training
- modifying company culture and human resource practice to reflect local differences (in culture and geography)
- democratic, participative management cultures
- recognizing the link between human resource management and quality.

It is important to persuade private companies to recognize that the ideas put forward by Baum make good business sense by reducing turnover and improving customer service.

There will clearly be a role for the State, not only in terms of encouraging good practice, but also in regulation to prevent bad practice. This means legislation on discrimination, minimum wages, maximum working hours and trade union recognition.

At the same there is also a role for educational institutions in providing courses which are more closely geared to the needs of the tourism industry, in terms of both course content and the mode of delivery, such as the use of open and distance learning. This is the only way by which the majority of staff in the industry can gain access to educational opportunities. Management courses should also stress the importance of sustainable human resource management policies and practices.

Finally, national and local tourist boards should devise human resource management strategies for their areas to encourage the development of more sustainable forms of human resource management that recognize the role of human resources in the creation of more sustainable forms of tourism.

Conclusions

We began by saying that the human resource dimension is often ignored in the sustainable tourism debate. Yet if we define sustainable tourism as tourism which is socially equitable then it is clear that tourism makes unrealistic demands on its staff, and treats them poorly. At the same time, the problem of high staff turnover also threatens the development of sustainable tourism. If tourism is to be sustainable, it needs a workforce which is stable, satisfied and well trained.

We have noted that the situation is particularly difficult, where the market is dominated by major transnational corporations and in developing countries. In general, it also appears that the most serious problems are found in the hospitality and retail travel sectors.

The challenge to create more sustainable human resource management in tourism is clearly a major task. However, unless we succeed with this challenge, then it is hard to conceive of how we can develop truly sustainable, socially just tourism.

Discussion Points and Essay Questions

1. Discuss the likely reasons why many tourism organizations continue to offer poorer pay and working conditions than other industries.
2. Critically evaluate the suggestion that tourism organizations have responsibilities to the local community to provide employment for local people.
3. Discuss the arguments you might use to persuade a tourism organization to adopt more sustainable forms of human resource management.

Exercise

Select a tourism organization with which you are familiar, or for which you can easily gather data. Evaluate its current human resource management policies and practices to see if they are compatible with the concept of sustainability or not.

Case Study: Global Examples of Good Practice in Human Resource Management

Three times a year the World Travel and Tourism Human Resource Centre (WTTHRC) produces a publication which offers case studies of good human resource management practice in the tourism industry. The March 1998 issue included the following examples:

- The Skill New Zealand scheme which aims to improve standards of training. The country's Aviation, Tourism and Travel Training Organization (ATTTO) has become involved in this scheme for trades such as tour guiding, casino and adventure tourism, and information centre work.
- The Go Forward Plan introduced by Continental Airlines to help rejuvenate the airline company. The plan aimed to encourage staff to provide customers with a more reliable service. It was also built upon the principle of partnership between staff and management. Performance-related pay has been introduced and staff now receive a bonus if the airline achieves a good performance or productivity.
- Delta Hotels and Resorts has an Employee Service Guarantee which assures staff that: 'We promise to give you feedback on how you are doing or to give you a chance to tell us how we are doing . . . on a regular basis. This means you will have an Employee/Management Development Review within 30 days of your anniversary date. If we do not keep this promise, we will give you one week's pay.' (WTTHRC, 1998)
- Two modules worth of training for staff at the Disney Polynesian Resort at the Disney World theme park in Florida to make staff aware of the traditional Polynesian cultural values on which the hotel is based.
- Staff training courses at the Ka'anapoli Beach Hotel in Hawaii to make them aware of the natural culture of Hawaii. The hotel has also introduced empowerment measures to give staff more autonomy.
- Nevis Range Development plc, a Scottish ski facility operator, which has an 'open management system' and uses training to increase job satisfaction and provide a quality service for customers.
- The Four Seasons Resort, Bali, which provides language training facilities to help its staff to improve their spoken English. Staff are given financial incentives to follow these training courses.
- The Sky City Casino in New Zealand which provides specialized security training for its staff covering the adverse effects of alcohol consumption, for example.

These schemes, while all worthy, generally seem to be more about satisfying customers and improving the organization's financial performance than benefiting the staff or furthering the cause of sustainability.

22

Operations Management

The management of tourism operations, whether accommodation, attractions or air travel for instance, has major implications for sustainability in tourism. Once the hotel or the theme park is built, the way that it is managed on a day-to-day basis will determine its impact on the world around it, and whether or not it will be sustainable.

Operations management covers every aspect of the management of the operational side of tourism enterprises. It is:

> concerned with the design, operation, and control of the systems that matches the organizations resources to customers' service needs. (Rogers and Slinn, 1993)

> [concerned] with day-to-day management of the [hotel or attraction or air service]. It is about managing [the organization's] resources, notably the staff and physical equipment . . . to provide a satisfactory service for the customer, and an acceptable rate of return on the use of these resources. The goal of operations management . . . is [a] smooth and efficient operation. (Swarbrooke, 1995)

There is a tendency, therefore, for operations management to take a short-term view, being preoccupied with crisis management, responding to customer complaints and measures that will reduce current expenditure. Yet if we are to develop more sustainable forms of tourism, we have to encourage operations managers to take a

longer term view of how their organization operates.

Environmental Practice

Most aspects of operations management have implications for the environment. Tourism operations involve the purchase and use of a wide variety of goods and consume considerable amounts of energy and water resources. The industry also creates great volumes of waste. Therefore it is very important that all tourism organizations have good environmental practices.

The first stage in this process should be the carrying out of an Environmental Audit, which has been defined as:

> A systematic, regular and objective evaluation of the environmental performance of an organization or area, its plant, buildings, and processes. Much like financial audits, environmental audits can provide a measure of the environmental performance of a company as regards management procedures, resources issues, waste production and disposal, and usually specifically ways in which this performance can be improved. (Middleton and Hawkins, 1998)

The same authors have also suggested 10 Rs that should form the basis of a corporate environmental management system, in tour-

Table 22.1. The main supplies required by different sectors of tourism.

Hotels	Museum	Airline
• Food and drink	• Artefacts	• Aircraft
• Furniture	• Glass cases	• Fuel
• Staff uniforms	• Interactive computer systems	• Staff uniforms
• Cutlery and crockery	for interpretation	• Pre-prepared meals
• Cleansing materials	• Souvenirs for sale in the shop	• Vehicles
• Laundry services	• Staff uniforms	• Chemicals
• Electricity	• Audio-visual programmes	• Electricity
	• Electricity	

ism as well as in other industries, as follows:

- recognition of the nature of the issues, the problems and the opportunities surrounding environmental impacts and sustainability has to come before action
- refuse to engage in activities, as soon as possible, when they are recognized to be environmentally damaging
- reduce current levels of usage, for example, using better portion control to reduce food wastage
- replace products or producers with ones which are more environmentally friendly
- re-use materials wherever possible, such as cotton laundry bags in hotels
- recycle where re-use is not an option
- re-engineer, in other words, changing traditional corporate management strategies and operations to reduce costs and achieve growth in ever more competitive activities
- retrain staff to help them behave in a more environmentally friendly manner and to help educate tourists about sustainability issues
- reward staff who perform particularly well in relation to environmental practices
- re-educate the tourist so that they modify their behaviour.

This model sees a progression from the first 'R'. However, many people might argue that the final 'R', which focuses on the customer, should come first for if consumers do not change their attitudes and become more concerned with environmental issues, then organizations will not seriously address the other nine Rs.

Purchasing Policies

A major aspect of operations management is purchasing the wide range of goods and services which are required by tourism organizations. Table 22.1 illustrates just some of the main supplies which are required by tourism enterprises.

Even these short simplistic lists show the range of supplies needed by organizations in these three sectors. For all tourism organizations a purchasing policy that furthers the cause of sustainability should have several key elements:

- Wherever possible, supplies should be sourced locally. This has two advantages:
  (i) it maximizes the economic benefits of tourism for the local community
  (ii) it reduces the need for transport and thus energy consumption.
- Providing the most environmentally friendly products available, such as cleansing materials and vehicles.
- Only buying goods and services from suppliers which operate good environmental management systems.

Table 22.2. Welcoming visitors with special needs at a museum.

Special needs	Operational requirements
Visitors who are wheelchair dependent	• Ramp access • Lifts • Wheelchair-accessible toilets
Visitors with mobility problems	• Minimum number of steps • Non-slip surface
Visitors with hearing difficulties	• The use of induction loop systems in areas where there is live first-person interpretation and audio-visual productions • The training of some staff to use sign language
Visitors with impaired sight	• Braille signs • Displays that make use of senses like touch and smell rather than just visual displays
Visitors with learning difficulties	• Specially produced signs and brochures • Use of live first-person interpretation and audio-visual programmes rather than a reliance on written text
Visitors with special diets	• Foods which are acceptable for health-related diets such as gluten-free meals • Foods which are acceptable to those whose diet is determined by their religion such as kosher or halal meals
Visitors with babies and very young children	• Baby-changing facilities in both mens and ladies toilets • Facilities to heat up baby bottles and meals • High chairs in catering outlets
Visitors who speak another language	• Signs and brochures in foreign languages • Some staff trained to be able to answer simple questions in other languages
School and college groups	• Classrooms • Work sheets relating to the museum • Advice for teachers and lecturers
Coach parties	• Parking facilities for coaches

The aim should also be to minimize the use of all kinds of goods to reduce the use of resources and the creation of waste. This also has the advantage of reducing the organization's costs.

Welcoming Customers with Special Needs

Most customers have special needs of one kind or another. The social equity dimen-sion of sustainable tourism means that we should endeavour to make sure that tourism experiences are equally available to every-one. This means ensuring that tourism operations are managed so that they are accessible to customers with different types of special needs. Table 22.2 illustrates what might be involved in welcoming visitors with special needs at a museum.

It is important, however, to accommodate the special needs of different groups of cus-tomers sensitively, so they are not made to feel like a problem or that they are being stigmatized in the eyes of fellow customers and staff.

Given that the needs outlined in Table 22.2 cover probably the majority of the population in one way or another, welcoming visitors with these needs is a good way for an organization to sustain its market into the future.

Good Neighbours

Sustainability is all about tourism organizations being a good neighbour to those who live around their operations. This point can be illustrated through several examples. Hotels which have discos and wedding parties should encourage their guests to be quiet when they leave the hotel late at night. Fast food restaurants should either persuade their customers not to drop litter or should arrange for staff to pick up the rubbish which results from their operations. Attraction and hotel car parks should be well landscaped so that they are not too much of an eyesore for those who live next to them.

As well as these measures which are designed to minimize the negative impacts of tourism, organizations may also take actions that are positively beneficial for local people. For example, visitor attractions might give free tickets to people living locally as a good will gesture.

Tourism organizations would, perhaps, be wise to set up consultative committees or meetings with local people to allow neighbours to voice their concerns and be willing to provide information for local people. Being a good neighbour can also help organizations improve their performance and improve their long-term prospects by reducing the likelihood of opposition from neighbours to both the current operation and any future expansion plans.

The Safety of Staff and Customers

In earlier chapters of this book we noted that sustainable tourism implies that staff have

rights, as do tourists. One of the most fundamental of these rights must be the right to safe working conditions and a safe leisure experience, respectively. Operations managers must therefore be dedicated to improving the safety of both staff and customers. This is a very important issue in some sectors of the tourism industry, including:

- In hotels, where there are a number of concerns such as:
  (i) fire safety
  (ii) swimming pool safety
  (iii) balconies in rooms where there are young children
  (iv) food hygiene.
- At theme parks where the major issue is the safety of rides.
- For zoos, where the main potential danger to both staff and visitors is the threat of attacks by animals.
- Airline safety, particularly in an era of de-regulation and cost-reduction strategies on the part of airlines.
- Tour operators making their customers aware of potential risks in some destinations such as health problems and crime.

However, while tourism organizations have a responsibility to operate as safely as possible, there is also a responsibility on tourists to behave sensibly and to take reasonable precautions. There is also a duty on staff to follow safety precautions and use whatever special clothing and equipment that is issued to them by the organization.

Conclusions

It is clear that the day-to-day operational management of tourism organizations has major implications for sustainable tourism in terms of the environment. However, it is also important in relation to the social dimension of sustainability such as customer safety and relations with neighbours.

Unfortunately, therefore, it is worrying to note that operations management is often short term and rarely takes the longer term perspective that is a vital pre-requisite for sustainable management.

cies can play in the development of more sustainable forms of tourism.

Discussion Points and Essay Questions

1. Critically evaluate the 10 Rs put forward by Middleton and Hawkins.
2. Discuss what the concept of welcoming customers with special needs might mean for hotels *or* airlines *or* tour operators.
3. Discuss the role which purchasing poli-

Exercise

Choose a visitor attraction with which you are familiar. Then visit this attraction and talk to the person or people who are responsible for operations management at the attraction. Produce a report evaluating the operations management procedures and policies at the attraction in relation to the principles of sustainable tourism.

Case Study: Energy Conservation in Hotels

A major area in which operations management can contribute towards sustainability is in the field of energy conservation. Reducing energy consumption helps sustainability by:

- reducing the impact of the operation on the world's resources
- reducing the organization's costs which helps make it more economically sustainable.

Hotels have been at the forefront of energy conservation in the tourism industry. Several examples will illustrate this point.

- Between 1987 and 1995, Inter-Continental Hotels cut its energy costs by 27%. In 1995 alone it achieved a saving in its energy bills of some $3.7 million. The hotel's unit in Vienna, for example, has
  (i) installed computer-controlled air-conditioning and heating
  (ii) introduced energy-saving light bulbs
  (iii) brought in equipment that recycles warm air and reduces the overall demand for energy for heating
  (iv) started to share its cooling system with a neighbouring ice skating rink.
- The Pelican Resort on the island of St Maarten in the Caribbean which now uses solar power to heat water for its 300 rooms, the kitchens and the laundry
- The Kahala Mandarin Hotel in Hawaii where the air-conditioning is powered by hydro-electricity to conserve energy
- Research designed to help hoteliers reduce their energy consumption such as the 1995 Energy Efficiency and Conservation Survey of New Zealand Hotels, conducted by Richards and Ward.

Some professional bodies have devised checklists for hotels to help them conserve energy, one of which is reproduced below:

A checklist of energy-efficiency options has been developed by Environmental Hotels of Auckland (EHOA) (*Green Hotelier*, January 1997).

Space and water heating	• Ensure only occupied areas are heated • Set water heater temperature to 60°C
Lighting	• Make sure someone responsible for switching off lights when areas are not in use • Make the best use of daylight
Ventilation	• Ensure kitchen fans are switched off when kitchens are not in use
Air conditioning	• Set temperature controls for cooling to 24°C or higher • Ensure refrigeration plant, such as chilled water systems, runs only when required
Equipment	• Encourage staff to turn off equipment when it is not needed

	• Switch off fluorescent lights when an area will be unoccupied for longer than 5 minutes
	• Remove unnecessary lamps
Laundry	• Set washing machine temperature to 60°C
	• Encourage staff to run laundry equipment only with full loads
Controls	• Clearly label controls to indicate their function and their reduced settings
Catering	• Inform kitchen staff of start-up times for cooking equipment and discourage them from using hobs and ovens for space heating
Maintenance	• Check plant operation and controls regularly
	• Check that thermostats and humidistats are accurate
	• Check calibration of controls
	• Look for water leaks from mains, taps and showers and carry out necessary repairs
	• Clean light fittings regularly

23

Financial Management

It is surprising that very little has been written about the role of financial management in sustainable tourism. After all, all tourism organizations and tourism developments have financial objectives which, if they are not met, will ensure that either the organization or the development will have no long-term future. In this chapter we will examine several financial management issues which are relevant to the idea of sustainability in tourism. They cover matters relating both to the development of new tourism projects as well as the everyday financial management of existing tourism organizations and developments.

Investment Appraisal

Many capital projects in tourism are viewed by potential investors as relatively high risk in relation to residential property or retail complex investment for example. This may be because:

- There have been a number of well publicized 'failures' in the attractions sector, for example, such as Windsor Safari Park and the early development proposals for the Battersea Power Station site in the UK. Even the powerful Disney Corporation has been experiencing problems with making its Disneyland

Paris project a success. Likewise many relatively newly built hotels in South-East Asia are, at the time of writing, experiencing very low occupancy levels due to the economic crisis in that region.
- Tourism developments are highly specialized and inflexible and cannot easily be adapted for new uses.

It would be difficult and expensive, for example, to convert most theme parks to a new use. Furthermore the market is seen to be volatile and fickle with ever shortening life cycles.

For these reasons investors in tourism projects tend to want to get their money back very quickly to balance the risk. This emphasis on short-term return forces organizations to behave in non-sustainable ways to exploit the environment, staff, local communities, suppliers and tourists for short-term gain, with little thought for the future. At the same time, many new tourism project proposals are not evaluated in terms of their true costs to society as a whole. As we have seen earlier in the book, the host community often subsidizes new hotels or attractions, for example, through public investment in infrastructure. It is only fair that those organizations which develop new projects should pay the full cost of their project.

It is also important that we ensure that new project proposals also recognize the costs of development to the environment although at the moment there is often no obligation on them to do so because again these costs are met by others. This also has to change in the spirit of equity which is implicit in the idea of sustainable development.

Ethical Investment and Tourism Projects

Tourism projects have increasingly been seen as attractive investment opportunities by individuals and organizations whose ethical beliefs are highly questionable. It is alleged that organized crime syndicates in the USA have invested heavily in hotels in resorts like Las Vegas, where gambling is the main attraction.

At the same time, there can be controversies over investment in tourism in foreign countries by entrepreneurs from countries which are seen as undesirable by the international community. For example, in spring 1998 there was controversy over alleged Libyan investments. One UK-based newspaper reported that:

> The American Embassy in the Czech Republic last week warned its citizens not to stay in nine of the country's smartest hotels because they are allegedly owned by a Libyan company.
> The hotels, which include the Forum, where President Clinton stayed in 1994, and the Panorama were recently bought by a Maltese-based company, Corinthia, that is on a US government list of Libya-owned companies and is therefore subject to sanctions. Any US citizen caught breaking the sanctions, imposed after the Lockerbie bombing of the Pan-Am flight in 1988, could face up to 10 years' jail and fines of $250,000.
> The embassy's announcement has caused chaos in the city. B.B. King, the blues guitarist, who was playing in Prague, cancelled his booking at the Forum Hotel and several companies have postponed conferences.
> The announcement should not affect British visitors, according to a spokesman

at the British embassy. 'As far as we are concerned these hotels are Maltese-owned', he said. 'The US, anyway, has tougher domestic laws on these sort of things'. The Czech authorities are waiting for reaction from Washington before they decide whether or not to freeze the assets of the company. The International Monetary Fund is scheduled to meet in Prague in the year 2000. The Czechs fear that a continued US boycott could jeopardise the meeting because the city would be left short of 5,000 beds. (Peter Shadbolt, *Daily Telegraph*, 4 April 1998)

This case highlights several interesting issues. Firstly, the boycott is based on alleged, not proven, links. Secondly, the action is affecting a third party, namely the city of Prague which has nothing to do with the dispute between Libya and the USA. Finally, the proposed boycott could be seen as an unethical act in its own right with a government seeking to use tourists and foreign entrepreneurs as simply an extension of its own foreign policy regardless of the interests of these groups.

Nevertheless, sustainability must be about ethical investment in new tourism projects or it will lack the integrity and idea of justice that must be at the centre of all sustainable development.

Short-term Budgeting

Most budgeting takes place over a 12-month cycle, whereby the short-term financial objectives of an organization have to be met within a 1-year period. These objectives might include:

- profit maximization, in other words, creating as large a surplus of income over expenditure as possible
- breaking even, so that income and expenditure equal each other
- operating within a given level of subsidy or grant aid, so that expenditure exceeds income by no more than the total subsidy available.

The fact that these objectives have to be met every year, might go against the fundamental principle of sustainable tourism which is about taking a longer-term perspective. The perspective taken by organizations tends to be little more than 12 months. This is particularly the case with smaller organizations which lack the resources to plan on a long-term basis, for whom life is generally a short-term 'hand-to-mouth' existence. How can organizations planning on such a short-term basis be realistically expected to take the longer-term view demanded by the concept of sustainability

Short-term budgeting also mitigates against organizations making large-scale capital investments that will 'green' the operation but may take many years to pay for themselves. Energy conservation measures and recycling facilities may well fit into this category. In many organizations any capital project that is so large that it dominates the budget is unlikely to be implemented, unless it has a guaranteed short-term payback period.

Cost Reduction and Sustainability

Many tourism organizations seek to meet their financial targets by rationalization and cost reduction. However, it is important to recognize that such action can be at odds with the idea of sustainability. In a service industry cost reductions usually mean cutting staff, reducing salaries or increasing productivity by making people work harder. Any cost reduction therefore can cost employees their jobs or reduce the multiplier effect of the organization in the local economy. It can also reduce the quality of experience for the tourists themselves as staff become demoralized and less enthusiastic about their jobs.

Cost reduction also means trying to extract lower prices from suppliers which in turn makes it harder for the suppliers to sustain their enterprises. Training is often one of the first victims of cost reduction strategies which affects the long-term sustainability of the business. Staff who are not trained continually will lack the skills to

take the business into the future and employees who are denied training opportunities may become demoralized and leave. General maintenance may be cut, such as painting, and this may ultimately shorten the life of the hotel, or the theme park ride, or whatever else is denied regular maintenance.

Conversely, cost reduction can provide a commercial motivation for tourism organizations to take action to make their operation more sustainable. This includes:

- increased recycling to reduce wastage
- initiatives to reduce the consumption of water and energy
- reducing mileage allowances for those staff who use their car for company business and/or phasing out company cars and replacing them with public transport passes, where appropriate.

Public Spending Cuts, Privatization and Sustainable Tourism

Two major trends in the public sector in recent years also have negative implications for sustainable tourism, as follows:

- The desire of central and local government, generally, to reduce public expenditure has led to them making cuts in the budgets of a range of public sector agencies which are key players in the tourism industry, notably publicly owned attractions like museums and theatres, together with tourist offices. This trend makes it more difficult for these organizations to compete in the market and this makes their future potentially less sustainable. Already some local authority owned museums in the UK have closed, while others are losing visitors because they cannot afford to invest in exhibitions and artefacts.
- The trend towards privatization and deregulation is leading to public sector agencies either being transferred into

the private sector, or at least having to compete with commercial organizations. This is being seen in the UK with organizations such as English Heritage. The need for organizations to behave more commercially can lead to them no longer taking the broader perspective which incorporates social objectives that reflect the needs of the whole community. At the same time, as we have seen with the privatization of British Rail, this process can lead to a lack of co-ordination in what is a national network. Both these situations are clearly against the concept of sustainability.

The two trends noted above are reducing the potential contribution of the public sector as a leading force in the growth of sustainable tourism.

Optimizing the Use of Resources

Most physical developments in tourism – hotels, visitor attractions and transport infrastructure – have high fixed costs, which means that most of their costs are incurred regardless of the number of users. They also mean that if the facility is unused or under-used at any time costs are still incurred. It could be argued therefore that sustainable tourism also means optimizing the utilization of tourism facilities and reducing the times when they are unused or under-used. This clearly means tackling the issue of seasonality and variations in demand, so as to make the best possible use of the staff and the premises. For example:

> Given that most attractions are very expensive to run and develop, it is amazing that many of them are only open from 10.00 a.m. to 5.00 p.m. and often for just 8 months a year. Thus for 17 hours a day and 4 months a year they are unused. (Adapted from Swarbrooke, 1995)

Such attractions are realising this and making themselves available for evening functions. It also means using the attraction for special events in the off-peak season. For example, when the author was the manager of the Wigan Pier heritage attraction in Greater Manchester, UK, a range of events were attracted to fill this role including:

- using the hard-surfaced otherwise under-used car park for caravan rallies in the winter months when grass-covered caravan sites are often too wet to be used
- boat rallies using the canal that runs through the site
- charity evenings ranging from a wedding dress exhibition to a clay-pigeon shoot using laser guns
- the use of the attraction's own acting company to put on evening performances of Victorian melodramas and pantomimes at Christmas.

Many hotels also seek to optimize use of their resources by using themed weekend breaks to bring in business when their corporate clients have gone home on Friday evenings.

The rise of the winter sun market has also helped Mediterranean hotels stay open all year, thus optimizing the use of their resources. It also helps the staff by guaranteeing them permanent all-year-round jobs. However, this trend has yet to really benefit the industry in places like Greece where many resorts still close for up to 5 months every year. Interestingly, the Greek National Tourism Office has announced that developing off-peak season business in the country is one of its major policy priorities. This is good news for the concept of sustainability in tourism.

Some would argue that off-peak closure is more sustainable because it allows the destination to 'recover' from tourism. However, the need for such recovery, the author believes, reflects those places where the types of tourism are clearly not sustainable or effectively managed. Sustainable tourism should instead, the author suggests, mean tourism which is all-year-round, is well balanced between seasons and optimizes the use of resources as evenly as possible across the seasons.

Grant-aided Projects: Tomorrow's White Elephants?

The author is concerned at the number of tourism projects where much of the funding is provided by grant aid from a range of governmental and charitable bodies. The fear is that the availability of this grant aid is encouraging destinations and individuals to develop projects that are not sustainable in the long term and would not be considered viable if it were not for the availability of grant aid.

Two examples can illustrate this problem very well, as follows:

- In the UK, the National Lottery is ploughing tens of millions of pounds every year into new visitor attraction projects, particularly in disadvantaged regions. Many of the projects are large scale, often out of keeping with the general scale of attractions in that area. Local authorities are spending time and money preparing bids for funding for such projects. Yet they are being introduced in a highly competitive market where there is no strong evidence that there is demand for them. While each one is required to submit a business plan there is a danger that over-ambitious plans are submitted to try to ensure that the projects are awarded funding. Much less grant aid is available for running costs so if these projects run into financial difficulties there may be no money available to support them. Or the public sector, in spite of other spending priorities, may have to divert funds to support these 'flagship' projects.
- The European Union has invested millions of ECUs in heritage centre projects in Ireland in recent years. Most centres have received European Union money. Yet again most of the money is for capital purposes, rather than revenue. With the enlargement of the European Union, this funding will fall dramatically in the future. Already visitor numbers at many heritage centres are disappointing and there are real fears over their long-term

sustainability when the European money is no longer available.

While grant-aid can help 'pump-prime' innovative new projects designed to develop more sustainable forms of tourism, it can, as we have seen, lead to the growth of projects which may not be sustainable. This issue needs addressing, particularly by those who advocate more use of grants in the funding of tourism projects.

Conclusions

It is clear that while often ignored in the sustainable tourism debate, financial management is at the heart of the issue of sustainable tourism. This is true in terms of both new development projects and the day-to-day operations of existing tourism organizations. We have seen the importance of resource use optimization and the problems associated with cost reduction and the grant-aiding of tourism projects. Overall, the main discrepancy between financial management and sustainable tourism is the fact that the former tends to be based on short-term perspectives while sustainability is about taking a long-term view.

Discussion Points and Essay Questions

1. 'Sustainable tourism can only be built on ethical investment'. Discuss this statement.
2. Evaluate the ways in which a museum *or* a theme park might optimize the use of their resources.
3. Discuss the ways in which cost reduction measures can be at odds with the concept of sustainable tourism.

Exercise

Select three tourism projects which have been developed with significant contributions of grant aid from sources such as the government, state lotteries or the European Union. For each project you should try to answer the following questions:

- Would the project have been developed if the grant aid had not been available?
- To what extent do you believe that the project is sustainable?

Conclusions to Part Five

In Part Five we have seen that sustainability is a challenge for all four functional management areas, namely, marketing, human resources, operations and finance.

As in this field of ethical management as a whole the emphasis is upon:

- taking a longer term perspective than has been traditional
- being environmentally friendly
- behaving in ways which are socially responsible
- reducing the waste of human resources as well as the earth's resources
- being fair to tourists, the industry and the host community.

Part Six

Sustainable Tourism and Different Sectors and Types of Tourism

---

The chapters in this part look at the concept of sustainable tourism in relation to nine sectors or types of tourism, namely:

(i)   tourist destinations
(ii)   visitor attractions
(iii)   tour operations
(iv)   transport
(v)   hospitality
(vi)   cultural tourism
(vii)   ecotourism
(viii) all-inclusive and self-contained resort complexes
(ix)   business tourism.

24

Tourist Destinations

Sustainable tourism, in relation to destinations, means ensuring the future success of existing destinations and planning new destinations, with their long-term future development in mind. This chapter will explore a range of issues relating to sustainability and destinations.

Firstly, we will look at the reasons why managing destinations is so difficult, and secondly we will consider the positive and negative impacts of tourism in destinations and how they vary according to the type of destination.

The Complexity of Destination Management

Destinations are complex phenomena to manage for a number of reasons including the following:

- They exist at different, but inter-related, geographical levels. This is illustrated in Fig. 24.1 in the case of the small French town of Sarlat, which is at the heart of the immensely popular Dordorgne or Périgord area. There is overlap and possible duplication in destination marketing and management functions, and there is often conflict over tourism policy between local and central government.

- Most destination management is in the hands of public sector agencies that only own or control a small proportion of the destination product. Most of the product is in the hands of the private sector over whom the public sector agencies have little or no control.

- Many destinations are managed and marketed by government agencies with limited budgets that cannot match the spending power of foreign tour operators, hotel chains or airlines.

- The destination is not a single homogeneous product but is rather a 'kit' made up of lots of individual products. Each tourist puts these individual products together to create their own specific 'do-it-yourself' holiday product.

- Destination management involves a bewildering range of stakeholders, all with their own interests including local residents, the local tourism industry, externally based companies, tourists and elected representatives. Most decisions on tourism planning and management in destinations are taken by elected representatives who are usually untrained and make decisions on the basis of political considerations rather than in the interests of sustainable tourism.

This complexity and diversity makes it difficult to make generalizations about desti-

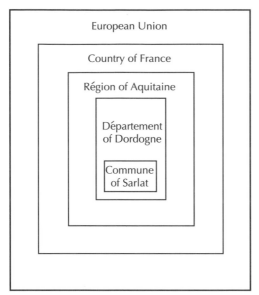

Fig. 24.1. The different geographical levels of destinations.

nations but that is what we must now endeavour to do.

The Positive and Negative Impacts of Tourism in Destinations

The negative and positive impacts of tourism in destinations have been well summarized by Middleton and Hawkins. Their ideas are detailed in Table 24.1.

Clearly the sustainable tourism challenge is to manage tourism in destinations in ways which maximize the positive impacts while reducing the negative ones. However, every destination is different and the actual impacts will vary between different types of destination, depending upon:

- when the resort was developed and how well the development was initially planned
- the types of tourism and tourist which the destination attracts
- the level of development of the local tourism industry and its relations with externally based tourism organizations

- public sector policy
- the fragility or otherwise of the local environment, economy and culture.

Sustainability and Different Types of Destination

Using sustainability in the broadest sense of the term, the word means different things in different types of destination. In wilderness areas where tourism is new, it often means developing tourism in ways which do not destroy the fragile ecosystem.

In rural and urban areas, where traditional activities like agriculture or heavy industry are in decline it means developing forms of tourism that will replace the income and jobs being lost in the traditional industries, thus ensuring that the community can sustain itself into the future. In established destinations it means developing forms of tourism which increase the ability of the destination to sustain both its environmental resources and its tourism market to prevent the onset of decline.

In other words, tourism must be sustainable in itself but it must also help to sustain the local community and environment.

The Tourist Area Life Cycle

The idea that destinations have life cycles was first suggested in 1980 by Butler through his model of the 'tourist area life-cycle', which is illustrated in Fig. 24.2.

This concept has become very influential in tourism and clearly has major implications for sustainable tourism, particularly as the model also suggests that each stage of the cycle has implications for:

- tourist numbers and types
- the level and nature of contact between hosts and guests
- the degree of change in the destination
- who is in control of the local tourism industry.

This aspect of the model is illustrated in Fig.

Table 24.1. The negative and positive impacts of tourism in destinations. Source: Middleton and Hawkins (1998).

Negative	Positive
Physical	
• Erodes natural spaces through construction of airports, marinas, resort complexes and so on.	• Provides a long-run justification for the protection, preservation and enhancement of natural and built resources, including the protection of biodiversity
• Pressures of overdevelopment and too many visitors erodes and damages fragile natural, and built environments – from Alpine ski resorts, coral reefs, to cathedrals and heritage cities such as Venice	• Provides access to internationally recognized quality standards for environmental resources
• Produces congestion and overcrowding leading to loss of wildlife habitats and damage to ecosystems	• Stimulates improvements to the quality of the physical environment available to residents
• Generates litter, sewage, noise emissions and use of chemicals and pollutants for maintaining landscapes, golf courses, laundries and visitor transportation	• Provides an economic justification and means for the regeneration of degraded/disused heritage environments based, for example, on 19th century harbours, railways, warehouses, and manufacturing sites for which the original economic rationale has disappeared
• Leads to ugly uniformity of buildings and townscape with no respect for architectural integrity or for such traditional styles as may exist	
• Diverts local resources and amenities such as water and land for tourism developments which disadvantage residents	
Social/economic	
• Commercializes the environment for profits which are diverted from the destination and do not accrue to local residents	• Creates economic value/generates markets for natural or built environments that otherwise may have no direct economic contribution to resident populations
• Employment at management level often goes to non-residents leaving only low-paid menial jobs. Tourism employment disrupts traditional employment patterns and the community structures they created	• Generates revenue which may be used for conservation goals
• Economic benefit leaks away from destinations through imports of materials and food and beverage, exacerbated by imposition of Western business methods alien to many local communities in the developing world	• Provides employment and opportunities for small businesses. Stimulates compatible new economic activity to supply tourism businesses
• Tourism provides a market for prostitution and is associated with drugs and crime	• Raises the standard of living for resident populations, especially if tourism generates otherwise unobtainable foreign currency and tax revenues
• Introduces developed country moral standards into local communities, generating greed, indolence,violence and crime	• Underpins the provision of restaurants, sports recreation facilities, local transport and generally improves the quality of life for residents
• Effectively lowers traditional qualities of life by introducing an alien, dominant, all-pervasive industry imposed upon and controlled from outside the community	
• Generates tension and animosity between visitors and residents	

Table 24.1. *continued*

Negative	Positive
Cultural/educational	
• Undermines local arts and cultural traditions of local residents by removing their original rationale and turning them into artificial staged events for profit • Undermines and eventually destroys original local identities and traditions of place • Communicates messages of environmental destruction, by examples of bad practice	• Supports and helps to fund local music, theatre, the arts, folk traditions, festivals and events • Provides a market for local crafts and manufacturing • Reinforces and focuses local identifies and the traditions of particular places. Helps to sustain and focus pride of place • Provides a medium for demonstrating and communicating environmental appreciation and values to both visitors and residents

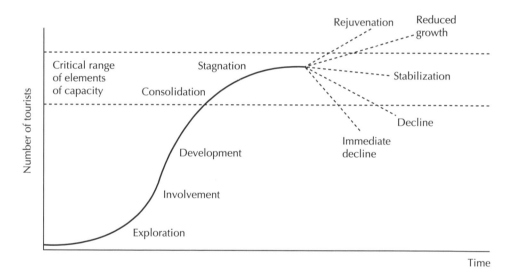

Fig. 24.2. Tourist area cycle of evolution.

24.3. Clearly, Butler believes that as the destination develops, problems arise in relation to the fact that outsiders begin to take control of the local tourism industry, and contact between locals and visitors becomes more formal and institutionalized. These could all be seen as negatives in relation to the concept of sustainable tourism. Conventional wisdom appears to be that we should develop destinations in ways which retard or even prevent these things occurring.

At the same time the tourist area life cycle also shows that resorts can decline which is

a threat to the idea of sustainability because it leads to:

• reduced income and less employment
• under-used infrastructure
• under-used or even derelict buildings
• the demoralization of the local population.

This phenomenon is clearly evident in some UK seaside resorts today.

Butler's model, in relation to sustainable tourism, therefore, reminds us of the need to

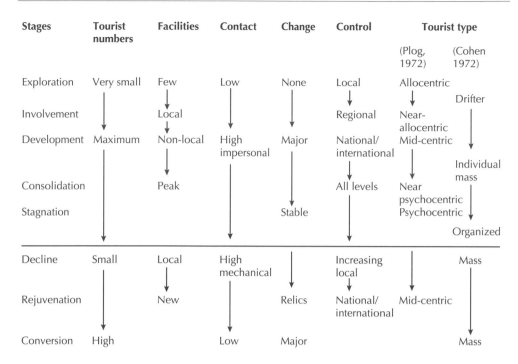

Fig. 24.3. Hypothetical cycle of tourist areas.

rejuvenate destinations constantly, preferably before the decline sets in. In the chapter on coastal tourism, there is a case study of how Benidorm has rejuvenated itself as a successful resort.

In terms of sustainability, one of the increasing trends is that the tourist area life cycle is getting ever shorter due to:

- the desire of tourists to constantly find new places to visit
- competition and the growth of new destinations.

Stagnation and decline, because of these factors, can sometimes be seen in a matter of a few years after the destination first began to attract significant numbers of tourists. This shortening of the life cycle is clearly a threat to sustainability and could lead to resort investment never being repaid.

A further important point is that as Middleton and Hawkins comment, Butler's theory

      supports the view that destination

managers can arrest or change this 'normal' development pattern by the management strategies that they adopt. (Middleton and Hawkins, 1998)

However, the fact is that a tourist area life cycle is rarely a neat curve and is often affected by factors which are largely outside the control of the destination managers. This point is illustrated in the hypothetical life cycle illustrated in Fig. 24.4.

Furthermore, just like the concept of the product life cycle on which it is based, the tourist area life cycle idea has a number of limitations. It:

- Tends to see the market as homogeneous and does not recognize that a single resort can have as many tourist area life cycles as it has market segments. For example, for elderly British tourists, Benidorm may be in the 'rejuvenation phase' while amongst Russian tourists, it may be in the 'involvement' or 'development' stage.

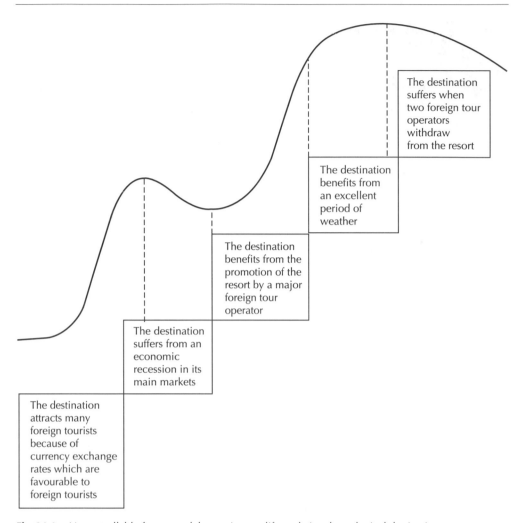

The destination
suffers when
two foreign tour
operators
withdraw
from the resort

The destination
benefits from
an excellent
period of
weather

The destination
benefits from the
promotion of the
resort by a major
foreign tour
operator

The destination
suffers from an
economic
recession in its
main markets

The destination
attracts many
foreign tourists
because of
currency exchange
rates which are
favourable to
foreign tourists

Fig. 24.4. Uncontrollable factors and the tourist area life cycle in a hypothetical destination.

● May be of only limited help in planning terms because it is difficult to predict when a stage begins. Often, the time when a particular stage begins can only be recognized some time *after* the event, which is little help in relation to forward planning.

From this it appears, therefore, that rather than being a precise technique used in the planning process, the concept of the tourist area life cycle is simply a useful way of conceptualizing how destinations develop and the key issues which arise at each stage of their development.

Doxey's Irridex

Another influential model that is relevant to sustainable tourism is Doxey's Irridex (Doxey, 1976). This model, based on what Doxey found in Barbados and Majorca, suggested that as tourism developed in destinations the attitude of local people towards tourists changed for the worse, as follows:

● The level of euphoria. People are enthusiastic and thrilled by tourist development. They welcome the stranger and there is a mutual feeling of satisfaction. There are opportunities for locals and money flows in along with the tourist.

- The level of apathy. As the industry expands people begin to take the tourist for granted. He or she rapidly becomes a target for profit-taking and contact on the personal plane begins to become more formal.
- The level of irritation. This will begin when the industry is nearing the saturation point or is allowed to pass a level at which the locals cannot handle the numbers without expansion of facilities.
- The level of antagonism. The irritations have become more overt. People now see the tourist as the harbinger of all that is bad. 'Taxes have gone up because of the tourists'. 'They have no respect for property'. 'They have corrupted our youth'. 'They are bent on destroying all that is fine in our town'. Mutual politeness has now given way to antagonism and the tourist is 'ripped off'.
- The final level. During this time people will have forgotten that what they cherished in the first place was exactly what drew the tourist; but in the wild scramble to develop, this has been overlooked and the environment allowed to change. What people must now learn to live with is the fact that their ecosystem will never be the same again. They might still be able to draw tourists but of a very different type from those they so happily welcomed in early years. If the destination is large enough to cope with mass tourism it will continue to thrive.

Clearly, in terms of the social dimension of sustainable tourism this progression is a problem. Our aim must be to focus on finding ways of slowing down or even reversing this process. This might involve:

- ensuring that local people do not subsidize the tourist and that the tourist is seen to pay a fair price for their holiday
- trying to educate both guests and hosts about each other to reduce the chances

of antagonism based on ignorance or misunderstandings
- involving the local community in tourism development decisions
- making sure that the volume of tourists never rises to the point where it threatens to overrun the local population.

This latter point brings us to the issue of destination carrying capacity.

The Concept of Carrying Capacity: a Useful Tool?

Those who advocate sustainable tourism seem to place great faith in the concept of carrying capacity, and numerous studies have been conducted around the world to establish the carrying capacity for different destinations. The idea is simple, that if it can be decided how many tourists an area can accommodate before the volume of visitors begins to cause problems then we may be able to manage tourism so that this number is never exceeded. The author argues that there are, perhaps, as many as six types of carrying capacity. These are illustrated in Fig. 24.5.

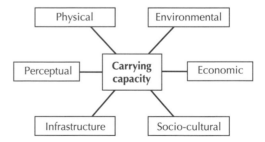

Fig. 24.5. The six types of carrying capacity.

We will now look at each of the types of carrying capacity in a little more detail.

- **Physical** capacity is the number of people that can be physically accommodated in a given area or site. It would mean, for example, how many people could be packed on to a beach, shoulder to shoulder. It is a simple, crude measure that has nothing really to do with sustainability or the quality of the tourist experience.

- **Environmental** capacity is the number of people an area or site can accommodate before damage to the physical environment begins to occur. This could be footpath erosion or disturbance to the habitat of wildlife for instance.
- **Economic** capacity is the number of tourists an area or site can absorb before the economic life of the local community begins to be adversely affected. This could mean traffic congestion slowing down business-related journeys.
- **Sociocultural** capacity is the volume of visitors that can be accommodated before the host community society and/or culture begins to be irreversibly affected by the impact of the tourist. This might involve affecting migration patterns, or trivializing traditional events, for example.
- **Infrastructure** capacity is the number of tourists that can be received before the infrastructure becomes incapable of coping adequately. This might mean everything from sewage and water services to road and airport capacity.
- **Perceptual** capacity, in contrast to the other five types is demand – rather than supply – oriented. It is the number of people an area or site can absorb before the quality of experience for the tourist is adversely affected. On a romantic beach for a couple, this could mean the arrival of a third person, while for a gregarious person the same beach could accommodate thousands with no loss of quality of experience. This is a very subjective measure of capacity.

Carrying capacity is an important idea because it is clearly related to the idea of de-marketing, which has been discussed in more detail in Chapter 20. The de-marketing of destinations should, presumably, begin when the area begins to reach its carrying capacity. However, the concept and the practical side of the idea of carrying capacity

can be criticized on a number of fronts. While these criticisms have been covered earlier in Chapter 3, they are relevant at this stage. They include the following:

- Even if we can measure the capacity accurately, how can we implement it in practice? Can we really close destinations when they are full or introduce systems whereby you must pre-book your trip? Probably not.
- Some of the types of capacity, such as perceptual and social, are very subjective.
- The current techniques for measuring capacity are rather crude and tend not to take account of key factors such as:
  (i) the type of destination and the fragility or otherwise of the environment and local community
  (ii) the type of tourism and market segments which the destination attracts.
- It is too simplistic in that it suggests that a few extra tourists can change a destination from an acceptable to an unacceptable situation. The situation is far more complex.
- The measurement of the capacity does not take into account the cost of *reducing* tourist volumes in terms of jobs and income if de-marketing is undertaken once the carrying capacity is reached. Keeping tourist volumes in popular destinations within its carrying capacity brings costs to the local community which must surely be taken into account when decisions are taken about de-marketing.

Therefore, although a useful idea, carrying capacity is fraught with difficulties when it comes to putting it into practice.

Destinations: the Human Rights Dimension

In terms of the social equality dimension of sustainable tourism, we simply cannot ignore the political situation in the destination and the human rights record of host governments in destinations. There is little point in worrying about the environmental impacts of tourism in a destination and ignoring the nature of the political regime in a destination and how it treats its own citizens.

This subject has so far received very little attention in most literature on sustainable tourism. However, political pressure groups have not been slow to seize on this point. Before the end of apartheid in South Africa, tourists were encouraged to boycott that country as a tourist destination, while today tourists are being asked to think about the human rights record of the government of Myanmar (Burma) before deciding whether to visit the country.

Sustainable tourism should clearly mean that:

- tourism development should not lead to the human rights of the indigenous population being taken away, or to them being deprived of resources for the sake of the tourists
- tourists and the tourism industry should seriously consider boycotting countries which clearly have a poor record on human rights
- tourists and the tourism industry should not allow themselves to be used as political propaganda by authoritarian regimes trying to persuade the outside world how wonderful their regime is by showing happy foreign tourists enjoying their visit
- tourism industry employees must be properly treated and reasonably paid
- tourist's freedom of movement should not be restricted by host governments providing that they behave reasonably
- heritage tourism products must tell the stories of ethnic minority communities as well as those of the majority community
- tourists should be protected from the effects of terrorism.

If these ideas were to be accepted today then tourism in many parts of the world would undoubtedly be under threat. However, tourism is now a major industry in many countries which have a poor human rights

record. It could therefore be a strong bargaining tool in persuading governments in these countries to improve their stance on the human rights of their own population and the tourists.

Maybe we will soon enter the era of **liberation tourism** where tourism and tourists become active agents of liberty for the oppressed people of the world. It is an attractive idea but that day is probably still a long way away.

Partnership: the Key to Success?

At the end of Part 3 of this book we noted that the only way for us to succeed in developing more sustainable forms of tourism will mean all the stakeholders in tourism working together. The destination is the natural focus for this partnership because it is where the stakeholders tend to all come together.

In destinations, partnerships are required between:

- public sector strategists and planners and private sector enterprises whose actions will either lead to the implementation of public sector strategies and plans, or will ensure that they simply gather dust on a shelf
- the local tourism industry and externally based tourism organizations, given that the former services the clients of the latter
- the host community and the tourists to ensure that tourism creates harmony and understanding between both groups, rather than irritation and conflict.

Several examples of apparently successful partnerships are illustrated in a case study at the end of this chapter.

Conclusions

In this chapter, we have seen that destinations are a complex phenomena involving a bewildering range of stakeholders. It has also to be recognized that several classic models in tourism such as tourist area life cycle, carrying capacity and Doxey's Irridex are very relevant to the idea of sustainable tourism in destinations. The author has also suggested that sustainability also means destinations being seen to take a positive stance on human rights. Finally, it has been suggested that partnership is the key to the successful development of sustainable tourism in destinations.

Discussion Points and Essay Questions

1. Discuss the implications of Butler's model of the tourist area life cycle for sustainable tourism management.

2. Critically evaluate the idea that sustainable tourism cannot be developed in a destination where the host government has a poor record on human rights.

3. Discuss Doxey's Irridex in terms of how applicable it is in different types of destinations, and how it relates to the concept of sustainable tourism.

Exercise

Choose a destination with which you are familiar. Attempt to calculate its carrying capacity, in terms of the six types of capacity outlined in this chapter. Present your findings in a report which highlights the problems you faced when undertaking this task.

Case Study: the Carrying Capacity of Venice

Given its popularity as a destination and the fragility of its environment, it is not surprising that several attempts have been made to measure the carrying capacity of Venice. It is interesting for us to look at these alternatives in a little detail given that in Chapter 20 we discussed the de-marketing of Venice.

In 1991, Canestrelli and Costa suggested that the optimal daily capacity for Venice would be:

- 9780 staying visitors in hotel accommodation
- 1460 staying visitors in non-hotel accommodation
- 10,857 day trippers.

The same authors estimated that the maximum carrying capacity for Venice should be set at 25,000 per day. However, research quoted by these authors showed that every day in August the city welcomed around 37,800 day trippers alone in the late 1980s. Even in 1987 van der Borg and Costa (1993) found that the 25,000 capacity was already being exceeded on 156 days. On 6 days they found the number even exceeded 50,000 visitors. Furthermore, van der Borg forecast that by the year 2000 the figure of 25,000 would be exceeded in 216 days and that on 7 days the number would exceed 100,000 tourists, four times the supposed maximum capacity.

Page has noted some of the effects of exceeding the 'carrying capacity' in Venice together with the problems of trying to take action to improve the situation:

> ... the negative impact of tourism on the historic centre of Venice is now resulting in a self-enforcing decline as excursionists, who contribute less to the local tourism economy than staying visitors, supplant the staying market as it becomes less attractive to stay in the city. Ironically, changing the attitude of the city's tourism policy-makers is difficult: it is heavily influenced by the pro-tourism lobby while hotel owners have sought to get the city council to restrict the booming eastern European day trip market which contributes little to the tourism economy. A number of positive measures have been enacted to address the saturation of the historic city by day visitors including denying access to the city by unauthorised tour coaches via the main coach terminal, and withdrawing Venice and Veneto region's bid for Expo 2000. Even so, the city continues to promote the destination thereby alienating the local population. A range of positive steps are needed to provide a more rational basis for the future development and promotion of tourism in the 1990s.
>
> Clearly, Venice is a small historic city under siege from a new marauding army in the late 20th century: the tourist and excursionist. In this case, tourism *has not* been a stimulus for urban growth, but has actually contributed to urban decline as residents have continued to leave. The excessive numbers of day trippers have also led to a deterioration in the quality of the tourist experience. (Page, 1994)

The Venice example does little to improve ones faith in our ability to turn the concept of carrying capacity into practical action.

Case Study: Partnerships in Practice

One theme which has emerged in this book is the view for partnerships between the key stakeholders in tourism in destinations. These partnerships should, according to Middleton and Hawkins, have seven major roles, as follows:

- Deciding local sustainable goals using information when it is available and common sense judgements and experience where it is not.
- Agreeing and communicating rolling 5-year capacity targets, type and volume of products offered for sale and key segments to be attracted.
- Devising and implementing planning guidelines and co-ordinating the available tools to integrate environmental assessment with planning. Where additional legislative/regulatory powers are required, it is essential that these are negotiated and implemented jointly by the public and private sector.
- Devising and implementing local visitor management programmes from the business perspective.
- Drawing up community awareness programmes.
- Co-ordinating visitor-awareness programmes to be implemented by local businesses and their partner organizations such as tour operators.
- Monitoring progress in achieving targets, undertaking research as necessary for this purpose. (Middleton and Hawkins, 1998)

There are a growing number of examples of partnerships in destinations worldwide of which a few are highlighted below.

The South Lakeland Tourism Partnership
Based in the UK – between 1992 and 1994 it had the following achievements:

For the resident community:
- conceiving and establishing, with South Lakeland District Council, a Residents Open Week: almost 40 attractions were involved with 5000 passes issued (6000 in 1995)
- establishing a visitor attractions forum, with the National Park Authority, for local guest house owners and hotel managers to learn about and promote 'heritage on your doorstep'
- supporting the district council and the National Park Authority in holding a Craft Fair; giving an opportunity for local crafts people to promote their work
- developing and presenting, with consultation, submissions to the Cumbria and Lake District Structure Plan and the Local Government Review Commission.

For the natural environment:
- 'The Lakes and Beyond'; a collaborative marketing project with British Rail to encourage increased use of trains
- 'Hilltop to the Lake' footpath scheme; a fund-raising venture to finance the building of an off-the-road footpath for residents and visitors from Beatrix Potter's house to the shores of Windermere.

For the visitor:
- special local offers for purchasers of British Rail Intercity tickets from Euston to Windermere
- development of itineraries for the travel trade
- integrated presence at British Travel Trade Fairs in 1992 and 1993, with awards for stand and promotion

- integrated presence at World Travel Market from 1992 onwards
- facilitating an 'Action Kendal' initiative to enable and encourage partnership work in the town.

(Source: McCormick quoted in Stabler, 1997)

Grecotel, Greece

The leading Greek hotel chain has taken a high profile pro-active stance on environmental issues. Its approach has been based on the concept of partnership with a range of organizations, including:

- foreign tour operators such as TUI and Thomson
- bodies such as the International Hotels Environmental Initiative
- local authorities in the districts where they have hotels
- the tourists themselves, whose behaviour they have sought to influence.

The Annapurna Conservation Area Project, Nepal

A government-sponsored initiative, that has involved:

- funding from outside agencies such as the Worldwide Fund for Nature and The Netherlands Development Organization
- local trekking lodge owners
- some 70 Village Development Committees
- tour operators.

The Wanuskewan Indian Heritage Inc., Canada

This is a non-profit-making organization run by native Canadians which has been developing heritage tourism in the region of Saskatchewan, in cooperation with the Wanuskewan Heritage Park Corporation. It brings together representatives of city, federal and provincial government, the local university and the park's 'Friends' organization.

25

Visitor Attractions

Visitor attractions are the heart of the tourism industry; they are motivators that make people want to take a trip in the first place. It is clear, therefore, that visitor attractions should have a central role to play in the development of more sustainable forms of tourism. However, before we look at this role, we must begin by recognizing that there are different types of visitor attractions. A typology of four different types of attraction is offered by the author below in Fig. 25.1.

In terms of sustainable tourism, attractions are divided into two main categories:

- those where tourism is seen as a problem and there is a need to manage tourism to limit its negative impact. This tends to be the case with natural environment attractions and those man-made attractions such as cathedrals which were not developed to attract tourists, but have become visitor attractions over time
- those man-made attractions where attracting the tourist is the sole reason for the development of an attraction, such as theme parks.

Special events and festivals can fall into either category. They can be traditional events which are in danger of being 'taken over' by tourists or may be new themed festivals designed to put a place on the tourist map.

Visitor Attractions in the Public, Private and Voluntary Sectors

A major consideration in respect of sustainability and attractions is the question of who owns an attraction. Attractions are owned by three types of organization, namely public, private and voluntary sector bodies. Public sector attractions, which are operated on behalf of the community as a whole and do not have an overt profit margin could perhaps be expected to take the longer term, broader perspective that sustainable tourism requires. Conversely, private sector operators with their short-term financial pressures, and need to impress a small group of shareholders or investors, could perhaps be expected to be less interested in sustainability. Finally, voluntary owned attraction, which tend to be owned by groups with a single shared interest, could probably be expected to have a narrow, single issue interest in sustainability. The National Trust, for example, focuses on the environmental conservation dimension of sustainability. However, things are not as simple as this and there are many exceptions. Nevertheless, who owns an attraction is clearly an issue in the stance an individ-

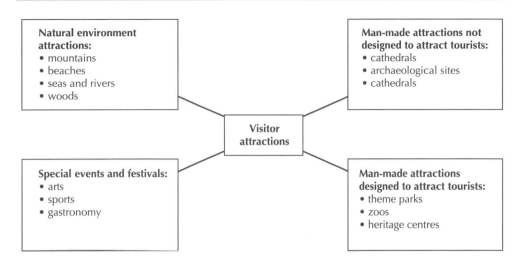

Fig. 25.1. A typology of visitor attractions.

ual attraction decides to take on the issue of sustainability.

Visitor Attractions, Ethical Issues and Sustainability

Some types of visitor attraction can be viewed negatively in relation to ethical considerations and the concept of sustainable tourism, in that they:

- appear not to have a sustainable future due to changes in consumer tastes
- are, in some ways, irreconcilable with the principles of sustainable tourism.

A good example of these two phenomena are **zoos** and **safari parks**.

> The question of zoos and whether it is right to keep animals in captivity for the entertainment of visitors is a long standing debate. Many zoos, recognising growing public distaste for traditional zoos, have responded ... [and now] sell the idea that their main purpose is education and conservation. As many zoo owners are voluntary sector bodies acting on behalf of the 'public interest' it is vitally important to their credibility that they are seen to behave in a socially responsible manner. It is

> interesting ... that one of the first tourism-related applications of virtual reality that has been talked about is the ... animal-less 'Virtual Zoo'! (Horner and Swarbrooke, 1996)

There are other examples of this apparent disparity between some visitor attractions and the concept of sustainable tourism.

In its early days, **Disneyland Paris**, was out of tune with the idea of sustainability in terms of its:

- apparent policy of not wishing to employ local people from the Paris area
- late payment of local contractors who worked on the development of the park
- 'Americanized' labour practices which were allegedly enforced on the staff.

Finally, the location and environmental impact of new sporting attractions such as golf courses is also a controversial topic in relation to the debate on sustainable tourism. Golf courses take up large amounts of land, require water to irrigate them and are often not accessible to local people who are not members of the club, even when they have been built on land to which the public previously had free access.

The Positive Role of Visitor Attractions in Relation to Sustainable Tourism

Attractions can also play a very important positive role in the development of more sustainable forms of tourism in two main ways. New attractions can breathe life into tired old destinations which were previously in decline. Examples of this include the casinos in Schevenigen in Holland, and Atlantic City in the USA. Furthermore, newly developed attractions can spearhead urban regeneration strategies and can help put rural areas on the tourism map for the first time. In recent years, for example, we have seen attractions used as a strategy to rejuvenate industrial cities, including the Albert Dock in Liverpool, UK, and the Oceanopolis Aquarium in Brest, France.

At the same time, certain attractions are also examples of good practice in relation to sustainability. These include **Center Parcs**, in the UK, which has created new wildlife habitats and planted trees on-site, and also ensures that, wherever possible, that it sources all the goods and services it needs from local suppliers.

A good example of the role that can be played by attractions, albeit in a small way, is the Mizen Head project, a case study of which can be found at the end of this chapter.

The Potential Role of Special Events and Festivals in Sustainable Tourism

So far we have focused upon physical attractions but special events and festivals can also play a positive role in the development of sustainable tourism, as the following examples illustrate:

- **Cinéscénie, the Vendée, France**. In this case a voluntary group, involving several thousand local residents, puts on a lavish spectacle on a heritage theme, which is viewed each year by several hundred thousand tourists. The income from the event is in turn used for the benefit of the local community, in terms of grants for local students and funding a radio station.
- **Spain 1992**. The Spanish government supported three major events in 1992. They were all designed to diversify the product and broaden the appeal of the Spanish tourism industry. These events were:
  (i) the Olympics in Barcelona
  (ii) Expo '92 in Seville
  (iii) Madrid, as the European City of Culture.
- **Oyster Festival, Galway, Ireland**. This annual event is a showcase for the local oyster-rearing industry and brings considerable economic benefits to the host community.

However, events and festivals can bring problems in relation to sustainability, of which perhaps the greatest is caused by their temporary nature. The challenge is to keep up the momentum of tourist numbers once the one-off event is over. This problem is faced by a range of places such as Olympic host cities to those cities which are designated as European City of Culture each year. If the volume of numbers cannot be sustained after the event, then there can be major problems of under-used infrastructure, including hotels and airports. This is particularly unfortunate where this infrastructure has been paid for by local taxpayers.

Towards More Sustainable Visitor Attractions

We will look at how the use of visitor attractions can contribute even more positively to the development of more sustainable forms of tourism, under two headings:

- the development of new attractions
- the types of attractions.

The Development of New Attractions
Figure 25.2 illustrates the issues which need to be taken into account when new attractions are developed.

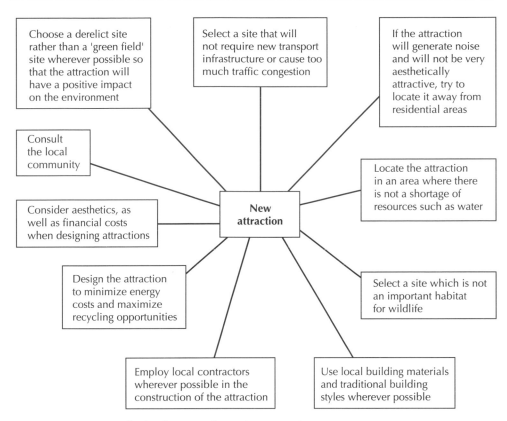

Fig. 25.2. Key issues in the development of new visitor attractions.

A major problem with most attractions is that they are designed for a single, specific purpose, and are therefore very difficult to adapt to other uses. What other use, for example, could one make of a Disney theme park or Legoland? Therefore, if an attraction fails, it would leave a serious problem of a blighted, derelict site.

Types of Visitor Attraction

Certain types of attraction are particularly close to the concept of sustainable tourism, especially those which reinforce and support the current life of the local community. Such types of attraction include the following:

- **Industrial tourism attractions**, such as workplaces which open their doors to visitors, and factory shops. These attractions bring economic benefits through the direct sales to visitors. They can also help improve the morale and feeling of self-worth of employees when they see the tourists valuing what they do for a living. Popular industrial attractions include food and drink factories and craft workshops.

- **Farms** which welcome visitors to see the work of the farm, buy the farm's products directly, take part in activities, or eat a meal cooked on the premises. Such attractions provide extra income for the farmer but can also help reduce rural de-population by making the farmer's family's life more interesting through meeting the tourists who may come from many different countries.

There are a range of other characteristics which mean some types of attractions are more sympathetic to the idea of sustainable tourism than others. The best types of attractions from a sustainable point of view include those which:

- are owned and controlled locally so there is little leakage of benefits to non-local corporations
- maximize the potential for spending by visitors on souvenirs and refreshments to ensure the economic benefits of tourism are optimized
- are locally 'rooted', and, in the case of heritage centres, for example, are directly related to the local area and culture, not to a 'foreign' culture.

Conclusions

In this chapter we have seen that visitor attractions can play a positive role in the development of more sustainable forms of tourism, both physical attractions and events and festivals. We have also considered some of the ways in which attractions can be in conflict with the principles of sustainable tourism. Finally, we have seen what good practice might mean in the attractions sector in terms of the development of new attractions and the management of existing attractions.

Discussion Points and Essay Questions

1. Discuss the contribution which attractions might make to the development of sustainable tourism in either a city where traditional industries are declining *or* a coastal resort which is in decline.
2. Discuss which of the following types of attraction are the most, and the least, compatible with the concept of sustainable tourism:

- a traditional zoo
- a theme park
- a heritage centre
- a casino
- a cathedral.

3. Evaluate the factors which might limit what an attraction operator can do to make their attraction totally sustainable.

Exercise

Think about your local area. Identify a type of attraction that might be developed successfully there. Produce a report suggesting how this attraction could be made as sustainable as possible.

Case Study: Mizen Vision Project, County Cork, Ireland

Mizen Head is the most south-westerly point in Ireland. In 1908 a fog signal station was opened which provided significant direct and indirect employment until it was auctioned in 1993.

A local voluntary association, the Mizen Tourism Association, decided to try to obtain a lease to operate the station as a visitor attraction to help retain, or even increase employment, in this area of high unemployment. In November 1992, the Association was granted a short lease on the site by the Irish Commission of Light. The West Cork Leader programme granted the Association £30,000 which had to be matched locally. In December 1992, at a public meeting, the Mizen Tourism Co-operative Society Ltd was formed as a friendly society to develop the site as a rural employment scheme. A full lease was eventually signed in June 1993.

The Visitor Centre was opened on 1 June 1994, and in 1995, it attracted 38,000 visitors. In its early days, the Visitor Centre employed:

- Mr O'Sullivan, the ex-keeper on a full time basis
- two ladies on a part-time basis, who also had farms in the area
- nine local young people, seasonally, as tour guides.

For the first time since the signal station opened in 1908, the public have access to this beautiful piece of coastline.

Apart from the beautiful views and walks along the clifftops, the Visitor Centre has a number of elements, including:

(i) the kitchen and bedroom of the keeper which have been refurbished to their original state
(ii) an audio-visual programme
(iii) exhibitions on the flora and fauna of the Mizen Head
(iv) a display about the building of the Fastnet Lighthouse and the Fastnet Race, the whales and underwater life in the surrounding sea, and what it is like to spend a stay right in the Fastnet Lighthouse.

The Mizen Head Vision is a good example of a community initiative in tourism, although it is, admittedly, on a very small scale.

Case Study: Industrial Tourism in France

Most communities in developed countries have been built upon a few industries, many of which are now facing problems of competition and decline, particularly in developed countries.

At the same time, in recent years, we have witnessed a growing interest in industrial tourism in terms of both visits to workplaces and direct sales of goods from factory outlets at low prices.

In the context of sustainable tourism, industrial tourism can help by:

- providing an additional income for enterprises where they charge an entrance fee
- increasing sales by direct sales from producer to final customer
- raising the profile of the brand image which should result in increased sales eventually
- raising staff morale as they see tourists valuing the product of their labour.

Industrial tourism can provide a lifeline for some businesses, while for others it may simply be the 'icing on the cake'.

In France, this form of tourism, which is called 'tourisme industriel et technique', is a major phenomenon. The publishers, Solar, have produced 12 guides to industrial tourism in the regions of France, which feature well in excess of 1000 enterprises which open their doors to tourists.

In the Bretagne-Pays de la Loire guide, published in 1996, for example, the following enterprises were featured:

- several specialist hand-made furniture workshops
- local traditional food producers such as specialist meat producers and biscuit makers
- wine and spirit producers
- oyster growers
- fishermen's cooperatives.

As well as consumer products the guide also included those utilities that support people's everyday lives such as electricity generation together with the airport in Nantes.

There were also entries for industrial heritage museums including 'ecomusées' dedicated to oyster-rearing, metallurgy, printing, wine production, mushroom growing and mining.

However, it is good to see that the guide also features examples of very modern, thriving industries such as computer-aided design, high-tech printing, and the production of animated films and audio-visual programmes.

Industrial tourism provides a 'shop window' for a community and its industries that celebrates their heritage and their present achievements and helps ensure the future survival of their industries.

Case Study: the Niagara Winter Festival of Lights, Canada

Reid, in 1996, produced a study of the internationally renowned Annual Light Festival in Niagara, which first took place in 1982. The festival lasts from November to January and attracts around one million people (Reid, 1996). It is organized by a voluntary sector non-profit-making organization, and involves two full-time staff, seasonal staff, and around 300 volunteers.

In 1994 the festival budget was, in Canadian dollars, $741,050 which came from grants (76%), sponsorship (13%) and other sources (11%) (Reid, 1996).

Research indicates that in 1993 the festival generated something over 13.7 million Canadian dollars. Given the grants received by the festival, the ratio of money generated to grant aid received was nearly ten to one, a good ratio (Reid, 1996). These figures relate to the nearly 175,000 visitors who stayed overnight when visiting the festival.

Almost one-third of all staying visitors spent at least 150 Canadian dollars on their trip, most of which was spent on accommodation and meals.

The profile of visitors to the festival was as follows:

- two-thirds of visitors were repeat visits
- around a half of visitors were over 40 years of age
- the event was most popular with visitors in the middle to lower income bands
- parents with children made up 40% of all visitors, with tour groups representing only 4% of visitors
- 95% of visitors arrived by private car
- 57% of all visitors visited the lights as a day trip with no overnight stay.
  (Source: Reid, 1996)

A survey of 433 local residents indicated high levels of support for the festival. Many attended the programme of special events that accompanied the lights themselves, including the opening ceremony, concerts, horse-and-carriage rides, fireworks and a car show. Indeed over 90% of respondents believed that it would be a loss if the festival were to cease to exist (Reid, 1996).

This seems a good example of a cultural tourism attraction that both satisfies local people and brings in tourists from outside the area.

26

Tour Operations

Tour operators are in many ways the key to the drive towards more sustainable forms of tourism, because they:

- design the itineraries which tourists will follow and thus decide where they will and will not go, and what excursions they will take
- contract services from local suppliers in the destination, notably hotels
- provide the representatives in each resort who advise tourists on what to do in the destination
- sell the destination to potential tourists via promotional messages in their brochures
- have relatively little capital invested in most destinations and are therefore foot-loose in that they can move from one destination to another with relative ease.

When discussing tour operations in the context of the sustainable tourism debate, the distinction is often made between mass market and specialist tour operators. However, this is rather a simplistic view. A more realistic typology is perhaps those illustrated in Fig. 26.1.

We will now consider the implications of these different types of tour operators for the concept of sustainable tourism.

In general, the conventional wisdom would appear to suggest that foreign operators selling products to a mass market are the least desirable in relation to sustainable tourism and vice versa. Table 26.1 illustrates the perceived differences between large-scale mass market operators and small-scale specialist operators in relation to sustainability.

This is a highly simplistic view but it is one which is seen implicitly in the writings of many authors on sustainable tourism.

The Negative Side of Tour Operations

Tour operators are the key element in the tourism system, they are the connection between the tourist and the destination. As such they exert a great deal of influence in relation to sustainable tourism. At their worst they can cause major problems in relation to the concept of sustainability. Mass market operators are in a high volume, low profit margins business so they need guaranteed high volumes. This means sending tourists to established honey-pot destinations which are already crowded with tourists. The price sensitive nature of much of the tour operation market often leads to a situation where tour operators use their power to negotiate contracts with local suppliers which ensure that the tourist pays a very low price for their holiday. This both minimizes the economic benefits of tourism

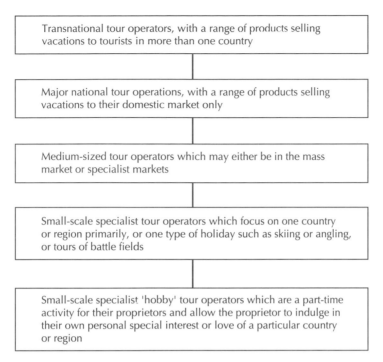

Fig. 26.1. A typology of tour operations.

Table 26.1. The perceived differences between large mass market tour operators and small specialist operators.

	Large-scale mass market operators	Small-scale specialist operators
Environmental impact	• High	• Low
Economic impact	• Low per head expenditure • Benefits relatively few enterprises • High leakage from community	• High per head expenditure • Benefits spread quite widely through the community • Low leakage from community
Sociocultural impact	• High	• Low
Host community relations	• Formal • Institutionalized	• Informal • Personal
Commitment to destination	• Low	• High
Types of tourist	• Generally insensitive • Disinterested in destination specifically	• Generally sensitive to/ interested in destination specifically

for local communities and makes it difficult for suppliers to improve quality.

Tour operators tend to exploit historic sites and natural resources simply as excursion opportunities, worsening the problem of large numbers of coach-based tourists visiting sensitive sites.

Many tour operators use their own employees as guides when they are in the destination region so that tourists are told about an area often by outsiders whose knowledge and interest in the area may be very limited, rather than by more knowledgeable and enthusiastic locals. Tour operators generally show little long-term commitment to destinations and will leave at the first sign that customers are losing interest or if prices rise too high for their market. Most tour operators are based outside their destinations so that much of the price paid for their holiday by the tourist never reaches the host community.

Towards More Sustainable Tour Operations

The author proposes a three-pronged strategy to help tour operation play a more effective role in the development of more sustainable forms of tourism:

- local communities in destinations should develop their own tour operation enterprises as a way of reducing the power of externally based tour operators
- destinations should try to ensure that as much of their inbound tourism as possible is handled by small-scale specialist tour operators
- attention should be made to encourage mass market tour operators to act in a more responsible and sustainable manner.

Reducing the Power of Externally Based Operators

Maximizing the benefits of tourism for the host community means reducing the power of externally based tour operators. This implies that the local tourism industry needs to work together to develop and market the destination product. This could involve:

- developing marketing consortia that represent local accommodation providers who will negotiate with foreign operators, with one voice, to increase

their bargaining power in contract negotiations
- creating local privately owned or co-operative tour operations enterprises to devise and sell packages based in the destinations directly to consumers.

Klemm and Martin-Quiros have written about an interesting initiative in their report on Spain:

Both the central and regional governments encouraged Spanish companies to assert greater control over their own industry by reducing dependence on foreign tour operators, increasing marketing and management skill levels, and overcoming local rivalries through pooling expertise. One example of this was the establishment of an independent marketing organization in Catalonia in 1991. Catalonia, which receives around 20 per cent of foreign visitors to Spain, has depended heavily on British and German tour operators.

The members of the hotel marketing organization, called the Costa Brava Centre, were 26 small (under 150 rooms), locally owned, independent, and most family-owned hotels on the northern part of the Costa Brava. The group began marketing in 1992 using a four-language brochure and a purpose-built communications centre for direct booking by computer reservation. The brochure contained information on local cultural and sporting activities that reflected the Catalan heritage of the area. The target market was mobile independent travellers from France, Spain, Germany, Italy, and to a lesser extent, the United Kingdom. The hotels, which represented a distinctly local character, differed in the degree of luxury (ranging from one to five stars) and in their location (some were on the coast while others were inland). This presented a challenge in that hotels were not a single brand and the office staff needed to develop expertise in guiding enquirers to the right product.

The establishment of the group and its communications centre involved considerable investment, both financially and in terms of business risk for the members. Prior to joining the organization they could rely on tour operators to fill their hotels, particularly in the low season. This was no longer the case.

In 1993 the group moved into the short holiday market by offering themed packages in the spring and autumn (e.g. hiking, sailing, golf, and gastronomic weekends). Developing such packages is the norm for tour companies, but it was an important step forward for a group of independent businesses and former rivals. For example, persuading local restaurants to join forces for a gastronomic weekend holiday was a major hurdle. In the words of one of the founding members, 'the Centre has made us think beyond our own petty rivalries to work together to control our own industry'.

This small, but interesting, venture represented a new independent and co-operative spirit in Spain. One measure of success was that overall bookings for the group increased threefold in 1993 compared to 1992. However, by 1994 a new demand pattern was emerging, with a larger percentage of tourists coming from the Spanish market, particularly from the nearby city of Barcelona. This demand is highly seasonal. Moreover access to the international market remains a problem. Some hotels in the group have linked up with smaller independent tour operators in Northern Europe, but this cannot provide the 'shop window' mass package that tour operators have at their disposal through their vertically integrated travel agencies. (Klemm and Martin-Quiros in Harrison and Husbands, 1996)

However, unless such initiatives are replicated in other destinations there is always the danger that tour operators will simply move on to other resorts where such groups do not exist. Furthermore, unless a large number, or even all, of the accommodation units in a resort join such a scheme, the operators will still be able to carry on as normal with those units that are not involved in the initiative. This will undermine the scheme and could lead to its collapse.

Attracting Small Specialist Tour Operators

Even allowing for the over-simplification in Table 26.1 it also follows that if small-scale tour operators are not exactly beneficial they are probably less harmful to destinations than their mass market counterparts. Therefore it is not surprising that some destinations are keen to attract more small-scale operators instead of mass market operators.

Small operators tend to survive through:

- selling holidays at prices which generate a higher profit margin per customer than mass market vacations
- relying heavily on repeat purchases by loyal customers
- offering high levels of personal service
- providing niche market, specialist products that are not offered by the mass market operator.

These four characteristics clearly make small-scale operators attractive to destinations.

While newly emerging destinations can consciously try to ensure that smaller operators play a major role in their development, the potential role of small operators in established destinations is more limited. Most established destinations, whether they be seaside resorts, ski centres or safari bases, have been developed to a point where they are attracting mass market customers, for whom price and security are important. They are looking for a psychocentric rather than an allocentric experience. The destinations will have reached that stage in Butler's tourist area life cycle where control is in the hands of externally based mass market tour operators. Small operators will therefore be made to compete for the custom of the resort's existing customers who are looking for the standardized low-priced product offered by the mass market operators.

However, even in that situation, small specialist tour operators could play a valuable two-part role. They might develop medium volume, medium priced special interest tourism in the off-peak season that will help to keep hotels open all year round. Secondly, destinations could then slowly seek to reposition their resorts over time by bringing in new tourists on higher priced more specialist holidays to replace the lower spending traditional visitors. Small operators could play a pivotal role in this campaign but it would be a risky process that may not be successful.

Towards More Responsible Mass Market Tour Operations

From what we have seen in the past two sections, it would seem that for the foreseeable future, in established resorts at least, mass market tour operators are going to continue to play a major role. It is important, therefore, that if we are to develop more sustainable forms of tourism, we need to persuade the mass market operators to behaviour more responsibly in the future.

This means encouraging such operators to:

- enter into longer term 'contracts' with local suppliers that would allow both to plan ahead more and work together to improve quality
- undertake initiatives designed to both protect the destination environment and increase the benefits of tourism for the host community
- raise awareness of sustainable tourism amongst customers and try to persuade them to behave in a more sustainable manner
- put pressure on governments and local authorities to develop sustainable tourism policies
- wherever possible, make use of more environmentally friendly forms of transport such as bicycles, horses and even the tourists' own feet, on excursions
- make sure that local suppliers pay their staff a reasonable wage and treat them properly
- only contract local hotels which operate in an environmentally friendly way
- help de-market overcrowded sites by not offering excursions to them at peak times, and instead finding alternatives where tourism is more welcome
- not offer holidays which overtly encourage irresponsible and offensive behaviour such as the hedonistic 'lager lout' type of trip
- boycott destinations where tourism development infringes the human rights of the indigenous population such as those places where local people are displaced to make way for new hotels
- not promote those all-inclusive holidays and self-contained resort complexes which separate tourists from hosts and take business away from small-scale local enterprises.

This sounds fine but why should tour operators do these things? There seems little evidence that their customers are demanding that they take such action in most countries, so why should commercial operators take action that might harm their sales and their profits? In any event there are clearly a number of obstacles that stand in the way of tour operators behaving in a more sustainable manner.

Obstacles to More Responsible Tour Operations

A survey of 36 UK tour operators, both large and small, reported in the publication *Practice makes Perfect*, identified ten reasons why tour operators (% of sample of 36) felt that they were unable to act in a more responsible or sustainable manner. These were as follows:

- perceived responsibility of others, especially governments (50%)
- fear of taking steps not matched by competitors (25%)
- lack of awareness amongst tourists (25%)
- perceived powerlessness of tour operators (22%)
- no perceived demand in the British market (22%)
- perceived intransigence and corruption in host authorities (22%)
- need to fill charter flights (19%)
- confusion over correct practices of recycling, etc. (19%)

- sustainable tourism seen as academic and irrelevant (11%)
- rapid staff turnover (6%).

Clearly, while some of these may be excuses rather than reasons, they need to be tackled if tour operators are to be encouraged to take a more pro-active stance on sustainable tourism. The implications of the results of this survey are that tour operators are not taking voluntary action because of a perceived lack of interest amongst tourists. They are also concerned that any steps they take may not be matched by competitors and that they will result in them being disadvantaged.

It is clear that the operators also feel that sustainable tourism in destinations is the responsibility of others, particularly governments. Perhaps, therefore, little will change until destination governments accept their responsibility and introduce regulations to control the activities of tour operators. However, unless there is concentrated action by all or most destination governments, tour operators will simply withdraw from those areas where they are regulated and move on to unregulated destinations. This could be self-defeating for those destinations which pioneered regulation.

However, if it proved effective, regulation could severely curtail the profits of tour operators. It would, perhaps, be in their interest, therefore, to practice voluntary self-regulation before the case for regulation becomes overwhelming.

Conclusions

We have seen that tour operators are crucial players in the tourism system and must therefore be involved in the development of more sustainable forms of tourism. The author has identified three ways in which the tour operation function could be made more sustainable.

However, it is clear that tour operators feel that at present, they have little real motivation to behave in more sustainable ways. Perhaps, therefore, the future role of tour operators will have to be shaped by tourist demand, government regulation or both.

Discussion Points and Essay Questions

1. Discuss the assertion that small-scale tour operators are intrinsically more sustainable than large-scale tour operators.
2. Evaluate the potential advantages and disadvantages of government regulation of tour operators.
3. Discuss those difficulties that might be experienced by marketing consortia of local tourism businesses which try to replace the role of externally based tour operators.

Exercise

Select a destination with which you are familiar, for which you are able to collect information. For your chosen destination:

- evaluate the role played by externally based tour operators
- assess the scope for the replacement of these operators by locally based tour operators and marketing consortia.

Finally, evaluate the benefits that are likely to accrue from the replacement of externally based tour operators by those which are locally owned and controlled.

Case Study: Ecotourism Tour Operators in Australia

Between 1992 and 1995 Burton conducted an intensive study of tour operators of various kinds, who were operating in areas of Queensland and the Northern Territory, where nature-based tourism is the core of the product.

Finally, Burton classified the operators according to the Ziffer (1989) spectrum, which distinguishes between nature-based (shallow green) tourism and eco (dark green) tourism. In the case of the Northern Territory this resulted in a pattern that is illustrated in Exhibit 1.

Burton found that most of the operators classified as eco-operators were:

- small in size, employing up to three guides only
- offering only small group tours for up to 25 tourists at a time
- relatively expensive
- generally run by people within a professional background such as teachers, as they are used to living and working in the 'bush'.

The study then went on to look at how the tour operators responded to growth in

Exhibit 1. Top end classification of tour operators (Northern Territory). Source: Burton in Stabler (1997).

Operator continuum	Ecotourism	Tourism operators	Nature-based tour operators
Nature-based tourism Selling nature, unaware/uncaring of impact			**
Aware of impact Abide by rules, do not seek to educate			* *****
Shallow green Sensitive, aware of impact		* *	
Educate to alter attitude, and influence behaviour, member of conservation group	****	*****	
Sensitive, positive action Minimum impact tourism, rotate sites	***	*	*
Donors Constructive action to improve environment, e.g. pack out others' rubbish, plant trees, donate % trip costs to conservation, support local initiatives		*	
Doers Initiate conservation projects, involved in policy-making Deep green: ecotourism	***		*

Note: each asterisk represents an individual tour operator.

Exhibit 2. Top end tour operators' response to increasing tourism. Source: Burton in Stabler (1997).

	Ecotours	Tour operators		Nature-based tourism
Actively avoids crowded place	***	*	*	*
Avoids crowded times	***	***		
Offers new products, new pristine environments	***			
Business decreasing	**	*	*	
Business static	**	*		**** **
Business increasing		*	*	**

Note: each asterisk represents an individual tour operator.

overall tourist numbers to the destinations in question. The responses of these operators involved in the Northern Territory are shown in Exhibit 2.

It appears that as overall tourist numbers increase the ecotour operators find it difficult to maintain their business and they tend to move on and go looking for opportunities to sell packages to less crowded places. The danger then is that the cycle of destination, discovery, growth and over-crowding will simply begin all over again in a new place, thanks to the so-called ecotour operators.

Case Study: TUI, Germany

The major German tour operator, TUI, is often seen to be an example of an externally based, mass market tour operator which operates in a responsible manner. There can be little doubt that TUI has been very pro-active in relation to the destinations and hotels to which it sends its clients. It is also clear that it communicates the information to its customers, as we can see from Exhibit 1, which contains extracts from information given to TUI clients through its brochures.

Exhibit 1.   General information for customers on TUI's environmental policy in the TUI travel catalogues.

TUI: Working for Better Environmental Conditions at Destinations

An intact environment is the very basis for a good holiday. TUI has been facing up to this responsibility for many years. **TUI's Environment Director, Dr Wolf Michael Iwand, and his team, work** together locally with the TUI Service, and with experts and environmentalists, local authorities and hotel partners **to ensure that your holiday is environment-friendly**.

We tackle this task with great care. We analyse the state of our destinations, and give them an environmental rating.

This process starts with the monitoring of water and beach quality, encompasses checks on sewage treatment plants and landfills, and includes energy- and water-saving measures in the hotels, to name but a few points among many others.

Nature conservation, animal welfare, species preservation, reforestation and the use of renewable sources of energy are also among the important issues on which we concentrate in our **environmental work**.

TUI Destination Criteria

- Bathing water and beach quality
- Water supply and water-saving measures
- Waste water disposal and utilization
- Solid waste disposal, recycling and prevention
- Energy supply and energy-saving measures
- Traffic, air, noise and climate
- Landscape and built environment
- Nature conservation, species preservation and animal welfare
- Environmental information and offers
- Environmental policy and activities.

The extensive information surveyed by us in destinations all around the globe is collected in our **TUI Environmental Database**, and used in our planning and catalogues.

We are **particularly concerned that you should be informed** about our findings in the destinations.

Concerning this, we would like to draw your attention to the "**Nature + Environment**" texts on the pages introducing the individual destinations.

Our contract hotels, too, are examined using a comprehensive **environmental acceptability checklist**.

TUI Hotel Criteria

- Waste water treatment
- Solid waste disposal, recycling and prevention
- Water supply and water-saving measures
- Energy supply and energy-saving measures

- Environmentally oriented hotel management (focus on food, cleaning and hygiene)
- Quality of bathing waters and beaches in the vicinity of the hotel
- Noise protection in and around the hotel
- Hotel gardens
- Building materials and architecture
- Environmental information and offers of the hotel
- Location and immediate surroundings of the hotel.

Look out for the "**Environmentally Sound Hotel Management**" destinations of selected hotels in the hotel descriptions in our catalogues.

In our local "**environmental actions**" we must be particularly sensitive to local concerns. In order to allay problems such as malfunctioning sewage plant or improper tipping of rubbish, we must put a lot of work into **convincing people of the necessity of taking action**. We bring tourist officials, local authority representatives, local politicians and hoteliers together at "round table" meetings in order to **find joint solutions**. In seminars with our hotel partners, we give ideas and support for environmentally sound hotel management.

Over the past years, our airline partners have spent millions on improving their fleets in accordance with environmental criteria (see also the section "**Airplanes and the Environment**"). With its "Holiday Express" and "Tourist Train", German Rail is continually adjusting its services due to ecological demands (see also the section "**Trains and the Environment**"). Our bus partners, too, are devoting great attention to the issues of transport and environment (see also the section "**Buses and the Environment**").

Together with carrier representatives, we are working on improving their environment-friendliness on the basis of the following criteria.

TUI Carrier Criteria

- Energy consumption
- Pollutant and noise emissions
- Land use and paving over
- Vehicle/craft, equipment and line maintenance techniques
- Catering and waste recycling and disposal
- Environmental information for passengers
- Environmental guidelines and reporting
- Environmental research and development
- Environmental co-operation, integrated transport concepts
- Specific data: vehicle/craft, type, motor/power unit, age.

In addition to our on-site efforts in the destinations, our consulting of hoteliers and our co-operation with rail, bus and air carriers, environment protection also means reducing the impacts of our facilities at home, and training our in-house and field staff accordingly. In pursuance of our **corporate principle of "Commitment to the Protection of our Natural Environment"**, we have implemented a system for the efficient promotion, with combined forces, with the goals of environmental protection. A network of committed staff members actively pursuing environmental issues in their fields of work has been set up, cutting across all departments of the company.

Co-operation with national and international environmental associations, professional and trade associations, universities and many other bodies is a further part of our daily work. It is, however, frequently difficult to push through low-pollution technologies, as these often involve high financial cost – environmental protection is not always to be had for free.

You, too, can make a personal contribution to **protecting the environment in the country you have chosen for your holiday**. One way is to get informed about the situation in the country before the journey. The "**Sympathy Magazines**" produced for many holiday countries and regions by the Study Group for Tourism and Development in Ammerland/Starnberger See are a good source of such information. In the TUI hotel folder, you will find **practical tips** on the proper approach to your destination's environment on the green page headed "**The environment needs a holiday too**".

Have you discovered environmental problems, or do you have further questions or suggestions? Then please contact your local tour guide, or write to us:

TUI
Department of Environment
Karl-Wiechert-Allee 23
D-30625 Hannover

We will continue to commit ourselves to ensuring that **the environment does not have to pay for our holiday!**

Protect **the environment!**
Please pass on catalogues that are still in good condition to friends and relatives, or back to your TUI travel agency.

This *reduces* paper consumption and *prevents* waste!
The price section is printed on 80% recycled paper. In the colour section, the recycled content is lower. All catalogue paper is bleached without chlorine.

Nature and Environment

Extracts from TUI catalogues, explaining the "Nature and Environment" situation for the exemplary cases of Fuerteventura, La Palma and Namibia.

Fuerteventura. Fuerteventura's beaches are acclaimed by our guests as the best in Europe. They are regularly cleaned, and the coastal waters are monitored within the international Coastwatch Network. Five bathing beaches on Fuerteventura were awarded the European Blue Flag in 1995. Due to the low amount of precipitation, the island is one of the driest in the archipelago. The extensive grazing of the many goats has intensified the island's desert character, and erosion, which is perhaps its greatest problem, is increased. Water supply is difficult. Because of the geological conditions, groundwater is scarce. The population is supplied by four seawater desalination plants, while the larger hotels often have their own facilities. For a renewable supply of energy, the "Parque Eolico" with 45 wind turbines came into operation in 1994. A second wind park is planned. A Nature Conservation Act designates 13 protected zones, amongst which are the unique and particularly endangered dune landscapes of Corralejo and Jandia. Together with the ASCAN environmental organization, TUI supports the ECO ISLA Fuerteventura project.

La Palma. La Palma boasts one of the ten Biosphere Reserves on Spanish territory, a piece of nature that is unique world-wide ... 40% of the island is already protected under nature conservation law. Last year, however, forest fires took toll of some 5,000 hectares ... Although the "Green movement" is strongly represented on La Palma, environmentally sound measures such as the construction of new sewage plants or the introduction of controlled waste management systems are currently only at the planning stage. The new Development Plan makes a positive step forward: this stipulates that 80% of the island must be held free from development.

Namibia. The government of Namibia has limited the number of tourists per annum to a maximum of 650,000 to preserve the country's unique landscape. Tourist accommodation in nature reserves will continue to be owned by the government in future; ecologically sensitive areas like the skeleton coast are protected by strict environmental legislation. More and more lodges are using solar energy for producing hot-water! On account of natural conditions (e.g. climate) Namibia suffers from water shortage. Therefore our request: please use water economically!

'Ecologically Sound Hotel Management'

Extracts from TUI catalogues, explaining "Ecologically Sound Hotel Management" for the exemplary case of Cyprus.

Columbia Pissouri, Pissouri. Own biological sewage plant with re-use of purified water for garden irrigation. Use of solar energy for hot-water supply. Waste separation and composting. Avoidance of disposable products.

The Annabelle, Paphos. Own biological sewage plant; re-use of purified water for garden irrigation. Use of solar energy for hot-water supply, waste separation and use of returnable bottles. Automatic tailor-made air-conditioning equipment.
(Source: Touristik Union International GmbH & Co. KG)

While this initiative is clearly excellent in relation to the environment, it says little or nothing about the social and economic dimensions of sustainable tourism. There is no mention of the wages paid to hotel staff, the cultural impact of tourism or the importance of maximizing the economic benefits of tourism for the host community.

Although valuable, therefore, the TUI approach could be seen to simply be based on their own self-interest, ensuring the satisfaction of their customers and the quality of their holiday. The company admit this freely. The link between ecological and economic objectives are seen clearly in Exhibit 2.

If tour operators can be persuaded to take a broader view of sustainable tourism that encompasses economic viability and social equity, then the hard-headed TUI approach of enlightened self-interest could offer us the best prospect of developing more sustainable tourism operations. Perhaps the motivations for action are less important than the actions which can be achieved.

Time period	Ecological objectives	Measures	Economic objectives
Short term	Reduction of environmental pollution and impairment	• Education/consulting • Programme organization • Hotel management	• Quality control • Product optimization • Ensuring returns
Medium term (up to 2000)	• Environmental relief • Prevention of environmental pollution and impairment	• Environmental standards • Eco-labelling • Environment information system • Environmental quality goals	• Management of risk and opportunities/innovation
Long term (up to 2005/10)	• Environmental relief • Prevention of environmental pollution and nuisance • Environmental improvements	• Eco-controlling • Ecological product control • Environmental impact assessment	• Securing the future • Securing and improving revenues

Exhibit 2. TUI's planning objectives, 1996.

27

Transport

Because we cannot take the tourism product to tourists in their home areas, we have to take the tourists to the tourism product. Therefore, all tourism requires transport in one form or another.

The need for transport services puts great pressure on the environment in several respects, notably:

- the resources used and the pollution involved in air transport. This problem is increasing as tourists travel ever further for their vacations
- the demands placed on the environment by the development of new transport infrastructure such as airports, motorways and high speed railway lines
- the resources used, pollution, and congestion caused by the huge growth, worldwide, in the use of the car to take leisure trips
- the use of taxis, buses and cars within tourist destinations
- the use of cars by staff in the tourism industry when going about their everyday work.

At the same time, we must recognize that the most frequent use of transport by tourists is perhaps not by leisure tourists, but rather by business tourists. The issue of business tourism is dealt with in more detail in another chapter.

Before we move on to consider some of the key issues, we will look briefly at the nature and scope of transport. Figure 27.1 offers a typology of tourist transport.

The Negative Impacts of Tourist Transport

The negative impacts of tourist transport are well documented, particularly in relation to air transport and the private car in particular. They include:

- the use of non-renewable resources such as oil and coal in the construction and operation of aircraft, ships, coaches, trains and private cars
- the contribution made by emissions to the problem of acid rain
- the apparent destructive effect on the ozone layer of aircraft emissions
- the air pollution caused around roads and airports
- water consumption and water pollution caused by airport operations and ferries
- noise pollution surrounding transport facilities such as airports and roads
- the degrading of landscapes by poor quality transport infrastructure development
- the use of green field sites for transport facilities and the use of agricultural land for new roads.

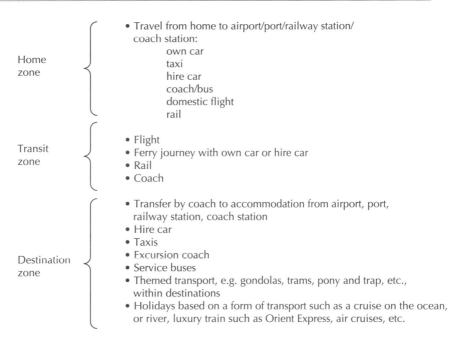

Fig. 27.1. A typology of tourist transport.

Measuring and Comparing the Impacts of Different Modes of Tourist Transport

Firstly, we need to get the problem in proportion for tourism is not the only – or indeed the major – activity which stimulates forms of transport that harm the environment. While air travel is largely tourism-related, other activities also make great demands on the transport system, particularly in relation to surface transport. Most use of the private car is for non-leisure purposes such as journeys to work, shopping and taking children to school. Manufacturing industries use heavy lorries to move most of their products from factory to shop. Agricultural products are transported around the world, by ship, air and lorry. At the same time it has to be said that developing more sustainable forms of tourist transport is not made any easier by the problems involved in measuring the impact of different modes of transport to see which are the best from an environmental point of view. For instance:

- Are four modern cars fitted with catalytic converters, each with three passengers, better or worse for the environment, than a 20-year old coach with a dozen people on board?
- How does the environmental cost of a train journey compare with a bus journey?
- On a journey across the English Channel, how does a trip on the Eurostar or Le Shuttle, compare with the ferry journey?
- Are petrol vehicles less environmentally friendly than diesel vehicles?

In a field which has so many partisan interest groups it is vital that we have more reliable and objective data on which to base our decisions.

Towards Sustainable Tourist Transport Systems

It is clearly impossible to make transport wholly green or sustainable, but pressure has been growing for it to become more

sustainable. The importance of making tourist transport more sustainable was put
succinctly by the Tourism Society in 1990 as
follows:

> no analysis of the relationship between
> tourism and the environment can ignore
> transportation. Tourism is inconceivable
> without it. Throughout Europe some 40%
> of leisure time away from home is spent
> travelling, and the vast majority of this is by
> car ... Approaching 30 per cent of the UK's
> energy requirements go on transportation
> ... [and] ... the impact of traffic congestion,
> noise and air pollution ... [will] ...
> diminish the quality of the experience for
> visitors. (Tourism Society, 1990)

Developing more sustainable forms of tourist transport implies action on a number of
fronts, including:

- regulatory controls which provide statutory limits on emissions for example
- fiscal incentives that favour more
  energy-efficient forms of transport
- the use of new technologies to improve
  the performance of aircraft, ships,
  trains, buses and cars from an environmental point of view
- pricing mechanisms that ensure that
  prices reflect the environmental cost of
  the mode of transport.

Sustainable transport, and these ideas in
particular, imply an important role for government as regulator and tax authority.
Given that tourists often have a choice of
transport mode, it is also important that we
take a holistic view of tourist transport,
planning it as an integrated whole.

One sector where progress has undoubtedly been made is in the airline business so
it is to that sector that we will now turn our
attention.

Towards Making Air Transport More Sustainable

Air travel is more tourism-related than any
other form of transport, with virtually every
air journey being made by a tourist. Furthermore, it was developments in air
transport that helped create mass tourism in
the 1950s, 1960s and 1970s.

However, unfortunately, air travel is one
of the most environmentally unfriendly
forms of transport. Its environmental
impacts relate to both the aircraft themselves and the airports and infrastructure.
While progress has been made in relation to
the aircraft themselves, airports still cause
major environmental problems.

Aircraft have undoubtedly become more
environmentally friendly thanks to technological developments. Engines are now
more fuel efficient and are less noisy than
their predecessors. More powerful engines
have also meant that large aircraft can now
fly on two rather than four engines. The
modern aircraft engine also produces less
emissions than those of 20 years ago.

The improvement of aircraft performance
in relation to the environment has been
partly due to international regulations. Airlines have to abide by these standards or
they face heavy financial penalties. Many of
these regulations are enforced strictly by the
International Civil Aviation Organisation.

At the same time airlines have been
encouraged to act because many of the changes to aircraft have also reduced their costs,
through the reduction of fuel consumption
for example.

Conversely, there are still major problems in relation to the environment in
respect of airports and the air transport
infrastructure. Much damage is caused to
the environment because some airports are
increasingly over-crowded so that aircraft
wait around on the tarmac with their
engines running. Likewise, congested air-
space also leads to aircraft being 'stacked'
waiting in an aerial traffic jam for a landing
slot. This again leads to increases in emissions and fuel consumption.

These problems underpin the plans to
build new runways at existing airports, and
even the development of new airports. At
the same time, these plans are opposed by
those whose concerns focus upon the
adverse impacts of airport operations on the
environment, such as the use of land and
increased noise.

We need also to recognize that airport
operations themselves involve practices
which are not friendly to the environment.

They involve heavy consumption of resources like water and electricity, and the use of toxic chemicals, for instance.

One example of an organization which has taken an effective, holistic view of air transport and the environment is British Airways, and readers will find a case study of this company at the end of this chapter. However, as we will see in the next two sections, there are trends in the airline market which are not conducive to the development of more sustainable tourism transport.

The Threat of Long-haul Holidays

A major problem in the air transport sector is the rise of the long-haul holidays. British people who used to holiday in Benidorm and Torremolinos in the 1970s, discovered the Greek islands, Turkey and the Canary islands in the 1980s. In the 1990s long-haul destinations such as Florida, the Dominican Republic and Thailand, are popular with British holidaymakers. Clearly, long-haul travel is more expensive in resource terms than short-haul trips, and it is therefore less sustainable.

At the same time, many of the 'new' long-haul destinations are developing countries where the growth of tourism, while bringing in income, has also forced these countries to spend valuable resources on the development of new airports and transport infrastructure, for the benefit largely of foreign tourists.

The growth of long-haul holidays has been stimulated by the fact that air fares no longer reflect the distance to these destinations. In spring 1998 the author looked for low cost flights and found the following prices:

- Prague £179
- New York £179
- Moscow £299
- Miami £299
- Barbados £339
- Perth £499.

These prices bear little relation to the distance involved in the flight. If Prague costs £179, then according to the distance involved, New York should cost around £600 and Perth nearly £2000!

Competition and the growing role of charter airlines in long-haul travel have all helped to create the situation where long-haul travel is becoming cheaper. This is a major threat to the concept of sustainable transport, because tourists are not being asked to pay the *real* cost of their long-haul trip.

Airline Liberalization in Europe

Not only is long-haul travel falling in price but in Europe airline liberalization is leading to lower prices on high volume routes, and new 'no frills' carriers are entering the market too. In terms of sustainable transport this trend has two negative aspects:

- it is likely to increase overall demand for air travel within Europe
- airlines which are trying to reduce their costs to allow them to compete on price may be tempted to buy and use older less environmentally friendly aircraft.

So we can see that liberalization may be good news for consumers but bad news for the environment.

The Private Car: from Liberator to Enslaver?

The private car has over the years given mobility and the freedom to travel to tens of millions of tourists around the world. Indeed car ownership created whole new forms of tourism such as caravan touring.

However, today, the car has moved from being a liberator to an enslaver in society in general with traffic jams and air pollution in towns and cities and the building of new roads across the countryside. Tourism is clearly not the major cause of traffic pollution compared to commuting and shopping but there are aspects of the use of the car for leisure purposes which are particularly problematic in respect of sustainability, including the following:

- the car is used to reach many remote rural areas which would not otherwise be accessible to tourists, and where the infrastructure is often not capable of accommodating them
- cars can damage buildings through vibration and their emissions in historic towns and villages
- large numbers of cars can destroy the atmosphere and sense of peace in a destination or at an individual visitor attraction
- parking on roadside verges causes damage to vegetation.

In the most extreme cases some forms of recreation now involve driving four-wheel drive vehicles 'off-road' in other words, across rough ground. This is particularly destructive to vegetation and wildlife in fragile ecosystems. However, it is the general use of the car as a means of leisure transport that is the main problem.

For more than 20 years this problem has been recognized and attempts have been made to persuade tourists to use other forms of transport. This has particularly been the case in the countryside as can be seen from the case study at the end of this chapter.

The alternative means of transport available to tourists as a substitute for the car are generally coach and rail travel. However, neither is as convenient as the private car because:

- trains and buses operate on a set timetable that may not suit the needs of the tourist
- service frequencies, in rural areas particularly, may not match the tourist's travel plans
- some destinations may not even be available by rail or coach service
- many rail and bus stations are not pleasant or safe places to wait around on cold days or dark evenings
- journeys may involve changing from one train or bus to another which adds to the inconvenience.

It is difficult to see how these problems can be overcome so that public transport can ever be as convenient as the private car, which in terms of short commuter trips from home to the city centre a few kilometres away may not be a major issue. However, for a tourist wanting to take a touring holiday in the French countryside from their home in Birmingham or Manchester, it is difficult to argue that public transport would be just as convenient.

Perhaps, therefore, the emphasis should be upon trying to divert people from their car when journeys are from city to city where train services, for instance, might be quite convenient. However, it will be difficult to persuade people to move from public to private transport, while:

- use of the private car is often underpriced because of indirect government subsidies and the fact that car drivers pay little or nothing towards the cost of the pollution they cause. Also many drivers do not take into account issues like depreciation when mentally calculating the cost of a trip by car
- public transport, in many countries, is experiencing significant price rises as state subsidies decline.

We need to see more use of pricing mechanisms that make public transport a more attractive option.

However, in many cases where we cannot make public transport an attractive option we should consider the need to use sticks as well as carrots. In other words, in situations where the problems caused by cars are particularly severe we need to be willing to control access by car. While this is a difficult decision to take given the political influence of car drivers it may be the only solution.

More Sustainable Ways of Moving Around in Destinations

Tourists use a variety of modes of transport to move around in their destination and to take excursions. Some of the most common such as taxis and coaches are rather environmentally unfriendly. In the interests of sustainable tourism, therefore, the aim should perhaps be to:

- introduce forms of transport which are more environmentally friendly and also more interesting for the tourist, including:
  (i) horses and carriages
  (ii) donkeys
  (iii) electric cars which use batteries
- combine transport with the desire of people to improve their health through exercise. In particular this could mean providing bicycles and encouraging walking as means of transport around destinations and for exercise
- combine transport with special interests such as horse-riding and canal boats
- use historic forms of transport that are also environmentally friendly, such as trams.

More Sustainable Tour Itineraries

At the same time, tour operators could also help by not devising itineraries which involve travelling between different countries. Instead packages should be developed which minimize the need for transport services once the tourist has arrived in their destination. This would clearly be much more sustainable than the following itinerary which is quite typical of some of today's multi-centre holidays:

14 Night Tour of Central Asia
- Day 1: flight London – Moscow – $3\frac{3}{4}$ hour flight
- Day 2: coach tour of Moscow
- Day 3: flight to Tashkent – 5 hour flight
- Day 4: coach tour of the city
- Day 5: flight to Samarkand – 1 hour flight
- Day 6: coach tour of the area
- Day 7: flight to Urgench for Khiva – 1 hour flight
- Day 8: flight to Bukhara – 1 hour flight
- Day 9: coach tour of the area
- Day 10: flight to St Petersburg via Tashkent – $6\frac{1}{2}$ hour flight in total
- Day 11: coach tour of the city
- Day 12: coach tour of the region
- Day 13: rail journey to Moscow – 8 hour journey
- Day 14: coach tour to nearby historic towns
- Day 15: flight to London – $3\frac{3}{4}$ hour flight.

Towards More Sustainable Infrastructure

There is still also work to be done to make the transport infrastructure more sustainable. Airports, ferry ports, rail and bus stations need to be designed to:

- be energy efficient
- ensure that they produce as little waste as possible
- take up the minimum possible amount of land
- be aesthetically attractive, be easy to use for tourists and provide decent working conditions for staff.

It is particularly important, too, for airports in particular to become better neighbours for those who live around them. Too often they can be seen as large powerful bodies which pay little attention to the views and concerns of local residents.

The Sustainable Tourist Transport Charter

There are no easy answers but there are some simple principles that should help us achieve more sustainable forms of tourist transport, as follows:

- Encourage tourists to take fewer long-haul holidays; this will mean actively promoting short-haul destinations.
- Make sure that pricing mechanisms reflect the full true cost of the journey, and are fair to all types of transport.
- Raise tourist's awareness of the negative impacts of different types of tourist transport and try to encourage them to

choose more environmentally friendly forms of tourism.

- Take measures to maximize the convenience and competitiveness of public transport, as a means of travelling to destinations.
- When tourists have arrived in their destinations offer them alternative, more environmentally friendly ways of getting around the area such as bicycles, horses and sailing boats.
- Conduct more research to help us identify, clearly, what the most sustainable forms of tourism are, on particular routes.
- We must be willing to place restrictions on the use of the private car in those situations where its use is particularly damaging.
- Encourage the media to publicize the benefits of travel by rail rather than by car.
- Encourage tour operators to put together packages that use rail travel rather than coaches or short flights.
- Try to persuade the industry and tourists to take touring holidays that allow them to discover a small area in depth on foot, bicycle or horseback rather than trying to see a whole country by coach and air in a week!

The Negative Dimension of Sustainable Tourist Transport

We must be careful to ensure that the pendulum does not swing too far in the opposite direction with widespread bans on cars in the countryside and exhortations to people to stay at home rather than travel at all. While such a development might sound ideal it would have drastic social and economic implications in terms of lost business and jobs. Tourist transport is a labour-intensive sector that employs a wide range of people in a variety of reasonably well paid occupations.

The need therefore is for a balanced approach that focuses on tackling the most acute problems through more radical action such as car bans while trying to use less drastic means to prevent the worsening of the general situation.

Conclusions

In this chapter we have seen that tourist transport brings great challenges in relation to sustainability in terms of both how tourists travel to their destinations and how they travel around once they have arrived in their holidays areas. It is also clear that the private car and air travel are perhaps the two biggest problems in the transport sector. However, while positive action is taking place in relation to the latter, the difficulties caused by the car appear to be increasing all the time. Transport is perhaps the most important aspect of the sustainable tourism debate because all tourists use transport. Yet it is also a sector where the problems are difficult to resolve for in many ways they are inherent in the concept of transport and are perhaps inevitable.

Discussion Points and Essay Questions

1. Discuss the ways in which tourists might be persuaded to use public transport instead of their own cars.
2. Evaluate the negative impacts of air transport and discuss the ways in which these may be reduced.
3. Critically evaluate the ten ideas outlined earlier in this chapter under the heading, 'The Sustainable Tourism Charter'.

Exercise

Select an airline or a car hire operator or a ferry company or a coach operator. Develop a report for your chosen organization, highlighting its current environmental policy, if it has one, identifying what you perceive to be its main strengths and weaknesses. If it does not have such a policy, you should seek to explain the absence of a policy.

Case Study: British Airways

British Airways is one of the world's largest and most profitable airlines. It has recognized the importance of environmental issues for over 20 years. Today it has an Environmental Department and environmental issues are at the heart of its management system.

Its mission and goals include the 'Good Neighbour' goal which it first adopted in the early 1990s. The goal states that the airline aims to be:

> a good neighbour, concerned for the community and the environment (Laws and Swarbrooke in Bramwell et al., 1996)

British Airways has a holistic environmental management programme that includes:

- publishing an annual environmental report together with reports on airport operations at Heathrow, Gatwick and Manchester
- reducing the number of 'Chapter II' aircraft which are noisier than 'Chapter III' aircraft
- reducing the number of infringements of noise regulations at Heathrow
- aiming to have fewer incidents where fuel is jettisoned in flight
- reducing waste, particularly in relation to the airline's catering operations
- reducing water consumption and effluent disposal at both Gatwick and Heathrow airports
- decreasing use of chlorofluorocarbons or CFCs.

The actions of British Airways have been recognized through a series of awards from bodies such as the Pacific Asia Travel Association, the Chartered Association of Certified Accountants, the Smithsonian Institution and the Royal Geographical Society.

British Airways has also gone out of its way to keep its stakeholders informed of its activities, as follows:

> In 1996 the airline published a booklet, *Aviation and the Environment*, in which space was allocated for comments from the Aviation Environment Federation, which represents a number of interest groups. The airline published a separate Community Relations report in 1997, reflecting initiatives in the communities around its main operational locations. Passengers are informed of the environmental programme by in-flight information and attitudes are monitored regularly as part of BA's market research programme. Approach and departure procedures are under ongoing review with a view to identifying changes that can reduce the noise impact on communities without compromising safety. Recent research illustrated that stakeholders – including the public – are well informed about the programme. A surprising 25 per cent of passengers questioned at Heathrow in the late 1990s were aware of BA's initiatives and many of these expressed an interest in receiving further information. (Middleton and Hawkins, 1998)

Furthermore, interestingly, the company uses:

> Environmental Champions (a designated network of staff to promote environmental activity within their particular departments to tackle environmental issues within the airline). (Middleton and Hawkins, 1998)

In terms of the wider world, the airline has a record of philanthropic activities in relation to the environment, through its Assisting Conservation Programme. Under this scheme free travel has been given to individuals working on conservation projects from Belize to the Seychelles.

No figures are available to show the cost of British Airways' environmental policies. However, in 1993–94, we do know that:

> the Environment Department's running costs were £409,000; measures to comply with noise standards on UK airports cost £3.2 million. (Laws and Swarbrooke in Bramwell *et al.*, 1996)

Conversely, we also know that the airline's activities in the 1990s have already saved £2 million from the energy bill and £100,000 on waste disposal costs (Middleton and Hawkins, 1998).

British Airways has achieved a worldwide reputation for its environmental policies as a result of:

- its desire to be seen as a 'good neighbour' to the community who live around the major UK airports
- its wish to reduce its costs
- international regulations.

Case Study: P&O Steam Navigation Company

Middleton and Hawkins in 1998 identified key elements of the environmental policy of the P&O organization as follows:

- the elaboration of a formal environmental policy in February 1991, which was reviewed and re-issued in 1994 and 1997
- the trialling in selected subsidiary companies of the new ISO 14001 Environmental Management System Standards, taking a leading role in the creation of an Environmental Code of Conduct for the General Council of British Shipping (now British Shipping)
- the widespread use of environmental activities throughout the organization
- awareness raising amongst staff through the publication, 'Environmental Briefing'
- appointing an Environmental Officer on each vessel, all of whom go through their in-house environmental training course
- reducing water consumption by up to one quarter on the organization's Dover–Calais ferries
- using the latest technologies to dispose of waste responsibly
- introducing environmentally friendly factors into its new flagship cruise ship, the 'Oriana'.

The actions of the company won it the prestigious Smithsonian Environmental Award, the first cruise company to win this award.

By and large the company has not acted in response to statutory regulation but rather from a desire to reduce costs, and perhaps from a desire to improve their public image.

Case Study: Approaches to Rural Tourist Transport

We can, perhaps, best explore the different approaches that might be taken to make tourist transport in rural areas more sustainable by taking a hypothetical example of a national park that is within driving distance of several major cities.

It attracts millions of day visitors per annum, who come almost exclusively by car. Few bus services serve the area, and those that do exist link the cities to the market towns, rather than the picturesque villages and the natural attractions the tourists like to visit. A railway line crosses the park but the trains are expresses that stop nowhere in the park. The measures that might be taken include:

- introducing 'tourist trains' on the railway line which would stop at key points to set down and pick up tourists at key tourist attractions. These services would be subsidized and available on all peak days such as weekends and holiday times
- running local tourist buses, on peak days, that offered tours around popular villages and sites, starting from local railway stations with their times being co-ordinated with those of the rail services, and with combined rail/bus tickets being available
- bringing in more environmentally friendly buses including electric-powered vehicles
- operating 'park-and-ride' schemes at honey-pot destinations that do not allow cars to enter, and instead transporting tourists around by either bus or horse and carriage or even on foot
- offering bicycle hire services at places where the 'tourist trains' stop
- encouraging tourists to travel as short a distance into the national park as possible by providing attractions and services such as visitor centres and picnic sites in the peripheral zone of the park
- using special events at key locations within the national park to encourage tourists to park their car in one place and stay there all day, rather than using their car to drive around the park all day, visiting several different places
- using differential pricing in car parks to penalize short stay visitors and reward those who stay in one place all day.

Clearly all of these initiatives would require planning and funding, and while several might generate income others would be costly, and perhaps unpopular with local tourism businesses as well as car owners. They would not solve the problem in our hypothetical national park but at least they would help to ameliorate the problem.

Perhaps, then, the income from the last two schemes, for instance, could be ploughed back into either public transport subsidies or conservation projects.

In some extreme cases there may be a case for saying cars would actually have to be banned from certain areas of the park on particular days.

28

Hospitality

The hospitality sector interfaces with the concept of sustainable tourism, in four main areas:

- the location and design of new accommodation units
- operational management practices in relation to the environment such as energy conservation and recycling
- given that hospitality is the largest employment sector in tourism, the human resource management practices in terms of equal opportunities, pay, seasonality, casual employment, particularly, together with the crucial issue of local labour versus immigrant labour
- the food and drink which tourists are offered in catering establishments and the extent to which it is local and authentically traditional or 'international' and/or trivialized versions of well-known local dishes.

Firstly, though, we need to look at the nature and scope of hospitality. Figure 28.1 shows a simple typology of the hospitality sector. Clearly, this is a generalized picture. Some types of establishments can fall into more than one category, such as hotel apartments, which offer both serviced and non-serviced accommodation.

In general, the hospitality industry has focused largely on 'green issues' rather than broadening its view to embrace the wider concept of sustainable tourism. Furthermore, the industry has been concerned primarily with operational matters rather than with the issues involved in the development of new units, or human resource management practices.

The Development of New Accommodation Establishments

We have already looked at the issue of environmentally friendly building design in Chapter 5. Nowhere is this issue more relevant than in the case of the hospitality sector. In recent decades, hospitality organizations have been guilty of developing new units which have been at odds with the principles of sustainable development, including:

- developing high-rise hotels which are aesthetically unattractive and which are often not in keeping with the scale of surrounding buildings
- utilizing architectural styles which are foreign to the area
- using non-local materials such as concrete which may not be suited to the local climate and may weather in a way which makes the buildings visually unattractive
- developing units on sites which are existing wildlife habitats, and not taking

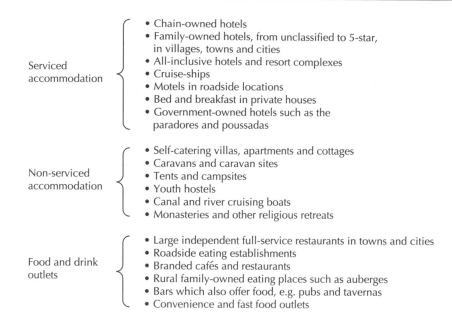

Fig. 28.1. A typology of hospitality.

this fact into account in the development of the site

• building units on sites in prominent locations where the construction destroys, forever, a wonderful view

• designing units with large swimming pools which make great demands on what may be limited local water supplies, in many locations

• creating resorts, with large-scale private grounds surrounding the hotel unit which can restrict the access of the locals to beaches and/or use up valuable land.

In the past few years, the industry has responded to criticisms of its new-build design practices. It has begun to develop hotels, especially in developing countries, using designs which are based – loosely – on local traditional architectural styles. For example, the Premier Holidays 1998 Asia holidays brochure included the following hotel and resort descriptions:

Marriott Royal Garden Riverside, Bangkok ... The hotel consists of three low-rise Thai-style buildings. Le Meridian Baa Boran, Golden Triangle, Thailand. This hotel is designed in traditional native Thai style. Pelangi Beach Resort, Malaysia. The hotel is designed in Malay Kampala style chalets to blend with its environment. Santian Beach Resort, Bali. Built in Balinese style as cottages and houses. (Premier Holidays Asia Brochure, 1998)

Tour operators clearly think that tourists today like to think that they are staying in accommodation which is designed in the traditional local style. However, this is open to the charge of tokenism for, often, the idea of traditional architecture is at odds with the reality of the development, particularly when we look inside the buildings. For example, the Santian Beach resort mentioned above, was described as being built in the style of Balinese style cottages and houses. However, the description failed to mention that:

• the complex has two swimming pools with poolside bars

• each room has air conditioning, a mini-bar and a shower.

Both of these features are, one suspects, rarely found in authentic Balinese dwellings.

However, in the era of consumer-led marketing the industry would argue that tourists would not pay to stay in a truly authentic Balinese cottage. On the other hand, more and more tourists appear to be choosing to stay with local people in 'authentic' houses, from bed and breakfasts in 'brownstone' houses in New York, to the 'long houses' of Borneo.

This tension between the real or perceived demands of tourists and the authenticity of hospitality architecture is also being seen in the self-catering sector with the conversion of traditional buildings for tourist accommodation, in rural areas. In the case of France, for example, many Britons go there claiming they are seeking a 'simple rural life'. Yet increasingly they are rejecting simple authentic gîtes in favour of privately owned villas with swimming pools, dishwashers and satellite television.

If we want to develop more sustainable forms of tourism, therefore, perhaps we should be encouraging tourists to stay only in authentic accommodation, wherever possible. We should also be encouraging hospitality organizations to develop new units, if possible, by converting existing buildings rather than building on green field sites, particularly in urban locations. For example, in the French city of Albi there is an excellent example of this where an old textile mill has been converted into an attractive riverside three-star hotel by the Accor chain. Hotels have also been created in former warehouses, port buildings and railway stations.

Rather than simply copying historic architectural styles, sustainable tourism principles mean we should also be encouraging good quality modern architecture which enhances the aesthetic environment. While this is subjective to some extent, the author believes that this idea is well illustrated in the new Antigone quarter in the southern French city of Montpellier.

However, the drive for more sustainable forms of architecture in hospitality will have to first overcome the short-term financial pressures under which new accommodation units are designed. The aim is generally to minimize development costs and design units so that the investment cost can be recovered as quickly as possible. This is often at odds with the idea of more sustainable forms of architecture.

Operations Management and Sustainable Tourism

The hospitality industry has been a leading sector in the development of more environmentally friendly operational management practices. Chains such as Inter-Continental and Canadian Pacific have been pioneers in this field. Their activities led to the creation of the very influential International Hotels Environmental Initiative.

Many hotel operators have been carrying out environmental audits and have then taken a range of initiatives designed to 'green' the operation including (adapted from Horner and Swarbrooke, 1996):

- developing recycling systems for packaging materials, paper, bottles and organic waste
- using recycled supplies like stationery and toilet paper
- installing water-saving devices in showers and toilets
- only using low energy light bulbs
- making full use of energy-conservation measures such as insulation
- using unbleached and undyed fabrics
- developing solar-powered water heating systems.

It is interesting to note that almost all of the actions outlined above also bring cost reductions for the hospitality organizations. This may be the main motivating force behind the decision to undertake such actions.

There are other aspects to sustainable operational management in the hospitality sector, namely:

- purchasing practices and the idea that, wherever possible, hotels and other accommodation establishments should

source supplies they need from local suppliers, to maximize the economic benefits of tourism, for the local economy
- being a good neighbour to the local community, minimizing noise and litter, as far as possible, for example.

Human Resource Management in the Hospitality Sector

We saw in Chapter 21 that the hospitality sector has some major human resources challenges in relation to the concept of sustainability. These include high staff turnover, the concept of equal opportunities, and pay levels and working conditions.

The seriousness of these challenges is clear in the fact that in many destinations today there is:

- a shortage of labour for the hospitality sector and/or
- a problem in retaining good staff
- a reliance on labour from other countries who are willing to accept lower rates of pay and poorer working conditions.

Some hotel organizations such as the Marriott organization have tried to improve the situation through the concept of empowerment. However, in many other companies it is all too easy for empowerment to turn into exploitation as large numbers of junior and middle management are removed and more pressure is put on front-line staff.

If the human resource problems outlined above are not taken seriously there is a danger that the hospitality industry may be unsustainable because it will simply run out of people who will want to work in the sector.

While this problem can be partly alleviated by the use of technology to remove the need for labour, hospitality is after all about service, and looking after guests. Tourists like to be looked after by other human beings rather than just machines.

Providing a good quality service only happens where staff:

- feel adequately rewarded for their efforts
- think they are valued
- have pride in their own work
- have a positive image of their self-worth.

Creating these four conditions is the challenge facing the hospitality industry today.

Food, Catering and Sustainable Tourism

The issue of sustainability in relation to the hospitality sector has generally focused on the accommodation side, but there are also major issues in relation to the catering side of the industry. The modern catering sector could be criticized in relation to sustainability on several fronts, as follows:

- many resort hotels and restaurants offer either 'international' menus or parodies of traditional local dishes, rather than authentic local food
- the use of imported ingredients rather than utilizing local food products
- the growth of standardized fast food and restaurant chains at the expense of small locally owned enterprises.

If we are to develop more sustainable forms of tourism then these problems have to be overcome.

However, there have been some positive developments in the broader relationship between the food and catering sectors and tourism. These include:

- encouraging tourists to visit local food producers, such as farms which make cheese, and wineries, to buy the produce directly from the producers. This means that the producer obtains the full value of their product without giving away a proportion of the price to an intermediary retailer

- the growth of farm-based restaurants where meals are provided using local ingredients such as the Fermes-Auberges of France.

Another positive development is the growth of self-catering holidays. This could potentially really help the creation of more sustainable forms of tourism by encouraging tourists to experiment with local foods.

Going around markets in a foreign country is always enjoyable for tourists and buying from markets ensures the money paid by the tourist goes directly to the producer. However, to maximize the potential for this to happen there is a need to educate tourists about what ingredients are available, what they are called in the local language and how they can be turned into tasty local dishes.

The growing demand of some tourists for organic food and drink might also help to make the local food industry in tourist destinations become more environmentally responsible in relation to its agriculture and food processing industries.

Conclusions

We have seen that there are four major ways in which hospitality and the concept of sustainable tourism interface with each other. Most attention so far has focused upon environmental management practices at hotels. However, the author has suggested that we also need to pay attention to the development of new units, human resource management policies and the catering side of the hospitality industry. In respect of sustainability, the record of the hospitality industry is not particularly good. Unless it

improves, the very future of the sector may be in doubt.

Discussion Points and Essay Questions

1. Devise a 'Code of Good Practice' that should guide the development of new accommodation units, in keeping with the principles of sustainability.
2. Discuss the suggestion that hospitality organizations have only taken action on environmental issues where these actions reduced their costs.
3. Evaluate the extent to which current human resource management problems in the hospitality industry are in conflict with the concept of sustainable tourism.

Exercise

Imagine that you have been engaged as a consultant by a large hospitality organization. Your brief is to advise them on the development of a new hotel in terms of its size, design and building materials, together with the layout of the grounds and the selection of the site.

They are considering the following locations for their development:

- a major city
- a beach in a tropical region
- a village in mountains which are used for skiing in the winter
- a lakeside location in a national park.

Select *one* of the locations and produce a report for the organization advising them how they can develop the new unit in the most sustainable manner.

Case Study: New Sustainable Developments – the Anderson Group of Architects in the USA

In 1984, Gail and Dave Anderson set up their own business, the Anderson Group of Architects, specializing in the architecture and planning of ecotourism. They have been involved in many projects with the aim of designing environmentally friendly resort complexes. Their story was told in the November/December 1993 issue of *Architecture Minnesota*.

Their first major project was the **Lapa Rios Resort in Costa Rica**. The site is just over 1000 acres of tropical rainforest. The owners wanted to build a resort that would provide the revenue to help them conserve the rest of the surviving rain forest. The main elements of the Anderson's design for the site included:

- designing the complex so none of the living trees on the site had to be cut down, thus preserving the habitat of the birds and monkeys
- using local materials – hard wood and palm thatch – for the construction of the accommodation units
- electricity being produced by a small hydro-electric generator while hot water was provided by a solar-powered system
- using local labour to build and maintain the resort.

The resort has also helped further the concept of sustainability by funding a small school for local children.

However, the resort has faced the dilemma of whether or not it should expand to meet demand. It has decided not to grow beyond its 16 existing bungalows, so it will never be able to play a large role in developing sustainable tourism in Costa Rica. It would take hundreds of Lapa Rios-type resorts to soak up the demand for ecotourism in Costa Rica!

The Anderson Group have also been involved in other projects, some of which were described in *Architecture* journal in June 1996. For example:

- **Sand Creek Resort, Belize**, where 'wind, solar and tent technologies are combined with romantic nautical images in [an] ecological machine which offers living, sleeping, and toilet facilities for visiting shell divers. The folding fabric roof of nautically inspired shelters provide sleeping and living platforms while diverting rainwater to a cistern at the resort'.
- **Visitor Centre at Korime Creek Lodge, Guyana**. 'The design is based on indigenous Amerindian notions that value the space between buildings more than the buildings themselves. Paths are designed as boardwalks that protect the fragile rainforest soil from erosion, and cleverly conceal utility lines'.

The work of the Anderson Group is trying to develop examples of good practice in relation to the design of new resort complexes.

Case Study: Grecotel – The Environmental Policies of a Major Hotel Chain

Grecotel, the largest Greek hotel chain which is associated with the German tour operator, TUI, has developed an ambitious environmental programme that encompasses several elements. They have appointed a professional environmentalist to head up the initiative, and undertook eco-audits and implemented the findings. Furthermore, they have developed environmentally friendly purchasing policies, and encouraged their staff and managers to think about environmental issues. They also sponsor a variety of external environmental and heritage projects, and are an active member of the International Hotels Environmental Initiative.

Amongst the actions which Grecotel has undertaken are the following:

- reducing the purchase of disposable materials in favour of materials which can be recycled
- introducing special tap regulators which reduce water flow
- reducing the frequency of laundering guest towels to reduce the use of water and detergents
- replacing traditional light bulbs with energy-efficient low energy bulbs
- installing bedroom electrical systems which are operated by key-controls so that when the guest goes out all the lights go off automatically
- investing in biological sewage treatment plants
- installing fridges which are CFC-free.

Grecotel has also tried to educate guests about environmental issues through guest bulletin boards or information points in bedrooms. They have also tried to raise awareness through the media and talks at local schools.

Overall, the Grecotel approach is interesting in that:

> it is not only concerned with the internal operations of the company, but also with the wider environment and community within which the hotels exist. As well as the physical environment, the company has become involved with cultural issues such as the conservation of heritage attractions. (Horner and Swarbrooke, 1996)

It is likely that the pro-active stance taken by Grecotel has also been influenced by the fact that:

- they receive large numbers of German tourists who are renowned for their interest in environmental issues
- they are associated with German tour operator, TUI, which is well known for its environmental policies.

29

Cultural Tourism

To many commentators, cultural tourism and sustainable tourism are seen as virtually synonymous. The former is seen as sensitive, soft 'intelligent' tourism that is complementary to the concept of sustainable tourism. However, there are several aspects to cultural tourism which mean it may well not be a sustainable activity in its own right, and may be incompatible with the principles of sustainable tourism.

Firstly, however, we must define what we mean by cultural tourism. Figure 29.1 illustrates the main types of cultural tourism resources. While not comprehensive, it is clear from Fig. 29.1 that the different types of cultural tourism resources are interrelated; for example, in the arts where resources can be a theatre, or a concert that takes place within it. Likewise, themed food trails will usually include visits to working food factories and food shops.

Cultural tourism is a multi-faceted subject, as we can see from Fig. 29.2.

There is clearly a cultural tourism system which is shown in Fig. 29.3. Within this system, the public, private and voluntary sectors all have a role to play. The public sector manages many cultural resources and promotes them through destination marketing. The private sector, as well as managing some cultural tourism resources, also makes up the vast majority of the intermediaries and suppliers of support services. The contribution of the voluntary sector is generally seen in the management of certain types of cultural tourism resources, such as historic buildings and festivals.

Finally, it is interesting to note how cultural tourism varies between the different geographical areas. Urban areas are the heartlands of cultural tourism, with a focus on large-scale physical attractions, and the performing arts. In coastal areas, it is often the 'artificial' culture of established seaside resorts which is the attraction, while in rural and mountainous areas, cultural tourism focuses on observing traditional life styles.

Threats to the Future of Cultural Tourism

Cultural tourism has grown dramatically around the world in recent decades, but its future is not guaranteed for it faces threats.

Pressures on Cultural Diversity

Firstly, it is threatened by pressures on cultural diversity due to the increasing homogenization of culture worldwide resulting from the effects of global popular cultures such as television, music and films. This reduction in cultural diversity may reduce the motivation of people to travel to experience other cultures. This process of homogenization has also been facilitated in other ways, notably:

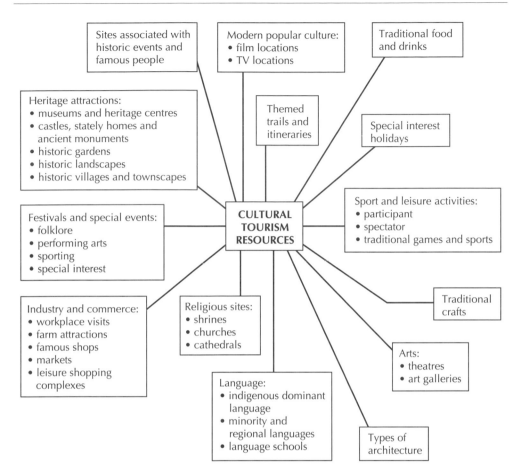

Fig. 29.1. Cultural tourism resources.

- the actions of major multinational corporations, who in order to grow must sell their products to consumers in other countries. It is easier to sell a standardized product than to customize it for each country. These organizations therefore devote much of their marketing budget to developing 'Euro-markets' so that people in Mannheim, Manchester and Malmo may well all be eating the same brands of cereal for breakfast and frozen pizza for dinner! This process threatens national, regional and local industries
- the failure of some governments to value and protect traditional cultures within their own countries. For example, the

UK government's failure to protect its traditional foods, so that while producers such as Roquefort cheese makers and Burgundy wine growers enjoy protection under French law, the label Cheddar is seen on cheeses purchased from Canada to New Zealand

- in some countries, regional and minority cultures have been suppressed rather than encouraged. Members of cultural minorities are encouraged to conform to the culture of the majority. Education systems have been used widely for the task, particularly in relation to minority languages. This has occurred in both western and eastern Europe.

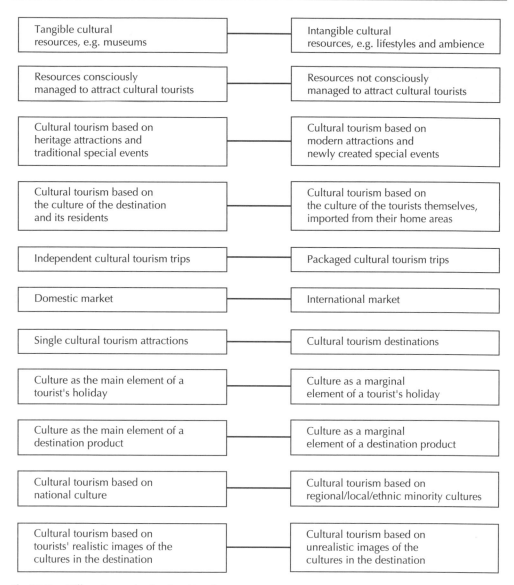

Fig. 29.2.   Different aspects of cultural tourism.

Changes in Education

While it is generally agreed that education levels are rising across Europe, with more people progressing to higher and further education, the emphasis in education has moved generally towards the vocational and away from the purely academic. Children and students across many European countries are learning more about business and computers and less about the arts and his-tory. Thus, it could be argued that the general citizen's knowledge of 'culture' as a subject may actually be falling.

Preserving Old Cultures, not Encouraging New Cultures

Much of the world at the moment is seeing widespread nostalgia in all aspects of its cultural life, for a variety of reasons. The manifestations of this nostalgia include:

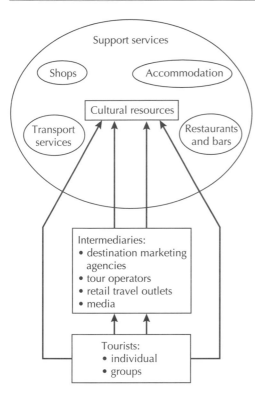

Fig. 29.3. The cultural tourism system.

- the use of old architectural styles in new housing developments in the UK
- the resurgence of traditional crafts in France and Norway
- the revival of Christianity in Russia.

Perhaps for the first time in our history, we are consciously trying to preserve or bring back old cultures and values. At its worst, this can impede the 'natural' evolution of new cultures.

Social Change

The process of social change, particularly in rural areas through de-population, is also a threat to culture within Europe. In some regions there may be no indigenous culture left as the original population disappears, to be replaced by a second home and seasonal holiday culture. This is true, for example, of parts of the west of Ireland, the Massif Central in France and large swathes of southern Europe.

Pressures on the Future of Cultural Tourism

There are also the threats to the future of the cultural tourism 'industry'.

Competition from Other Leisure Activities

The development of new leisure products, and the impact of technological innovations such as virtual reality, are providing competition for cultural tourism, particularly in the important day trip market. In the case of virtual reality, if it continues to develop it may lead, to some extent, to the substitution of Virtual for real cultural tourism experiences. Why go to the Pyramids with the problems of over-booked internal flights, the heat and stomach upsets, when you can enjoy the virtual experience from your local high street or your own home? Likewise, why go to Milan for a Pavarotti concert, when you can pretend to be Pavarotti in your own living room? Clearly this is some way off in the future but it is perhaps nearer than we think. It may be that those who put forward such scenarios are ignoring the social dimension to travel and the status which is gained from visiting the real site or event.

The Danger of Cultural Tourism Overload

It now appears that every country, region, city and village is trying to attract cultural tourists. Vast sums of money are spent every year on building new theatres and museums, devising new cultural tourism itineraries, and organizing special events. One is left wondering how long this rapid growth can continue before a state of saturation is reached. This could result in under-use and obsolete infrastructure which could tarnish the reputation of cultural tourism, such as we have seen happen in the UK seaside resorts.

Product Standardization

The growth of cultural tourism products has been based largely on copying those which have succeeded elsewhere. This has resulted in a certain standardization of the product. Heritage interpretation must be a classic example of this, with a proliferation of live first-person interpretation and interactive computer programs. In an industry where customers seem to be always looking for novel products, this standardization could, in the longer term, be a threat.

Poor Quality

While much cultural tourism is of a high standard, there is sometimes a quality problem, where entrepreneurs have sought to gain short-term benefits from exploiting the market. This can be seen in terms of poorly trained guides at historic monuments, for instance. On a wider scale, rapid development of cultural tourism can lead to overcrowding and unmanaged growth. In this situation, the quality of the visitor's experience may be poor, so that they will not return nor will they recommend a visit to their friends and relatives.

Safety and Security

Cultural tourism, like all forms of tourism, only survives if tourists feel safe and secure. This is a problem for cultural tourism as many destinations are large cities with serious crime problems. Furthermore, cultural tourists, who tend to be relatively affluent, are a particularly attractive target for criminals. At the same time, terrorists are increasingly realizing that the best way to undermine a government is to damage its tourism industry. In many countries, this means attacking cultural tourism attractions and cultural tourists, as we have seen in Egypt. If this develops further, it could be a threat to cultural tourism across the world.

Over-commercialization

The commodification of culture is being widely used to bring extra income to public, private and voluntary organizations. If it goes too far, however, there may be a consumer backlash against what could be seen as over-exploitation. This may be stimulated not so much by the cultural attractions themselves, but by the plethora of catering and merchandising operations that often accompany them.

The Non-sustainable Dimension of Cultural Tourism

As well as the threats to cultural tourism, there are also aspects of cultural tourism which are not compatible with the principles of sustainable tourism.

The Over-use of Sites and Places

This is a particular problem with older forms of cultural tourism such as heritage tourism, but it can also be seen in newer forms such as leisure shopping. This over-use can result in both damage to buildings and landscapes and a poor experience for visitors. The problem can be caused by too many visitors in total, too high a proportion of consumers visiting at the same time or the wrong kind of visitors whose behaviour is not appropriate.

All of these are management problems, but often their solution may be beyond the skill or financial resources of those who own the cultural tourism resources in question.

Lack of Local Control

The stimulus and funding for the development of cultural tourism in any location often comes from outside the local area. Examples of this include:

- government economic development agencies developing existing or new facilities or special events
- schemes by urban regeneration bodies to convert derelict industrial buildings into cultural attractions
- national archaeological trusts opening up archaeological sites to visitors
- foreign tour operators creating cultural tourism packages to a destination.

In most cases, local people, and even local government, may have little say in the process, which is clearly at odds with the concept of sustainable tourism. It is perhaps especially a problem in the heritage field, where the story of a community is told to tourists by outside professionals rather than by local people. In any event, the lack of local control can often lead to situations where developments take place which are inappropriate in their location, due to the lack of knowledge of the outside agencies. Furthermore, it can lead to some or most of the benefits of the development being exported from the local area.

Trivialization or Loss of Authenticity

The needs of the tourism industry, and the tastes of tourists, can lead to the trivializing of culture and a loss of authenticity. Traditional dances are shortened to meet the schedules of tour groups and traditional cuisine is internationalized to make it acceptable to the palates of visitors. For instance, the regionally diverse richness of Italian cuisine too easily becomes bland pasta dishes and the vast range of Spanish traditional dishes is represented often solely by paella. Likewise, folk songs are presented purely as musical entertainment rather than as part of the jigsaw of a complex traditional culture.

Fossilization of Cultures

The tourism industry and tourists have a vested interest in fossilizing cultures which are picturesque or interesting because of their novelty value, or the contrast with the tourists' own culture. Brochures are full of phrases like 'unchanged' and 'timeless'. Yet culture is always changing and it is probably impossible and undesirable to attempt to conserve cultures. It seems strange to speak emotionally and nostalgically of the need to conserve a traditional culture, which is already being rejected by local young people, keen to adopt the culture of the tourists' own country. There is a danger that our current interest in conserving the cultures of yesteryear may ensure that the new cultures of tomorrow are rather artificial or lacking in dynamism.

Controversial and Morally Difficult Tourism

Most cultural tourism tends to focus on non-controversial subjects. Too often it chooses to ignore controversial or morally difficult issues such as the role of immigrant communities and the repression of minorities. This denies the human rights of these communities to have their story told, fairly.

The challenge is, therefore, to find ways of making cultural tourism more sustainable in itself, and be more able to contribute towards the development of sustainable tourism in general. It is to that challenge that we now turn our attention.

Potential Approaches to Developing More Sustainable Cultural Tourism

There are many different potential approaches to the development of more sustainable forms of cultural tourism, of which we can only discuss a few here.

De-marketing

We need to de-market less sustainable forms of cultural tourism, which can mean de-marketing places, times and even people. Two examples may illustrate this point, in relation to places and times:

- the de-marketing of places such as cathedrals where the sheer volume of numbers can destroy the sense of place or the spirituality of the building
- discouraging tourists from visiting traditional events on specific days of the year when locals celebrating a festival as part of their religious observance may be swamped by tourists, insensitive to the religious significance of the festival.

However, while increasingly fashionable the concept of de-marketing does have its problems. Who decides when it should be practised and how it will be implemented? There are also doubts about how feasible de-marketing is in cultural tourism, where tourists are determined to visit cultural attractions which bestow status on visitors. Most of these attractions are so famous that it is very difficult to remove the desire to visit them or persuade tourists to 'forget' about them. Perhaps the most controversial area of de-marketing is the de-marketing of people. Until now, this concept has usually been related to so-called 'lager-louts', but it could theoretically be applied to cultural tourists. It could be said that only those who really understand the arts or history, for example, should be allowed to visit those places which are currently over-used. Or high prices might be used to discourage less well-off tourists in destinations which want to maximize the economic benefits of cultural tourism. These are clearly very sensitive issues, both morally and politically.

Encouraging Local Initiatives

Local control is a key element of sustainable tourism ideology, so it is clear that locally generated initiatives should be applauded. An excellent example of a sustainable cultural tourism project is La Cinéscénie at the Ecomusée de la Vendée at Puy-du-Fou, in France. La Cinéscénie is a live interpretation of scenes from the history of the region. It is wholly performed by local volunteers in the grounds of an old chateau, and it is managed purely by the local community.

The income from the event is used to help protect the area's heritage, but also to support today's community and its cultural activities. In recent years, profits have been used to fund an archaeology club, set up a research centre concerning local traditions, support a school of popular dance, expand the Ecomusée, and finance a local radio station.

Innovative Public Sector Projects

The Futuroscope theme park in western France is an excellent example of a public sector project that has forwarded the cause of sustainable cultural tourism, and has helped promote the cause of modern popular culture. Futuroscope is a theme park dedicated to moving images, but it is also home to a high technology industrial complex and a range of educational institutions. It was developed by the local authority, the Conseil Général de la Vienne, and opened in 1987. Since then visitor numbers have grown from 220,000 to more than 2,000,000 per annum.

Futuroscope contributes to the goal of sustainable cultural tourism in several ways. It promotes the film, television, video and multi-media industries which are becoming a crucial element of cultural tourism, both as a product and as a means of communicating with visitors. Furthermore, it provides spin-off benefits for the region as a result of the money spent by tourists visiting the theme park. Finally, visitors to the theme park are tending to spend several days in the area, during which they are visiting other cultural attractions, such as the Romanesque churches of the Poitou, and enjoying the artisan food products of the region.

Celebrating Emerging Cultures

Future cultural tourism will depend on us recognizing and promoting emerging modern cultures, rather than simply continuing to promote long-established cultural resources which have become the icons of modern tourism. This may mean being willing to embrace low-brow popular culture rather than just being concerned with high-brow cultural attractions and activities. This change of attitude should attract new younger people into cultural tourism as consumers, which in itself helps ensure the long-term sustainability of cultural tourism, rather than simply relying on older people. This change of attitude is illustrated by several examples relating to different types of destination in Table 29.1. The table illustrates another apparent development in cultural tourism, namely the growing emphasis on popular culture rather than physical cultural facilities.

Maximizing Local Benefits

This means consciously setting out to maximize the economic, social and environmental benefits of cultural tourism for the host community. Farm and gastronomic tourism in France are a good example of this phenomenon. In recent years, the public sector and the food industry have worked together to promote gastronomy in France in a way which maximizes the benefits for the local community, including:

- developing the 'fermes-auberges' scheme which allows farmers to add to their income by providing meals for tourists, based on locally produced foodstuffs

Table 29.1. Established cultural tourism attractions and modern emerging cultural tourism attractions, in selected destinations. Source: Swarbrooke (1996).

Destination	Established cultural tourism attractions	Modern, emerging cultural tourism attractions
Leeds and Bradford	• Victorian museums and art galleries • Parks • Industrial heritage	• Ethnic cuisine such as Asian food in Bradford • New museums, e.g. Royal Armouries, in Leeds
Montpellier	• Historic buildings • Long-established museums, e.g. the Fabre art museum • Opera House	• Modern architecture, e.g. the Antigone quarter • Ethnic minority influences, e.g. African music and cuisine
Dublin	• Following in the footsteps of great writers • Great museums	• Good leisure shopping opportunities • Modern Irish music
Prague	• Restored buildings	• Lively arts scene
St Petersburg	• Opera and ballet company performances • Great art museums such as the Hermitage	• Watching cultural changes resulting from political change in Russia

• creating themed trails linking food and drink producers and retailers such as the wine routes of Burgundy and the cheese routes of Normandy. These schemes help producers sell directly to customers without having to rely on intermediaries. They thus retain a higher proportion of the price the customer pays.

Ensuring Tourists Pay a Fair Price

It is important to ensure that tourists receive value for money, but it is also vital that tourists pay the full price of the product they enjoy. Otherwise cultural tourism cannot be sustainable, for either local people will become aggrieved at having to subsidize the visitors or insufficient income will be generated to support the cultural resources adequately. This may be a particular issue in the less affluent countries of Europe which have a wealth of cultural attractions, such as Greece and the countries of Eastern Europe, for example.

There are a number of other approaches which are worthy of mention, including:

• The need to improve quality to ensure that cultural tourists will make repeat visits and make positive recommendations to friends and relatives.

• Attempting, wherever possible, to link past, present and future on a continuum, rather than simply focusing on the past. For example, in the industrial heritage field this might mean developing linkages between industrial heritage museums, factory or workplace visits, and economic development and inward-investment policies.

• Educating tourists, professionals and local residents about cultural tourism and the attitudes and needs of the other stakeholders in cultural tourism.

• Tackling sensitive and controversial issues openly rather than seeking to ignore them, whether they be ethnic or religious conflicts or traditions like hunting.

• Democratizing cultural tourism so that more and more people take an interest in it, rather than maintaining it as a rather elitist activity.

Table 29.2. Sustainable cultural tourism: prerequisites and outcomes. Source: Swarbrooke (1996).

	Tourists	Destination	Host community	Tourism industry	Government	Cultural industries
Pre-requisites	• Knowledge • Concern • Willingness to modify behaviour	• Adequate infrastructure • Appropriate management structure and financial resources to manage initiatives	• Strong sense of identity and coherence • General agreement on aims and objectives • Well developed dynamic culture	• Recognition of problems • Viable businesses • Willingness to engage in debate and contribute to initiatives	• Recognition of problems • Clear objectives for tourism • Willingness to fund initiatives • Mechanisms for managing initiatives • Willingness to legislate to prevent major problems	• Dynamic • Recognition of wider implications of cultural activities including their role in tourism
Outcomes	• More interaction with hosts • Greater respect for local people, places, and traditions • Consciously seeking to behave in ways which maximize benefits for local people, e.g. buying goods at locally owned shops • Enhanced quality of visitor experience	• Reduced negative environmental impacts caused by over-use of sites and infrastructure	• Larger share of economic and social benefits of cultural tourism than previously • Satisfaction with level and type of tourism • Tourism aiding rather than threatening the development of local culture	• More interaction with local community in destination • Long term commitment to destination	• Ongoing partnerships with host communities, tourism industry, cultural industries and tourists	• Tourism contributing more to the development of cultural facilities and activities

Table 29.2 outlines some key prerequisites and projected outcomes in relation to the development of more sustainable forms of tourism.

Conclusions

Cultural tourism and sustainable tourism are often perceived as being inherently compatible entities. Yet we have seen in this chapter that:

- it is far from certain that the future of cultural tourism can be guaranteed in the face of a range of threats
- cultural tourism has elements which conflict with the guiding principles of sustainable tourism.

However, we have also outlined some ways in which cultural tourism can be made more sustainable and can make a more positive contribution towards sustainable tourism.

Discussion Points and Essay Questions

1. Discuss the obstacles which make it difficult to achieve the outcomes identified in Table 29.2.
2. Evaluate the contention that we are approaching the point of 'cultural tourism overload'.
3. Discuss the suggestion that cultural tourism and sustainable tourism are compatible forms of tourism.

Exercise

Obtain the brochure of a tour operator which specializes in cultural tourism holidays. Select one of the holidays on offer and evaluate the extent to which it is in line with the principles of sustainable tourism. Suggest how it might be modified to make it more sustainable.

Case Study: Hunting, Cultural Tourism and Sustainability

In the chapter we saw that there are many controversial and morally difficult aspects in the field of cultural tourism. Nowhere is this seen more clearly than in relation to hunting.

Hunting takes many forms, including:

- the practice of shooting migrating birds in southern European countries
- fox and other hunting in the UK
- sea-angling and coarse fishing worldwide.

In the latter case, fishing holidays are a rapidly growing type of special interest tourism product.

All of these activities are deeply rooted in their respective cultures. It could easily be argued that any tourist indulging in them could simply be trying to immerse themselves in an authentic local cultural experience. Yet in most circumstances, such action would bring condemnation from those who promote the concept of sustainable tourism.

Hunting is usually attacked on the grounds that:

- it has a negative impact on the environment by reducing the wildlife
- it is not socially acceptable to many tourists who come from different cultures.

However, in other circumstances the proponents of cultural tourism would simply argue that tourists should respect local cultures. It could thus be argued that hunting should be accepted as one particular form of cultural tourism, providing that it is not illegal in the country concerned.

Certainly, hunting is associated with distinct subcultures which have their own cultural traditions such as traditional songs and, in many countries, hunting has shaped the features of the landscape we see today. It is also a source of employment and revenue for local people, particularly native people such as the Sami of Lapland.

It is therefore clear that one could argue that hunting is comparable with some aspects of the concept of sustainable tourism while conflicting with others.

Case Study: the Commodification of Culture in Ireland

Ireland undoubtedly has a rich cultural heritage ranging from its native language and the prehistoric sites through its great castles to the world famous writers of the last few centuries.

The country has clearly used this heritage to help boost its tourist industry. Irish culture, both past and present, is a major attraction for tourists today. However, the way in which the country's heritage is 'sold' to tourists raises questions as to how far this 'commodification' of heritage should go. Some heritage products appear to be in danger of trivializing Irish history, such as the 'medieval banquets' and sentimental entertainments based on Irish folklore.

At the same time, many new 'heritage centres' have been developed, usually with European Union financial assistance. It has to be said that some of these centres are very 'thin' in terms of both the quantity and the quality of their exhibitions. Visitor numbers for many of these heritage centres also appear to be very modest, particularly in relation to the value of capital investment involved in their development.

The heritage–entertainment sector in Ireland received a jolt in the mid-1990s when the 'Celtworld' theme park ceased trading.

Conversely, some of the new centres appear to be attempting to provide an authentic view of local history in an entertaining manner. An example of this phenomenon is the 'Kerry the Kingdom' exhibition in Tralee. In a few cases, such as the Mizen Head Vision project, community-led institutions have helped develop cultural tourism products, which are more in keeping with the concept of sustainable tourism. A case study on this project is included elsewhere in this book.

On a very positive note, Ireland has been successful in promoting its modern culture as a tourist attraction rather than simply relying on its cultural heritage. Films such as *The Commitments* have been exploited as a cultural attraction, as has the *Riverdance* phenomenon and the current film and rock music scene.

The designation of Dublin as one of the earliest official 'European Cities of Culture' and the development of the Temple Bar quarter have helped establish the city as a major cultural tourism destination.

Ireland appears well placed to develop a balanced form of sustainable cultural tourism if it can control the excesses of its heritage industry and continue to encourage new dynamic cultural attractions.

30

Ecotourism

Perhaps the most controversial aspect of the sustainable tourism debate is the concept of 'ecotourism'. Some writers use the two terms interchangeably while others see the two phenomena as diametrically opposed. In this chapter, we will look at the pros and cons of ecotourism in relation to the idea of sustainable tourism, and see how the two might be brought closer together. However, firstly we must begin by defining 'ecotourism'.

The Definition of Ecotourism

Ecotourism is a term which is widely used today, but is rarely defined. It is often used interchangeably with other terms such as soft tourism, alternative tourism, responsible tourism and nature tourism.

In simple terms, ecotourism simply means that the main motivation for travel is the desire to view ecosystems in their natural state, both in terms of wildlife and the indigenous population. However, ecotourism is often taken to be more than this with its proponents claiming that it is also concerned with a desire to see the ecosystems conserved and the lives of local people improved through the effects of tourism.

Even without this latter aspect, many people would see ecotourism and sustainable tourism as being closely related, as ecotourism is seen to be:

- inherently small scale
- more active than most other forms of tourism
- less reliant on the existence of sophisticated tourism infrastructure
- undertaken by 'enlightened' well-educated tourists who are aware of the issues of sustainability, and are keen to learn more about the issues
- less exploitative of local cultures and nature than 'traditional' forms of tourism.

However, as we will see later in this chapter, there is nothing inherently sustainable about ecotourism.

It is also interesting to note that most ecotourism appears to involve travelling to destinations in developing countries. Here there is a chance to see wildlife which is different to that in the tourist's own country, and indigenous people who may appear 'exotic', 'picturesque' or even 'primitive' to the tourist.

One of the problems of defining ecotourism is that it varies depending on who you are, as we will see later in the chapter. To the tourist, ecotourism is a fashionable, high status type of holiday that is often equated with quality tourism. For industry, ecotourism is a product which offers attractive profit margins and has a large and growing market. Meanwhile, to newly emerging destinations, ecotourism is high yield, low volume tourism that allows them to differentiate themselves from their competitors.

The advantages of ecotourism for tourism organizations and destinations can, as we will see later, lead to the development of forms of 'alleged' ecotourism which are large-scale, exploitative and, in short, the opposite of the principles of ecotourism outlined earlier. This is the source of much of the confusion that surrounds ecotourism, namely, the gap between theory and practice, tourists' views and the supply side of tourism.

The Ecotourism Market

As there is no clear definition of ecotourism, it is virtually impossible to produce statistics on the size of the ecotourism market. In 1992, Filion tried to quantify the market for ecotourism. Filion stated that between 40 and 60% of all international tourist trips were 'nature tourists', in other words, tourists using a destination to experience and enjoy nature. Filion also talked about wildlife tourists who were those people travelling to a destination specifically to view wildlife, and estimated that this group represented between 20 and 40% of all global tourism trips. In other words around half of the natural tourists were more specialist wildlife tourists. The figures are very vague but there are more figures that illustrate the size of the market, perhaps more realistically.

The United States Travel Department Center, in 1992, estimated that some 8 million ecotourism trips took place that year. Some 35 million Americans claimed they would be taking such a trip within the next 3 years. A 1994 survey reported by Wight also indicated that 77% of North American travellers had already taken a holiday that could be described largely as ecotourism in the broadest sense of the term.

Ecotourism is so vague a term that we perhaps should take a very broad view of what it means. With this in mind we can perhaps say there are different forms of ecotourists. The author has attempted to illustrate this in Fig. 30.1.

When looking at the motivations of ecotourists, Wight has also noted the overlap between culture tourists, adventure tourists and nature tourists. She has also looked at the difference between specialist and general tourists. Her model of ecotourism motivations is illustrated in Fig. 30.2. It is clear from this model that such 'ecotourists' are not very concerned about the issue of sustainability.

The Case for Ecotourism

In spite of the reservations expressed by some authors, there is no doubt that there are aspects that are positive about ecotourism in relation to sustainable tourism. It:

- provides economic benefits for local people and can provide revenue for conservation projects
- tends to be quite small scale and carefully managed
- involves tourists who are well aware of the potential dangers of tourism and at least should behave more sensitively than many other tourists
- raises awareness of issues amongst the tourists because of their first-hand experience of the issues in the field. These tourists may then become involved in active campaigning on these issues when they come home. It is also a form of tourism which is very popular with tourists.

Nevertheless there are aspects of tourism which we need to seriously consider, and which may make it seem much less compatible with the concept of sustainable tourism, as we shall now see.

The Case against Ecotourism

The author believes that, in spite of the positive aspects of ecotourism outlined above, ecotourism has several major negative aspects in relation to the concept of sustainable tourism. It is to these issues that we will now turn our attention.

People who want to view wildlife and/or indigenous people with little or no concern about the impact of their trip on either the wildlife or the people

People who want to view wildlife and/or indigenous people and consciously try not to cause damage to either the wildlife or the people

People who wish to not only view wildlife and/or indigenous people, but also want to make a positive contribution to conservation and sustainable development by their presence in the area

Specialist tourists such as conservation project workers

Fig. 30.1. The ecotourist continuum.

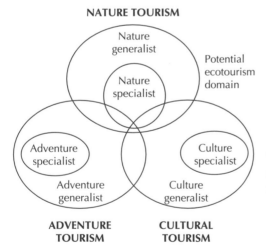

Fig. 30.2. Model of potential ecotourism motivations, with generalist and specialist dimensions.

Ecotourism or Ego-tourism?

A few commentators have chosen to criticize the concept of ecotourism by challenging the motives of ecotourists themselves, and exposing the potential hypocrisies involved in ecotourism. For example, Wheeler has said that:

> Ecotourism is synonymous with ego-tourism. [Ecotourism allows] the thinking tourists [to] behave much as before with a clear conscience – the blame still lies essentially with the mass tourist. Aren't we falling into the trap of automatically assuming that the more alternative, more custom designed, more up-market the product is, . . . then the better it is in sustainable terms? . . . This is the ego trip-product demand acceptably correct for the environment, for as we all know, the traveller is at one with nature. The ecotourist, so concerned to ostentatiously behave sensitively in the vulnerable destination environment is not generally concerned about the danger to the overall environment they cause in actually reaching the destination. Here convenience takes precedence over conscience – a car to the airport and a jumbo jet are hardly paradigms of virtue in the environmental stakes. A number of . . . supposedly ecofriendly holidays seem to be two centre trips. With . . . [for example] one week in the bush being supposedly ecofriendly followed by one week recovery afterwards in pampered luxury on the beach – a sort of let us spoil you in unspoilt Africa. No doubt . . . the package as a whole would be deemed ecofriendly and statistically categorised under nature tourism. (Wheeler, 1993, 1994, 1996)

These quotes sum up well the doubts that exist over the sustainability, and even the morality of ecotourism.

Today's Ecotourism, Tomorrow's Mass Tourism?

Today's ecotourism package can easily become tomorrow's mass market tourism product with all the accompanying problems of mass tourism that we know well.

In the 1960s and 1970s those taking safaris in Kenya were a small number of concerned, aware ecotourists, who had relatively little adverse impact on either wildlife or the host population. Then the local community, the government and foreign tour operators realized the potential and began to develop the Kenyan safari product. The number of safari holidays in Kenya has grown ever since, and the old specialist tourist has been replaced by the mass market package tourist mixing a week's safari with a week's relaxation on the coast.

The safaris have led to disturbance of the wildlife and even tourist and traffic congestion in some areas, while many of the economic benefits have 'leaked' to external operators.

Tourism has now grown too rapidly and has swamped certain locations. At the same time the fact that tourism now contributes a large proportion of Kenya's foreign earnings means that the government feels the need to take action to protect the interests of the tourism industry. This can even lead to local people being moved on or forcibly removed to help the wildlife flourish. This is not only morally unacceptable but is also interfering with an element in the ecosystem which has existed for centuries.

Safari tourism in Kenya today is largely mass tourism with few of the benefits of 'true' ecotourism outlined earlier in the chapter. Action is now underway to reduce the resulting problems but much of the damage has already been done.

Often the phenomenon of ecotourism has grown so that it has more in common with the worst aspects of mass market tourism. Trekking in Nepal, another form of ecotourism, started out as an almost spiritual quest in the 1960s by those seeking inspiration from the Nepalese culture. Now it has become part of the mass tourism market, with the number of trekkers rising over 250% between 1980 and 1991 (Gurung and De Coursey, 1994). Furthermore, Gurung and De Coursey have estimated that on a standard conservation trek in the Annapurna region, every group of 12 trekkers sets off with a support staff of around 50 people. The results of this volume of tourists in such a fragile environment have been:

- deforestation as wood is used for fires lit for the benefit of tourists

- the need to import food and household items to meet tourists' demand. This has caused local inflation and has introduced non-nutritious diets
- non-biodegradable material littering local towns and hills
- contamination of water courses by sewage
- the importing of inappropriate Western values.

Now projects costing millions of dollars are being undertaken to put right the results of ecotourism which simply became too big for its boots. In a sector where tourism organizations are more powerful than many governments in developing countries who is to say that this will not happen elsewhere?

The Ecotourist 'Locusts'!

There is always the danger that once an ecotourism destination has become well established, receiving large numbers of more mainstream tourists, it loses its appeal for ecotourists. The more sensitive, aware tourists who value 'unspoilt' areas and will pay highly to visit such a place may well move on, leaving behind the lower spending, less sensitive package tourist.

The 'ecotourist' will then simply move on to another destination to start the same process going all over again. From Kenya to Tanzania, on to Botswana, and then Namibia, perhaps then leaping the oceans to the Indonesian archipelago or China.

No Hiding Place from the Ecotourist!

The ecotourist gains prestige and satisfaction from visiting new off-the-beaten track destinations and seeing things that other tourists have not seen. They are thus driven to seek out ever more remote, obscure destinations with ecosystems and cultures wholly different from their own.

Because of this nowhere is safe from the ecotourist. It is their very sense of discovery that makes them dangerous. Instead of staying on the beaten track where their activities can be managed, they are always longing to escape into uncharted (and unmanaged) destinations.

Ecotourism is More than Just Wildlife

Very often it appears that ecotourism is just about wildlife. Tourists appear generally to be more interested in watching animals than they are in meeting and seeking to understand people of different cultures. Seeing an elephant or lion in Africa is seen as more important than meeting Maasai tribespeople. Observing the whales which live below the sea off Iceland and Norway is more interesting than finding out about the fishermen who work above the waves. Yet, ecotourism should be about ecosystems and ecosystems are about both wildlife *and* people. Indeed people are simply another form of animal life. In many ecotourism destinations the landscape and the wildlife are a direct result of the interaction between humans and the rest of the wildlife. To ecotourists, therefore, both people and wildlife should be of equal importance.

The Good, the Funny, the Big, the Bad, but not the Ugly and the Boring

Ecotourists, when it comes to animals, prefer the 'good' and the funny, are in awe of the big, fascinated by the bad, but are not interested in the ugly or the dull. Creatures like dolphins and monkeys are seen as good perhaps because they are the nearest creatures to us in terms of intelligence. We also find them aesthetically attractive in the case of dolphins and funny in the case of monkeys, while elephants impress us with their size. We see creatures like snakes and lions as bad and evil killers, but they are still fascinating. However, no one is really interested in taking a trip to see wildlife which is seen as boring or ugly. No one goes tuna watching, we just want our supermarkets to ensure that when fishermen go hunting tuna, no 'nice' dolphins get caught in their nets! Ecotourists do not seem to want to spend good

money to go and see pygmy shrews, anteaters or antelopes. Yet in ecological terms such creatures are as important and worthy as the elephant or the whale. It seems that ecotourism is a beauty contest where beauty is in the eye of the beholder and the losers have few friends or protectors.

Ecotourism can also lead to the commodification of indigenous wildlife and people, so both are seen as just tourism resources, whose main role in life is to fulfil the desires of tourists. Both people and animals can then be priced so that a chance to meet a tribe in the forests of Borneo can be judged to be worth a $30 boat trip. Tourists have to choose if this is better value than a $30 trip to an orang-utan sanctuary. In this process both people and animals are not treated with the dignity which both deserve.

Patronizing Indigenous People

Ecotourism can lead to indigenous people being patronized by the tourists, often innocently. The indigenous people who are most popular with tourists are those who may:

- be physically very different from the tourist or may dress in what the tourists see as eccentric ways
- live in unusual homes
- eat what the tourist sees as odd foods
- engage in dances and rituals which are picturesque.

Tourists can patronize local people in two different ways:

- by treating them as backward 'primitives' who are to be looked down upon in some way, so that while seen as 'entertaining' the tourist does not see them as an equal
- by viewing them as super-human beings with some almost supernatural ability to commune with nature, who have not changed their life style for generations. This is almost always inaccurate and perhaps reflects a wistful longing in the

heart of the tourist that such people might still exist on the planet.

While the latter may seem less offensive, it is still patronizing in its own way.

The Role of Tour Operators

Tour operators have increasingly sought to jump on the ecotourism bandwagon. At first involvement was confined to small operators where the owner was simply a person with a deep concern for the destination and its ecosystems. However, large operators are now becoming increasingly involved selling ecotourism trips as excursions and short add-ons to traditional package holidays. These larger operators may have less interest in, or knowledge of, the ecosystems concerned and will probably generate more tourist trips than the small operators. Operators, understandably, focus on the positive aspects of ecotourism trips for the tourist rather than on the problems caused by ecotourism. They sell the idea of ecotourism as 'good' tourism to give their customers a 'feel good' factor about their choice. This simply reinforces the 'ego-tourism' problem identified by Wheeller and discussed earlier in this chapter.

The Role of Governments

Governments, particularly in developing countries, are keen to attract the high spending ecotourists. They have also been told by international bodies that ecotourism is a relatively beneficial type of tourism. Often they develop ecotourism zealously, but in doing so, they often fail to recognize the rights of indigenous people living in the destination area, who may be moved to other areas to make way for tourism development. They may also spend money on infrastructure that might be better spent on education and health and they might inadvertently give too much power to major corporations based outside the destination, which limits the benefits enjoyed by the local population.

Towards Sustainable Ecotourism

We have seen that ecotourism and sustainable tourism are not the same thing. However, ecotourism can be a sustainable form of tourism, if properly managed. The aim should be to manage ecotourism so that it is:

> an enlightening nature travel experience that contributes to the conservation of the ecosystem while respecting the integrity of the host community. (Scace et al., 1992)

An ideal model of sustainable ecotourism is offered in Fig. 30.3, based on the views of Sadler (1990) and Wight (1993).

Wight (1993) identified nine principles that should underpin sustainable ecotourism, as follows:

- it should not degrade the resource and should be developed in an environmentally sound manner
- it should provide first hand, participatory and enlightening experiences
- it should involve education among all parties – local communities, government, non-governmental organizations, industry and tourists (before, during and after the trip)
- it should encourage all-party recognition of the intrinsic values of the resource
- it should involve acceptance of the resource on its own terms, and recognition of its limits, which involves supply-oriented management
- it should promote understanding and involve partnerships between many players, which could include government, non-government organizations, industry, scientists and locals (both before and during operations)
- it should promote moral and ethical responsibilities and behaviour towards the natural and cultural environment, by all players
- it should provide long-term benefits – to the resource, local community and industry (benefits may be conservation, scientific, social, cultural or economic)

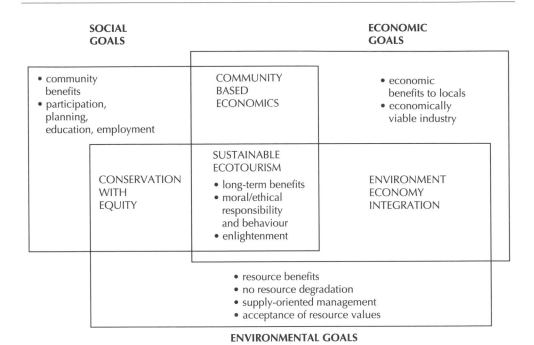

Fig. 30.3. Sustainable ecotourism values and principles model. (After Sadler, 1990; Wight 1993).

- ecotourism operations should ensure that the underlying ethics of responsible environmental practices are applied not only to the external (natural and cultural) resources which attract the tourists, but also to their internal operations.

There is also a need for governments to both effectively control poor quality ecotourism, and actively encourage good quality sustainable ecotourism.

The move towards more sustainable forms of ecotourism will also require a move from what Ziffer called nature-based tour operators to true ecotourism operators. The distinction between the two extremes and the points in between are illustrated in Table 30.1. Already, there are examples of good practice emerging that appear to be examples of sustainable ecotourism. These include:

- the controlled development of ecotourism as a whole in Belize, together with individual projects like the baboon sanctuary on Bermuda Landing and the Toledo Ecotourism Association Project (see Edington and Edington in Stabler, 1997)

- the partnership-based Annapurna Conservation Area Project in Nepal (see Gurung and De Coursey in Cater and Lowman, 1994)

- the Danube Delta Biosphere Resource project on ecotourism (described by Hall and Kinnard in Cater and Lowman, 1994).

Ultimately, however, ecotourism will only become more sustainable if tourists either demand such change or are at least willing to accept its implications for their holiday experiences.

Conclusions

We have seen that ecotourism and sustainable tourism are not necessarily the same thing. Indeed we have discussed conflicts between the two phenomena. However,

Table 30.1. Ziffer's spectrum of ecotourism. Source: Ziffer (1989), quoted in Burton (1997).

Nature-based tourism	Added subdivisions
Tour operators that sell nature	• Those who are unaware or uncaring about its impact • Operators that are aware of impacts, do the minimum to abide by any management rules, who do *not* seek to educate or change tourists' attitudes, but may provide information
Sensitive tour operators	• Aware of impacts, actively seek to educate tourists by providing information • Actively seek to influence tourists' attitudes and behaviour. Support conservation, e.g. members of conservation groups • Practice minimum impact tourism (over and above management requirements) e.g. pack away rubbish, rotate sites
Donors (in that they give something back to the environment)	• Act positively to improve the environment they use and restore damage, e.g. pack up other people's rubbish, participate in restoration schemes, voluntarily donate a proportion of trip costs to conservation or management of the resource, plant trees, support local community
Doers	• Those who initiate conservation projects or research • Those involved actively in influencing policy and management towards sustainable practices

towards the end of the chapter, ideas were outlined which might close the gap and make ecotourism more sustainable. As tourists travel to ever more remote parts of the world to view the wildlife and see indigenous peoples, the need to develop more sustainable ecotourism will become ever more urgent.

Discussion Points and Essay Questions

1. Critically evaluate Wight's model of ecotourism motivators illustrated in Fig. 30.2.
2. Discuss the issues raised by Wheeller in the section entitled 'Ecotourism or Ego-tourism?' in this chapter.
3. Discuss the ways in which ecotourism can be in conflict with the concept of sustainable tourism.

Exercise

Compile a list of tour operators which claim to offer ecotourism or ecotourism type holidays. You should then see where they lie on Ziffer's spectrum, as shown in Table 30.1. Finally, produce a report noting what this exercise has demonstrated to you about the link between ecotourism and sustainable tourism.

Case Study: Codes of Conduct for Ecotourists

The growing concern over the potentially negative aspects of ecotourism has led to the growth of various codes of conduct for ecotourists and the ecotourism 'industry'. Exhibits 1, 2 and 3 illustrate three examples of such codes of conduct, all of which were included in the World Tourism Organization publication, *Sustainable Tourism Development*, published in 1993.

While all of them contain sound advice, they rarely deal with the fundamental underlying issues and tend to be rather superficial.

Exhibit 1. ASTA's ten commandments on ecotourism.

Whether on business or leisure travel:

- **Respect the frailty of the earth.** Realize that unless all are willing to help in its preservation, unique and beautiful destinations may not be here for future generations to enjoy.
- **Leave only footprints. Take only photographs.** No graffiti! No litter! Do not take away 'souvenirs' from historical sites and natural areas.
- To make your travels more meaningful, **educate yourself about the geography, customs, manners and cultures of the region you visit.** Take time to listen to the people. Encourage local conservation efforts.
- **Respect the privacy and dignity of others.** Inquire before photographing people.
- **Do not buy products made from endangered plants or animals**, such as ivory, tortoise shell, animal skins and feathers. Read *Know Before You Go* the US Customs list of products which cannot be imported.
- **Always follow designated trails**. Do not disturb animals, plants or their natural habitats.
- Learn about and **support conservation-oriented programmes and organizations** working to preserve the environment.
- Whenever possible, **walk or utilize environmentally sound methods of transportation**. Encourage drivers of public vehicles to stop engines when parked.
- **Patronise those** hotels, airlines, resorts, cruise lines, tour operators and suppliers who advance energy and environmental conservation; water and air quality; recycling; safe management of waste and toxic materials; noise abatement; community involvement; and which provide experienced, well-trained staff **dedicated to strong principles of conservation.**
- Ask your ASTA travel agent to **identify those organizations which subscribe to ASTA Environmental Guidelines for air, land and sea travel**. ASTA has recommended that these organizations adopt their own environmental codes to cover special sites and ecosystems.

Exhibit 2. Guidelines for nature tourism.

Nature tourism is of growing importance to those countries and regions interested in sustainable tourism. It is one segment of the industry which is difficult to define because it covers a wide range of activities. Nature tourists can be people casually walking through an undisturbed forest, or scuba divers admiring coral formations, or bird watchers adding birds to their lists. But, it is a segment of the market that will respond to environmental issues. The following guidelines can be used by the local planner to encourage community, environmental and tourism constituencies to work together toward a common goal.

- **The success of nature tourism depends on the conservation of nature.** Many parks are threatened, and it is critical for everyone involved with nature tourism to realize that intact natural resources are the foundation.

- **Nature tourism sites need revenue for protection and maintenance, much of which can be generated directly from entry fees and sale of products**. Many protected areas charge nominal or no entrance fees and provide few if any auxiliary services. Nature tourists also desire gift shops, food services and lodging facilities and expect to pay for them.
- **Tourists are a valuable audience for environmental education**. In many parks, opportunities are missed to provide environmental education. Whether 'hard-core' nature tourists or 'new' visitors with little background in natural history, all tourists can enhance their appreciation of the area through information brochures, exhibits and guides.
- **Nature tourism will contribute to rural development when local residents are brought into the planning process**. For nature tourism to be a tool for conservation and rural development, a concerted effort must be made to incorporate local populations into development of the tourism industry. In some cases, tourism to protected areas is not benefiting the surrounding population because they are not involved.
- **Opportunities are emerging for new relationships between conservationists and tour operators**. Traditionally, these groups have not worked together; often they have been in direct opposition. However, as more tourists come to parks and reserves, tour operators have the opportunity to become more actively involved with the conservation of these areas through education for their clientele and donations to park management.

(Source: E. Boo (1990) *The Potentials and Pitfalls*, Volumes 1 and 2, World Wildlife Fund, Washington, DC).

Exhibit 3. Environmentally responsible safaris – guidelines for tour operators.

- State your commitment to conservation in brochures and other pre-departure information.
- Conduct orientations on conservation and cultural sensitivity before and during the trip. Arrange to meet with wildlife rangers for all safari tours, not only for special-interest tours.
- Provide guidance about endangered species products sold in souvenir shops and why to avoid them in pre-trip printed materials. During the trip patronize only appropriate craft concessions that sell locally produced goods that benefit the local economy. Explain when it is or is not appropriate to bargain or barter for goods.
- Build in a contribution to a conservation, cultural or archaeological project. Or encourage donations by clients directly to the reserve, wildlife service or non-profit projects. Or adopt a specific project. Or hold a fund-raising drive to donate specific equipment or meet other needs. Or give a membership to a wildlife organization as a tour benefit. Provide an opportunity for clients to see what project they are helping to support.
- Equip clients with information to help minimize any negative impact (e.g. don't wear bright colours, distracting patterns, or perfume, don't smoke, talk loudly, or crowd the animals with more than five vans at one time, stay on the roads). This encourages clients not to pressure drivers to break the rules of the reserve. Stop at the visitor centre. Provide copies of park rules for clients and explain why they are important.
- Discourage negative social ramifications that result by giving candy and inappropriate gifts to children along the route. If there is something to donate, have the tour guide give it to a village elder or school teacher to distribute.
- Ensure that ground operators train drivers/guides. Give recognition or monetary awards for safety excellence and sensitivity to the rules of the reserve. Ask drivers to turn off the engine to alleviate noise and reduce diesel fuel exhaust when viewing wildlife or scenery.

- Follow up the safari with newsletters and information on wildlife appeals. Give a progress report on any adopted project the client helped support. Ask clients for feedback after the safari.
- Explain your commitment to the environment to tour operator colleagues, travel agents during office visits and at trade shows, and in-bound operators. Share ideas on materials, driver training, and ethical standards for the industry. By presenting the company's commitment as a competitive selling point, it can serve to heighten awareness and others may be persuaded to evaluate their practices too.

(Source: Laurie Lubeck (1991) *Wildlife Tourism Impact Project Materials*, California.)

Case Study: Whale-watching

Whale-watching has increased dramatically on a worldwide scale in recent years. Day trips and whole holidays are now devoted to this activity from California to New Zealand, Iceland to South Africa. It can be seen as part of the growth of ecotourism.

In several ways, it can be seen to be quite sustainable in that:

- It helps tourists increase their understanding of this endangered species. This could lead them to become actively involved with whale conservation groups when they return home.
- It provides an alternative living, potentially, for whaling ships and crews, and is surely better than killing the whales. Indeed, as whaling and fishing have declined, whale-watching has been viewed as the economic and social salvation of some small fishing ports.

Conversely, whale-watching can be seen as exploitation, an extension of the safari park concept. If the scale of it gets out of hand, it can also disturb the whales.

Perhaps, therefore, the challenge is to find better ways of regulating whale-watching, following the example of New England, for example, in the USA. Here there are conditions on boat operators and how close to the whales their boats can go.

We also need a clearer idea of the 'carrying capacity' of whale habitats in terms of whale-watchers, so that we can perhaps begin to impose constraints on the volume of whale-watchers in particular areas of sea.

31

All-inclusive and Self-contained Resort Complexes

In the 1990s, all-inclusive resort complexes have increased dramatically in popularity. Many tourists clearly value the concept of paying one price before they depart on holiday, after which all their meals, drinks, entertainment and sporting activities will be 'free'.

It is important to recognize that there are several types of all-inclusive complex, including the following:

- Large purpose-built resort complexes that are designed to be all-inclusive are generally located in established destinations and have been in existence for a number of years. They are generally owned by well-known brand name chains such as Club Med and Sandals. These tend to have developed up-market reputations and are valued for their quality image.
- Complexes that can be simply a single hotel or may be somewhat larger, but are located in new destinations, usually in developing countries such as the Dominican Republic. Here the all-inclusive concept may be attractive to tourists because the local tourism infrastructure is still under-developed and/or the tourist does not feel safe in the local environment.
- Older hotels in well-established Medi-

terranean destinations which are seeking to use all-inclusive packages to differentiate them from their competitors and achieve competitive advantage. These hotels tend to be priced at the middle to lower end of the market.

It is important to recognize that in this chapter, we are using the term 'resort' in the American sense of a large accommodation complex, not as an alternative term for a tourist destination.

However, there are resort complexes which are attempting to be self-contained mini destinations in their own right, even though they do not offer all-inclusive packages. Nevertheless, by setting out to meet all the needs of the tourist on their own site, they discourage tourists from leaving to explore other parts of the region. There are three main types of such self-contained complexes:

- branded names such as Center Parcs in the UK, France, Belgium and The Netherlands
- theme parks which have on-site accommodation units within the same complex such as Disneyland Paris
- fantasy themed tourism complexes such as the hotels in Las Vegas, which are

keen that gamblers should not leave the hotel!

The Negative Aspects of All-inclusive Resort Complexes

The main criticism of all-inclusive resort complexes is that they greatly reduce the spin-off benefits of tourism for local businesses. As the all-inclusive package tends to include all meals, drinks, entertainment and all or most sporting activities, tourists do not need to spend money on eating out in local restaurants, drinking in bars and watersport activities.

Compared to a tourist on a bed and breakfast package at a hotel in the Caribbean, the all-inclusive package could deprive local traders of around £200 to £300 per tourist per week. Multiplying this figure by the number of tourists means the growth of all-inclusive resorts could be costing local communities as much as several million pounds per annum. This could be enough to send local enterprises into bankruptcy.

At the same time, the fact that tourists know everything is paid for may encourage them to eat and drink too much. This could lead to bad behaviour influenced by over-indulgence in alcohol.

Once they have paid for everything that is delivered on site, there is often also a reluctance to leave the complex which reduces contact between host and guest.

The all-inclusive concept can also make the resort complexes themselves too complacent because they already have the tourist's money and do not need to impress them to ensure that they do not go off and spend their money elsewhere in the area. This can therefore result in poor quality standards in relation to food, for example.

The Positive Aspects of All-inclusive Resort Complexes

All-inclusive resort complexes are good news for their operators. They can help rejuvenate an existing establishment by allowing it to gain a share of this growing market. The concept also makes financial planning easier because the operator knows how many meals they will need to make and can estimate the demand for drinks. This should minimize wastage and help with the cashflow situation.

From the tourist's point of view, the all-inclusive concept is very attractive, hence its growing popularity in the market place. The tourist knows, in advance, exactly how much their holiday will cost. They do not, therefore, have to worry about over-spending. At the same time, it takes away the need to take cash or credit cards with them, which may make them more relaxed and reduce their fear of being robbed.

While all-inclusive complexes, in general, reduce the demand for the services of local small enterprises, they can bring great benefits to local traders who supply the resort complex, by giving them guaranteed business.

The Negative Aspects of Self-contained Resort Complexes

Self-contained complexes encourage the tourist to believe they have no need to leave the sites throughout their holiday. Again, this reduces the opportunities for local traders to sell their services to tourists, and ensures that tourists see relatively little of the destination region. In relation to the principles of sustainable tourism, this lack of interaction between host and guests has to be seen as negative.

They also isolate tourists from the realities of local everyday life which can lead to them leaving with an unrealistic view of the local area.

Self-contained complexes may even be tempted to exaggerate local health and crime risks to discourage tourists from leaving the complex. This can lead to the tourists returning home with an unrealistically negative image of safety in the destination, which may in turn put other people they talk to off visiting the resort.

The Positive Aspects of Self-contained Resort Complexes

However, if one views tourism as a form of social pollution, it is possible to put forward a persuasive argument that self-contained complexes are a beneficial phenomenon in terms of sustainable tourism. They allow tourists from one culture to take a holiday in a country with a very different culture and ensure that the tourist's culture does not affect the local culture. They can drink and dress immodestly without offending local residents. Tourists often see self-contained complexes as ideal for a relaxing holiday, particularly in areas where they may feel vulnerable to crime if they leave the complex.

Resort Complexes: the New Apartheid?

One of the most controversial aspects of resort complexes, whether they be all-inclusive, or simply self-contained, is the issue of access for local people to the complexes. In many developing countries, these complexes are built on land from which the original residents may have been forcibly displaced by a government keen to attract foreign tourists. The complexes may use local people as labour, but otherwise the host community may be denied access to the site. Armed guards may even patrol the perimeter to keep out local people. Thus, the development of resort complexes across the world can in many ways, be seen as the new form of apartheid, enforcing the separation of tourists and hosts, and giving greater rights to the immigrant tourists than to the indigenous population. Clearly, such tourism apartheid is not in keeping with the underlying principles of sustainable tourism.

Making All-inclusive and Self-contained Resort Complexes More Sustainable

Given the popularity of the all-inclusive and self-contained resort complexes outlined in this chapter, it is perhaps naive to talk about whether they should be allowed or not. They are unlikely to disappear as most of them are backed by major corporations or even governments.

Realistically, therefore, the best we can perhaps hope for is that such complexes may endeavour to adopt the following principles of good practice. They should, wherever possible, source all their supplies from local traders, and pay them a fair price. Food and drink that cannot be sourced locally should perhaps not be offered. However, it will be difficult to get tourists to accept this if their holiday is in a region where the scope of agricultural produce is rather narrow. Reasonable access should be allowed to the site for local people, subject to the legitimate need to protect the safety of tourists. Tourists should be encouraged to leave the site to explore the region. This should be offered as part of the package of the all-inclusive resort complexes. Governments ought to ensure that resorts are either locally owned or are partnerships between local entrepreneurs and external organizations, to maximize the local benefits of these complexes.

Finally, complexes should be encouraged to become involved in the local community and contribute to local development projects.

Conclusions

In general we have seen that all-inclusive and self-contained resort complexes are very popular with tourists and the large-scale tourism industry. However, they tend to be viewed negatively by local small and medium-sized enterprises. We have noted that they have to modify their operations in several ways if they are to become more compatible with the concept of sustainable tourism.

Discussion Points and Essay Questions

1. Identify the main beneficiaries and losers from the growth of all-inclusive and self-contained resort complexes.
2. Discuss the motivations that have led to more and more tourists choosing to take

holidays at all-inclusive, self-contained resort complexes.

3. Discuss the ways in which resort complexes might be made more sustainable.

Exercise

Choose an organization which operates all-inclusive *or* self-contained resort complexes (e.g. Butlins, Club Med, Center Parcs, Sandals, Oasis, etc.). For your selected organization, produce a report detailing:

- how sustainable their complexes are at present
- what could be done to make the complexes more sustainable.

Case Study: All-inclusive Hotels in the 1998–1999 Thomson *Winter Sun* Brochure

In recent years, most UK tour operators have begun to offer brochures of all-inclusive holidays. Even in general brochures, all-inclusive hotels or resort complexes or all-inclusive options are on offer. For example, the 1998–1999 Thomson *Winter Sun* brochure included 22 hotels or resort complexes offering an all-inclusive package which included:

- all you can eat buffets for breakfast, lunch and dinner
- soft drinks
- locally produced alcoholic drinks
- a variety of sports, a range of daytime activities and evening entertainment
- in addition, snacks and afternoon tea are available in most units.

(Source: Thomson, 1998–1999 *Winter Sun* brochure.)

The 22 units are located as follows:

- Tenerife (2)
- Gran Canaria (1)
- Lanzarote (2)
- Fuerteventura (1)
- Costa Blanca (2)
- Costa del Sol (1)
- Majorca (2)
- Malta (2)
- Cyprus (2)
- Tunisia (2)
- Mexico (2)
- Israel (1)
- Jamaica (1)
- Gambia (1).

The rapid rise in popularity of such packages is demonstrated by the fact that previous client satisfaction scores were not available for 15 of these units because of their only recent conversion from 'traditional' hotels to all-inclusive package providers. Thomson seems to be dealing mainly with existing establishments which are seeking to use their conversion to all-inclusive operations to enhance their market position. Most are in traditional short- and medium-haul winter sun destinations, and appear to be aimed at the mid-market tourist looking for a value-for-money three-star level holiday.

The brochure stresses the benefits of staying on site at the hotel complexes, but also occasionally promotes shopping and bars in local towns. One even offers discounts on local taxis and in shops in the neighbouring resort.

Prices are modest considering the all-inclusive nature of the package offered. The cost of a 14-night holiday for an adult in the 1998–1999 season ranged from £355 in Spain to £1138 in Jamaica.

It is clear that Thomson assume that most clients will spend most of their time on the site, taking advantage of everything that is included in the price of their holiday, but Thomson do not seem to be overtly encouraging tourists to stay on the site.

Case Study: Center Parcs

While Center Parcs certainly aim to be self-contained complexes, encouraging tourists to stay on site, they are often held up as an example of good practice in relation to sustainability. This reputation has been built on the following factors:

- The company tries to choose the least environmentally sensitive sites for its new holiday villages.
- Wherever possible, existing trees on site are retained.
- New wildlife habitats are developed, such as lakes and woods, which help conserve indigenous wildlife.
- The villages are traffic free, with guests leaving their cars in peripheral car parks. During the holiday the only form of on-site transport is the bicycle.
- Sourcing labour and suppliers from the local area, wherever possible.

In the UK, Center Parcs' environmental policies and practices have earned them a range of awards. At the same time, the guests also benefit from the high quality environment and relaxing atmosphere.

Center Parcs claim their complexes bring a range of benefits. For example, they:

- provide a family-friendly environment
- emphasize the health-enhancing aspects of a stay at a Center Parcs village
- offer a non-weather-dependent facility.

This latter point helps to offer one of the perceived reasons why more British people apparently now holiday outside the UK. This aspect of Center Parcs probably persuades people to take a domestic holiday in the UK, The Netherlands, France or Germany when they might otherwise take a foreign vacation, thus benefiting the country's balance of payments situation.

Center Parcs also do not neglect their staff. Two of their six corporate goals are framed in terms of having:

- a positive approach to the genuine recognition of our own employees
- a commitment to invest in the personal development of each and every individual in the organization.
  (Center Parcs, quoted in Horner and Swarbrooke, 1996.)

Nevertheless, we must remember that Center Parcs are self-contained complexes which do not encourage their guests to leave the site. Many of their visitors will see little of the region in which the village is located, except the roads that bring them to the site!

32

Business Tourism

In most discussions of sustainable tourism, little or no mention is made of business tourism. Yet, business travel is growing worldwide and represents a large slice of the global tourism cake. It is vital therefore that if we want to develop more sustainable forms of tourism we also give attention to the business tourism phenomenon.

If we take the simple definition that business tourism is that tourism which is undertaken as a part of an individual's occupation, then we can see from Fig. 32.1 that it is a broad and diverse sector.

There are several specific characteristics of business tourism which make it particularly problematic in relation to the concept of sustainable tourism. Firstly, most business tourists take more trips in a year than the average leisure tourist, thus making more demands on transport infrastructure, and destination services. Business tourists tend to be very demanding and want high quality facilities, even in towns and cities in developing countries. While both of these are difficult to reconcile with the concept of sustainable tourism, the positive side of business tourism is the fact that business travellers tend to be higher spending than leisure tourists.

The Negative Side of Business Tourism

Business tourism can bring a range of problems in its wake. It:

- demands infrastructure such as convention and exhibition centres which are expensive to develop and require large tracts of land
- generally involves travel by private car rather than public transport so that it is very demanding in terms of fuel consumption and is a serious cause of tourism-related pollution
- involves consumers who tend to want standardized service and facilities, wherever they are in the world. This creates pressure for standardization that does not take account of local differences in culture and geography
- attracts crime such as prostitution and mugging
- may involve morally dubious trading activities such as the illegal smuggling of animals or animal products, drugs or arms
- creates waste; because the business tourist is usually not paying the bill they

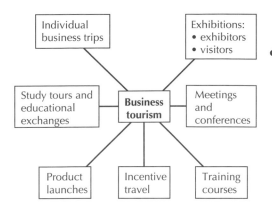

Fig. 32.1. The nature and scope of business tourism.

are often willing to buy more than they need and create waste

- business tourism makes heavy use of resources. For example, large amounts of electricity are required by the audio-visual aids used at conferences and the computers used by those making individual business trips.

Of all the sectors of business tourism, incentive travel is particularly problematic in relation to sustainable tourism. The key to incentive travel is offering one's client a unique experience which means going where other tourists do not go and doing things which other tourists do not get to do. This can lead to tourism trips to particularly fragile natural environments which are unsuitable destinations for tourists.

Two Key Audiences: Customers and Consumers

When we try to make business tourism more sustainable we have to impress two audiences, as follows:

- The **customer** who is the employer who decides where and when business trips will be taken and who pays the bill. They will be influenced by messages and initiatives that will:
  (i) reduce the cost of business travel to the organization

(ii) improve the organization's reputation in its market.

- The **consumer**, the business traveller, who actually is the one who travels and consumes the various products and services of business tourism suppliers. This person wants to travel in as much comfort as possible, and is often concerned with their status. Therefore, business travellers will react badly to any suggestion which threatens to make their travel more difficult or reduces their status.

Proposals such as the idea of heavily taxing company cars to reduce their use, for the sake of the environment, thus often leads to opposition from both audiences, for different reasons.

New Communications Technologies: the Key to More Sustainable Business Tourism?

The needs of these two audiences is clearly an issue when we consider the extent to which the new, emerging communications technologies may lead to more sustainable forms of business tourism. It could be argued that the growth of satellite and video-conferencing, computer-conferencing and CD-ROMs should reduce the demand for business travel. Likewise virtual reality technologies are also allowing people to train to do everything from fighting fires to carrying out surgical operations, without the need to travel to a training centre or another hospital.

Clearly, this should appeal to the employers or customers who stand to save money if this becomes more common. Conversely, the business traveller may resent these developments. They will reduce the number of trips they take to interesting places, when they might often take a partner along, as we shall see later, mixing business with pleasure. This could reduce their job satisfaction and their status. At the same time, fewer trips will mean fewer points for the consumer from frequent flyer programmes and thus fewer free leisure flights for them and their partner.

However, as yet the substitution of new technology for business trips has not become widespread because of:

- the limited quality of the technologies as yet and the high cost of using them
- the idea that some business can only be done on a personal, face-to-face basis.

Nevertheless, as the technologies improve, they could play a role in reducing business travel, and the use of resources which it consumes.

Mixing Pleasure with Business: the Real Problem?

Some would argue that many of the problems surrounding business tourism relate to the interface between business travel and leisure travel. This relationship has four elements:

- business travellers become leisure travellers when the working day is over
- partners often accompany business tourists on their trips and while the business traveller is working, the partner is free to act as a leisure tourist
- many conferences have social programmes of leisure activities for delegates
- incentive travel is actually leisure travel for business purposes.

While the latter three are generally positive characteristics it is the first one which causes many of the problems associated with business tourism.

People working under pressure can tend to go a little wild when the working day is over. Business tourists, for instance, are the core market for most 'red light' districts around the world, from Amsterdam to Bangkok. The demand for sex by business people leads to young women being forced – economically or physically – into prostitution, and also helps spread the HIV and hepatitis B viruses.

The fact that business tourists are high spending also attracts muggers, professional gamblers, and drug dealers to major business tourism destinations. Business tourism thus can have a negative social impact on destinations.

Business Tourism – a Better Class of Tourism for Destinations?

Conversely, in terms of the economic and social aspects of sustainable tourism, business tourism has a number of advantages over leisure tourism. As they are usually not paying the bill, business tourists tend to spend two or three times as much money per day as leisure tourists. However, they are more likely to spend their money with transnational companies so that a higher proportion of their expenditure may be lost to the local community. Business tourists demand a high level of personal service so accommodating them is a labour-intensive activity which creates more jobs than leisure tourism. Business tourism spreads its benefits widely around local enterprises because of its demand for everything from florists to secretarial services, photographers to security people. Business tourism tends to be less seasonal than leisure tourism, and it is complementary to leisure tourism in that it:

- is in full swing in the months which are the off-peak season for leisure tourism
- fills hotels on weekdays but leaves them empty for the leisure tourist at the weekends.

There is also the idea that if business people and entrepreneurs are impressed by a place they visit for business, then they may invest in the place or even re-locate their business there.

Towards More Sustainable Business Tourism

We have seen that business tourism brings social and environmental costs as well as economic and social benefits. In order to make it more complementary with the principles of sustainable tourism, a number of changes would be beneficial. There is a need to:

- replace as many trips as possible by the use of new communications technologies
- persuade the business tourist to use public, rather than private, transport whenever possible
- educate business travellers about the social problems caused in destinations by prostitution and about the risks to their own health involved in having sex with prostitutes
- make business travellers aware of the need to spend their money with local enterprises rather than with multinational corporations, wherever possible
- encourage business tourists to welcome local cultural differences rather than searching for standardized products and services.

In this way, business tourism could reinforce its position as potentially one of the most sustainable forms of tourism.

However, we must always recognize that, by and large, its future in any destination lies not in how well it is managed there. Instead it relies on economic and industrial factors which will be outside the control of those who promote business tourism destinations.

Conclusions

We have seen that, in many ways, business tourism is a potentially highly sustainable form of tourism. However, we have also noted that it also brings some social and environmental problems. It has also been discussed that there is a need to influence two audiences – employers and the business travellers themselves – if these problems are to be overcome.

Discussion Points and Essay Questions

1. Discuss which of the types of business tourism outlined in Fig. 32.1 are the most beneficial in relation to sustainable tourism.
2. Critically evaluate the main social and environmental costs associated with business tourism.
3. Discuss the reasons why tourist destinations might wish to attract business tourists rather than leisure tourists.

Exercise

Identify an organization within your local area which generates a significant volume of business travel, of different types, over a year. Then interview the key 'customers' and 'consumers' within the organization, to see to what extent they think new, emerging communications technologies will reduce the demand for business travel within the organization.

Case Study: a Day in the Life of the Business Tourist!

In the chapter we saw that business tourists bring higher than average economic benefits for destinations than leisure tourists, but that they also bring problems with them. The following hypothetical example of a day in the life of the business tourist working in a foreign country, seeks to illustrate this point:

- 07.10: Mr A wakes up and complains that the alarm call he ordered did not materialize.
- 07.30: Mr A showers using the complementary toiletries provided in plastic, disposable containers by the hotel. He puts other bottles of the rather nice shampoo in his case to take home for his daughter, a keen vegetarian and animal rights campaigner, unaware of the fact that it was tested on animals.
- 08.00: Mr A goes down to breakfast. He rejects fresh local fruit in favour of imported yoghurts and marmalade, all packed in plastic, disposable portion packs.
- 09.00: Mr A leaves for his appointment with a client in a large luxury car that guzzles petrol as it sweeps past the poor local people waiting in the bus queue.
- 12.00: Mr A spends a large amount of money on an expensive business lunch with his clients in a luxurious international-style hotel restaurant.
- 14.00: Mr A finishes his business and goes to the shopping area by taxi to buy gifts for his wife and daughter. Ignoring the local traders he spends several hundred pounds at the local branch of a well-known international clothes chain such as Benetton.
- 16.00: Mr A then spends a further £100 buying a very old piece of pottery that has been stolen from an archaeological excavation elsewhere in the country.
- 17.30: Mr A returns to his hotel room by taxi, switches on the air conditioning and gets changed. He forgets to switch off the air conditioning when he leaves the room.
- 18.30: Mr A goes to MacDonald's for a snack.
- 19.00: Mr A starts drinking in a nearby hotel bar in a country where alcohol is not drunk by local people because of their religion.
- 21.00: Mr A goes to a well-known local massage parlour where he spends some of his expenses on some rather unusual 'extras'. The masseuse is about the same age as his daughter!
- 22.30: Mr A goes to a casino and spends the last of the expenses given him by his company on a little gambling.
- 00.30: Mr A returns to his hotel, and realizes that he has been robbed of his credit cards. Mr A is surprised that all the people who smiled at him and obeyed his requests when he had money no longer seem interested in him.

While this is a very stereotypical and extreme picture, it does contain some relevant points in relation to business tourism and its relationship with the concept of sustainable tourism.

Conclusions to Part Six

In Part Six we have seen what the concept of sustainable tourism means in relation to different sectors of tourism and different types of tourism.

We have noted that:

- for destinations the challenge is to give the lcoal community a fair share of the benefits of tourism
- there is a need to reduce the negative environmental impacts of the operations of transport and hospitality organizations
- ecotourism is not necessarily complementary to the concept of sustainable tourism
- cultural tourism and business tourism have both positive and negative aspects
- the growth of all-inclusive and/or self-contained resort complexes is a threat to the development of sustainable tourism.

It is now time for the author to endeavour to draw together some general conclusions from the first six parts and 32 chapters of the book, after which there will be a final chapter on different aspects of the future of sustainable tourism.

Part Seven
Conclusions

In Chapter 33, the author will attempt to draw together the key conclusions from this lengthy and wide-reaching book.

He will also try to evaluate to what extent the book has met the objectives set out for it in the preface.

33

Conclusions

This book has taken a broad view of sustainable tourism management. It has also endeavoured to offer an objective, balanced perspective on sustainable tourism management. While it has attempted to offer positive suggestions for making tourism more sustainable it has also hopefully been realistic about the obstacles to achieving this end.

The author has written this text based on a belief that there is a need for more critical evaluation of existing thinking and techniques in the field of sustainable tourism. He has sought to question the numerous 'conventional wisdoms' and 'sacred cows' which are found everywhere in the sustainable tourism debate.

A conscious effort has also been made to produce an overview of the subject rather than focusing on any one aspect such as the physical environment or particular types of place such as developing countries. This is partly because the author believes that sustainable tourism has to be viewed as an holistic whole. We cannot understand the physical environment unless we understand the social and economic dimension of tourism and the challenges in developing countries are largely the result of the demands made by tourists from developed countries.

However, the book can be criticized because of this breadth. Given the limited length of the text it could be accused of being rather superficial with no issue being dealt with in great detail.

Conversely, the author brings to the reader's attention, many detailed, more specialized books and articles so that the interested reader may then read further about more specific issues.

Some readers might criticize the book on the grounds of repetition and duplication in places. However, the author would agree that where this occurs it demonstrates the essentially inter-dependent, inter-related nature of sustainable tourism.

While trying to draw together general conclusions from a book as broad as this one is a very difficult task, there are key points which the author believes have emerged from the text, as follows:

- Sustainable tourism cannot be separated from the wider debate about sustainable development in general. Likewise, tourism cannot be viewed in isolation from other industries and activities.
- Tourism is an integrated system in which all the elements are linked so that changes in one element affect the other elements. This means that sustainable tourism requires an holistic approach.
- Sustainable tourism is not just about the physical environment. It is also about the cultural environment and social jus-

tice as well as being concerned with long-term economic viability.

- Sustainable tourism involves a wide range of stakeholders, all of whom have *both* rights *and* responsibilities. This means that host communities have responsibilities as well as rights, while the tourism industry and tourists have rights as well as responsibilities.

- To date, there has been a surplus of wishful thinking and perhaps a lack of realism and pragmatism in the sustainable tourism debate.

- There has been too much emphasis on formulating sustainable tourism strategies rather than on how such strategies could be implemented. This has led to the lack of large-scale success stories to date in the field of sustainable tourism management.

- We need to recognize that initiatives designed to achieve sustainable tourism bring benefits to some people and costs to others. It is important to ensure that sustainable tourism strategies do not bring benefits to those who are already privileged at the expense of those who are currently disadvantaged.

- Because sustainable tourism policy is largely about the distribution of finite resources it is important to recognize that it is an overtly political issue. Solutions must therefore be political solutions, not merely technocratic ones.

- We need to place a much greater emphasis upon the social dimension of sustainable tourism, in terms of social equity and the sociocultural impacts of tourism. Tourism must be seen to be fair from the point of view of all the parties involved.

- There can be no sustainable tourism unless there is long-term economic viability in respect of tourism organizations and destinations.

- Perhaps too much faith is being placed in public sector planning given that such planning has become discredited in recent years because of its apparent failures.

- We need to recognize that the future of tourism will largely be determined by the tourism industry which is dominated by the private sector.

- Currently, there appears to be little real concern about sustainable tourism amongst consumers. It is highly unlikely that sustainable tourism will develop unless there is pressure for it from tourists.

- Consumer interest will probably only rise if the media gives more attention to the subject of sustainable tourism.

- We must seriously question the common apparent assumption that the host community is always in the right and is always the most important stakeholder in tourism. There are, perhaps, times when the host community is either wrong or has less rights than some other stakeholders.

- There is a need for partnership between the various stakeholders in tourism. However, this principle of partnership must be based upon the realistic recognition that the different stakeholders have different and often conflicting interests and views.

- While there are similarities between the key issues in sustainable tourism between different types of area, there are also clearly differences in terms of the nature and scope of sustainable tourism in different geographical milieux.

- Sustainable tourism affects all the main functional management areas, namely, finance, marketing, human resources and operations.

- Those in developed countries should put their own houses in order rather than seeking to lecture those in developing countries on what they should do in their own countries.

- Tourism in developing countries should be based on the principles of 'fair trade'.

- Sustainable tourism is not just about developing new products and destinations in ways which are sustainable. It is also about sustaining existing products and destinations given the investment of resources, which are tied up in them and the jobs which depend upon them.

- We need to critically evaluate the relationship between sustainable tourism and ecotourism and recognize that the latter can be diametrically opposed to the former.
- In terms of sustainable tourism there is a need to recognize the threat posed by the growth of all-inclusive and self-contained resort complexes.
- There is a need for official standards and sustainable-tourism labelling systems to be developed to help those consumers who want to purchase more sustainable tourism products make their decisions.
- We should endeavour to develop market mechanisms which ensure that tourists pay the full price of the products they purchase and the resources they consume.
- Sustainable tourism has the potential to become a divisive force in society if we continue to make distinctions between so-called 'good' tourism (independent travel) and 'bad' tourism (mass market package holidays).
- Sustainable tourism is about conservation and managed change rather than preservation and fossilization. It should seek to ensure that tourism operates in line with the concept of 'limits to acceptable change'.

- We should see sustainable tourism as one aspect of the concept of ethical business and socially responsible management. However, if we define sustainable tourism in the broadest sense of the term then it could be argued that it encompasses most of the different ethical issues in tourism.
- There is a clear requirement for more research about what constitutes sustainable tourism, and how the concept can be implemented in different countries, sectors and geographical milieux.
- There is no real hard evidence that sustainable tourism is an achievable goal.

Perhaps the most important, if rather contentious conclusion is that no one type of tourism is inherently more sustainable, or better than any other. Managed well, probably any kind of tourism can be highly sustainable while managed badly all tourism is, perhaps, unsustainable. We should, therefore, concentrate on approaches to tourism management rather than types of tourism.

Having drawn conclusions from the current situation the author will now attempt, in Part Eight, to look into the future and make some predictions about sustainable tourism in the years to come.

Part Eight
The Future of Sustainable Tourism

The final chapter in the book looks at different aspects of the future of sustainable tourism, as follows:

(i)   the relationship between sustainable tourism and the wider debate on ethics in business, and the growing idea of ethical marketing
(ii) the link between sustainable tourism and sustainable development
(iii) the potential role of technological innovations, notably virtual reality, in the development of more sustainable forms of tourism
(iv) the issue of implementation, particularly monitoring and performance indicators
(v)   the question of whether sustainable tourism is an impossible dream or whether it may in the future be seen as an irrelevant issue.

34

The Future of Sustainable Tourism

It seems likely that the future of sustainable tourism will be inextricably linked with several key issues which will be discussed in the following sections.

Sustainable Tourism, Ethics in Business and Ethical Marketing

There are a number of ways in which sustainable tourism will be influenced by wider questions relating to ethics, as follows:

- The existence of a range of other ethical challenges which are currently facing the tourism industry at the same time as sustainable tourism. Some of these issues are illustrated in Fig. 34.1. Clearly some of these issues are heavily related to the broader concept of sustainable tourism. What is more they are all issues which, while evident today, will become more significant challenges for the tourism industry in the future. We must therefore ensure that sustainable tourism is seen in the context of other ethical issues.
- The debate over ethical standards in business in general. This issue has become a high profile concern on a global scale following numerous highly publicized political and business scan-

dals in the early 1990s. Tourism organizations, like those in other industries, when faced by ethical dilemmas and changes, can respond in a number of ways, as we can see from Fig. 34.2.

- The attitudes of consumers, the media and politicians towards the responsibilities it is felt corporations should take in relation to society as a whole. These attitudes may well largely determine the stances corporations choose to adopt in terms of the options displayed in Fig. 34.2.
- The concept of ethical marketing and the extent to which it may develop in the future. Ethical marketing is an approach to marketing that recognizes an organization's social responsibilities and seeks to minimize the negative impacts, and enhance the positive impacts, of the organization's activities, on the world outside the organization. This may mean society or the physical environment. It is also about taking a longer term view of the influence of today's marketing activities on tomorrow's society and the physical environment of the future. This appears very much at odds with the short-term financial imperative that determines most marketing activities.

While it is still a relatively new concept, ethical marketing has been used as a com-

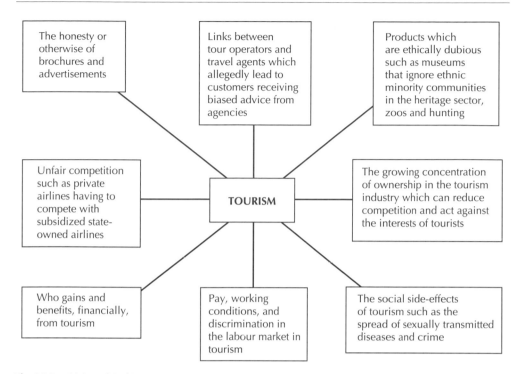

Fig. 34.1. Major ethical issues in tourism.

petitive advantage strategy by organizations in a number of industries. The following few examples will serve to illustrate this point:

- The Body Shop, with its products which are not tested on animals, and the involvement of its founder in aid projects in developing countries.
- The ethical stance taken by the Co-operative Bank on its investments, and the organizations it is willing to accept as customers.
- The car company, Daewoo, with its emphasis on integrity and soft-selling, as opposed to the traditional hard sell in the car industry.

There may be many other companies which behave ethically in their marketing. What is different about the three organizations above is that they have chosen to promote their ethical stances as a way of seeking to gain competitive advantage. This means they have made a conscious effort to communicate what they are doing, or claim to

do, to potential customers, in the hope that it will lead to them attracting more customers.

As yet there has been little attempt to apply the concept of ethical marketing to tourism. Yet it is easy to see the scope for ethical marketing in tourism particularly if we bear in mind the ethical issues shown in Fig. 34.1. In relation to sustainable tourism ethical marketing might involve:

- adopting equal opportunities policies covering the staff who deliver the service which is the core of the tourism product
- providing services designed to meet the requirements of consumers with special needs such as the disabled
- pricing the product in ways which do not discriminate against groups such as single parent families
- being honest in brochures and providing ample information for tourists that will lead to them having realistic expectations.

Problem denial. The organization does not agree there is a problem, for example, tobacco firms in the USA claiming that tobacco is not addictive

Responsibility denial. The organization accepts there is a problem but says the task of resolving it is someone else's responsibility. For example, a tour operator may say that it is government's responsibility to tackle the environmental problems caused by tourism

Putting the other side of the argument. The organization stresses the positive impacts of its activities to counter criticism of the negative aspects. For example, it might talk about the jobs created by tourism which is at the same time damaging the environment

Legal compliance. The organization complies with any relevant legislation but goes no further. An example might be complying with equal opportunities legislation when recruiting staff but not going further in terms of positive discrimination, for instance

Tokenism. Minor actions are taken to counter criticism and make customers feel better about purchasing a product. For example, the organization might donate £2 of the price of a holiday to a conservation project

Public relations. This involves just doing those things that offer the best potential, in public relations terms, such as being seen to be helping a popular charity

Cost reduction. An organization may take quite drastic action but only where it leads to a reduction in costs, such as a hotel introducing energy conservation measures

Competitive advantage. Organizations that take whatever action is necessary to allow them to use their stance on ethical issues as a basis for achieving competitive advantage, which will bring extra custom. This could mean selling products on the basis that they are not tested on animals for example

Ideological conversion. The organization changes its policies and practices radically, even if this may lead to short term competitive disadvantage, because it becomes convinced that its current activities are morally wrong. This phenomenon is rare!

Fig. 34.2. Organizational responses to ethical dilemmas and challenges.

These examples are all related to the concept of sustainable tourism which the author has espoused in this book. Ultimately, however, the rise or otherwise of ethical marketing will probably depend upon the level of consumer concern about ethical issues.

The Relationship between Sustainable Tourism and Sustainable Development

As we saw at the beginning of the book, sustainable tourism is simply part of the broader concept of sustainable develop-

Fig. 34.3. Sustainable tourism and sustainable development.

ment. Yet rarely does the literature on sustainable tourism discuss it in the context of sustainable development as a whole. Figure 34.3 illustrates the relationship between the two aspects of sustainability.

There is a need to start seeing sustainable tourism as part of a larger sustainable development system, an open system where every element affects the other elements. Change in any element of the system will have knock-on effects on other elements of the system. In other words, if we do something to try to develop more sustainable forms of tourism it will affect other non-tourism elements in the system. For example, seeking to reduce the number of tourists may reduce the negative impacts of tourism on the environment but may also harm the host community by reducing the economic benefits of tourism in terms of jobs and salaries. Likewise, trying to reduce immigrant labour by employing more local people, might make local people leave their family farm to work in a hotel. Ultimately the removal of their labour from the farm may make it no longer viable.

This is why it is vital that we do not attempt to tamper with any aspect of tourism unless we understand how it relates to other aspects of sustainable development.

There are two clear links between sustainable tourism and sustainable development:

● Sustainable tourism is a powerful

potential tool for helping achieve sustainable development by acting as a catalyst for small business development and providing a market for agricultural produce, in rural regions in developing countries, for example. In regions in developed countries where traditional industries are in decline, it can also help regenerate local economies and communities.

● Sustainable development is a prerequisite for sustainable tourism for non-sustainable development can severely reduce the quality of the tourism product through inadequate infrastructure and pollution from other industries, for instance.

While the first relationship has been well recognized we have not as yet fully acknowledged the importance of the latter. That is why we must become more interested in the broader issue of sustainable development.

Sustainable Tourism and Virtual Tourism

Some commentators are already arguing that virtual reality-based tourism could help develop sustainable tourism in a number of ways:

● By helping prepare and educate tourists before they take a trip to ensure that they are aware of key issues in relation to sustainability in the hope that they will modify their behaviour accordingly.

● By substituting a virtual reality experience for a visit to a destination which has exceeded its carrying capacity.

● By substituting a virtual reality experience for a visit to a site which is fragile and in danger of being damaged by tourism.

● By offering an alternative virtual reality experience to persuade tourists not to make a trip to destinations which are currently not visited by tourists, but which will undoubtedly be explored soon by adventurous 'ecotourists'.

- By substituting for an activity which is seen to be socially unacceptable, or even illegal, such as hunting, or more contentiously, sex tourism.
- By offering an alternative to people indulging in dangerous activities such as off-piste skiing.
- By the use of virtual reality experience attractions to rejuvenate declining resorts.

Some of these issues will now be considered in a little more detail.

However, there are a number of limitations currently to the role which virtual reality might play in sustainable tourism, as follows:

- The limitations of the technologies themselves, notably:
  (i) the technologies are largely only capable of being used by one person at a time rather than for shared group experiences, yet much of the pleasure gained from holidays comes from the interactions between different people
  (ii) as yet, the virtual reality technologies cannot deliver experiences where the experience involves smell and touch as these cannot be convincingly reproduced today. Furthermore, the sound effects and graphics, while improving, are still relatively crude
  (iii) the enjoyment of virtual reality technologies often involves the use of cumbersome, uncomfortable helmets or gloves and suits
  (iv) the emphasis to date has been on pursuits which appeal to younger males rather than to women, or older males.
- There is a lot of status value involved in visiting famous destinations and sites, or taking part in particular activities. It is hard to believe that a virtual reality experience available in every high street arcade worldwide could carry more status than actually visiting a remote location that only a small proportion of the population can ever hope to visit.
- Some market segments such as the elderly, may be suspicious of these new technologies and resist making use of them.
- The consumer would not be able to easily enjoy the unique nature of the authentic tourism experience which is the result of the combination of the place, the weather and the people one is there with.
- There will have to be a large perceived latent demand for tourism applications of Virtual Reality or the corporations which develop such products will not be induced to make major investment in new product development.

Some people agree that tourists will not readily accept artificial tourism experiences. Yet there is evidence to contradict this view. For example, over 200,000 people a year pay to see a facsimile of the Lascaux caves in France. However, maybe this is because the real caves are closed to the public and the facsimile is the only option.

Attempting to use virtual reality as a substitute for 'real' tourism experiences as a form of de-marketing does carry one major danger. In other words there is always the fear that virtual reality may make more people want to visit places or undertake activities, once they have experienced the virtual reality product. They could make people aware of tourism opportunities they did not previously know about.

Indeed there is little doubt that virtual reality could become a powerful promotional tool for the tourism industry. A sophisticated virtual reality experience could sell most holidays far more effectively than a glossy brochure. The danger therefore is that virtual reality could increase tourist numbers in already overcrowded destinations and at fragile sites.

The other danger is that if virtual reality does succeed in reducing demand for certain activities or visits to particular destinations and attractions, then the host community will suffer job losses and reduced revenue. Tourism-related buildings such as hotels could become disused and infrastructure could end up being underutilized.

Having now considered three key factors that will influence the approach we should

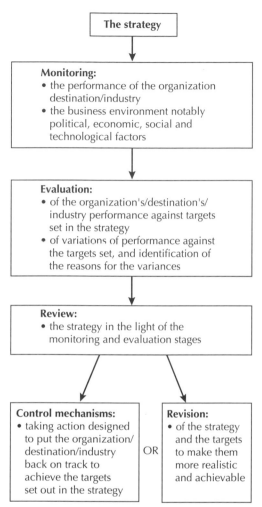

Fig. 34.4. The strategy implementation process.

take to sustainable tourism management in future, it is now time for us to look at the implementation of our desired approaches.

The Implementation of Sustainable Tourism Strategies

To date there has, perhaps, been too much emphasis placed on strategy generation rather than strategy implementation. Yet unless it can be implemented, there is no point in having a strategy. Figure 34.4 illustrates an ideal strategy implementation process. The outcome of the implementa-

tion stage then provides the input for the next cycle of strategic policy.

As yet there are relatively few sustainable tourism strategies at the level of individual tourism organizations. Most existing strategies tend to be public-sector led destination strategies or rather academic, generic 'strategies' for the tourism industry as a whole.

Therefore, in this chapter, we will focus on sustainable tourism strategies for destinations to illustrate points which would also be equally valid for individual organizations.

The two key issues in the implementation of every strategy, including those in the sustainable tourism field are:

- monitoring systems
- measurable performance indicators.

We will now look at both in the context of destinations.

Monitoring includes two stages:

- monitoring the actual performance of the destination itself
- identifying changes in the external business environment namely political, economic, social and technological factors.

Monitoring a destination's performance would involve looking at a range of issues including:

- the number, location, size and quality of new tourism developments
- the number and type of tourists visiting the destination and their spending levels and behaviour
- initiatives that help to build relationships between tourists and the host community
- the distribution of the economic benefits of tourism within the local population
- the wages and working conditions of the workforce in the local tourism industry.

At the same time, the destination should be scanning the external business environment, of which the following elements would probably be the most important from a sustainable tourism point of view:

- government policies, funding policies, and legislation relating to tourism
- the ownership structure of the industry and the rise of large, transnational corporations
- the state of the economy
- public opinion on social issues such as environmental issues and animal welfare
- the increasing sophistication of virtual reality technologies.

The monitoring system cannot be generalized, it must be specific to the situation of an individual destination. This means not only using published secondary data but also carrying out original primary research, which might take the form of:

- surveys of tourists
- interviews with key marketing intermediaries such as travel agents
- discussions with the local tourism industry, notably accommodation establishments and visitor attractions.

Monitoring needs to be carried out in a systematic way, continuously so that key changes can be easily and quickly identified.

Performance Indicators

Strategies can only be evaluated if actual performance can be measured against a set of performance indicators. These indicators need to be expressed in terms of measurable targets. Too often, sustainable tourism targets are vague and incapable of measurement, being expressed in terms of 'spreading the benefits of tourism more fairly', or 'attracting better quality tourists'. These objectives are impossible to measure.

For a coastal destination in the Mediterranean, a set of measurable performance

indicators might include:

- encouraging tourists to spend, on average, another £20 per week, at locally owned enterprises
- reducing visitor numbers at 'honey-pot' sites by 10% at peak times where overuse at these times is causing irrevocable damage
- ensuring that local hotel staff are all paid at least the average wage for the area
- reducing, by 50%, the pollution of the sea by tourist-generated sewage
- persuading 20% of tourists to use trains, bicycles or horses to take excursions rather than private cars or hire cars
- encouraging 3000 tourists using the destination to take a free 1-day course designed to increase their understanding of the local culture.

It is important to recognize that targets should relate to the whole planning period. As most strategies are designed to last for 5 or 10 years, for example, targets should be expressed on a year-by-year basis.

As well as performance indicators set by organizations themselves, another target that can be set as part of a strategy is the achievement of official standards and labels. Some standards are already well established, such as standards on environmental management and labels such as those on food products which are approved by the Soil Association.

However, as yet, while there has been progress on so-called 'ecolabelling' there has been little progress on official standards and labelling in the area of sustainable tourism.

If such standards and labels are to be developed, it will need action by one or all of the following:

- the International Standards Organisation (ISO)
- national governments
- professional bodies
- pressure groups.

Because of the diverse nature of sustainable

tourism, it will clearly be very difficult to create standards and/or labels for sustainable tourism products.

However, such standards and labels are essential to help consumers who want to purchase more sustainable tourism products to be able to do so, with confidence.

Control Mechanisms and Corrective Action

If a sustainable tourism strategy is going off course, a range of relevant control or corrective mechanisms may be required to put things right. For a destination this might include:

- more investment in the tourism infrastructure by public sector agencies
- stricter planning controls on new developments
- new regulations on minimum wages or maximum working hours
- restrictions on the activities of externally based tourism organizations such as tour operators, which contribute too little to the local community, or which take too high a share of the revenue from tourism out of the community
- fiscal incentives for new enterprises to be set up by local people.

For an individual tourism organization which controls every aspect of its own activities, corrective action should be reflected in its marketing mix. This might include:

- modifying existing products to make them more sustainable or developing new more sustainable products
- changing pricing policies to make prices fairer for consumers or to allow the generation of sufficient revenue to ensure the organization can pay its staff a fair wage
- altering promotional messages and changing the media used
- adding new distribution channels.

The implementation of sustainable tourism strategies is the key to success. Therefore we cannot afford to only start considering implementation, once we have developed a strategy. Instead we need to devise strategies which are realistic and capable of being implemented in the first place.

As more and more organizations, as well as destinations, create sustainable tourism strategies the issue of implementation will assume ever greater importance. This higher profile for implementation will in turn place more emphasis on the issues of monitoring and measurable performance indicators.

However, it is important to recognize that any sustainable tourism strategy is likely to involve taking a continuous journey rather than reaching an actual final destination.

The author would like to conclude by posing several contentious questions that need to be considered when we look at the future of sustainable tourism.

Sustainable Tourism: an Impossible Dream?

If we are to achieve sustainable tourism we need to:

- really know what we mean by sustainable tourism
- have the will to take action
- develop effective techniques that will allow us to achieve sustainable tourism.

The author is sceptical about what progress has been made to date on all three issues.

There still seems to be confusion about what forms of tourism are more or less sustainable. Is Benidorm package tourism really less sustainable than ecotourism in Belize? Are self-contained resort complexes tourist ghettos that reduce the benefits of tourism for the host community, or are they an excellent way of protecting local communities from the 'sociocultural pollution' which tourism can bring?

Too often, it seems that sustainable tourism is being defined in terms of the holiday-taking preferences of those who are doing the defining. Unless we can develop an agreed definition of sustainable tourism

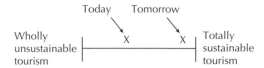

Fig. 34.5. The sustainable tourism continuum.

then there is no chance of us making much progress towards developing it in practice.

There also seems to be a distinct lack of will to develop more sustainable forms of tourism on the part of two key audiences. The first, governments, driven by short-term political timescales have little motivation to take the kind of long-term view of tourism that is implicit in the concept of sustainability.

However, it is the second audience, the tourist, where the interest in, let alone the will to develop, sustainable tourism, is perhaps the greatest barrier. At the time of writing there seems little evidence that tourists are becoming more concerned about sustainability and modifying their behaviour accordingly. Nor does there appear to be anything on the horizon that might make them more likely to take more interest in sustainable tourism.

Finally, as we have seen in earlier chapters, many of the techniques for achieving sustainable tourism in which we have placed great faith are flawed, including planning, de-marketing, carrying capacity and visitor management. Often the weaknesses of these techniques are based upon either a lack of knowledge of how tourism actually operates or the potentially negative implications of implementing the techniques.

Perhaps we should accept that totally sustainable tourism is an unattainable myth, and instead simply seek to make tourism more sustainable. In other words, we should not treat sustainable tourism as an absolute but rather as a relative term. We would then talk about the sustainable tourism continuum and continually seek to move tourism further along towards the right-hand side of the line shown in Fig. 34.5.

We should also, perhaps, acknowledge that *all* forms of tourism can aspire to move towards the right-hand side of this continuum, mass market passive tourism as well as small-scale, 'soft' cultural tourism.

We must accept that sustainable tourism is a continuous journey to a destination we will never reach, because wholly sustainable tourism is probably unattainable, and also because our idea of what constitutes sustainable tourism will undoubtedly change constantly.

Sustainable Tourism: a Potential Nightmare?

The author occasionally sees sustainable tourism as a potential nightmare rather than a dream. He thinks of the awful things that could be done in the name of sustainable tourism, such as:

- placing restrictions on the fundamental right of the freedom of movement
- 'outlawing' particular types of tourist or tourist behaviour.

There is a fear that sustainable tourism could also become a way for people from developed countries to influence what happens in developing countries so as to protect their own interests as tourists. Rather than being idealistic and altruistic, sustainable tourism has great potential to be selfish and even cynical. We must also be humble and not assume that we know today what will be best tomorrow. There is a danger that we could take action today that might cause great problems for future generations even though it is well intentioned.

We need look no further than the tower block housing in UK cities to illustrate this point. Idealistic planners in the 1950s and 1960s saw these tower blocks as solutions to the UK's housing crisis and as a way of improving people's living standards. By the 1980s these blocks were themselves at the heart of the UK's urban crisis, vilified and being demolished wherever possible.

Our decisions today must not make life worse for further generations and we must not do things now which gives them no chance to make their own decisions.

Sustainable Tourism: an Irrelevant Issue?

There seems little compelling evidence to suggest that in most places in the world, sustainable tourism is one of the most important issues today. In developing countries, perhaps, the issue is at its most important but these countries also face great problems ranging from health and disease to debt, water supply and education.

In developed countries, most people's concerns appear to revolve around crime and education and how the growing number of elderly people can be supported.

As more and more people around the world are able to enter the tourism market – from Eastern Europe, South-East Asia and Africa – it may be harder to convince tourists that what they are doing can have a negative side; and with life becoming ever more stressful it may become increasingly difficult to persuade tourists to behave sensibly and responsibly when they are on holiday.

Finally, if the harbingers of doom are right about global warming, and its implications then sustainable tourism may seem even less relevant to most people's lives than it does today.

Canute, King of Sustainable Tourism?

Are the proponents of sustainable tourism the King Canutes of our age, vainly trying to hold back the tide?

Is there really any point in believing in local control in an era characterized by globalization and the growth of transnational corporations? Can we hope to be successful if we place our faith in planning at a time when de-regulation and free trade are the dominant trends?

Perhaps it is time for the supporters of sustainable tourism to accept they cannot hold back the tide, but instead must concentrate on trying to channel it in the right direction and build defences to protect the most vulnerable areas from its worst effects.

Can Tourism be Made More Sustainable?

The author believes that tourism can be made more sustainable, but it will require fundamental changes that go far beyond tourism itself. It will mean:

- the concept of sustainable development being taken more seriously around the world
- action being taken to curb the impact of globalization, in other words, its tendency to lead to the homogenization of life styles, cultures, attitudes and even language across the world
- a further growth of interest in ethical issues, and socially responsible management generally.

This will require supra-governmental action and cooperation between states.

As far as the tourism industry is concerned, sustainability will mean changing the attitudes of both the demand side (tourists) and the supply side (tourism industry).

The Demand Side

Within tourism itself, the main challenge will be to raise tourist interest in sustainability. This can perhaps best be done by:

- appealing to their morality so that they modify their own behaviour to reduce the negative impacts of tourism
- stressing that more sustainable tourism also means better quality vacations in many cases
- persuading them that if they do not take this issue more seriously today their own children will suffer in the future.

The hope is that interested tourists will then help stimulate more sustainable forms of tourism by:

- putting pressure on the tourism industry as consumers, to make its practices more sustainable

- putting pressure on politicians, as voters, to legislate for regulation for sustainable tourism, whenever it is appropriate.

This is the only morally acceptable way of developing sustainable tourism in a democratic manner, although it will be very difficult.

Furthermore, sustainable tourism must not become a pre-occupation for a tiny minority of people, it must become an interest for everyone.

The Supply Side

Sustainable tourism will require tourism organizations to see how they can match sustainable tourism with their business objectives. They must be allowed and encouraged to use sustainability to make profits providing they are willing to take a long-term approach to their operations. Tourism organizations will also have to work more in partnership with, and show greater long-term commitment to, particular destinations.

As far as destinations are concerned, they must jealously guard their uniqueness. In an increasingly competitive market this uniqueness is their main selling point that differentiates them from other destinations. However, they must then take a global view of the market rather than a parochial one. In other words they should reverse the well-known marketing cliché and **Think Local, Act Global!**

Some Final Words

Completely sustainable tourism is probably a myth; we can only hope to make tourism more sustainable.

In this book we have looked at a number of ways in which we could move closer to the goal of sustainable tourism.

Whether or not we do move in that direction will depend upon us, you and me. We are the tourists who need to change our behaviour. Sustainable tourism should begin with yourself. If everyone simply undertakes to improve their own behaviour, tourism would become more sustainable.

Are you willing to deny yourself a visit to the beautiful rain forests of Belize? Or not dress in shorts in Greece or not drink alcohol in Islamic countries? Are you willing to pay more for your holiday to make sure that staff are paid a decent wage?

If you are, then the future for sustainable tourism looks bright. It all depends on you.

Bibliography

Agarwal, S. (1994) The life-cycle approach and south coast resorts. In: Cooper, C. and Lockwood, A. (eds) *Progress in Tourism, Recreation and Hospitality Management*, Vol. 5. John Wiley and Sons, Chichester, pp. 194–208.

Agarwal, S. (1998) What is new with the resort cycle? *Tourism Management* 19, 181–182.

Anon (1993) The Anderson Group architects: from Minnesota to the rain forest. *Architecture Minnesota* November-December, pp. 16–17.

Anon (1996) The Anderson Group architects. *Architecture* June, pp. 122–123.

Arnstein, S. (1965) A ladder of citizen participation. *Journal of the American Institute of Planners* 35, 216–224.

Ashworth, G. (1990) The historic sites of Groningen: which is sold to whom? In: Ashworth, G. and Goodall, B. (eds) *Marketing Tourism Places*. Routledge, London, pp. 138–155.

Ashworth, G.S. and Larkham, P.J. (1994) *Building a New Heritage*. Routledge, London.

Atkinson, H., Berry, A. and Jarvis, R. (1998) *Business Accounting for Hospitality and Tourism*. Chapman and Hall, London.

Baum, T. (1995) *Managing Human Resources in the European Tourism and Hospitality Industry: a Strategic Approach*. International Thomson Business Press, London.

Berlitz (1995) *Berlitz Complete Guide to Cruising and Cruise Ships*. Berlitz, Oxford.

Bleasdale, S. and Tapsell, S. (1996) Sahara tourism: Arabian Nights or tourist daze? The socio-cultural impacts of tourism in southern Tunisia. In: Robinson, M. *et al.* (eds) *Tourism and Cultural Change*. Tourism and Culture Conference Proceedings. Centre for Travel and Tourism/Business Education Publishers, Sunderland.

Boniface, P. (1995) *Managing Quality Cultural Tourism*. Routledge, London.

Boo, E. (1990) *Ecotourism: the Potential and Pitfalls*, Vols 1 and 2. World Wildlife Fund, Baltimore, Maryland.

Boyd, S.W. and Butler, R. (1996) Seeing the forest through the trees. In: Harrison, L.C. and Husbands, W. (eds) *Practicing Responsible Tourism: International Case Studies in Tourism Planning, Policy, and Development*. John Wiley and Sons, New York.

Bramwell, B., Henry, I., Jackson, G., Prat, A.G., Richards, G. and van der Straaten, J. (1996) (eds) *Sustainable Tourism Management: Principles and Practice*. Tilburg University Press, Tilburg, Netherlands.

Bull, A. (1995) *The Economics of Travel and Tourism*, 2nd edn. Longman, Melbourne.

Burton, R. (1997) The sustainability of ecotourism. In: Stabler, M.J. (ed.) *Tourism and Sustainability: Principles and Practice*. CAB International, Wallingford.

Butler, R.W. (1980) The concept of a tourist area cycle of evolution: implications for the management of resources. *Canadian Geographer* 24, 5–12.

Butler, R., Hall, C.M. and Jenkins, J. (1998) (eds) *Tourism and Recreation in Rural Areas*. John Wiley and Sons, Chichester.

Canestrelli, F. and Costa, P. (1991) Tourism carrying capacity: a fuzzy approach. *Annals of Tourism Research* 18, 295–311.

Cater, E. and Lowman, G. (1994) *Ecotourism: a Sustainable Option?* John Wiley and Sons, New York.

Clarke, J. (1997) A framework of approaches to sustainable tourism. *Journal of Sustainable Tourism* 5, 224–33.

Coccossis, H. (1996) Tourism and sustainability: perspectives and implications. In: Priestley, G.H., Edwards, J. and Coccossis, H. (eds) *Sustainable Tourism? European Experiences*. CAB International, Wallingford, pp. 1–21.

Cohen, E. (1989) Alternative tourism – a critique. In: Singh *et al.* (eds) *Towards Appropriate Tourism: the Case of Developing Countries*. European University Studies, Series X, Vol 11. Peter Lang, Frankfurt am Main, pp. 127–142.

Conlin, M.V. (1995) *Island Tourism: Management Principles and Practice*. John Wiley and Sons, Chichester.

Conlin, M.V. (1996) Revitalising Bermuda: tourism policy planning in a modular island destination. In: Hanson and Husbands (eds) *Practising Responsible Tourism: International Case Studies in Tourism Planning, Policy and Development*. John Wiley and Sons, New York.

Convery, F.J., Flanagan, S., Keane, M. and O'Cinneide, M. (1994) *From the Bottom Up: a Tourism Strategy for the Gaeltacht*. An Sagart An Daingean, Galway.

Cook, S.D., Stewart, E. and Repass, K. U.S. (1992) *Travel Data Centre. Discover America: Tourism and the Environment*. Travel Industry Association of America, Washington, DC.

Cooper, C.P. (1992) The life-cycle concept and strategic planning for coastal resorts. *Built Environment* 18, 57–66.

Cooper, C.P. (1994) The destination life-cycle: an update. In: Seaton, A.V. (ed.) *Tourism: the State of the Art*. John Wiley and Sons, Chichester, pp. 340–346.

Cooper, C. (1997) The environmental consequences of declining destinations. In: Cooper, C. and Wanhill, S. (eds) *Tourism Development: Environmental and Community Issues*. John Wiley and Sons, Chichester.

Cooper, C.P. and Lockwood, A. (1994) (eds) *Progress in Tourism Recreation and Hospitality Management*, Vol. 5. John Wiley and Sons, Chichester.

Cooper, C. and Wanhill, S. (1997) (eds) *Tourism Development: Environmental and Community Issues*. John Wiley and Sons, Chichester.

Cyprus Tourism Organisation (CTO) (1994) *Tourism Development, Planning and Sustainability*. Paper presented at the United Nations Economic and Social Council, Economic Commission for Europe, Committee on Human Settlements, 18th Meeting of Experts on Human Settlements Problems in Southern Europe, Nicosia, Cyprus, 6–8 June.

D'Amore, L.J. (1992) Promoting sustainable tourism. The Canadian approach. *Tourism Management* 13, 258–62.

Davis, D. and Harriott, V.J. (1996) Sustainable tourism development or a case of loving a special place to death. In: Harrison, L.C. and Husbands, W. (eds) *Promoting Responsible Tourism: International Case Studies in Tourism Policy, Planning and Development*. John Wiley and Sons, New York.

De Kadt, E. (1979) *Tourism: Passport to Development*. Oxford University Press, Oxford.

Dearden, P. and Harron, S. (1992) Tourism and the hilltribes of Thailand. In: Weiler, B. and Hall, G.M. (eds) *Special Interest Tourism*. Belhaven Press, London, pp. 96–104.

Department of Leisure Studies (1995) *Conference Proceedings: Expert Meeting on Sustainability in Leisure and Tourism*. December 1994. Tilburg University Press, Tilburg, The Netherlands.

Donert, K. and Light, D. (1996) Capitalising on location and heritage in tourism and Economic Regeneration in Argentière La Bessée, High French Alps. In: Harrison and Husbands (eds) *Practising Responsible Tourism: International Case Studies in Tourism Planning, Policy and Development*. John Wiley and Sons, New York.

Dower, M. (1968) *Fourth Wave: the Challenge of Leisure*. Civic Tour, London.

Doxey, G. (1975) A causation theory of visitor–resident irritants: methodology and research inferences. In: *The Impact of Tourism*. Proceedings of the 6th Annual TTRA Conference, San Diego.

Ecotourism Society (1993) *Ecotourism Guidelines for Nature Tour Operators*. North Bennington, Vermont.

Edington, J.M. and Edington, M.A. (1997) Tropical forest ecotourism: two promising projects in Belize. In: Stabler, M.J. (ed.) *Tourism and Sustainability: Principles and Practice*. CAB International, Wallingford.

Editions Solar (1996) *Guide du Tourisme Industriel et Technique: Bretagne-Pays de la Loire*. Editions Solar, Paris.

Elkington, J. and Hailes, J. (1992) *Holidays that Don't Cost the Earth*. Victor Gollancz, London.

English Tourist Board, Countryside Commission, Rural Development Commission (1991) *The Green Light: a Guide to Sustainable Tourism*. English Tourist Board.

Farrell, D.H. and Runyan, D. (1991) Ecology and tourism. *Annals of Tourism Research* 18, 26–40.

Farrell, B.H. and McLellan, R.W. (1987) Tourism and physical environment research. *Annals of Tourism Research* 14, 1016.

France, L. (ed.) (1997) *The Earthscan Reader in Sustainable Tourism*. Earthscan, London.

Frommer, A. (1996) *The New World of Travel*, 5th edn. Prentice Hall, Englewood Cliffs, New Jersey.

Gartner, W.C. (1996) *Tourism Development: Principles, Processes, and Policies*. Van Nostrand Reinhold, New York.

Gill, A. and Williams, P.W. (1994) Managing growth in mountain tourism communities. *Tourism Management* 15, 212–220.

Glasson, J., Godfrey, K. and Goodey, B. (1995) *Towards Visitor Impact Management*. Avebury, Aldershot.

GLOBE '92 Tourism Stream (1992) *Challenge Statement*. Vancouver, Canada.

Godfrey, K.B. (1994) *Sustainable Tourism – What is it Really?* Address to the 18th Meeting of Experts on Human Settlements Problems in Southern Europe, United Nations Economic and Social Council, Economic Commission for Europe, Committee on Human Settlements, Nicosia, Cyprus, 6–8 June.

Gurung, C.P. and De Coursey, M.D. (1994) The Annapurna Conservation Area project: a pioneering example of sustainable tourism? In: Cater, E. and Lowman, G. (eds) *Ecotourism: a Sustainable Option?* John Wiley and Sons, Chichester.

Hall, C.M. (1992) Adventure, sport and health tourism. In: Weiler, B. and Hall, C.M. (eds) *Special Interest Tourism*. Belhaven Press, London, pp. 141–158.

Hall, C.M. (1993) Sex tourism in South East Asia. In: Harrison (ed.) *Tourism and the Less Developed Countries*. Bellhaven, London.

Hall, C.M. (1994) *Tourism and Politics: Policy, Power, and Place*. John Wiley and Sons, Chichester.

Hall, C.M. and Lew, A.A. (1998) (eds) *Sustainable Tourism: a Geographical Perspective*. Addison-Wesley-Longman, Harlow.

Hall, C.M. and Page, S.J. (1996) *Tourism in the Pacific – Issues and Cases*. International Thomson Business Press.

Hall, P. (1975) *Urban and Regional Planning*. Penguin, Harmondsworth.

Hamzah, A. (1997) The evolution of small-scale tourism in Malaysia: problems and opportunities, and implications for sustainability. In: Stabler, M.J. (ed.) *Tourism and Sustainability: Principles and Practice*. CAB International, Wallingford.

Harris, R. and Leiper, E.N. (1995) *Sustainable Tourism: an Australian Perspective*. Butterworth-Heinemann, Chatswood, Australia.

Harrison, D. (1993) (ed.) *Tourism and the Less Developed Countries*. Bellhaven, London.

Harrison, L.C. and Husbands, W. (1996) (eds) *Practising Responsible Tourism: International Case Studies in Tourism Planning, Policy and Development*. John Wiley and Sons, New York.

Hawkes, S. and Williams, P. (1993) *The Greening of Tourism – from Principles to Practice. Globe '92 Tourism Stream: Case Book of Best Practice in Sustainable Tourism*. Sustainable Tourism, Industry, Science and Technology, Canada, and the Centre for Tourism Policy and Research, Simon Fraser University, Burnaby, BC.

Hiller, H. (1991) Environmental bodies edge closer to green ratings for travel. *Ecotourism Society Newsletter*, Summer, 1.

Hiltz, S. and Fitzgibbon, J. (1989) Sustainable development and rural resource planning. The challenge of the future in rural Canada. *Plan Canada* 29, 19–27.

Holder, J.S. (1994) *The Tourism Industry: a Global and Regional Perspective in the Context of Sustainable Development*. Keynote address to Tourism Industry Leadership Conference, Grand Bahamas Island, April.

Horner, S. and Swarbrooke, J. (1996) *Marketing Tourism, Hospitality and Leisure in Europe*. International Thomson Business Press, London.

Hughes, G. (1995) The cultural construction of sustainable tourism. *Tourism Management* 16, 49–59.

Hunter, C. (1997) Sustainable tourism as an adoptive paradigm. *Annals of Tourism Research* 24, 850–67.

Hunter, C. and Green, H. (1995) *Tourism and the Environment: a Sustainable Relationship*. Routledge, London.

Hunter-Jones, P.A., Hughes, H.L., Eastood, I.W. and Morrison, A.A. (1997) Practical approaches to sustainability: a Spanish perspective. In: Stabler, M. (ed.) *Tourism and Sustainability: Principles and Practice*. CAB International, Wallingford.

Ingram, C.D. and Durst, P.B. (1989) Nature-oriented tour operators: travel to developing countries. *Journal of Travel Research* 28, 11–15.

Inskeep, E. (1991) *Tourism Planning: an Integrated and Sustainable Development Approach*. Von Nostrand Reinhold. New York.

Inskeep, E. and Kallenburger, M. (1992) *An Integrated Approach to Resort Development: Six Case Studies*. WTO, Madrid.

Jenner, P. and Smith, C. (1992) *The Tourism Industry and the Environment*. The Economist Intelligence Unit Special Report No. 2453. Business International Ltd, London.

Jones, A. (1992) Is there a real 'alternative tourism?' *Tourism Management* 13, 102–3.

Keane, M.J., Ó Cinnéide, M.S. and Cunningham, C. (1996) Setting the stage to balance competing trade offs: identifying issues affecting tourism development and management in Inis Oírr. In: Harrison and Husbands (eds) *Practising Responsible Tourism: International Case Studies in Tourism Planning, Policy and Development.* John Wiley and Sons, New York.

Kerr, J. (1992) Making dollars and sense out of ecotourism/nature tourism. In: Weiler, B. (ed.) *Ecotourism: Incorporating the Global Classroom.* International Conference Papers. University of Queensland, Bureau of Tourism Research, Canberra, pp. 248–252.

Krippendorf, J. (1987) *The Holiday Makers: Understanding the Impact of Leisure and Travel*, English edition. Heinemann, Oxford.

Kulalis, E. (1993) Green resort. *Architecture Minnesota* November–December, pp. 28–29.

Lane, B. (1990) *Developing Sustainable Rural Tourism.* Paper presented at Planning and Tourism in Harmony. The Irish National Planning Conference. Newmarket on Fergus, Country Clare, Ireland.

Law, C.M. (1993) *Urban Tourism: Attracting Visitors to Large Cities.* Mansell, London.

LDR Commission (1994) *LDR International Committee on Competitiveness. Final Report.* LDR, Bermuda.

Lockhart, D.G. and Drakakis-Smith, D. (1997) (eds) *Island Tourism: Trends and Prospects.* Pinter, London.

Lowe, E., Faulkner, B. and Moscardo, G. (1998) (eds) *Embracing and Managing Change in Tourism: International Case Studies.* Routledge, London.

Lundberg, K. and Hawkins, D.E. (1993) (eds) *Ecotourism: a Guide for Planners and Managers.* The Ecotourism Society, North Bennington, Vermont.

MacLellan, R. (1997) The effectiveness of sustainable tourism in Scotland. In: Stabler, M.J. (ed.) *Tourism and Sustainability: Principles and Practice.* CAB International, Wallingford.

Martin, A. (1997) *Tourism, the Environment and Consumers.* Paper presented at the Environment Matters Conference, Glasgow, April 1997.

Mathieson, A. and Wall, G. (1982) *Tourism: Economic, Physical, and Social Impacts.* Longman, Harlow.

May, V. (1995) Environmental implications of the 1992 Winter Olympic Games. *Tourism Management* 16, 269–75.

Mayle, P. (1989) *A Year in Provence.* Hamish Hamilton, London.

McIntyre, G. (1993) *Sustainable Tourism Development: Guide for Local Planners.* World Tourism Organisation, Madrid.

McKercher, B. (1993) The unrecognised threat to tourism: can tourism survive sustainability? *Tourism Management* 14, 131–136.

Meadows, D.H., Meadows, D.L., Randers, J. and Behrens, W.W. III (1972) *The Limits to Growth.* Pan, London.

Middleton, V.T.C. and Hawkins, R. (1998) *Sustainable Tourism: a Marketing Perspective.* Butterworth-Heinemann, Oxford.

Ministry of Housing and Local Government (1969) *The Skeffington Report – People and Planning: Report of the Committee on Pubic Participation in Planning.* HMSO, London.

Morgan, M. (1991) Dresssing up to survive: marketing Majorca anew. *Tourism Management* 12, 15–20.

Mowforth, M. and Munt, I. (1998) *Tourism and Sustainability: New Tourism in the Third World.* Routledge, London.

Murphy, P.E. (1985) *Tourism: a Community Approach.* Methuen, London.

Murphy, P.E. (1994) Tourism and sustainable development. In: Theobold, W. (ed.) *Global Tourism: the Next Decade.* Butterworth-Heinemann, Oxford.

Nash, D. (1996) *Anthropology of Tourism.* Pergamon Press, Oxford.

Neale, G. (1998) *The Green Travel Guide.* Earthscan, London.

Opperman, M. (1998) What is new with the resort cycle? *Tourism Management* 19, 179–180

Opperman, M. and Chon, K.S. (1997) *Tourism in Developing Countries.* International Thomson Business Press.

Packard, V. (1960) *The Waste Makers.* Penguin, Harmondsworth.

Page, S. (1994) *Transport for Tourism.* Routledge, London.

Page, S. (1995) *Urban Tourism.* Routledge, London.

Pearce, D.W., Markandya, A. and Barbier, E. (1989) *Blueprint for a Green Economy.* Earthscan Publications, London.

Pearce, P., Moscardo, G. and Ross, G.F. (1996) *Tourism–Community Relationship.* Pergamon Press, Oxford.

Pigram, J.J. (1990) Sustainable tourism policy considerations. *Journal of Tourism Studies* 1, 2–9.

Pillman, W. and Predl, S. (1992) *Strategies for Reducing the Environmental Impact of Tourism.* The Proceedings of the Envirotour Vienna 1992 Conference. International Society for Environmental Protection, Vienna.

Porter, M.E. (1980) *Competitive Strategy.* The Free Press, New York.

Prentice, R. (1993) *Tourism and Heritage Attractions.* Routledge, London.

Price, M.F. (1996) (ed.) *People and Tourism in Fragile Environments.* John Wiley and Sons, Chichester.

Priestley, G.H., Edwards, J. and Coccossis, H. (1996) (eds) *Sustainable Tourism? European Experiences.* CAB International, Wallingford.

Prosser, G. (1986) The limits of acceptable change: an introduction to a framework for national area planning. *Australian Parks and Recreation* 22, 5–10.

Reid, L.J. (1996) Cultivating markets for economic spin-offs: the Niagara Winter Festival of Lights, Ontario, Canada. In: Hassan and Husbands (eds) *Practising Responsible Tourism: International Case Studies in Tourism Planning, Policy and Development.* John Wiley and Sons, New York.

Reimer, G. and Dialla, A. (1992) *Community Based Tourism Development in Pangnirtung, Northwest Territories: Looking Back and Looking Ahead.* Report prepared for the Department of Economic Development and Tourism. Government of the Northwest Territories and the Hamlet of Pangnirtung.

Ridzwan, A.R. (1994) Status of coral reefs in Malaysia. In: Wilkinson, R., Sudara, S. and Chou, L.M. (eds) *Proceedings of the Third ASEAN–Australia Symposium on Living Coastal Resources.* Chuialongkorn University, Bangkok.

Robinson, M., Evans, N. and Callaghan P. (1996) (eds) *Tourism and Culture: Towards the 21st Century.* Conference Proceedings (four volumes). Centre for Travel and Tourism and Business Education Publishers, Sunderland.

Rogers, H.A. and Slinn, J.A. (1993) *Tourism: the Management of Facilities.* M and E Handbooks, Longman, Harlow.

Romeril, M. (1989) Tourism and the environment: accord or discord? *Tourism Management* 10, 204–208.

Rural Development Commission (1996) *Green Audit Kit: the DIY Guide to Greening your Tourism Business.* Rural Development Commission.

Ruschmann, D.v.d.M. (1992) Ecological tourism in Brazil. *Tourism Management* 13, 125–128.

Ryan, C. (1991) *Recreational Tourism: a Social Science Perspective.* Routledge, London.

Saglio, C. (1979) Tourism for Discovery: a project in Lower Casamance, Sénégal. In: de Kadt, E. (ed.) *Tourism: Passport to Development.* Oxford University Press, Oxford.

Scace, R.C., Grifone, E. and Usher, R. (1992) *Ecotourism in Canada.* Canadian Environmental Advisory Council, Environment Canada, Quebec.

Seaton, T. (1996) Tourism and relative deprivation: the counter-revolutionary processes of tourism in Cuba. In: Robinson, M., Evans, N. and Callaghan, P. (eds) *Tourism and Culture: Towards the 21st Century Conference Proceedings,* one of the 4 volumes – *Culture as the Tourism Product.* Centre for Travel and Tourism and Business Education Publishers, Sunderland.

Shafer, E. (1995) *How to Win in Any Negotiation: the Key to Success in the Sustainable Ecotourism Business.* Presented to the 5th CTO Ecotourism Conference. Margarita Island, Venezuela, June.

Shaw, G. and Williams, A. (1994) *Critical Issues in Tourism.* Blackwell, Oxford.

Shaw, G. and Williams, A. (1997) *The Rise and Fall of British Coastal Resorts: Cultural and Economic Perspectives.* Pinter, London.

Slee, W., Far, H. and Snowdon, P. (1997) Sustainable Tourism and the local economy? In: Stabler, M.J. (ed.) *Tourism and Sustainability: Principles and Practice.* CAB International, Wallingford.

Smith, V.L. and Eadington, V.R. (1992) *Tourism Alternatives: Potentials and Problems in the Development of Tourism.* University of Pennsylvania Press, Philadelphia, Pennsylvania.

Stabler, M.J. (1997) (ed.) *Tourism and Sustainability: Principles and Practice.* CAB International, Wallingford.

Stadel, C. (1996) Divergence and conflict or convergence and harmony? Conservation and tourism potential in Hohe Tavern National Park, Austria. In: Harrison and Husbands (eds) *Praticising Responsible Tourism: International Case Studies in Tourism Planning, Policy and Development.* John Wiley and Sons, New York.

Swarbrooke, J. (1993) Attractions touristiques, grands évènements et régénération urbaine dans le Nord de l'Angleterre. *Hommes et Terres du Nord* 3, 91–99.

Swarbrooke, J. (1995) *The Development and Management of Visitor Attractions.* Butterworth Heinemann, Oxford.

Swarbrooke, J. (1996a) Towards the development of sustainable tourism in Eastern Europe. In: Richards, G. (ed.) *Tourism in Central and Eastern Europe: Educating for Quality.* ATLAS Tilburg, University Press, Tilburg, The Netherlands.

Swarbrooke, J. (1996b) Towards a sustainable future for cultural tourism: a European perspective. In: Robinson, M., Evans, N. and Callaghan, P. (eds) *Tourism and Culture: Towards the 21st Century Conference Proceedings,* one of the 4 volumes – *Culture as the Tourism Product.* Centre for Travel and Tourism and Business Education Publishers, Sunderland.

Svalbard Tourist Board (1996) *Svalbard*. Svalbard Tourist Board and Info Svalbard, Longyearbyen.

Taylor, G.D. (1991) *Tourism and Sustainability – Impossible Dream or Essential Objective?* Conference Proceedings of the TTRA Canadian Chapter. Tourism–Environment–Sustainable Development: an Agenda for Research. Hull, Quebec, 27–29 October, pp. 27–29.

Theobold, W. (1994) (ed.) *Global Tourism: the Next Decade*. Butterworth Heinemann, Oxford.

Travis, A. (1988) Alternative tourism. *Naturopa* 59, 25–27.

Tribe, J. (1995) *The Economics of Leisure and Tourism: Environments, Markets, and Impacts*. Butterworth Heinemann, Oxford.

Turner, J. (1994) Natural neighbour. BBC TV, 22 October 1994.

Valentine, P.S. (1993) Ecotourism and nature conservation: a definition with some recent developments in Micronesia. *Tourism Management* 14, 107–115.

Voon, P.K. (1994) Land use and sustainable development: the case of Pulau Tisman. In: *Proceedings of the Third International Conference on Geography of the ASEAN Region, Kuala Lumpur*, pp. 1–22.

Wall, G. (1996) One name, two destinations: planned and unplanned coastal resorts in Indonesia. In: Harrison L.C. and Husbands, W. (eds) *Practising Responsible Tourism: International Case Studies in Tourism Policy, Planning and Development*. John Wiley and Sons, New York.

Wall, G. and Long, V. (1996) Balineous 'homestays', an indigeneous response to tourism opportunities. In: Butler, R. and Hinch, T. (eds) *Tourism and Native Peoples*. Routledge, London.

Weaver, D.B. (1998) *Ecotourism in the Less Developed World*. CAB International, Wallingford.

Weiler, B. and Hall, C.M. (1992) Special interest tourism: in search of an alternative. In: Weiler, B. and Hall, C.M. (eds) *Special Interest Tourism*. Belhaven Press, London, pp. 199–204.

Wheeller, B. (1991) Tourism's troubled times: responsible tourism is not the answer. *Tourism Management* 12, 91–96.

Wheeller, B. (1992) Is progressive tourism appropriate? *Tourism Management* 13, 104–105.

Wheeller, B. (1993) Sustaining the ego. *Journal of Sustainable Tourism* 1, 121–129.

Wheeller, B. (1994) Tourism and the environment: a symbiotic, symbolic or shambolic relationship? In: Seaton A.V. *et al.* (eds) *Tourism: the State of the Art*. John Wiley and Sons, Chichester.

Wheeller, B. (1996) World Congress on Adventure Travel and Ecotourism. Conference Report. *Tourism Management* 17, 383–385.

Wheeller, B. (1997) Here we go, here we go, here we go eco. In: Stabler, M.J. (ed.) *Tourism and Sustainability: Principles and Practice*. CAB International, Wallingford.

Whelan, T. (1991) (ed.) *Nature Tourism: Managing for the Environment*. Island Press, Washington, DC.

Wight, P. (1993a) Ecotourism: ethics or ecosell? *Journal of Travel Research* 31, 3–9.

Wight, P. (1993b) *Improved Business Positioning: Environmentally Responsible Marketing of Tourism*. Paper presented at the 24th Annual TTRA International Conference, Whistler, British Columbia, 14 June.

Wight, P.A. (1993c) Sustainable ecotourism: balancing economic, environmental, and social goals within an ethical framework. *Journal of Tourism Studies* 4, 56–64.

Wight, P. (1994) Environmentally responsible marketing of ecotourism. In: Cater, E.A. and Lowman, G.A. (eds) *Ecotourism: a sustainable option?* Royal Geographical Society and Belhaven Press, London.

Wilson, D. (1997) Strategies for sustainability: lessons from Goa and the Seychelles. In: Stabler, M.J. (ed.) *Tourism and Sustainability: Principles and Practice*. CAB International, Wallingford.

Wood, K. and House, S. (1991) *The Good Tourist*. Mandarin, London.

World Commission on Environment and Development (1987) *Our Common Future*. Oxford University Press, Oxford.

World Tourism Organisation (1993) *Sustainable Tourism Development: Guide for Local Planners*. WTO, Madrid.

World Travel and Tourism Human Resource Centre (1998) *Steps to Success: Global Good Practices in Travel and Tourism Human Resource Development*. WTTHRC, North Vancouver, BC, Canada.

Worldwide Fund for Nature/Tourism Concern (1994) *Beyond the Green Horizon*. WWF, Godalming.

Yee, J.G. (1992) *Ecotourism Market Survey: a Survey of North American Ecotourism operators*. The Intelligence Centre, Pacific Asia Travel Association, San Francisco.

Young, G. (1973) *Tourism: Blessing or Blight?* Penguin, Harmondsworth.

Ziffer, K. (1989) *Ecotourism: the Uneasy Alliance*. Conservation International and Ernst and Young, Washington, DC.

Index